The
COMPLETE
LANGUAGE

~ *of* ~

HERBS

The

COMPLETE
LANGUAGE

~•~ *of* ~•~

HERBS

A Definitive & Illustrated History

S. THERESA DIETZ

wellfleet
press

First published in 2022 by Wellfleet Press, an imprint of The Quarto Group,
142 West 36th Street, 4th Floor, New York, NY 10018, USA
T (212) 779-4972 F (212) 779-6058 www.Quarto.com

This edition published in 2024 by Wellfleet Press, an imprint of The Quarto Group,
142 West 36th Street, 4th Floor, New York, NY 10018, USA.

Wellfleet titles are also available at discount for retail, wholesale, promotional, and bulk purchase. For
details, contact the Special Sales Manager by email at specialsales@quarto.com or by mail at The Quarto
Group, Attn: Special Sales Manager, 100 Cummings Center Suite 265D, Beverly, MA 01915 USA.

10 9 8 7 6 5 4 3 2 1

ISBN: 978-1-57715-412-9

Library of Congress Control Number: 2023939902

Publisher: Rage Kindelsperger
Creative Director: Laura Drew
Managing Editor: Cara Donaldson
Editors: James Jayo and Elizabeth You
Cover and Interior Design: Verso Design

Printed in China

This book provides general information on various widely known and widely accepted culinary and/
or medicinal herbs. However, it should not be relied upon as recommending or promoting any specific
diagnosis or method of treatment for a particular condition, and it is not intended as a substitute for
medical advice or for direct diagnosis and treatment of a medical condition by a qualified physician.
Readers who have questions about a particular condition, possible treatments for that condition, or
possible reactions from the condition or its treatment should consult a physician or other qualified
healthcare professional.

CONTENTS

INTRODUCTION

My interest in herbs started in the kitchen with my mom, Virginia, and her abiding love and praise for all the culinary seasonings that flavored her food and our family's life. I expanded my early love of culinary herbs over time to completely fill a large food cupboard and an entire drawer in my own kitchen. My daughter and son-in-law, each of my grandchildren, and my very young great-grandchildren are all foodies or foodies in the making. Every one of them has a palate that appreciates flavors. When I started exploring the language that might be inherent in culinary herbs, in particular I was thinking of my family and myself, and wondering what I might find out about what we were already using to elevate the flavors of our food.

All the while I was researching all the culinary herbs I ever knew about, I was simultaneously discovering other herbs that I had not seriously thought of as being so fascinating to explore. These other herbs were far outside the realm of my culinary interests, which is why I had not considered them before. I had not even realized that they were in the realm of herbs. And yet, there they were, just waiting to be investigated.

For the most part, there was not a thing edible about most of them. And yet, their contribution to our existence has been significant, even life-saving at times. We, on this good Earth, are quite fortunate to have so many interesting plants growing somewhere on it. Some of them have been growing to be contributions to our desire for delicious flavors, true. Thinking outside of that small circle, in some instances, they could even be the entire meal. Extend the circle a tiny bit and they could be a survival meal in desperate times. Widening it more can include herbs for plain old-fashioned safety, such as would be included in the early stuffing used in a life jacket. Or providing the perfect materials to make an enduring musical instrument. All in all, moving wider still, the circle will encompass most of the herbs that have been used as healing folk remedies for thousands of years, and as the base ingredients for contemporary medicinal formulas used today.

Over time, medicinal folk knowledge might have been handed down to me or gleaned from the advice of those around me. In some cases they were, and I would not hesitate to recommend sipping a hot tea brewed entirely of sliced lemons when sick with a cold. And I saw with my own two eyes how raw onion slices held with socks against the soles of bare feet could work to bring down a fever. There are many other herbs that I have tried for whatever reason, and many more that I'd be quite hesitant to ever try unless they were prescribed by a licensed physician. All in all, I just don't know enough about medicinal herbs yet. Maybe someday I will. I am certain that I do not know enough about the medicinal properties of herbs to seriously advise anyone of anything at all regarding them. So, I won't. What I have done in this book, though, is add a symbolic note when there was an herb that might be worth a further investigation of its inherent medicinal properties, on your own. It may not be worth the time to read another word about some of the herbs, although there are several herbs in this book that might be just what you needed to wonder more about, and that might encourage further investigation, so you have a point of reference for a deeper discussion about them with your physician.

There are also the essential oils. Not all plants provide them as we know and use them. Since I was still widely exploring herbs driven by my own curiosity, I made sure that I included the plants that do provide essential oils for whatever purposes they are utilized. I have and I use essential oils myself, so I have made sure I have included the plants that produced them. In researching these precious oils, I discovered much that I needed to know regarding what more these essential oils provide when I use them in my mist diffuser on any given day, for a plethora of various reasons. I knew that I was initially drawn to my wide range of essential oils based on my own preference for pleasant fragrances. What I had not really considered was, why was that? What was it about those aromas that triggered something positive in me? It was interesting uncovering the clues that led me onward towards the surprising answers to those personal questions. I also discovered how much more these essential oils can be used magically, for a variety of purposes I may not have ever considered.

Throughout this book I mention the making of herbal sachets to carry, wear, or tuck away in some particular, significant place. A magical sachet can be made any size, and either stitched into a pouch or pulled up into a bundle to be tied off to close it. Because it is an herbal sachet, a piece of a clean, pure, plant-fiber cloth, such as cotton or linen, is a good choice of fabric to employ. It can be tied off with a thin strip of the same fabric, or a piece of white or colored cotton embroidery thread. Most of the sachets that I have made and used for my own magical purposes are small. Most of them have been no larger than an oversized tea bag, but even being this small in size, they are still mighty powerful.

All of the herbs mentioned in this book mean something, and they just might have the power to actually manifest a magical effect if the enablement is, at the very least, a heartfelt wish. If you find an herb interesting, do take the time to do more research before employing it, keeping in mind before making that wish that it is important to know more about what you might be touching. Never touch a plant without knowing what you are getting yourself into. Some herbs, even in this book, exude such a deadly sap that just touching the plant can do grave harm. This book is merely a hint at which herbs are best to just look at. Any of these herbs can inspire the formulation of a mystical, vividly lucid, and very magical mental image of an herb, which can be utilized as a magical proxy. A sharply vivid mental image can be just as effective in a magical working if employed with well-focused intent.

As I mentioned in *The Complete Language of Flowers*, in folk magic the utilization of one particular plant over any other in any working is dependent upon the possible inherent power of any magically potent plant. Intuitively sensing which plant will create the effect you intend is part of the magic. Remember, too, the humble *Taraxacum officinale* growing on the front lawn, between the cracks in a sidewalk, or at the dusty cluttered edge of a vacant lot, might present the perfect Dandelion puff just waiting for a big wish to be made using it, as wishes have been made by the very young and the very old, for many generations past, throughout, and far into the distant future.

How to

USE THIS
BOOK

*T*f you do not know the scientific name of a plant, but you do know one of its common names, you will be able to find it in the Plant Names Index. There you will find the corresponding number that will refer to it in the body of the book. You can also locate the number of a specific plant (or several different plants) by determining which meaning and/or power you are researching.

There is no specific indication as to which part or parts of the plant are toxic, nor when they are toxic or if their toxicity is eliminated with ripening, etc. Please be acutely aware that some plants are so extremely poisonous that simply touching them or breathing in smoke where they may be burning can be fatal. In no way whatsoever is there a suggestion anywhere in this book that any plant represented should be inhaled, or put directly on the skin. Please do take the time to do further research of your own with regard to what you are going to touch or ingest before you dare to do so. The internet is a wonderful source for that kind of scientific information.

Be informed, stay safe, feel free to tap into the innate powers of trees, plants, and flowers, always let the recipients of your floral gifts know what significant thoughts and feelings are in your heart.. and please, whatever you do and whenever you do it: *do not even dare to vex the fairies!*

No. 000: (cross-reference number for searching from any index)

Specific primary scientific name

☠ (toxicity symbol)

⚗ (medicinal symbol) •┄┄┄┄┄┄┄┄┄┄┄┄┄┄┄┄

🍴 (culinary herb)

Other Known Scientific Names | Common Names

✳ **SYMBOLIC MEANING:** Come to me; I am shy; my heart aches for you; and so on.

🎨 **COLOR MEANINGS:** When applicable to particular colors of an herb.

🌱 **COMPONENT MEANINGS:** Associated with branches, leaves, seeds, or sprays of an herb.

🌀 **POSSIBLE POWERS:** Healing; love; protection; and so on.

🜨 **FOLKLORE AND FACTS:** Tidbits of factual, fanciful, mystical, magical, or plain silly information.

Note: With regards to the medicinal symbol, it indicates that either currently or at some time in the past, folk healers, herbalist practitioners, or traditional medicine physicians have used this herb or its derivative for medicinal purposes. Further research into this plant's full medicinal potential is ongoing and encouraged.

No. 001
✑*Abelmoschus moschatus* ⚗

Ambrette

Abelmoschus abelmoschus | Abelmoschus betulifolia | Abelmoschus chinensis | Abelmoschus ciliaris | Abelmoschus cubensis | Abelmoschus cucurbitaceus | Abelmoschus haenkeanus | Abelmoschus lanyunatus | Abelmoschus magnificus | Abelmoschus marianus | Abelmoschus palustris | Abelmoschus roseus | Abelmoschus sublobatus | Abelmosk | Annual Hibiscus | Bamia Moschata | Galu Gasturi | Hibiscus abelmoschus | Hibiscus cardiophyllus | Hibiscus ciliaris | Hibiscus flavescens | Hibiscus haenkeanus | Hibiscus moschatus | Hibiscus multiformis | Hibiscus pseudabel-moschus | Hibiscus ricinifolius | Hibiscus roxburghii | Hibiscus sublobatus | Musk Mallow | Musk Okra | Muskdana | Muskseed | Ornamental Okra | Rose Mallow | Tropical Jewel Hibiscus | Yorka Okra

✹ SYMBOLIC MEANINGS
Sweet disposition.

⚜ POSSIBLE POWERS
Alleviate anxiety; Aphrodisiac; Attract love; Honoring the dead; Love; Protection.

⬥ FOLKLORE AND FACTS
Carry or wear a sachet of Ambrette flower and leaf to alleviate intense anxiousness. • Woody musky scented Ambrette essential oil is used in aromatherapy for alleviating anxiety, depression, fatigue and other manifestations of stress.

No. 002
✑*Abies alba* ⚗

Silver Fir

Abies abies | Abies argentea | Abies baldensis | Abies candicans | Abies chlorocarpa | Abies metensis | Abies miniata | Abies minor | Abies nobilis | Abies pardei | Abies pectinata | Abies picea | Abies taxifolia | Abies vulgaris | Fir | Fir Tree | Peuce abies | Picea kukunaria | Picea metensis | Picea pectinata | Picea pyramidalis | Picea rinzi | Picea tenuifolia | Pinus abies | Pinus baldensis | Pinus heterophylla | Pinus lucida | Pinus pectinata | Pinus picea

✹ SYMBOLIC MEANINGS
Elevation; Friendship; Height; Honesty; Longevity; Manifestation; Perceptiveness; Progress; Remembrance; Resilience; Time.

⚜ POSSIBLE POWERS
Birth; Change; Christmas celebration; Feminine rebirth; Insight; Progression; Protection.

⬥ FOLKLORE AND FACTS
The Silver Fir was the original Christmas tree because the needles were fragrant and lasted a longer time. • Young Silver Fir trees have sharper needles.

No. 003
✑*Abies balsamea* ⚗

Balsam Fir

Christmas Tree | Fir | Fir Tree | Peuce balsamea | Picea balsamea | Pinus balsamea | Pinus taxifolia

✹ SYMBOLIC MEANINGS
Elevation; Friendship; Height; Honesty; Longevity; Manifestation; Perceptiveness; Progress; Remembrance; Resilience; Time.

⚜ POSSIBLE POWERS
Change; Dissolving negativity; Insight; Progress; Strength.

⬥ FOLKLORE AND FACTS
Other members of the pine family can be set apart from a Balsam Fir by how the Balsam Fir needles look flat and how they attach to the twig. • The needles of young Balsam Fir are sharper. • Balsam Fir essential oil smells like a fragrant Christmas tree. • For thousands of years, the Native Americans of various tribes have utilized the needles, bark, sap, wood and root of the Balsam Fir tree for a wide variety of medicinal remedies.

No. 004
✑*Acer saccharum* ⚗

Sugar Maple

Acer hispidum | Acer palmifolium | Acer saccharophorum | Acer subglaucum | Acer treleaseanum | Bird's Eye Maple | Curly Maple | Hard Maple | Rock Maple | Saccharodendron hispidum | Saccharodendron saccharum | Sugar Tree | Sweet Maple

✹ SYMBOLIC MEANINGS
Reserve.

⚜ POSSIBLE POWERS
Air element; Earth element; Jupiter; Longevity; Love; Masculine energy; Money.

⬥ FOLKLORE AND FACTS
The seed pods of the Sugar Maple tree are unusual in that they occur connected in pairs that spin as they fall from the tree. • The Sugar Maple tree seeds are called samaras, maple keys, helicopters, whirlybirds, or poly-noses. • The Maple leaf is the national flower and iconic national symbol of Canada. • The connected Sugar Maple seed pods are often gilded and worn as jewelry. • Sugar Maple trees are tapped during very early spring to gather the sap to be boiled down into maple syrup, and further on to make maple sugar. • The US Army developed an effective carrier based on the shape of the Acer tree seed. It could hold up to sixty-five pounds

of supplies that were dropped from planes. • It is believed that the use of pure maple syrup as a sweetener is more manageable for diabetics than other glucose sources that are in their diets. • Sugar Maple tree wood will make a fine centering first magic wand.

No. 005

Achillea ageratum ☠️⚗️

Sweet Yarrow

Achillea viscosa | *Conforata ageratum* | English Mace | *Santolina ageratum* | Sweet Maudlin | Sweet Nancy

❋ SYMBOLIC MEANINGS
Courage; Courageous.

✿ POSSIBLE POWERS
Banish negativity; Clarity; Confidence; Courage; Discernment; Divination; Exorcism; Feminine energy; Fragrance; Grounding; Healing; Lift melancholy; Love; Marriage; Protection; Psychic opening; Psychic power; Repel insects; Romance; Venus; Ward off fear; Water element.

✦ FOLKLORE AND FACTS
Sweet Yarrow was strewn on the floors of homes in the Middle Ages to add fragrance, but it was primarily relied upon to repel ticks, lice, moths, fleas, silverfish, and any other plague of insects that would regularly infest a medieval household. • Sweet Yarrow is often used during handfasting and alternative wedding rituals. • Make and then carry or wear a sachet of Sweet Yarrow to banish negativity. • Make a yellow sachet of Sweet Yarrow. Write your fears on a small piece of parchment in black ink to place inside the packet. Carry or wear the sachet to ward off and overcome those fears. • Make and then carry or wear a sachet of Sweet Yarrow for confidence and courage. • Make and then carry or wear a pink and red sachet of Sweet Yarrow to invite romantic love that could lead to marriage. • A newly married couple should make and then place sachets of Sweet Yarrow in places around the home that cannot be accessed by pets or children, such as under rugs, under both sides of the mattress, in the top kitchen

cupboards, down into the sofa and chair cushions, and on the front door. This is done as encouragement to keep their love alive, romantic, and respectful to each other, and to prevent upsets that could cause discord in the relationship.

No. 006

Achillea millefolium ☠️⚗️

Yarrow

Achi Uea | Achillea | *Achillea albicaulis* | *Achillea albida* | *Achillea alpicola* | *Achillea ambigua* | *Achillea anethifolia* | *Achillea angustissima* | *Achillea arenicola* | *Achillea bicolor* | *Achillea borealis* | *Achillea californica* | *Achillea compacta* | *Achillea coronopifolia* | *Achillea crassifolia* | *Achillea cristata* | *Achillea cuspidata* | *Achillea dentifera* | *Achillea eradiata* | *Achillea fusca* | *Achillea gigantea* | *Achillea gracilis* | *Achillea haenkeana* | *Achillea intermedia* | *Achillea lanata* | *Achillea lanulosa* | *Achillea magna* | *Achillea marginata* | *Achillea megacephala* | *Achillea nabelekii* | *Achillea nigrescens* | *Achillea occidentalis* | *Achillea ochroleuca* | *Achillea ossica* | *Achillea pacifica* | *Achillea palmeri* | *Achillea pecten-veneris* | *Achillea pratensis* | *Achillea pseudotanacetifolia* | *Achillea puberula* | *Achillea scabra* | *Achillea setacea* | *Achillea sordida* | *Achillea subalpina* | *Achillea subhirsuta* | *Achillea submellifolium* | *Achillea sylvatica* | *Achillea tanacetifolia* | *Achillea tenuifolia* | *Achillea tenuis* | *Achillea tomentosa* | *Achillea virgata* | *Achillios millefoliatus* | *Alitubus millefolium* | Arrowroot | Bad Man's Plaything | Blue Yarrow | Carpenter's Weed | *Chamaemelum millefolium* | *Chamaemelum tanacetifolium* | Cloth of Gold | Common Yarrow | Death Flower | Devil's Nettle | Eerie | Fern Leaf Yarrow | Field Hops | Gearwe | Gordaldo | Hundred Leaved Grass | Knight's Milefoil | Knight's Milfoil | Knyghten | Melefour | Milefolium | Milfoil | Military Herb | Millefoil | Millefolium | *Millefolium officinale* | *Millefolium vulgare militaris* | Noble Yarrow | Nosebleed | Old Man's Mustard | Old Man's Pepper | Plumajillo | *Ptarmica borealis* | *Santolina millefolium* | Seven Years' Love | Snake's Grass | Soldier | Soldier's Woundwort | Stanch Griss | Stanch Weed | Staunch Weed | Sweet Yarrow | *Tanacetum angulatum* | Tansy | Thousand Leaf | Thousand Seal | Wound Wort | Woundwort | Yarroway | Yerw

❋ SYMBOLIC MEANINGS
Courage; Courageous; Cure and recovery; Lasting love.

✿ POSSIBLE POWERS
Animal communication; the Arts; Attraction; Beauty; Courage; Cure for heartache; Divination; Exorcism; Friendship; Gifts; Harmony; Healing; Health; Joy; Love; Lucky; Pleasure; Protection; Psychic power; Sensuality; Venus; Water element.

✦ FOLKLORE AND FACTS
Homer's hero of the *Iliad*, Achilles, supposedly used Yarrow on wounded soldiers under his leadership. • In traditional Yi Jing, which is also known as I Ching, dried Yarrow stalks are

A

tossed to create the shape that is used to divine the future.
• It was also thought that if Yarrow was once used as a
wedding decoration and it was then hung over a marriage
bed, seven years of true love would be ensured. • Wear
Yarrow for courage and protection. • Carry Yarrow to attract
friends. • Yarrow is used to banish evil from any place, any
thing, and anybody. • The Druids used dried Yarrow stems
for divination. • Yarrow essential oil is known as Blue Yarrow
and its use for aromatherapy can be very helpful in easing
worries and for calming the anxious mind. • A divination to
learn of one's true love was to pick the first stem of Yarrow
seen on the grave of a young man, then to sleep with it under
the pillow to dream the answer. • There was a time in Ireland
when on May Day, unmarried girls would fill a stocking with
Yarrow to sleep with it under the pillow and dream of the
identity of their future husband. • Yarrow is believed by some
to be the first herb in the hand of the Baby Jesus, therefore
making Yarrow a lucky herb forevermore.

No. 007
Achillea ptarmica subsp. *ptarmica* 🌿

Sneezewort

Achillea acuminata | Achillea dracunculoides | Achillea fragilis | Achillea grandifolia | Achillea
grandis | Achillea ircutiana | Achillea lenensis | Achillea leucantherma | Achillea linearis |
Achillea maxima | Achillea multiplex | Achillea partheniflora | Achillea ptarmica | Achillea
serrulata | Alitubus pyrenaicus | Bastard Pellitory | Chamaemelum ptarmica | Chrysanthemum
ptarmicifolium | European Pellitory | Fair Maid of France | Goose Tongue | Matricaria
ptarmicifolia | Ptarmica | Ptarmica grandiflora | Ptarmica integrifolia | Ptarmica ircutiana |
Ptarmica lenensis | Ptarmica vulgaris | Ptarmica vulgaris | Santolina ptarmica | Sneezeweed |
Sneezewort Yarrow | White Tansy | Wild Pellitory

☀ SYMBOLIC MEANINGS
Tears.

⚘ POSSIBLE POWERS
Expel an evil spirit.

☘ FOLKLORE AND FACTS
The act of actually sneezing
is what gave Sneezewort the
supposed power of being able
to rid oneself of evil spirits by
sneezing them out.

No. 008
Acmella oleracea

Buzz Button

Anacyclus pyrethraria | Bidens acmelloides | Bidens
fervida | Bidens fixa | Bidens fusca | Bidens oleracea | Cotula
pyrethraria | Electric Daisy | Jambu Oil Plant | Pyrethrum spilanthus |
Sancho Button | Sichuan Button | Spilanthes acmella | Spilanthes fusca |
Spilanthes oleracea | Spilanthes radicans | Tingflowers | Toothache Plant

☀ SYMBOLIC MEANINGS
Attraction.

⚘ POSSIBLE POWERS
Healing; Toothache pain relief.

☘ FOLKLORE AND FACTS
When the small flowers of the Buzz Button plant are in
bloom, they attract fireflies. • Buzz Button plant extract
is called Jambu Oil, which is used as a flavoring, most
especially in India, for such things as chewing tobacco and
chewing gum.

No. 009
Acorus calamus ☠🌿

Sweet Flag

Bajai | Bhutanashini | Calamus | Calamus aromaticus |
Flag Root | Gladdon | Gora-bac | Haimavati | Jatil |
Lubigan | Myrtle Flag | Myrtle Grass | Myrtle Sedge |
Sweet Cane | Sweet Grass | Sweet Root | Sweet
Rush | Sweet Sedge | Vacha | Vadaja | Vasa | Vasa
Bach | Vashambu | Vayambu | Vekhand

☀ SYMBOLIC MEANINGS
Affection; Aflutter; Attract love;
Delusion; Fitness; Lamentation; Love; Lust.

⚘ POSSIBLE POWERS
Aphrodisiac; Emotions; Feminine energy; Fertility;
Generation; Healing; Inspiration; Intuition; Love; Luck;
Lust; Money; the Moon; Protection; Psychic ability; Sea;
Subconscious mind; Tides; Travel by water; Water element.

☘ FOLKLORE AND FACTS
Sweet Flag was a favorite plant of Henry David Thoreau.
• As an addendum to the third printing of *Leaves of Grass*,
Walt Whitman wrote a section of poems titled "Calamus"
that was inspired by Sweet Flag, devoted to affection, love,
and lust. • Sweet Flag seeds can be strung on thread as
beads and worn for healing purposes. • Place a small piece
of Sweet Flag in each corner of the kitchen to guard against
poverty and hunger.

A

No. 010

Actaea racemosa ☠️📦

Black Cohosh

Actaea | Actaea gyrostachya | Actaea monogyna | Actaea orthostachya | Black Bugbane | Black Snakeroot | Botrophis actaeoides | Botrophis pumila | Botrophis serpentaria | Bugbane | Cimicifuga americana | Cimicifuga racemosa | Cimicifuga serpentaria | Fairy Candle | Macrotrys actaeoides | Macrotrys racemosa | Megotrys serpentaria | Thalictrodes racemosai

✹ SYMBOLIC MEANINGS
Rough.

🌼 POSSIBLE POWERS
Courage; Fire element; Love; Lust; Mars; Masculine energy; Money; Potency; Protection.

🜂 FOLKLORE AND FACTS
Sprinkle an infusion of Black Cohosh and rainwater, natural spring water, or distilled water around the perimeter of your house or on door thresholds to protect your home against evil entering into it. • In the case of impotency, make and carry a sachet of Black Cohosh. • In the case of meekness, make and carry a sachet of Black Cohosh for strength.

No. 011

Adiantum pedatum ☠️📦

Northern Maidenhair Fern

Adiantum americanum | Adiantum boreale | Adiantum grandifolium | Five-Fingered Fern

✹ SYMBOLIC MEANINGS
Bond of love; Confidence; Traditional dancing.

🌼 POSSIBLE POWERS
Aphrodisiac; Attract love; Beauty; Dancing; Feminine energy; Invisibility; Love; Venus; Water element.

🜂 FOLKLORE AND FACTS
The Druids believed Northern Maidenhair Fern could bestow invisibility. • The Native American tribes believed that the Northern Maidenhair Fern was a symbol of their traditional dancing. • Northwest Coastal Native American tribes may include the Northern Maidenhair Fern as part of their traditional dance regalia. • There is an unproven belief that by holding a nosegay of self-gathered sprigs of Rue, Broom, Maidenhair Fern, Agrimony, and Ground Ivy, one can gain profound intuition of who is and who is not a practicing witch.

No. 012

Adonis annua ☠️📦

Adonis

Adonis abortiva | Adonis aestivalis | Adonis atrorubens | Adonis autumnalis | Adonis baetica | Adonis castellana | Adonis erosipetala | Adonis flos | Adonis Flower | Adonis maculata | Adonis perramosa | Adonis phoenicea | Adonis presli | Autumn Adonis | Autumn Pheasant's Eye | Blood Drops | Cosmarium autumnale | Flos Adonis | Pheasant's Eye | Red Chamomile | Red Morocco | Rose-a-Ruby | Soldiers in Green

✹ SYMBOLIC MEANINGS
Painful recollections; Recollection of life's pleasure; Sad memories; Sorrowful recollections.

🌼 POSSIBLE POWERS
Love; Sex; Promiscuity.

🜂 FOLKLORE AND FACTS
It is said that the Adonis flower contains the spirits of many women and many men living in the same flower. Regarding that belief, there was once a secret religious congregation called the Arioi or Areoi who lived on the islands of Tahiti prior to the arrival of nineteenth century missionaries in Polynesia. These people had a single promiscuous marriage of absolute sexual freedom among themselves before and after marriage that consisted of one hundred males and one hundred females. • The Adonis plant has gone extinct in the Flanders and Wallonia regions of Belgium.

No. 013

Aegopodium podagraria ☠️📦

Ground Elder

Aegopodium angelicifolium | Aegopodium simplex | Aegopodium ternatum | Apium biternatum | Apium podagraria | Bishop's Weed | Carum podagraria | English Masterwort | Gout Wort | Goutweed | Herb Gerard | Ligusticum podagraria | Pimpinella angelicifolia | Podagraria aegopodium | Podagraria erratica | Seseli aegopodium | Sison podagraria | Sium podagraria | Sium vulgare | Snow in the Mountain | Tragoselinum angelica | Wild Masterwort

✹ SYMBOLIC MEANINGS
Anticipation; Precaution.

🌼 POSSIBLE POWERS
Abundance; Assimilating newness; Connect closer to the higher self; Grounding; Healing; Higher goals.

🜂 FOLKLORE AND FACTS
Ground Elder is considered to be a seriously undesirable weed for any garden. Even though the plant

A

will attract butterflies, Ground Elder has an invasive, highly competitive habit. When conditions are optimal, Ground Elder prevents other groundcovers from thriving and even prevents seedlings for shrubs and trees to firmly establish.
• Because the highly attractive Ground Elder is so aggressive and difficult to control, new plantings have been banned in many places around the world. • Historically, Ground Elder was commonly used for various medicinal purposes that have waned in modern times. • Because European monks once used Ground Elder for various medicinal purposes, it can often be found growing near the ruins of European monasteries.

No. 014
Aerva lanata 💀☠

Mountain Knotgrass

Achyranthes lanata | Achyranthes villosa | Aerva arachnoidea | Aerva elegans | Aerva floribunda | Aerva mozambicensis | Aerva pubescens | Aerva sansibarica | Aerva tandalo | Aerva viridis | Alternanthera pubescens | Amaranthus aeruoides | Amaranthus lanatus | Ashmahabhedah | Asmei | Astmabayda | Bhadra | Bhui | Bili Himdi Soppu | Bui-Kaltan | Chaya | Cherula | Ciru-Pulai | Gorakhbuti | Gorakhganja | Gorakshaganja | Illecebrum lanatum | Illecebrum pubescens | Jari | Kapu-madhura | Kapurijadi | Kapurmadhuri | Khali | Khari | Khul | Kul-ke-jar | Paronychia lanata | Pasha-nabheda | Pinde-conda | Pindi-chetter | Pindidonda Pol Pala | Pol-Kudu-Pala | Polpala | Sasai | Shatakabhedi | Spirke | Tamdlo | Ulinai | Woolly Aerva | Woolly Illecebrum

☀ SYMBOLIC MEANINGS
Tightly bound.

🌀 POSSIBLE POWERS
Fend off an evil spirit; Good luck hunting; Healing; Snakebite; Protection and well-being for widows.

🜂 FOLKLORE AND FACTS
Mountain Knotgrass is one of the Ten Sacred Flowers of Kerala, India. • Mountain Knotgrass is a traditional folk medicine remedy for snakebite. • Carry or wear a sachet of Mountain Knotgrass flower, leaf, and root to fend off an evil spirit. • Carry or wear a sachet of Mountain Knotgrass flower, leaf, and root for good luck when hunting. • A widow or widower can carry or wear a sachet of Mountain Knotgrass flower, leaf, and root for comfort and assurance of well-being.

No. 015
Aframomum corrorima 🝆🍴

Korarima

Aframomum korarima | Aframomum usambarense | Amomum corrorima | Amomum korarima | Ethiopian Cardamom | False Cardamom

☀ SYMBOLIC MEANINGS
Familiar comfort.

🌀 POSSIBLE POWERS
Aphrodisiac; Love; Luck; Lust; Money; Wishing.

🜂 FOLKLORE AND FACTS
Korarima is a very popular spice used in Ethiopian recipes, Middle Eastern spice blends, and to spice coffee. • Make then carry or wear a pink and red sachet filled with Korarima seeds to entice romantic love.

No. 016
Aframomum melegueta 🝆🍴

Grains of Paradise

Aframomum grana-paradisi | Aframomum melegguetella | African Pepper | Alligator Pepper | Amomum elatum | Amomum grana-paradisi | Amomum melegueta | Atare | Cardamomum grana-paradisi | Guinea Grains | Guinea Pepper | Hepper Pepper | Mbongo Spice | Melegueta Pepper | Torymenes officinalis | Zerumbet autranii

☀ SYMBOLIC MEANINGS
Judge.

🌀 POSSIBLE POWERS
Determining guilt; Divination; Fire element; Love; Luck; Lust; Mars; Masculine energy; Money; Wishing.

🜂 FOLKLORE AND FACTS
For the Melegueta plant it is all about the seeds which are usually obtained by the pod, with the seeds within known as Grains of Paradise or Mbongo Spice. • Grains of Paradise spice seeds, either whole or ground into a powder, can be used to make wishes by holding the spice in the hand to make the wish, then tossing a little of it in each of the four directions beginning with North and ending with West. • In Igboland, Nigeria, Grains of Paradise and Kola Nuts are part of nearly every ceremony as the primary element before anything else, since Igbo traditional religious prayers and offerings always involve Grains of Paradise along with the revered Kola Nuts.

No. 017

Agastache foeniculum 🍵

Blue Giant Hyssop

Agastache anethiodora | Anise Hyssop | Fragrant Giant Hyssop | Giant Hyssop | *Hyptis marathrosma* | Hyssopus anethiodorus | Hyssopus anisatus | Hyssopus discolor | Hyssopus foeniculum* | Lavender Giant Hyssop | *Lophanthus anisatus* | *Lophanthus foeniculum* | Perilla marathrosma* | Stachys foeniculum | Vleckia albescens | Vleckia anethiodora | Vleckia anisata | Vleckia bracteata | Vleckia bracteosa | Vleckia discolor | Vleckia foeniculum* | *Vleckia incarnata*

✹ SYMBOLIC MEANINGS
Cleanliness.

✹ POSSIBLE POWERS
Plenty; Provision.

☾ FOLKLORE AND FACTS
Blue Giant Hyssop blooms prolifically, feeding hummingbirds, butterflies, and honeybees. One acre can easily support one hundred beehives from summer until frost.

No. 018

Agathosma betulina ☠🍵

Buchu

Agathosma | *Barosma betulina* | *Barosma orbicularis* | Boegoe | Bookoo | Bucco | *Bucco betulina* | Bucoo | Buku | Diosma | *Diosma betulina* | *Diosma crenata* | *Hartogia betulina* | *Parapetalifera betulina* | Pinkaou | Round Leaf Buchu | Sab

✹ SYMBOLIC MEANINGS
Good fragrance.

✹ POSSIBLE POWERS
Divination; Feminine energy; the Moon; Prophetic dreams; Psychic power; Water element; Wind spell.

☾ FOLKLORE AND FACTS
Buchu plants are prized for their pleasant herbal fragrance. • To prepare to effectively peer into the future requires preparation. A few drops of Buchu essential oil or some Buchu leaves in the bathwater will imbue additional power into a seer while soaking in the tub. Add nothing else to the water. Allow the moisture from the magical bath to dry on the body without aid of a towel. Then a few drops of Buchu essential oil in a diffuser will additionally relax and help open the Mind's Eyes and the Mind's Ears.

No. 019

Agave amica 🍵

Tuberose

Agave polianthes | *Agave tuberosa* | Azucena | Bone Flower | Bunga Sedap Malam | *Crinum angustifolium* | Gole Maryam | King of Fragrance | Mary Flower | Mixochitl | Nilasambangi | Nishi Ghanda | Omi-xochitl | *Polianthes gracilis* | *Polianthes tuberosa* | Raat ki Rani | Rajnigandha | Ronjoni Ghanda | Sambangi | Sampangi | Scent of the Night | Sugandaraja | *Tuberosa amica* | Wan Xiang Yu | Ye Lai Xiang | Yue Xia Xiang

✹ SYMBOLIC MEANINGS
Dangerous pleasures; Funerary; Pleasures that inevitably cause pain; Sweet voice; Voluptuousness.

✹ POSSIBLE POWERS
Amorous madness; Calms the nerves; Harmony; Lost virginity; Lucid sexual dreams; Peace; Psychic stimulation; Restore happiness; Seduction; Ward off evil or negativity.

☾ FOLKLORE AND FACTS
There is a legend around the power of the Tuberose's fragrance and its ability to seduce a young girl into losing her virginity. • It was believed that breathing in the fragrance of the Tuberose throughout the night in a bedroom would incite sexually indecent lucid dreams. • Tuberoses were coveted by young women, who wore them in their hair and tucked them in the cleft of their bosom. • Tuberose essential oil is a favorite scent used by the finest quality perfumers.

A

No. 020

Agrimonia eupatoria ☠️☕

Agrimony

Agrimonia | Agrimonia adhaerens | Agrimonia adscendens | Agrimonia canescens | Agrimonia elata | Agrimonia humilis | Agrimonia minor | Agrimonia officinalis | Agrimonia officinarum | Agrimonia sulcata | Agrimonia vulgaris | Church Steeples | Common Agrimony | Garclive | Ntola | Odermenning | Philanthropos | Sticklewort | Stickwort | Umakhuthulas

✴ **SYMBOLIC MEANINGS**
Gratitude; Thankfulness.

⚜ **POSSIBLE POWERS**
Aid sleep; Air element; Banish entities or negative energy; Barrier against negative energies; Break a hex; Colorize; Enhance psychic healing; Jupiter; Masculine energy; Overcome emotional obstructions or fear; Protection; Protection against evil, goblins, poison, or psychic attack; Reverse spells; Send spells back to the hexer; Ward off witchcraft.

🜃 **FOLKLORE AND FACTS**
Since ancient Roman times, Agrimony has been believed to have medicinal and magical powers. • A sachet that has a bit each of Agrimony and Mugwort sewn into it then placed under the pillow will promote dreaming. • It was believed that if Agrimony is placed under the head of a sleeper, it must be removed for the sleeper to fully awaken. • It was believed that scattering Agrimony seeds around the perimeter of one's home would fend off witchcraft. • Agrimony seeds carried in one's pockets or in a pouch around the neck or waist will fend off witchcraft. • Agrimony was believed to be able to offer protection against evil, poison, and goblins as well as banish negative energies and negative spirits. • A yellow vegetable dye that can be used to dye wool is made using the Agrimony plant. • There is an unproven belief that by holding a nosegay of self-gathered sprigs of Rue, Broom, Maidenhair Fern, Agrimony, and Ground Ivy, one can gain profound intuition of who is and who is not a practicing witch.

No. 021

Agropyron repens ☠️☕

Witch Grass

Braconotia officinarum | Common Couch | Couch Grass | Couchgrass | Dog Grass | Elytrigia repens | Frumentum repens | Hairy Panic | Quack Grass | Quick Grass | Quitch | Quitch Grass | Scutch Grass | Triticum infestum | Triticum repens | Twitch | Witchgrass | Zeia repens

✴ **SYMBOLIC MEANINGS**
Remove a curse or hex.

⚜ **POSSIBLE POWERS**
Curse removal; Exorcism; Happiness; Hex removal; Jupiter; Love; Lust; Masculine energy.

🜃 **FOLKLORE AND FACTS**
When it comes to hex removal, Witch Grass does its best work at removing and eliminating a hex or a curse without blindly retaliating by sending it back to where it came from, which is a knee-jerk reaction and best avoided. • Prior to the steady emmigration from England, Witch Grass was virtually unknown in North America until it was introduced into the newly planted English gardens in the New World.

No. 022

Alcea rosea ☠️☕

Hollyhock

Alcea cretica | Alcea microchiton | Althaea caribaea | Althaea chinensis | Althaea coromandeliana | Althaea cretica | Althaea flexuosa | Althaea meonantha | Althaea mexicana | Althaea microchiton | Althaea rosea | Althaea sinensis | Common Hollyhock | Malva florida | Malva hortensus | Malva rosea

✴ **SYMBOLIC MEANINGS**
Abundance; Ambition; Ambition of a scholar; Cycle of life; Fecundity; Fruitfulness; Growth; Liberality; Rebirth.

⚜ **POSSIBLE POWERS**
Death; Fertility; Funerals; Life.

🜃 **FOLKLORE AND FACTS**
The Hollyhock is a beautiful, surprisingly tall, narrow plant with large flowers along its stalk that is often found in gardens planted behind the shorter plants. The Hollyhock can grow to a stunning eight feet tall. • As a form of the Wild Marshmallow, the Hollyhock got its name from "Holy Hoc," with Hoc meaning Mallow. • Hollyhocks were often planted

A

along fence-lines surrounding cemeteries. The ancient Egyptians sometimes buried Hollyhock flower wreaths with mummies to indicate the Circle of Life and what was hoped to come for the deceased after death. • It was believed that fairies used Hollyhock blossoms as skirts. • Because the Hollyhock seed looks like a cheese wheel, it was called Fairy Cheese. • In Victorian times it was very common to find tall Hollyhocks growing near the outhouse that had been mass planted as a privacy screen. If a guest to the house needed to use the privy they would only need to look for the Hollyhocks. • A charm dating from around the mid-1600s that supposedly allows a mortal to see fairies combines Wild Thyme, Hazel flower bud, Marigold, and Hollyhock. • Plant Hollyhocks near the home to encourage power and wealth in abundance to all those who reside within. • Plant Hollyhocks near the home to encourage fertility. • It is believed that Hollyhock seeds found their way to Europe from the Middle East when they were carried home by Crusaders.

No. 023

Alchemilla vulgaris

Lady's Mantle

Alchemilla acutangula | *Alchemilla acutiloba* | *Alchemilla latifolia* | *Alchemilla pontic* | Bear's Foot | Dewcup | Dew-cup | Leontopodium | Lion's Foot | Nine Hooks | *Potentilla acutiloba* | Stellaria

SYMBOLIC MEANINGS

Soft.

POSSIBLE POWERS

Attract love; Feminine energy; Femininity; Love; Venus; Water element.

FOLKLORE AND FACTS

In the Middle Ages, drops of dew that were on Lady's Mantle leaves were collected every day as they were considered sacred and magical. • The precious Lady's Mantle dewdrops were, and still are, sometimes used in many different magical potions. • The dewdrops have given the Lady's Mantle the name Dew-cup. • Lady's Mantle is believed to have the ability to attract fairies. • A pillow containing Lady's Mantle leaves or placing Lady's Mantle leaves under a pillow supposedly promotes a good night's sleep. • In the Middle Ages it was seriously believed that Lady's Mantle could actually restore a girl's lost virginity. • Lady's Mantle dewdrops were used by many eighteenth century alchemists in experiments attempting to mystically transform various metals into gold.

No. 024

Aletris farinosa

Unicorn Plant

Ague | Ague Grass | Ague Root | Ague Weed | Aletris | *Aletris alba* | *Alétris Farineux* | *Aletris lucida* | Aloeroot | Backache Root | Bettie Grass | Betty Grass | Bitter Grass | Black Root | Blazing Star | Crow Corn | Huskwort | Maïs des Corbeaux | Mealy Starwort | Rheumatism Root | Star Root | Stargrass | Starwort | True Unicorn Root | Unicorn Horn | Unicorn Root | White Stargrass | White-tube

SYMBOLIC MEANINGS

Complete; Powerful.

POSSIBLE POWERS

Break a hex; Gain protection of good spirits; Keep evil away; Preserve virginity; Protection; Restore innocence of the soul; Reverse a negative spell; Trust; Turn away evil.

FOLKLORE AND FACTS

If evil is plaguing your home, form crosses using Unicorn Plant roots and place them outside each entry to your house • Unicorn Plant can be used in love spells to attract one's soul mate. • Unicorn Plant has been carried to fend off evil. • Use Unicorn Plant to help remember past-life lovers. • The Unicorn Plant is useful in uncrossing rituals and is believed to be an effective hex breaker. • The Unicorn Plant is a visionary herb that can promote fantasy in magical working. • Carry or wear an amulet or sachet of Unicorn Plant to retain virginity. • Make and wear a Unicorn Plant sachet for personal protection against evil energy.

No. 025

Aleurites moluccana

Candlenut

Aleurites javanicus | *Aleurites pentaphyllus* | *Aleurites remyi* | *Aleurites trilobus* | Buah Keras | Candleberry Tree | Indian Walnut | *Jatropha moluccana* | Kemiri | Kuki | Kukui Nut Tree | Nuez de la India | Varnish Tree

SYMBOLIC MEANINGS

Enlightenment.

POSSIBLE POWERS

Enlightenment.

FOLKLORE AND FACTS

The ancient Hawaiians would open a Candlenut and extract the nutmeat that is slightly smaller than that from a shelled Walnut. They would skewer the oily nutmeats then set them afire. These candles burned for close to forty-five minutes. • Native Hawaiians may still use Candlenut oil for lighting stone lamps. • All parts of the Candlenut tree have been deemed very useful in the day-to-day life of many Polynesian people. • The polished nuts can be unpainted, painted, or polished to a gleam, drilled through with a hole then strung as a beautiful highly prized Candlenut bead necklace.

No. 026
Alkanna tinctoria ☠🏺

Alkanet

Alkanna arietinella | Alkanna bracteolata | Alkanna lehmannii | Alkanna matthioli | Alkanna tuberculata | Alkannawurzel | Alkermeswurzel | Anchusa | Anchusa bracteolata | Anchusa rhizochroa | Anchusa tinctoria | Anchusa tuberculata | Baphorhiza tinctoria | Buglossum tinctorium | Dyer's Alkanet | Dyers's Bugloss | Languedoc Bugloss | Lithospermum commutatum | Lithospermum lehmannii | Lithospermum obtusum | Lithospermum tinctorium | Lycopsis cyrenaica | Onochilis tinctoria | Orchanet | Racine d'Alcanna | Racine d'Orcanette | Radix anchusea | Ratan Jot | Rhytispermum tinctorium | Rote Ochsenzungen Wurzel | Schminkwurzel | Spanish Bugloss

✹ SYMBOLIC MEANINGS
Falsehood.

✤ POSSIBLE POWERS
Attract prosperity; Colorize; Feminine energy; Healing; Prosperity; Protection; Protection from a snakebite; Purification; Repel negativity; Replace negativity with positivity; Water element.

❦ FOLKLORE AND FACTS
Alkanet creates a noble color for a red vegetable dye that attracts all kinds of prosperity. • Alkanet is used for its rich red color for dye and also to colorize wine. • When Alkanet is mixed with oil it will make a rich stain for wood that is found on many red shades close to the color of rosewood. • Wear an amulet of Alkanet to help overcome an overwhelming fear of snakes.

No. 027
Alliaria petiolata ☠🏺

Jack-by-the-Hedge

Alliaria alliacea | Alliaria alliaria | Alliaria fuchsii | Alliaria mathioli | Arabis alliaria | Arabis petiolata | Clypeola alliacea | Crucifera alliaria | Erysimum alliaceum | Erysimum alliaria | Erysimum cordifolium | Garlic Mustard | Garlic Root | Hedge Garlic | Hesperis alliaria | Jack in the Bush | Pallavicinia alliaria | Penny Hedge | Poor Man's Mustard | Sauce-Alone | Sisymbrion alliarium | Sisymbrium alliaria | Sisymbrium truncatum

✹ SYMBOLIC MEANINGS
Pushy.

✤ POSSIBLE POWERS
Abundance; Assertive; Healing.

❦ FOLKLORE AND FACTS
Every part of Jack-by-the-Hedge smells like Garlic. • In Europe, Jack-by-the-Hedge is considered to be one of the oldest spices used. • Jack-by-the-Hedge was brought into North America by settlers from Europe in the 1800s. • Jack-by-the-Hedge is considered to be a troublesome invasive species due to the fact it can undermine the biodiversity of forests by dominating the undergrowth area. • Jack-by-the-Hedge is toxic to most herbivores.

A

No. 028

Allium ampeloprasum 🏺🍴

Leek

Ail à Grosse Tête | Alho Bravo | Alho Inglês | Alho Porro | *Allium adscendens* | *Allium albescens* | *Allium ascendens* | *Allium babingtonii* | *Allium bertolonii* | *Allium byzantinum* | *Allium duriaeanum* | *Allium durieuanum* | *Allium gasparrinii* | *Allium halleri* | *Allium holmense* | *Allium kurrat* | *Allium laetum* | *Allium leucanthum* | *Allium multiflorum* | *Allium polyanthum* | *Allium porraceum* | *Allium porrum* | *Allium pylium* | *Allium scopulicola* | *Allium spectabile* | *Allium syriacum* | *Allium thessalum* | Antillais Poireau | Broadleaf | Broadleaf Wild Leek | Cebolla Puerro | Elephant Garlic | Great-headed Garlic | Iraakuuccittam | Kurrat | Pearl Onion | Perpétuel | Petit Poireau | Poireau | *Porrum amethystinum* | *Porrum ampeloprasum* | *Porrum commune* | *Porrum sativum*

✴ SYMBOLIC MEANINGS
Lingering presence.

⚜ POSSIBLE POWERS
Exorcism; Fire element; Love; Mars; Masculine energy; Protection.

☘ FOLKLORE AND FACTS
It has been suggested that if two people eat Leek together, they will fall in love. • Leek can be carried for protection. • Leek is believed to have been brought into Southwest England and Wales by Prehistoric people. • One of the national emblems of Wales is the Leek. One reason as to how that came to be is attributed to a Welsh legend. When an ancient battle against the Saxons took place in a Leek field, King Cadwaladr ordered the soldiers to indicate which side they were fighting on by attaching a Leek to their battle helmet. Another legend says that, when fasting, Saint David, patron saint of Wales, only ate Leeks. • The British one pound coin in 1985 and 1990 both depicted a Leek in its design as a tribute to Wales. • The Welsh Guards wear a beautiful design of the Leek symbol on their caps. • To break a hex and drive its evil away from you, bite into a Leek.

No. 029

Allium ampeloprasum var. *ampeloprasum* 🏺🍴

Elephant Garlic

Ail à Grosse Tête | Alho Bravo | Alho Inglês | Alho Porro | *Allium adscendens* | *Allium albescens* | *Allium ascendens* | *Allium babingtonii* | *Allium bertolonii* | *Allium byzantinum* | *Allium duriaeanum* | *Allium durieuanum* | *Allium gasparrinii* | *Allium halleri* | *Allium holmense* | *Allium kurrat* | *Allium laetum* | *Allium leucanthum* | *Allium multiflorum* | *Allium polyanthum* | *Allium porraceum* | *Allium porrum* | *Allium pylium* | *Allium scopulicola* | *Allium spectabile* | *Allium syriacum* | *Allium thessalum* | Antillais Poireau | Broadleaf | Cebolla Puerro | Great-Headed Garlic | Iraakuuccittam | Kurrat | Leek | Pearl Onion | Perpétuel | Petit Poireau | Poireau | *Porrum amethystinum* | *Porrum ampeloprasum* | *Porrum commune* | *Porrum sativum* | Wild Leek

✴ SYMBOLIC MEANINGS
Lingering presence.

⚜ POSSIBLE POWERS
Exorcism; Fire element; Love; Mars; Protection.

☘ FOLKLORE AND FACTS
Human man fist-sized Elephant Garlic tastes like mild Garlic, but is more closely related to the Leek. Under those conditions, even as big as a bulb of Elephant Garlic is, it is unlikely to have what it takes to fend off a vampire. However, it still offers other magical protections as well as folk medicinal usefulness.

No. 030

Allium ascalonicum 🏺🍴

Shallot

Allium carneum | *Allium fissile* | *Allium hierochuntinum* | *Cepa ascalonica* | Eschalot | French Gray Shallot | French Red Shallot | Griselle | Kanda | Musir | Persian Shallot | *Porrum ascalonicum* | True Shallot

✴ SYMBOLIC MEANINGS
Land of Astolet; Unrequited love.

⚜ POSSIBLE POWERS
Cure misfortune; Fire element; Luck; Mars; Masculine energy; Purification.

☘ FOLKLORE AND FACTS
The ancient Greeks believed that the Shallot comes from a city called Ashkalon, which was an ancient city in Biblical Canaan. • Shallot-infused bathwater is used for a good luck bath when a lot of it is needed the most.

No. 031

Allium cepa 🌱🍴

Onion

Allium angolense | Allium aobanum | Allium cepaeum | Allium commune | Allium cumaria |
Allium esculentum | Allium napus | Allium nigritanum | Allium pauciflorum | Allium salota |
Ascalonicum sativum | Brown Onion | Bulb Onion | Cepa alba | Cepa esculenta | Cepa pallens |
Cepa rubra | Cepa vulgaris | Common Onion | Kepa esculenta | Oingnum | Onyoun | Porrum
cepa | Purple Onion | Red Onion | Unyoun | White Onion | Yellow Onion | Yn-Leac

☀ SYMBOLIC MEANINGS
Emotional release; Multi-layered protection.

✦ POSSIBLE POWERS
Colorize; Exorcism; Fire element; Healing; Isis; Lust; Mars;
Masculine energy; Money; Prophetic dreaming; Protection;
Purification; Remove aggressive energy; Remove negative
energy; piritual cleansing; Spirituality.

☘ FOLKLORE AND FACTS
The ancient Egyptians worshipped the Onion, as the round
shape, the layers, and the concentric rings when sliced easily
symbolized Eternal Life. • The ancient Egyptians included
Onions in burials. • In the Middle Ages, Onions were so
valuable that people gave them as gifts and could even pay
their rent with them. • An Onion is commonly used as an
antidote for an aggressive psychic attack. By keeping an
Onion on the mantlepiece or hung in a room it will strongly
attract and absorb negative energy and possibly even a
malicious spirit, to be removed by burying or burning the
Onion after the anxiety dissipates and the process feels as
though it has been completed. If the problem returns, use a
fresh Onion. • When sensing that there is negative energy in
the home, an Onion can be used to remove it. This is done by
cutting an Onion into quarters and placing the pieces where
negativity feels present. It is often settled in the sleeping
areas, but it can be anywhere. Remove the Onion's quarters
twelve hours later by taking the pieces all the way out of the
house to throw them away, preferably by burying or burning
them. Use a fresh Onion every night until it feels like it is no
longer necessary. • Early
American settlers would
hang strings of Onions
over the doors to protect
the inhabitants of the
home from infections.
• An interesting divination
when you have a decision
to make is using an Onion
to make the decision for
you. Using a separate
Onion for each option,

scratch a possibility on each one. Put them all into a dark
place, checking them one time each day. The first one
that sprouts will provide the answer. • Grow Onions as a
protection against evil. • Sleep with an Onion under the
pillow to encourage revealing dreams. • Onions were an
ingredient in ancient Egyptian mummification. • Ancient
Romans believed Onions were a sleep aid. They also believed
that Onions could heal dog bites, toothaches, backaches,
and much more. • The Pilgrims brought Onions over to
America from England, only to find that they were already
being enjoyed by Native Americans. • An easy to do favorite
school project to teach the nature of vegetable dyes involves
using Onion skins to produce a brown color. • One folk
remedy for bringing down a fever is to lightly tie the slices
of an Onion to cover over the bottoms of bare feet by first
wrapping them around once with a damp paper towel to
hold them in place, then covering them over with a sock to
hold them snug to the skin of the soles. By the time the
Onion slices are limp the fever should be gone.

No. 032

Allium cepa
var. *proliferum* 🌱🍴

Egyptian Tree Onion

Allium multiabulatum | Egyptian Onion |
Topsetting Onion | Tree Onion | Walking Onion

☀ SYMBOLIC MEANINGS
Emotional release; Multi-layered
protection.

✦ POSSIBLE POWERS
Exorcism; Healing; Lust; Money;
Prophetic dreams; Protection;
Purification; Spiritual cleansing;
Spirituality.

☘ FOLKLORE AND FACTS
To make a difficult decision, gather
as many Egyptian Tree Onions as
there will be options and scratch a
possibility on each one. Put them in
a dark place and check them once a
day. The first to sprout provides the
answer.

A

No. 033

Allium fistulosum 🌿🍽

Everlasting Onion

Allium bouddae | *Allium kashgaricum* | Bunching Onion | *Cepa fissilis* | *Cepa fistulosa* | *Cepa ventricosa* | Here Today Here Tomorrow | Japanese Bunching Onion | *Kepa fistulosa* | Long Green Onion | *Phyllodolon fistulosum* | *Porrum fistulosum* | Scallion | Sibies | Small Bunching Onion | Spring Onion | Welsh Onion

✴ SYMBOLIC MEANINGS
Strength; You're elegant; You're perfect.

✦ POSSIBLE POWERS
Enhance psychic ability; Prophetically dream; Protection.

✦ FOLKLORE AND FACTS
The only time of the year that an Allium can be planted is in the autumn. The flower of the narrow Everlasting Onion plant is globular and the stem is tall, making it possible to tuck at least a few plants into even the most densely crowded garden. • Tuck an Everlasting Onion into a sachet and sleep with it under the pillow to enhance one's psychic ability with the hope of perhaps having a prophetic dream.

No. 034

Allium sativum 🌿🍽

Garlic

Ajo | *Allium arenarium* | *Allium controversum* | *Allium longicuspis* | *Allium ophioscorodon* | Artichoke Garlic | Creole Garlic | Crow Garlic | Field Garlic | Hard Necked Garlic | Meadow Garlic | Porcelain Garlic | *Porrum ophioscorodon* | *Porrum sativum* | Purple Stripe Garlic | Rocambole Garlic | Sativum | Silverskin Garlic | Soft-Necked Garlic | Stinking Rose | Wild Garlic | Wild Onion

✴ SYMBOLIC MEANINGS
Courage; Get well; Strength.

✦ POSSIBLE POWERS
Anti-theft; Aphrodisiac; Attract love; Exorcism; Fire element; Healing; Hecate; Lust; Mars; Masculine energy; Protection; Protection against an evil spirit, vampire, or werewolf; Unrequited love; Ward off evil, the evil eye, illness, a vampire, or werewolf.

✦ FOLKLORE AND FACTS
Traditionally compiled by Confucius, the *Shih Ching*—also called *Shijing*, the *Classic of Poetry*, or *Book of Odes*—mentions it. • The earliest Sanskrit writings refer to Garlic too. • Wear Garlic as protection against monsters. • A superstitious matador will wear a clove of Garlic on a string around his neck for his protection prior to a bullfight. • Some mountain climbers wear Garlic amulets to fend off bad weather. • To dream of Garlic is good fortune. • To dream of giving away Garlic is bad luck. • Garlic wreaths outside a home's door are put there to ward off witches and psychic vampires. • A clove of Garlic worn on a string around the neck protects a traveler. • There was a time when brides actually tucked a clove of Garlic somewhere on themselves as protection against anyone or anything that could ruin their wedding day. • Magical Garlic would supposedly only grow during a waning moon. • Garlic's sticky juice can be used as a natural glue to mend hairline cracks in glass. Cutting a clove in half then gently rubbing it across the crack forces the juice into the cracks and helps keep them from extending any farther. • Sailors should carry Garlic on board to protect themselves and the ship against shipwreck. • To protect oneself against hepatitis, string thirteen cloves of Garlic into a necklace then wear it for thirteen days. In the middle of the night on the thirteenth day, walk to the nearest intersection, and toss the Garlic necklace behind you. Don't look back. Run all the way home.

A

Allium schoenoprasum

Chives

Allium acutum | Allium alpinum | Allium broteri | Allium buhseanum | Allium carneum | Allium coloratum | Allium foliosum | Allium glaucum | Allium Herb | Allium idzuense | Allium lusitanicum | Allium montanum | Allium palustre | Allium punctulatum | Allium purpurascens | Allium raddeanum | Allium reflexum | Allium riparium | Allium roseum | Allium sibiricum | Allium tenuifolium | Allium ubinicum | Allium udinicum | Ascalonicum schoenoprasum | Cepa schoenoprasa | Cepa tenuifolia | Porrum schoenoprasum | Porrum sibiricum | Rivas | Rush Leek | Schoenissa rosea | Schoenissa schoenoprasa | Schoenoprasum vulgare | Sweth

✹ **SYMBOLIC MEANINGS**
Usefulness; Why are you crying?

✸ **POSSIBLE POWERS**
Exorcism; Healing; Promotes psychic powers; Protection from evil or negativity.

☘ **FOLKLORE AND FACTS**
There was a time when bunches of Chives were hung in homes with the sole intention of repelling evil spirits. • Early American Dutch settlers deliberately planted Chives in the fields used for grazing their dairy cows so they could enjoy milk naturally flavored with the distinctive taste. • Carry or wear a sachet of Chives to push away a clinging bad habit.

Allium scorodoprasum

Rocambole

Allium arenarium | Allium contortum | Allium neglectum | Allium obscurum | Allium persicum | Allium supranisianum | Allium violaceum | Ascalonicum scorodoprasum | Korean Pickled-Peel | Porrum arenarium | Porrum scorodoprasum | Sand Leek

✹ **SYMBOLIC MEANINGS**
Patience.

✸ **POSSIBLE POWERS**
Flavoring; Healing; Protection against evil; Strength.

☘ **FOLKLORE AND FACTS**
What was once cultivated Rocambole can be found growing somewhat wild near very old homes where, once upon a time, it might have been grown for use as a culinary herb.

Allium tuberosum

Garlic Chives

Allium angulosum | Allium argyi | Allium chinense | Allium roxburghii | Allium tricoccum | Allium uliginosum | Allium yesoense | Chinese Chive | Chinese Leek | Jeongguji | Jiu Cai | Ku Chai | Nira | Nothoscordum sulvia | Oriental Garlic Chive | Sol

✹ **SYMBOLIC MEANINGS**
Courage; Strength.

✸ **POSSIBLE POWERS**
Prophetic dreams; Protection; Psychic power.

☘ **FOLKLORE AND FACTS**
Although the leaves smell like Onions when they are cut or crushed, the fragrance of the Garlic Chives flower resembles that of a Violet.

Alnus glutinosa

Alder

Black Alder | European Alder | European Black Alder | Common Alder

✹ **SYMBOLIC MEANINGS**
Giving; Nurturing; King of the woods.

✸ **POSSIBLE POWERS**
Colorize; Decision making; Divination; Education; Music; Poetry; Protection for the dead; Teaching; Weather magic; Wind magic.

☘ **FOLKLORE AND FACTS**
Appreciated for its bright tone, Alder wood has been used for the bodies of Fender Stratocaster and Telecaster electric guitars since the 1950s. • Alder is strongly connected to both elemental fire and elemental water, making it unusual, which makes Alder wood a fine choice for a self-protective healing wand that is gifted in divination and anything regarding the magical elements of fire and of water. • Nearly all of the pilings that support the city of Venice, Italy are made of Alder wood. • Alder bark produces a brown vegetable dye for fabrics. • Include Alder in rituals for the dying and the deceased to provide protection in their transition as they leave the physical realm.

No. 039
Aloe vera ⚱

Aloe Vera

Aloe | Aloe barbadensis | Aloe chinensis | Aloe elongata | Aloe flava | Aloe indica | Aloe lanzae | Aloe maculata | Aloe rubescens | Aloe variegata | Aloe vulgaris | Barbados | Barbados Aloe | Burn Plant | Crocodile's Tail | Crocodile's Tongue | Curaçao Aloe | First-Aid Plant | Gheekvar | Ghiu Kumari | Ghrtakumari | Guar Patha | Gwar Patha | Immortality Plant | Katraazhai | Kattar Vazha | Korphad | Kumari | Lidah Buaya | Lily of the Desert | Lu Hui | Medicinal Aloe | Medicine Plant | Miracle Plant | Plant of Immortality | Quargandal | Sabila | Saqal | Savia | Savila | Single Bible | True Aloe | Zabila

✴ SYMBOLIC MEANINGS
Bitterness; Dejection; Grief; Integrity; Luck; Most effective healer; Religious superstition; Small talk; Sorrow; Superstition; Wisdom.

✿ POSSIBLE POWERS
Bring good luck or success; Feminine energy; Guard against evil influences; Healing; Luck; the Moon; Prevent household accidents; Prevent loneliness; Protection; Repel evil; Security; Shelter from harm; Water element; Worldly success.

✾ FOLKLORE AND FACTS
Aloe Vera has been planted on graves to help promote pre-reincarnation peacefulness. • Drawings of Aloe Vera plants have been discovered on the walls of the tombs of Egyptian pharaohs. • There are ongoing studies into the extensive benefits of the Aloe Vera plant. • To bring forth a new lover by the time of the new moon, burn Aloe Vera on a Friday night during a full moon. • Growing Aloe Vera as a houseplant will protect against household accidents and evil. • Use fresh Aloe Vera gel to anoint above doors and windows to both keep out evil and bring in luck. • Aloe Vera is believed to be able to alleviate loneliness. • The Aloe Vera plant is know as the Burn Plant because the sticky gel within the fleshy leaf has been applied to millions of burns as a healing salve for thousands of years. • Sunburn can be soothed with a coating of Aloe Vera gel.

No. 040
Aloysia citrodora ⚱🍴

Lemon Verbena

Aloysia triphylla | Cedron | Hierba Luisa | Lemon Beebrush | Lippia citriodora | Louisa | Louiza | Verbena triphylla | Yerba Luisa | Zappania citriodora

✴ SYMBOLIC MEANINGS
Attraction; Attracts the opposite sex; Love; Sexual attraction; Sexual attractiveness.

✿ POSSIBLE POWERS
Air element; Art; the Arts; Attraction; Beauty; Friendship; Gifts; Harmony; Joy; Love; Masculine energy; Mercury; Pleasure; Protection; Purification; Sensuality.

✾ FOLKLORE AND FACTS
Lemon Verbena can be added to your bath water to purify yourself of negative energies. • Lemon Verbena is often added to give a lemony flavor to beverages, alcohol, liqueurs, and some dishes.

No. 041
Althea officinalis ⚱

Althea

Althaea balearica | Althaea kragujevacensis | Althaea multiflora | Althaea pulchra | Althaea sublobata | Common Marshmallow | Heemst | Malva althaea | Malva maritima | Malva officinalis | Marsh Mallow | Marshmallow | Marshmellow | Mortification Root | Slaz | Sweet Weed | Wymote

✴ SYMBOLIC MEANINGS
Dying for love; Maternal tenderness; Unmarried.

✿ POSSIBLE POWERS
Applying knowledge; Astral plane; Attract good spirits; Beneficence; Controlling lower principles; Feminine energy; Finding lost objects; Overcoming evil; Persuasion; Protection; Psychic power; Regeneration; Removing depression; Sensuality; Uncovering secrets; Victory; Water element.

✾ FOLKLORE AND FACTS
Carry Althea as a sachet to stimulate psychic power. • Althea is believed to be capable of drawing in good spirits. • A vase of Althea in the window will attract a lover who is straying. • Carry Althea in a sachet or small blue pouch to stimulate psychic power. • Althea is believed to have the power to calm an angry person.

A

No. 042

Alyssum maritima ⚱

Alyssum

Adyseton halimifolium | Adyseton
maritimum | Adyseton orbiculare |
Alison | Alyssum halimifolium | Alyssum
halimifolium | Alyssum maritimum |
Alyssum minimum | Alyssum odoratum |
Alyssum strigulosum | Clypeola
halimifolia | Clypeola maritima |
Crucifera koniga | Draba maritima |
Glyce maritima | Koniga halimifolia |
Koniga maritima | Koniga maroccana |
Koniga strigulosa | Lepidium
angustifolium | Lepidium fragrans |
Lobularia halimifolia | Lobularia strigulosa |
Lunaria halimifolia | Madwort | Octadenia
maritima | Ptilotrichum strigulosum |
Sweet Alyssum

❋ **SYMBOLIC MEANINGS**
Worth beyond beauty.

🌼 **POSSIBLE POWERS**
Calm anger; Moderate anger; Protection.

🜨 **FOLKLORE AND FACTS**
Alyssum will expel negative charms if worn as an amulet.
• Alyssum can calm an angry person if it is placed in their
hand or on their body. • When Alyssum is hung in the
house it supposedly can protect those in it against magically
imposed illusions and psychic fascinations of any kind,
whether they be fancifully amusing or intensely disturbing.

No. 043

Amaranthus cruentus ⚱

Amaranth

Amarant | Amaranthus anacardana | Amaranthus arardhanus | Amaranthus aureus |
Amaranthus brasiliensis | Amaranthus carneus | Amaranthus farinaceus | Amaranthus flavus |
Amaranthus guadelupensis | Amaranthus incarnatus | Amaranthus montevidensis |
Amaranthus paniculatus | Amaranthus purgans | Amaranthus rubescens | Amaranthus
sanguineus | Amaranthus sanguinolentus | Amaranthus speciosus | Amaranthus spicatus |
Amaranthus strictus | Amaranthus violaceus | Blood Amaranth | Flower Gentle | Flower
Velour | Huautli | Kiwicha | Lady Bleeding | Mexican Grain Amaranth | Pilewort | Prince's
Feather | Prince's Feathers | Purple Amaranth | Red Amaranth | Red Cock's Comb | Spleen
Amaranth | Velour Flower | Velvet Flower

❋ **SYMBOLIC MEANINGS**
Desertion; Endless love; Fidelity; Hopeless; Hopeless, not
heartless; Hopelessness; Immortality; In waiting; Love; Never
fading.

🌼 **POSSIBLE POWERS**
Artemis; Feminine energy; Fire element; Guard against evil;
Healing; Healing broken hearts; Immortality; Invisibility;
Magical attack; Magical protection; Protection; Protection
against bullets, cooking burns, or household accidents;
Saturn; Summon spirits.

🜨 **FOLKLORE AND FACTS**
Wearing an Amaranth wreath will supposedly give the
wearer the power of invisibility. • Ancient Greeks believed so
intensely in Amaranth being a strong symbol of immortality
that they would commonly spread Amaranth flowers
over graves. • Make then carry or wear a sachet of dried
Amaranth flowers to heal a broken heart. • Zuni people
use the plume of the Amaranth plant to color ceremonial
bread. • Most often planted in garden borders, Amaranth
flowers resemble curved chenille
pipe-cleaners. • Amaranth was once
outlawed in Mexico by the colonial
Spanish authorities because it was
used in Aztec rituals. • A circlet of
Amaranth flowers worn on top of
the head was believed to accelerate
healing. • Uprooting an Amaranth
plant on a full moon Friday, making
an offering, then wrapping the plant
into a white cloth before binding it to
one's chest will supposedly make one
magically bullet-proof. Don't try it!

A

No. 044
Amaranthus hypochondriacus 🝣
Love Lies Bleeding

Amaranthus bernhardii | Amaranthus chlorostachys erythrostachys | Amaranthus frumentaceus | Amaranthus hybridus | Amaranthus leucocarpus | Amaranthus leucospermus | Amaranthus macrostachyus | Blero | Floramon | Flower of Immortality | Huauhtli | Love-Lies-Bleeding | Prince's Feather | Prince of Wales Feather | Princess Feather | Quelite | Quintonil | Red Cockscomb | Velvet Flower

✳ SYMBOLIC MEANINGS
Desertion; Hopeless; Hopeless, not heartless; Hopelessness; In waiting; Love.

⚘ POSSIBLE POWERS
Healing; Invisibility; Magical attack; Magical protection; Protection.

☾ FOLKLORE AND FACTS
Love Lies Bleeding was once outlawed in Mexico by the colonial Spanish because it was frequently used in Aztec rituals. • A circlet of Love Lies Bleeding flowers worn on top of the head is believed to accelerate healing. • Love Lies Bleeding is believed to be able to cure a broken heart. • Wearing a Love Lies Bleeding wreath is said to give the wearer the power of invisibility.

No. 045
Ambrosia artemisiifolia ☠🝣
Ragweed

Ambrosia chilensis | Ambrosia diversifolia | Ambrosia elata | Ambrosia elatior | Ambrosia glandulosa | Ambrosia monophylla | Ambrosia paniculata | Ambrosia senegalensis | Ambrosia umbellata | American Ragwood | American Wormwood | Annual Ragweed | Bastard Wormwood | Bitterweed | Blackweed | Bloodweed | Canhlogan Onzipakinte | Canhlogan Wastemna | Carrot Weed | Common Ragweed | Hay Fever Weed | Hogweed | Iva monophylla | Low Ragweed | Popipiye | Roman Wormwood | Short Ragweed | Stammerwort | Stickweed | Tassel Weed

✳ SYMBOLIC MEANINGS
Courage; Immortal; Love is reciprocated; Love returned; Mutual love; Love is given back; Love is returned to you.

⚘ POSSIBLE POWERS
Banish a negative spirit; Courage.

☾ FOLKLORE AND FACTS
Ragweed is a damaging, invasive weed. If cows eat it they will produce bitter-tasting milk. • Healers among the Lakota people of North America brewed Ragweed as a tea to reduce swelling. • Ragweed pollen causes misery for many who suffer from hay fever. Before people scientifically understood allergies, they considered the physical reactions it can induce as proof that it possessed magical power. • Make and carry or wear a sachet of Ragweed to break a hex. • As it turns out, science has discovered that Ragweed can remove heavy metals from soil.

No. 046

Ananas comosus ✥

Pineapple

Abacaxi | Alanaasi | Anaasa | Ananá | Ananas | Anarosh |
Anay'nus | Annachi Pazham | *Bromelia comosa* | Kaitha
Chakka | Nanas | Nanasi | Nenas | Piña | Piña de Indes |
Pine Apple | Sapuri-PaNasa

❋ **SYMBOLIC MEANINGS**
Chastity; Hospitality; Joy;
Perfection; You are perfect.

❦ **COMPONENT MEANING**
Flower: You are perfect.

❀ **POSSIBLE POWERS**
Chastity; Fire element;
Luck; Masculine energy;
Money; the Sun.

❧ **FOLKLORE AND FACTS**
The Pineapple is not related to the Pine or Banana, but
people used to call the fruit of all three "apples." • It takes
two years for the Pineapple plant to produce one fruit,
which resembles a pinecone with a bromeliad on it. • Each
section of the whole Pineapple fruit has a tip containing
what remains of the flower that developed into that section
of the fruit. Botanically each section is a fruit unto itself,
making it a multiple fruit, or a joined collection of them,
like Jackfruit. • Christopher Columbus brought Pineapple
from the New World to Spain. • The Pineapple fruit juice
contains bromelain, an enzyme that can tenderize meat. • If
your dog is eating its own feces, add small amounts of ripe
fresh Pineapple fruit to its food. Going in, it tastes delicious.
Coming out, not so much. • Eating the fresh ripe Pineapple
fruit reportedly relieves laryngitis. • Make an infusion with
the core of the Pineapple fruit and distilled or filtered water
and add it to bathwater to encourage chastity or luck before
gambling. Spray this same infusion at the front door of your
home to encourage luck and a spirit of chaste respectfulness
to its inhabitants.

No. 047

Anemone coronaria ☠✥

Anemone

Anemone alba | *Anemone albiflora* | *Anemone coccinea* | *Anemone cyanea* | *Anemone
grassensis* | *Anemone kusnetzowii* | *Anemone messarensis* | *Anemone nobilis* | *Anemone
oenanthe* | *Anemone pusilla* | *Anemone regina* | *Anemone rosea* | *Anemone variata* | *Anemone
ventreana* | *Anemone versicolor* | Calanit | Calanit Metzouya | Crown Anemone | Dag Lalesi |
Kalanit | Kalanit Metzuya | Poppy Anemone | *Pulsatilla coronaria* | Shaqa'iq An-Nu'man |
Spanish Marigold

❋ **SYMBOLIC MEANINGS**
Abandonment; Forsaken; Immortal
love; Sickness; Withered hopes.

❀ **POSSIBLE POWERS**
Adonis; Aphrodisiac; Attract love;
Fire element; Healing; Health; Mars;
Masculine energy; Protection; Venus.

❧ **FOLKLORE AND FACTS**
The Anemone has a long history of
superstition around it. In ancient times, people thought it
caused all forms of pestilence, bringing diseases so deadly
that people ran through blooming fields of it, holding their
breath, because they believed that even the air around it
would bring death. • The Scots believed that picking the
Anemone flower triggered a thunderstorm. • The English
believed that you should pick the first Anemone you saw,
then wrap it in a piece of clean white silk to carry as an
amulet against pestilence. • In old Russian folk magic,
placing an Anemone blossom under the pillow in April
induces dreams as premonitions. • Some legends claim that
the same wind that passes over the Anemone flowers to open
closed petals will blow the dead petals off others. • Some
believe that, at night, fairies sleep inside the closed Anemone
flowers. • In spring, wrapping the first Anemone you see
in a red cloth, then wearing or carrying it supposedly will
prevent disease. • The first warm wind of spring is associated
with Anemones. • Use the Anemone blossoms in healing
rituals. • There is a legend that Aphrodite had followed
Adonis when he went into a forest to hunt. Ares disguised
himself as a wild boar and followed them both. In a crime
of passionate jealousy, Ares viciously attacked Adonis with
the intent to kill him. Aphrodite tried to save Adonis by first
covering his open wounds with nectar before running him
out of the forest, but Adonis' soul had already left his body
to go into The Underworld. In the forest, where every drop
of Adonis' blood or some of the nectar had fallen, the red
Anemone grew. • Growing red Anemone flowers in your
home garden offers protection to the garden and the home.

No. 048

Anethum graveolens 🐦🍴

Dill

Anethum | *Anethum arvense* | *Anethum involucratum* | *Anethum sowa* | Aneton | *Angelica graveolens* | Buzzalchippet | Chathakuppa | Chebbit | Dill Weed | Dillia | Dilly | Endro | *Ferula graveolens* | *Ferula marathrophylla* | Garden Dill | Hariz | Hulwa | Keper | Lao Cilantro | Laotian Coriander | Mirodjija | *Pastinaca anethum* | *Pastinaca graveolens* | *Peucedanum anethum* | *Peucedanum graveolens* | *Peucedanum sowa* | Phak Chee Lao | Phak See | Sada Kuppi | Sapsige Soppu | Sathakuppa | Savaa | *Selinum anethum* | *Selinum graveolens* | Shevid

☀ SYMBOLIC MEANINGS

Good cheer; Luck.

🌐 POSSIBLE POWERS

Aphrodisiac; Fire element; Love; Lust; Masculine energy; Mercury; Money; Protection; Soothing; Survival; Ward off evil.

🍄 FOLKLORE AND FACTS

In the Middle Ages, Dill was frequently used in magic spells and witchcraft. • Hanging Dill at a door offers protection against harm and will keep out anyone who is envious of you or unpleasant in nature. • A sprig of Dill attached to a cradle is supposedly able to protect the child in it. • Dill is said to stimulate the libido if it is eaten or even smelled. • Dill is an entirely beneficial herb that is always a good omen. • The Ancient Norse people gave Dill seeds to their babies to help them sleep.

No. 049

Angelica archangelica ☠🐦🍴

Angelica

Amara Aromatica | Angel Plant | *Angelica commutata* | *Angelica discocarpa* | *Angelica intermedia* | *Angelica norwegica* | *Angelica officinalis* | *Angelica procera* | *Angelica sativa* | Archangel | Archangelica | *Archangelica littoralis* | *Archangelica norwegica* | *Archangelica officinalis* | *Archangelica slavica* | *Archangelica spuria* | Arznei-Engelwurz | Bellyache Root | Boska | Dead Nettle | European Wild Angelica | Fádnu | Garden Angelica | Goutweed | Grote Engelwortel | Herb of the Angels | Herb of the Holy Ghost | High Angelica | Holy Ghost | Holy Ghost Root | Holy Herb | Hvonn | Hvönn | Kuanneq | Kvan | Kvanne | *Ligusticum angelica* | Masterwort | Norwegian Angelica | Purple Angelica | Rássi | Sonboi-e Khatayi | Väinönputki

☀ SYMBOLIC MEANINGS

Gentle melancholy; Inspiration; Inspire me; Symbol of good magic; Symbol of poetic inspiration.

🌐 POSSIBLE POWERS

Courage; Eliminate the effects of intoxication; Exorcism; Fire element; Healing; Magic; Masculine energy; Protection; Remove curses, enchantments, hexes, or lust; Render witchcraft and the evil eye harmless; Strength; the Sun; Venus; Visions; Ward off disasters, evil spirits, or lightning strikes.

🍄 FOLKLORE AND FACTS

Exercise serious caution before touching *Angelica archangelica*. The plant closely resembles Poison Hemlock and Poison Parsnip, both being among the deadliest of poisonous plants. If you planted Angelica in your garden and you're quite certain of what it is, it's logical to consider it to be safe. Otherwise, beware! • During the first year of growth, Angelica produces only leaves. In the second year, the stalks can reach more than eight feet tall. • Angelica is a blessing to the garden because, when it flowers, it attracts bees. • Legend holds that, in the 1300s, Angelica protected entire villages from the bubonic plague, which has since been called the Black Death. • Another legend from the Middle Ages tells of a monk who dreamt of an angel who gave him a recipe for a tonic to cure any sickness. Angelica was one of the ingredients. • Some believe that angels smell exactly like Angelica. • Plant Angelica at the four corners of a house to protect against wickedness and pestilence. • Make an infusion of Angelica and rainwater, natural spring water, or distilled water and sprinkle that around the home as protection against evil. • Gamblers carry Angelica in their pockets for protection against losing their money and increasing their luck. • In a bath, Angelica will remove any kind of curse, hex, or negativity cast against the bather. • Aromatherapists call Angelica the oil of angels because of its peacefully calming influence.

A

No. 050

Angelica sinensis ☠🗡

Dong Quai

Chinese Angelica | Dang Gui | Dānggui | Empress of Herbs | Female Ginseng | Proper Order

✸ SYMBOLIC MEANINGS
Defender of women.

🌸 POSSIBLE POWERS
Alleviate fatigue; Aphrodisiac;
Attract love; Break a hex;
General blessing; Lift low
vitality; Protection against
an evil spirit.

☙ FOLKLORE AND FACTS
Traditional Chinese medicine has used
Dong Quai for millennia. • Dong Quai has anticoagulant
and antiplatelet properties that can affect the uterus as well
as cause photosensitivity. • Although the complications of
the herb are well documented, Dong Quai has been an herb
used in traditional Chinese medicine for thousands of years.
• Make then carry or wear a sachet of Dong Quai as a general
blessing when meditating about any issue concerning women.

No. 051

Annona muricata ☠

Soursop

Annona bonplandiana | Annona cearensis | Anón | Anón de Corcho | Anoncillo | Durian
Belanda | Durian Salat | Graviola | Guanábana | Guanábana Cimarrona |
Guanábana de Pozo | Guanabanilla | Guyabano | Lampun | Maiolo |
Mãng Cầu | Mãng Cầu Xiêm | Tearb Barung

✸ SYMBOLIC MEANINGS
Sour custard.

🌸 POSSIBLE POWERS
Release from oppression;
Unblock desperate
emotions.

☙ FOLKLORE AND FACTS
The Soursop flower is especially fragrant
in the morning. • Claims that Soursop is a cure or valid
treatment for cancer continue to be proven completely
without merit. • Make then carry or wear a sachet that holds
a Soursop flower and a leaf to help push off and send away
the heavy overwhelming sensation of oppression.

No. 052

Anthriscus cerefolium 🗡🍴

Chervil

Anthriscus chaerophyllus | Anthriscus longirostris | Anthriscus sativa |
Anthriscus trachysperma | Anthriscus trichosperma |
Cerefolium cerefolium | Cerefolium sativum | Cerefolium
sylvestre | Cerefolium trichospermum | Chaerefolium
cerefolium | Chaerefolium trichospermum | Chaerophyllum
cerefolium | Chaerophyllum nemorosum | Chaerophyllum
sativum | French Parsley | Garden Chervil | Gourmet Parsley |
Myrrhodes cerefolium | Salad Chervil | Scandix cerefolium | Scandix
tenuifolia | Selinum cerefolium

✸ SYMBOLIC MEANINGS
Serenity; Sincerity.

🌸 POSSIBLE POWERS
Sense of the higher, divine, immortal spirit.

☙ FOLKLORE AND FACTS
It was Roman soldiers who spread Chervil by planting it
close to all their camps across the entire Roman empire
because they hated being without it. • Make and carry
or wear a white sachet of Chervil that can be used when
attempting to make contact with a loved one on "the other
side" via any method. • Chervil is in the Nine Sacred Herbs
healing charm that was originally written in the dialect used
in Wessex, England around the time of the tenth century.

A

Antirrhinum majus ♂

Snapdragon

Antirrhinum grandiflorum | Antirrhinum hendersonii | Antirrhinum murale | Antirrhinum vulgare | Calf's Snout | Common Snapdragon | Dog's Mouth | Lion's Mouth | Orontium majus | Termontis racemosa | Toad's Mouth | Toadflax

✳ SYMBOLIC MEANINGS
Creativity; Deception; Force of will; Gracious lady; Indiscretion; Never; Presumption.

❀ POSSIBLE POWERS
Break a hex; Clairaudience; Fire element; Mars; Masculine energy; Protection; Protection against curses, deceit, or negativity; Strength.

❦ FOLKLORE AND FACTS
If you sense evil near you, step on or hold a Snapdragon flower in your hand until you feel the evil pass by. • If someone has sent their negative energy to you or cursed you, place a vase of Snapdragon flowers in front of a mirror and the negativity and the curses will be sent back to the sender. • Wear Snapdragon seed around your neck to protect yourself from being bewitched. • It was thought that if you hid a Snapdragon on your person, you would appear to be gracious and quite fascinating. • Wear or carry any part of a Snapdragon to protect yourself against deception.

Apium graveolens var. graveolens ♂🍴

Celery

Aipo | Apium | Apium celleri | Apium decumbens | Apium dulce | Apium integrilobum | Apium lobatum | Apium lusitanicum | Apium maritimum | Apium palustre | Apium rapaceum | Apium vulgare | Carum graveolens | Celeri graveolens | Elma | Helosciadium graveolens | Helosciadium ruta | Helosciadium rutaceum | Karafs | Marshwort | Pascal | Selinum graveolens | Seseli graveolens | Sison ruta | Sison trifidum | Sium apium | Sium graveolens | Smyrnium laterale | Wild Celery

✳ SYMBOLIC MEANINGS
Banquet; Entertainment; Feast; Festivity; Lasting pleasures; Merriment; Rejoicing; Useful knowledge.

❀ POSSIBLE POWERS
Aphrodisiac; Attract love; Balance; Calm; Concentration; Fire element; Lust; Masculine energy; Mental clarity or power; Mercury; Psychic power; Sleep; Virility.

❦ FOLKLORE AND FACTS
The ancient Greeks regarded Celery with the same esteem as Bay Laurel, using it in wreath making for the crowning of athletes. • Carry or wear a sachet of Celery leaves to encourage lust. • Chewing Celery seeds before flying off on a broom will keep you aright so you will not fall off. • Put Celery seed into a sleep pillow to fall asleep easier. • Celery has been cultivated for use as food or folk medicine for many thousands of years. • The stalks of Wild Celery can grow to be three feet tall. • To help concentrate, chew teeny tiny Celery seeds; better yet, if that proves difficult, make and then carry or wear a Celery seed sachet.

Apium graveolens var. *rapaceum* 🌾🍴

Celeriac

Celery Root | Knob Celery | Selinon | Turnip-Rooted Celery

✹ SYMBOLIC MEANINGS

Feast.

✹ POSSIBLE POWERS

Balance; Fire element; Masculine energy; Mercury.

✦ FOLKLORE AND FACTS

In the *Iliad,* horses graze on Celeriac in marshes near Troy. In the *Odyssey,* Celeriac grows outside Calypso's cave. • If stored properly, Celeriac's shelf life can exceed six months. • As a culinary herb, Celeriac functions much the same as Celery. It also can serve as a mashed substitute for Potatoes.

Apium graveolens var. *secalinum* 🌾🍴

Leaf Celery

Chinese Celery | Nan Ling Celery

✹ SYMBOLIC MEANINGS

Banquet; Entertainment; Feast; Festivity; Lasting pleasures; Merriment; Rejoicing; Useful knowledge.

✹ POSSIBLE POWERS

Aphrodisiac; Attract love; Balance; Calm; Concentration; Fire element; Lust; Male virility; Masculine energy; Mental clarity or power; Mercury; Psychic power; Sleep.

✦ FOLKLORE AND FACTS

Although having thinner stalks, Leaf Celery is used in many of the same ways as Common Celery, with the difference being so much more leafiness for use. • Leaf Celery leaves are dried and readily available for culinary use as Celery leaf and for the seeds. • Leaf Celery essential oil is useful for its calming effect.

Aquilaria malaccensis ☠🏺

Agar-Agar

Agallochum malaccense | Agallochum officinarum | Agallochum praestantissimum | Agallochum sylvestre | Agarwood | Aloeswood | Aloexylum agallochum | Aquilaria agallocha | Aquilaria moluccensis | Aquilaria ovata | Aquilaria secundaria | Aquilariella malaccensis | Cynometra agallocha | Eaglewood | Gharuwood | Lignum Aloes | Lolu | Mapou | Oodh | Wood Aloes

✹ SYMBOLIC MEANINGS

Spirit of life.

✹ POSSIBLE POWERS

Attract good fortune, love, or opportunities; Bring blessings; Feminine energy; Love; Promote joy; Spirituality; Venus; Water element.

✦ FOLKLORE AND FACTS

Agar-Agar is so spiritually significant that it is revered in the holy texts of virtually all major religions in the world. • Agar-Agar attracts love if carried or worn. • Agar-Agar has been used in magic for centuries to attract good fortune and bring love forward. • Due to the loss of its habitat in the wild and increasing illegal harvesting and trade, the Agar-Agar tree is so highly threatened that it is considered to be extinct in the wild. • Agar-Agar is used in the making of perfume and incense. • Carry or wear a sachet of Agar-Agar when you go to the casino, play bingo, or are participating in any chance-type games to promote an advantage of a winner's good luck and success being on your side. • Place an amulet of Agar-Agar over the doors and windows of the home to attract blessings into it.

A

No. 058

Arbutus unedo

Strawberry Tree

Apple of Cain | Arbutus cassinifolia | Arbutus crispa | Arbutus intermedia | Arbutus laurifolia | Arbutus nothocomaros | Arbutus procumbens | Arbutus salicifolia | Arbutus serratifolia | Arbutus turbinata | Arbutus vulgaris | Cain Apple | Cane Apple | Irish Strawberry Tree | Killarney | Texas Madrone | Tick Tree | Unedo edulis | Unedo globosa | Unedo oviformis

☀ SYMBOLIC MEANINGS
Esteemed love; I love only you; Only love; True love.

☙ POSSIBLE POWERS
Cardea; Exorcism; Fidelity; Fire element; Mars; Masculine energy; Protection.

☙ FOLKLORE AND FACTS
There have been reported incidences of bears becoming intoxicated from eating fermented Strawberry Tree berries that had been left on or under the trees. • The ancient Romans used the Strawberry Tree to protect small children by chasing off any evil lurking around them. • Strawberry Tree regularly sheds bark, leaves, and berries. • Strawberry Tree bark is rich in tannin that is used for tanning hides. • When Strawberry Tree berries shrivel they grow barbs which attach to animals that unwittingly disperse them. • The smooth Strawberry Tree wood has been used for making weaving spindles as far back as 350 BCE.

No. 059

Areca catechu ☠☙

Betel Nut

Areca catechu | Areca faufel | Areca himalayana | Areca hortensis | Areca macrocarpa | Areca nigra | Areca Nut Palm | Areca Palm | Betel Palm | Catechu | Indian Nut | Pinang Palm | Ping Lang | Siri | Sublimia areca | Supari

☀ SYMBOLIC MEANINGS
Loyalty in love; Strong bond.

☙ POSSIBLE POWERS
Aphrodisiac; Banishing negativity; Dependability; Fertility; Healing; Intensify; Love; Magnify; Uplift the spirit.

☙ FOLKLORE AND FACTS
In many Asian countries, people have been chewing Betel Nut, whole or chopped and wrapped with a Betel Leaf, for at least 2,000 years. Addictive, it stains the teeth of heavy users red or reddish-black. • The Puyama people of ancient China believed that they couldn't communicate with the spirits of their ancestors without it.

No. 060

Arenaria verna ☙

Irish Moss

Alsine subulata | Alsinella subulata | Arenaria calycina | Arenaria verna | Golden Moss | Moss Sandwort | Phaloe subulata | Sagina alexandrae | Sagina subulata | Sandwort | Spergella subulata | Spergula laricina | Spergula subulata | Spergularia nobreana

☀ SYMBOLIC MEANINGS
Sand-loving.

☙ POSSIBLE POWERS
Feminine energy; Luck; Money; the Moon; Protection; Water element.

☙ FOLKLORE AND FACTS
Irish Moss will grow into a thick three-inch high green living carpet that can be walked upon. • Make then carry or wear a sachet filled with bits of Irish Moss for very good luck. • Make and then carry or wear a sachet of Irish Moss for continued safety when traveling. • Make an infusion of rainwater, spring water, or distilled water and Irish Moss to sprinkle around a business, especially at the entrance door to increase business. • To take on some good luck before gambling, rub the hands with some Irish Moss. Also, make then carry or wear an Irish Moss good luck sachet. • Tuck bits of Irish Moss under the rugs of the home for good luck and money to come on a regular basis. • Make an amulet pouch stuffed with Irish Moss to keep in a safe place in the house to ensure good luck, protection, and a steady income for all who live there.

A

No. 061

Argentina anserina 🥣

Silver Cinquefoil

Argentina argentea | Argentina vulgaris | Cinquefoil | Dactylophyllum anserin | Dasiphora anserina | Five-Finger Blossom | Five-Finger Grass | Five Fingers | Fragaria anserin | Potentilla anserina | Potentilla argentina | Potentilla pratincola | Potentilla pseudoanserina | Potentilla viridis | Silverweed | Tormentilla anserina

✴ **SYMBOLIC MEANINGS**
Eternal love; Naiveté; Simplicity.

🌐 **POSSIBLE POWERS**
Fire element; Jupiter; Masculine energy; Ward off an evil spirit; Ward off witchcraft.

🜚 **FOLKLORE AND FACTS**
There is a legend that the five points of the Silver Cinquefoil leaf represent love, money, health, power, and wisdom. If carried about, these powers will be granted unto you. • If you happen to find a Silver Cinquefoil leaf with seven points, if you put it under your pillow you will dream of your future lover. • Worn or carried in a Silver Cinquefoil sachet, the herb is said to be able to give the ability to ask favors with a positive outcome. • Make then carry or wear a sachet of Silver Cinquefoil leaf to court with full hope for a positive outcome. • Silver Cinquefoil was once put into shoes to absorb perspiration.

No. 062

Armoracia rusticana 🥣🍴

Horseradish

Armoracia armoracia | Armoracia austriaca | Armoracia lapathifolia | Armoracia rustica | Armoracia sativa | Chrain | Cochlearia armoracia | Cochlearia lancifolia | Cochlearia lapathifolia | Cochlearia rusticana | Cochlearia variifolia | Crucifera armoracia | Horse-Radish | Horseradish Root | Khren | Moolee | Nasturtium armoracia | Radicula armoracia | Raphanis magna | Raphanus rusticanus | Rorippa rusticana | Stingnose | Western Wasabi

✴ **SYMBOLIC MEANINGS**
Bitterness of enslavement.

🌐 **POSSIBLE POWERS**
Exorcism; Fire element; Mars; Masculine energy; Purification.

🜚 **FOLKLORE AND FACTS**
Putting a piece of Horseradish in your pocket, purse, or wallet during New Year's Eve supposedly promises a year of adequate funds. • In Greek mythology it is written that the Oracle of Delphi once told Apollo that Horseradish was worth its weight in gold. • To clear all evil powers and dissipate negative spells cast upon your home, sprinkle ground dried Horseradish root around the house and on the entry steps into the home, on every windowsill, and in every corner. • A mural in Pompeii, Italy depicts a Horseradish plant in the artwork.

A

No. 063
Arnica montana ☠✣

Arnica Montana

Alaska Arnica | Aliseta | Arnic | *Arnica alpina* | *Arnica angustifolia* | *Arnica helvetica* | *Arnica lowii* | *Arnica petiolata* | *Arnica plataginisfolia* | Arnicula | Broadleaf Arnica | Chamisso Arnica | *Cineraria cernua* | *Doronicum arnica* | *Doronicum oppositifolium* | Epiclinastrum | Foothill Arnica | Hairy Arnica | Heartleaf Arnica | Heart-Leaf Leopardbane | Lanceleaf Arnica | Longleaf Arnica | Mallotopus | Mountain Tobacco | Mt. Shasta Arnica | Narrowleaf Arnica | Nodding Arnica | Orange Arnica | Parry's Arnica | Peritris | Rayless Arnica | Rydberg Arnica | Rydberg's Arnica | Serpentine Arnica | Shasta County Arnica | Shining Leopardbane | Smallhead Arnica | Spearleaf Arnica | Subalpine Arnica | Twin Arnica | Whitneya | Wolf Flower | Wolfsblume | Wooly Arnica |

✻ SYMBOLIC MEANINGS

Emotion; Memory; Will.

❀ POSSIBLE POWERS

Abundance; Apollo; Fend off unwanted spirits; Fire element; Freya; Healing; Increase psychic powers; Masculine energy; Protection; Psychic ability; Ra; the Sun; Willpower.

✿ FOLKLORE AND FACTS

Due to its extreme toxicity, the US Food and Drug Administration has declared Arnica Montana an unsafe herb. • Carry or wear a sachet of an Arnica Montana flower, leaf, and piece of root to keep unwanted spirits away. • According to an ancient German legend, the spirit of the Corn Wolf would imbibe his strength into the cornfields or grain fields as he wandered through them. Arnica Montana was planted around the fields to keep the Corn Wolf within them. When the last of the corn or grain stalks were cut and tied into a sheaf, the Corn Wolf would enter into it, to be carried to the village and displayed with gratitude and honors for an abundant crop and released until the next planting of the crops coaxed him in. • Because of Arnica Montana's correspondence to the sun and to fire, it is a sacred herb to Freya the Norse goddess, Ra the Egyptian god, and Apollo the Greek god. • To prevent a spirit from coming into or leaving an area, encircle it with living Arnica plants, although the power only lasts while the plant is alive. • Arnica is given the credit for driving the Norse demon, Bilwis, away from the wheat crops it was intent upon destroying.

No. 064
Artemisia abrotanum ☠✣

Southernwood

Abrotanum alpestre | *Abrotanum ambiguum* | *Abrotanum brachylobium* | *Abrotanum congestum* | *Abrotanum incanescens* | *Abrotanum mas* | *Abrotanum pauciflorum* | *Abrotanum pedunculare* | *Abrotanum platylobum* | *Abrotanum pulverulentum* | *Abrotanum rhodanicum* | *Abrotanum suave* | *Abrotanum virgatum* | *Abrotanum viridulum* | *Abrotanum xerophilum* | Appleringie | *Artemisia abrotanifolia* | *Artemisia altissima* | *Artemisia anethifolia* | *Artemisia angustifolia* | *Artemisia elatior* | *Artemisia elegans* | *Artemisia foeniculacea* | *Artemisia herbacea* | *Artemisia humilis* | *Artemisia naronitana* | *Artemisia paniculata* | *Artemisia procera* | *Artemisia proceriformis* | *Artemisia sabulosa* | *Artemisia tenuissima* | Boy's Love | European Sage | Garde Robe | Garden Sagebrush | Garderobe | Lad's Love | Lemon Plant | Lover's Plant | Maid's Ruin | Old Man | Old Man Wormwood | Our Lord's Wood | Sagebrush | Slitherwood | Southern Wormwood |

✻ SYMBOLIC MEANINGS

Absence; Aphrodisiac; Attract love; Bantering; Constancy; Fidelity; Jest; Jesting; Lustful bed partner; Pain; Seduction.

❀ POSSIBLE POWERS

Air element; Antidote for a magic potion; Aphrodisiac; Earth element; Exorcism; Feminine energy; Love; Lust; Male virility; Masculine energy; Mercury; Protection; Purification; Repel a snake or moths; Seduction; Sex appeal; Venus; Ward off an evil spirit.

✿ FOLKLORE AND FACTS

A Southernwood amulet is considered to be the most potent antidote for a magic potion. • Southernwood was supposedly used to keep snakes and thieves away. • One of the beliefs about Southernwood is that it can cause impotence in men. • In medieval times, a sprig of Southernwood was very often included in bouquets presented by young men to girls as a secret mode of seducing them. • A sprig of Southernwood placed under the mattress is supposed to arouse lust. • Southernwood amulets used to be carried around as protection against all manner of infection. • Southernwood used to be placed in courtrooms to ward off an imaginary malady called jail fever. • A Southernwood amulet was once believed to have the power to transform a smooth-skinned boy into one with man-hair on the face, chest, and elsewhere on the body.

A

No. 065
Artemisia annua

Sweet Wormwood

Annual Mugwort | Annual Wormwood | *Artemisia chamomilla* | *Artemisia exilis* | *Artemisia hyrcana* | *Artemisia plumosa* | *Artemisia stewartii* | *Artemisia suaveolens* | *Artemisia wadei* | Huanghuahao | Qing Hao | Qinghao | Sweet Annie | Sweet Sagewort

✹ **SYMBOLIC MEANINGS**
Unexpected pathway.

❀ **POSSIBLE POWERS**
Artemis; Calling a spirit; Diana; Fire element; Healing; Iris; Love; Mars; Masculine energy; Protection; Psychic power.

✦ **FOLKLORE AND FACTS**
The Chinese scientist, Tu Youyou, was awarded the Nobel Prize in Physiology or Medicine in 2015 for her discovery of the antimalarial properties of an extract of Sweet Wormwood, *Artemisia annua*, known as "artemisinin" or "artesunate" that has proven to be an effective treatment for malaria.

No. 066
Artemisia dracunculus 🏺🍴

Tarragon

Absinthium cernuum | Achillea dracunculus | Artemisia aromatica | Artemisia cernua | Artemisia dracunculiformis | Artemisia dracunculoides | Artemisia inodora | Artemisia nutans | Artemisia redowskyi | Artemisia simplicifolia | Draconia dracunculiformis | Draconia dracunculus | Dragon Herb | Dragon Wort | Dragon's Herb | Dragon's Wort | Estragon | French Tarragon | Fuzzy Weed | Green Dragon | Herbe Dragon | King of Herbs | Little Dragon | Oligosporus condimentarius | Oligosporus crithmifolius | Oligosporus dracunculiformis | Oligosporus dracunculinus | Oligosporus dracunculoides | Oligosporus dracunculus | Oligosporus nuttallianus | Petit Dragon | Russian Tarragon | Snakesfoot | Spanish Tarragon

✹ **SYMBOLIC MEANINGS**
Horror; Lasting commitment, interest, or involvement; Permanence; Shocking occurrence; Terror.

❀ **POSSIBLE POWERS**
Dragon magic; Hunting; Love; Snakebite cure.

✦ **FOLKLORE AND FACTS**
Tarragon is considered to be a desirable companion plant that protects the other plants near to it, because its taste and scent are disliked by common garden pests. • Carry Tarragon for good luck when hunting. • Tarragon is one of the four primary culinary herbs used in French cuisine.

No. 067
Artemisia pallens 🏺

Davana

Artemisia absinthii | Artemisia orientalis | Artemisia paniculate

✹ **SYMBOLIC MEANINGS**
Flower; Fruit.

❀ **POSSIBLE POWERS**
Aphrodisiac; Calming; Ease stress; Healing; Quiet a noisy mind; Soothe a rattled body.

✦ **FOLKLORE AND FACTS**
Davana is a religious plant in India. • Davana essential oil is useful in aromatherapy to help soothe rattled nerves and restore emotional calm to quiet a noisy mind, especially following a crisis. • Davana's fruity, floral, woodsy fragrance can smell quite different to different people, who variously compare it to balsam, licorice, apricot, or even fresh cut hay.

No. 068
Artemisia vulgaris ☠🏺

Mugwort

Absinthium vulgare | Artemis Herb | Artemisia coarctata | Chornobylnik | Chrysanthemum Weed | Common Wormwood | Felon Herb | Mugwyrt | Muggons | Naughty Man | Old Man | Old Uncle Henry | Sailor's Tobacco | St. John's Herb | St. John's Plant | Western Mugwort | White Mugwort | Wild Wormwood

✹ **SYMBOLIC MEANINGS**
Awareness of our spiritual path; Dignity; Good luck; Happiness; Tranquility.

❀ **POSSIBLE POWERS**
Artemis; the Arts; Astral projection; Attraction; Beauty; Diana; Earth element; Feminine energy; Friendship; Gifts; Harmony; Healing; Health; Joy; Longevity; Love; Pleasure; Prophetic dreams; Protection; Protection against dark forces; Psychic power; Sensuality; Strength; Venus.

✦ **FOLKLORE AND FACTS**
When worn or carried, Mugwort brings journeying loved ones safely home and offers protection along the way from wild animals, sunstroke, and fatigue. • If worn or carried, Mugwort will also increase fertility and enough lust to facilitate conception. • Mugwort was thought to have magical powers and would be worn as protection from evil powers. • It was believed that if Mugwort was collected on the evening before the Feast Day of Saint John the Baptist, it would offer increased protection against evil, misfortune, and diseases. • It is believed that if you place Mugwort in your

shoes for long runs you will get strength from it. • A pillow stuffed with Mugwort may give you prophetic dreams when you sleep upon it. • Place Mugwort beneath or around a crystal ball to help with psychic readings while using it. • The ancient Japanese and Chinese once believed that the evil spirits of disease hated the smell of Mugwort. • The ancient Japanese and Chinese would hang bunches of Mugwort over doors to keep illness out. • If a Mugwort amulet is put under the mattress, it is supposed to help achieve astral projection. • Carry or wear a Mugwort sachet to prevent backache. • Carry or wear a Mugwort sachet as a possible cure for madness. • Mugwort is part of the Nine Sacred Herbs healing charm that was originally written in the dialect used in Wessex, England around the time of the tenth century.

No. 069
Asclepias tuberosa ☠☕

Indian Paint Brush

Acerates decumbens | Asclepias decumbens | Asclepias elliptica | Asclepias lutea | Asclepias revoluta | Asclepias rolfsii | Butterfly Love | Butterfly Weed | Canada Root | Chigger Flower | Fluxroot | Indian Paintbrush | Indian Posy | Orange Milkweed | Orange Swallow-wort | Pleurisy Root | Prairie Fire | Silky Swallow-wort | Tuber Root | White-Root | Windroot | Yellow Milkweed

✹ **SYMBOLIC MEANINGS**
Heartache cure; Hope in misery; Let me go; Love.

🌐 **POSSIBLE POWERS**
Feminine energy; Gratitude; Heartache cure; Introspection; Love; Peacemaker; Venus; Water element.

☘ **FOLKLORE AND FACTS**
Asclepias plants such as Indian Paint Brush are the only ones that a Monarch butterfly will lay its eggs on. The hatched larvae caterpillar will feed upon the leaves, absorbing the toxins that protect them from bird predators by making them distasteful. • Tuck an Indian Paint Brush flower into a sachet to carry or wear to brush away heartache with a wide sweep. • It was believed that Indian Paint Brush had the power to completely end fighting and anger if it is carried in a talisman along with the heart of a mole. • It was believed that Indian Paint Brush could cause a dying person to sing from their deathbed. • The Indian Paintbrush is the state flower of Wyoming, USA. • It was believed that Indian Paint Brush could bring a healed person to the point of weeping with heartfelt gratitude for their restored health.

No. 070
Aspalathus linearis ☕

Rooibos

Bush Tea | Red Tea Bush | Redbush | Rooibosch

✹ **SYMBOLIC MEANINGS**
Natural.

🌐 **POSSIBLE POWERS**
Health.

☘ **FOLKLORE AND FACTS**
A tea known as Redbush Tea is brewed from the leaves of the Rooibos that has been consumed in South Africa for many generations. • There are archeological records that imply that the Rooibos plant was used thousands of years ago. • Harvesting the needle-like leaves from the Rooibos plant required climbing mountains to cut the leaves, bundling the leaves in a burlap bag, then toting the rolled bag down the mountain tied to the back of a donkey.

No. 071
Asparagus officinalis ☠☕

Asparagus

Ashadhi | Aspar Grass | Asparag | Asparage | Asparagio | Asparago | Asparagus | Asparagus acutifolius | Asparagus altilis | Asparagus caspius | Asparagus esculentus | Asparagus fiori | Asparagus hedecarpus | Asparagus hortensis | Asparagus littoralis | Asparagus oxycarpus | Asparagus paragus | Asparagus polyphyllus | Asparagus sativus | Asparagus setiformis | Asparagus vulgaris | Aspargo | Espárrago | Garden Asparagus | Grass | Love Tips | Majjigegadde | Mang Tây | No Mai Farang | Points d'Amour | Sipariberuballi | Spar Grass | Spárga | Spargel | Sparrow Grass | Sparrow Guts | Sperage | Wild Asparagus

✹ **SYMBOLIC MEANINGS**
Fascination; Phallus.

🌐 **POSSIBLE POWERS**
Aphrodisiac; Attract love; Change; Cleansing; Dreams; Fertility; Growth; Healing; Lucid dreaming; Lust; Masculinity; Passion; Rebirth; Renewal; Reproduction; Sex; Travel.

☘ **FOLKLORE AND FACTS**
Since ancient times, the rise of phallic Asparagus shoots in spring have signified male sexuality, stamina, and virility. • On an ancient Egyptian panel from around 3000 BCE, it appears as a type of ritual offering. • Mediterranean and European cultures have incorporated it into their spring festivals as food, wearable wreaths, and decorative arrangements. • Dioscorides, author of an influential medical book written between 50–70 CE,

A

touted that bits of ram's horn planted as mystical Asparagus "seeds" would sprout the plant in the spring. Then again, he also wrote that wearing an amulet of it around the neck would make the wearer barren. • Due to the distinctive odor of urine after eating Asparagus, Victorian wives could smell unfaithfulness on their husbands, knowing that they had consumed it as an aphrodisiac they enjoyed with others. • In *Swann's Way*, published in 1913, Marcel Proust wrote a flowery paragraph about eating Asparagus and the distinctively aromatic fragrance of his urine later.

No. 072

Astragalus gummifer ☠☡

Tragacanth

Astracantha adanica | Astracantha gummifera | Astracantha rayatensis | Astracantha tournefortii | Astragalus adanicus | Astragalus adpressus | Astragalus erianthus | Astragalus noemiae | Astragalus rayatensis | Astragalus tournefortii | Gum Tragacanth | Loco Weed | Milkvetch | Tragacantha eriantha | Tragacantha gummifera | Tragacantha tournefortii

☀ **SYMBOLIC MEANINGS**
Goat horn.

🌐 **POSSIBLE POWERS**
Binding; Burn care; Earth element; Fire element; Healing; Incense; Masculine energy; Thickening.

🜨 **FOLKLORE AND FACTS**
The sharply thorny Tragacanth plant produces a gum that lends itself well to medical uses related to burn care. • The water soluble natural gum from the Tragacanth sap has been used for thickening in such things as commercially produced sauces, as well as in ink, glue, watercolor paints, toothpaste, fabric waterproofing, for the printing of calico fabric, and in medicinal pill adhesion. • Plants in the *Astragalus* genus produce swainsonine, a toxin harmful to livestock that gives the group the nickname "locoweed." • Tragacanth has been used for medicinal purposes for thousands of years, hundreds of years preceding the Christian era.

No. 073

Atropa belladonna ☠☡

Belladonna

Atropa | Atropa Bella-Donna | Banewort | Black Cherry | Deadly Nightshade | Death Cherries | Death's Herb | Devil's Berries | Devil's Cherries | Divale | Dwale | Dwaleberry | Dway Berry | Dwayberry | Fair Lady | Naughty Man's Cherries | Sorcerer's Berry | Witches' Berry

☀ **SYMBOLIC MEANINGS**
Falsehood; Hush; Loneliness; Silence; Warning.

🌐 **POSSIBLE POWERS**
Astral projection; Bellona; Circe; Feminine energy; Forgetting past love; Hallucinations; Hallucinatory witch flight; Hecate; Saturn; Visions; Water element.

🜨 **FOLKLORE AND FACTS**
As one of the world's most toxic plants, all parts of Belladonna are deadly poisonous and should be completely avoided in every way. • Belladonna's genus name was taken from Greek mythology's Atropa, the sister among the Three Fates who would cut a human's life thread after her two sisters had carefully spun and measured it out. • There is a legend that ancient Rome's Emperor Augustus was murdered by his wife, Livia Drusilla, who is said to have used Belladonna to poison a fig while it was still hanging on the branch of the tree. • In the Middle Ages, Venetian women used the leaves to redden their cheeks. • Renaissance women, especially in Italy, used a tincture of its extract to dilate their eyes to appear more attractive.

No. 074

Avena fatua ⚗

Wild Oat

Anelytrum avenaceum | Aveia-Brava | Aveia-Fatua | Avena intermedia | Avena japonica | Avena lanuginosa | Avena Loca | Avena Matta | Avena meridionalis | Avena nigra | Avena occidentalis | Avena pilosa | Avena Selvatica | Avena septentrionalis | Avena Silvestre | Avena Silvestre Comun | Avena sterilis | Avena vilis | Balanco | Ballueca | Chahiki | Flug-Hafer | Folle Avoine | Fyghavre | Karasumugi | Oot | Owies Gluchy | Wilde Haver | Wind-Hafer | Yabani Yulaf

❋ SYMBOLIC MEANINGS
Music; Musical; the Witching soul of music.

🌚 POSSIBLE POWERS
Healing; Money.

🜨 FOLKLORE AND FACTS
Since the early years of the Iron Age, naturalized Wild Oat has been a harvested cereal grain. • It takes only a few invasive Wild Oat plants to start wreaking major havoc on a crop of cultivated Oats and other cereal grain crops, because it is highly competitive and will rapidly begin to deplete soil resources and moisture. It will also vie for the light to ultimately cause loss of the yield and overall quality of the harvest. • There is no herbicide available that can be used to selectively control a Wild Oat invasion within a cultivated Oat crop. • A concerted effect to manage and control the Wild Oat can be intensely laborious and expensive. • During the Middle Ages it was believed that Wild Oat would attract a vampire, which inspired the farm practice of draping a garland of Garlic over the doors and windows of their homes. • Wild Oat straw can be used to fashion a woven magical object such as a talisman, charm, or even a wand.

No. 075

Avena sativa ⚗

Oat

Avena algeriensis | Avena anglica | Avena cinerea | Avena dispermis | Avena distans | Avena flava | Avena fusciflora | Avena geogica | Avena georgiana | Avena grandis | Avena hungarica | Avena macrantha | Avena mutata | Avena mutica | Avena nodipilosa | Avena orientalis | Avena pendula | Avena podolica | Avena polonica | Avena ponderosa | Avena praeccocioides | Avena praecoqua | Avena pseudosativa | Avena racemosa | Avena sexflora | Avena shatilowiana | Avena tatarica | Avena thellungii | Avena trabutiana | Avena trisperma | Avena unilateralis | Common Oat | Groats | Joulaf

❋ SYMBOLIC MEANINGS
Music; Musical; Witching soul of music.

🌚 POSSIBLE POWERS
Anxiety reduction; Concentration; Earth element; Endurance; Enhance mental power; Feminine energy; Fertility; Healing; Health; Inner peace; Money; Rejuvenation; Stress relief; Venus.

🜨 FOLKLORE AND FACTS
An old folk warning intending to scare children and keep them from playing in the planted fields regarded a menacing spirit called the Oat Goat that would grab hold of them if they ventured into the fields. • October 29th is National Oatmeal Day in the United States. • During the Middle Ages it was believed that Oat would attract a vampire, which inspired the farm practice of draping a garland of Garlic over the doors and windows of their homes. • Oat straw can be used to fashion a woven magical object such as a talisman, charm, or even a wand.

No. 076
Averrhoa carambola

Star Fruit

Averrhoa acutangula | *Averrhoa pentandra* | Balimbing | Carambola | Carambolo | *Connaropsis philippica* | Kamaranga | Ma Fen | *Sarcotheca philippic*

✴ SYMBOLIC MEANINGS
Stars.

⊛ POSSIBLE POWERS
Call for spiritual forces; Conjure a spirit.

☘ FOLKLORE AND FACTS
The ridges along the sides of the fruit of the Star Fruit tree can number five, six, or even seven ridges. • When the five-ridged whole fruit is sliced across, the individual slices of the Star Fruit are in the shape of a star and can be used as a pentagram for magical purposes. A six-ridged fruit will produce a slice of Star Fruit with six points that is also known as a magical hexagram as well as the Seal of Solomon. With it, spirits or spiritual forces for many different purposes can be conjured. • A seven-ridged fruit will produce a slice of Star Fruit with seven points that is also known as a magical heptagram and also the elven star, fairy star, and elf-queen's daughters. Magically, it can mean seven directions which imply "North, South, East, West, Above, Below, and Within." It can also represent the seven days of the week. • Regardless of how many star points a slice of Star Fruit can produce, the fruit is magically powerful. • Star Fruit juice can also be used to clean rust and tarnish off brass and most other metals.

No. 077
Azadirachta indica ☠☙

Neem

Antelaea azadirachta | *Antelaea canescens* | *Antelaea javanica* | Arishta | Arya Veppu | Azad Dirakht | Bead Tree | Bevu | Cure Tree | Divine Tree | Dogon Yaro | Heal All | Holy Tree | Huile de Neem | Indian Lilac | Indian Neem | Kohomba | Lilas de Perse | Lilas des Indes | Margosa | Margousier d'Inde | *Melia azadirachta* | *Melia fraxinifolia* | *Melia hasskarlii* | *Melia indica* | *Melia japonica* | *Melia parviflora* | *Melia pinnata* | Muarubaini | Nature's Drugstore | Neeb | Neem Oil Tree | Nim | Nimba | Nimm | Nimtree | Panacea for All Diseases | Persian Lilac | Pride of China | Pride of India | Tamar | Tree of Good Health | Tree of Life | Tree of the Forty | Tree of the Forty Cures | Vempu | Vepa | Vepu | Village Pharmacy

✴ SYMBOLIC MEANINGS
Complete; the Cure; Freedom; Health; Imperishable; Life; to Live; Noble; Perfect.

⊛ POSSIBLE POWERS
Healing; Insecticide.

☘ FOLKLORE AND FACTS
Neem tree oil has a garlicky, very long-lingering odor when it gets on fabric. • Where the Neem tree leaves fall to the ground beneath it, there are supposedly no pests. • Dried Neem leaves are often placed in the cupboards in India to keep insects away from clothing and food. • In Hindu myth, the divine Devas sprinkled the elixir of immortality on the earth, thereby creating Neem.

A

No. 078

Backhousia citriodora ☠️🦠

Lemon Myrtle

Lemon Scented Backhousia | Lemon Scented Ironwood | Lemon Scented Myrtle | Lemon
Scented Verbena | Queen of the Lemon Herbs | Sweet Verbena Myrtle |
Sweet Verbena Tree

✳ SYMBOLIC MEANINGS
Chaste beauty.

🌀 POSSIBLE POWERS
Cleansing; Flavoring; Healing; Insect
repellant; Purification; Relaxation;
Relieve anxiety; Relieve stress.

🜨 FOLKLORE AND FACTS
The crushed leaves of the Lemon Myrtle
emit a strong lemony fragrance. • The essential oil of the
Lemon Myrtle is crisp and more lemony than Lemon.
• In aromatherapy Lemon Myrtle is uplifting while
simultaneously calming to someone who is anxious.

No. 079

Bambusa vulgaris ☠️

Bamboo

Arundarbor blancoi | Arundarbor fera | Arundarbor mitis | Arundarbor monogyna |
Arundarbor striata | Arundo fera | Arundo mitis | Bamboo Sprouts | Bambú | Bambusa
auriculata | Bambusa blancoi | Bambusa blumeana | Bambusa
fera | Bambusa humilis | Bambusa latiflora | Bambusa
madagascariensis | Bambusa mitis | Bambusa monogyna |
Bambusa nguyenii | Bambusa odashimae | Bambusa sieberi |
Bambusa striata | Bambusa surinamensis | Bambusa
thouarsii | Common Bamboo | Dendrocalamus latiflorus |
Fargesia spathacea | Gigantochloa auriculata | Nastus thouarsii |
Nastus viviparus | Oxytenanthera auriculata | Phyllostachys
bambusoides | Phyllostachys edulis | Phyllostachys mitis

✳ SYMBOLIC MEANINGS
Endurance; Flexibility; Good fortune; Longevity; Loyalty;
Luck; Protection; Rendezvous; Scientific research;
Steadfastness; Strength; Summer; Suppleness; Youth.

🌀 POSSIBLE POWERS
Break a hex; Classical elements (air, earth, fire, water);
Hinna; Luck; Masculine energy; Protection; the Sun;
Wishing.

🜨 FOLKLORE AND FACTS
Bamboo grows in tropical and subtropical regions on five
continents. It is often considered a tree. However, botanically
it's actually a spreading grass. • Because Bamboo grows

to its full height and diameter in one growing season, it
serves a multitude of commercial purposes, including in
construction, fabrics, flooring, foods, and furniture. • As
an edible herb, Bamboo ranks among the most toxic of all
plant foods, even more so than Apricot and Bitter Almond.
If consumed unprocessed or insufficiently processed, it can
result in cyanide poisoning that causes confusion, dizziness,
headache, weakness, nausea, abdominal cramps, vomiting,
rapid breathing, convulsions, circulatory irregularity,
cardiac arrest, coma, and death. • In 1945, a small grove of
Bamboo survived the radiation that killed all other plants in
Hiroshima, Japan, after the atomic bomb detonated there.
• Carve a wish on a piece of it then bury it in a quiet place.
What's to be will be. • Grown, carried, or burned, it can help
break a hex. • To protect your home and to receive good
fortune, lightly scratch symbols of protection and good luck
on a viable length of it, then plant it near your home and
nurture it to grow. • *Dracaena sanderiana*, the plant often
marketed as "lucky bamboo," isn't Bamboo at all.

No. 080

Banisteriopsis caapi ☠️🦠

Ayahuasca

Banisteria inebrians | Banisteria quitensis | Banisteriopsis
inebrians | Banisteriopsis quitensis | Caapi | Jagube | Yagé

✳ SYMBOLIC MEANINGS
Plant teacher.

🌀 POSSIBLE POWERS
Enlightenment; Insight.

🜨 FOLKLORE AND FACTS
The first references of Ayahuasca were written by the early
Spanish, Portuguese, and missionary explorers regarding
their visits to South America in the 16th century. They
each, in their own words, described their encounters with
concoctions brewed by tribal shamans as being "diabolically
dangerous." • Ayahuasca is a part of many of the rituals
practiced by the Brazilian religious sect, União do Vegetal.
• Ayahuasca is illegal in many countries, with no regard
or exemption for its use in religious ceremonies. • Among
various tribes that have resided in the Amazon rainforest for
thousands of years, Ayahuasca has been considered a plant
teacher; they believe that while affected by it, somehow
the meaning of life might be revealed. Or not. Many have
attempted to attain that deeper intuition or higher self,
depending on the extent of prior expectations. However, it
seems nothing that was previously articulated in one way
or another was improved upon when reflecting on the same
topics via a high on Ayahuasca.

ℬ

No. 081

Bellis perennis 💀🏺

Lawn Daisy

Aster bellis | Baimwort | *Bellis alpina* | *Bellis armena* | *Bellis croatica* | *Bellis hortensis* | *Bellis hybrida* | *Bellis integrifolia* | *Bellis minor* | *Bellis pumila* | *Bellis scaposa* | *Bellis validula* | Common Daisy | Daisy | English Daisy | *Erigeron perennis* | Eye of the Day | Eyes | Field Daisy | Garden Daisy | Llygady Dydd | Maudlinwort | Moon Daisy | Wild Daisy

☀ SYMBOLIC MEANINGS

Beauty; Candor; Cheer; Childlike playfulness; Contempt for worldly goods; Creativity; Decisions; Do you love me?; Faith; Forever-young attitude; Gentleness on behalf of both giver and recipient; Gentleness; Happy-go-lucky; I share your sentiments; I will think of it; I'll never tell; Innocence; Loyal love; Purity; Simplicity; Simplify; Strength; You have as many virtues as this daisy has petals.

❀ POSSIBLE POWERS

Divination; Divination for love; Feminine energy; Heightened awareness; Inner strength; Love; Lust; Venus; Water element.

☘ FOLKLORE AND FACTS

The Lawn Daisy is a sentimental and beloved flower among lovers, poets, and children. • It was once believed that if a Lawn Daisy chain were wrapped around a child, the flower chain would protect the child from being stolen by fairies • If you sleep with a Lawn Daisy root under your pillow your lost lover may return. • Wear a Lawn Daisy flower to bring you love. • It was once believed that whoever it is that picks the very first Lawn Daisy of the season will be uncontrollably flirtatious.

No. 082

Berberis vulgaris 💀🏺

Barberry

Berberis | *Berberis abortiva* | *Berberis acida* | *Berberis aethnensis* | *Berberis alba* | *Berberis angulizans* | *Berberis apyrena* | *Berberis arborescens* | *Berberis articulata* | *Berberis asperma* | *Berberis aurea* | *Berberis bigelovii* | *Berberis dentata* | *Berberis dulcis* | *Berberis dumetorum* | *Berberis edulis* | *Berberis hakodate* | *Berberis heterophylla* | *Berberis innominata* | *Berberis irritabilis* | *Berberis jacquinii* | *Berberis latifolia* | *Berberis marginata* | *Berberis maximowiczii* | *Berberis microphylla* | *Berberis mitis* | *Berberis nepalensis* | *Berberis nitens* | *Berberis obovata* | *Berberis orientalis* | *Berberis pauciflora* | *Berberis racemosa* | *Berberis rubra* | *Berberis sanguinea* | *Berberis sanguinolenta* | *Berberis sibirica* | *Berberis sieboldii* | *Berberis sylvestris* | *Berberis violacea* | Common Barberry | European Barberry | Pepperidge Bush

☀ SYMBOLIC MEANINGS

Ill temper; Petulance; Satire; Sharpness; Sharpness of temper; Sourness; Sourness of temper.

❀ POSSIBLE POWERS

Atonement; Cleansing; Colorize; Freeing oneself from the control of another; Sorcery.

☘ FOLKLORE AND FACTS

There are hundreds of *Berberis* Barberry species. Most of them have sharp spines on the stems and along the edges of the leaves. • Low or tall growing Barberry plants are often planted to show off ornamental leaves and flowers, but mostly the attractive red or dark blue-black berries. • Tall Barberry plants are thick and extremely thorny, which are often grown as hedges or under windows to thwart even the most persistent criminal. • Italian legend claims that Barberry was used in the crown of thorns that Jesus was forced to wear. • Barberry shrub thorns are sharp but soft enough to be used to safely remove corrosion from ancient coins by scrubbing and scraping with a green fresh cut piece of the thorny Barberry stem. • In the past, the stem, roots, and bark of the Barberry plant were used to make a strong yellow vegetable dye. The Barberry berries can also be used to make a coral and a yellow-colored dye. • Do not bring Barberry into any house. Barberry is an extremely dangerous herb to have in the house in even the tiniest amounts because by just being there, Barberry can provoke all manner of interpersonal problems with everyone who enters. With Barberry present, those living in the home will discover what chaos is really like by falling victim to irrational jealousy, fights over anything and just about everything, accusations of all kinds, and physical aggression that can and most likely will quickly get out of hand, violent, and even turn deadly. And in the end, each who suffered at the insidious magical whim of Barberry will be hard-pressed to truly explain why they, themselves, were involved in the pandemonium, when all the time it was the malignant influence of the Barberry. Blame it on the Barberry.

No. 083

Beta vulgaris subsp. *vulgaris* ☙

Beet

Acelga | Beetroot | Beta alba | Beta altissima | Beta atriplicifolia | Beta bengalensis | Beta brasiliensis | Beta braziliensis | Beta carnulosa | Beta cicla | Beta crispa | Beta decumbens | Beta esculenta | Beta foliosa | Beta hortensis | Beta hybrida | Beta incarnata | Beta lutea | Beta marina | Beta maritima | Beta orientalis | Beta purpurea | Beta rapa | Beta rapacea | Beta rosea | Beta sativa | Beta stricta | Beta sulcata | Beta triflora | Blood Turnip | Dinner Beet | Garden Beet | Golden Beet | Mangel | Mangold | Red Beet | Remolacha | Sugar Beet | Table Beet

☀ SYMBOLIC MEANINGS
Blood; Heart; Love.

✹ POSSIBLE POWERS
Aphrodisiac; Earth element; Feminine energy; Love; Saturn.

☙ FOLKLORE AND FACTS
Growers originally cultivated it only for the greens. • In Europe, only aristocrats could afford the luxury of sugar from Sugar Cane, which needs to grow for many months in a tropical climate. In the mid-1700s producers developed a method of extracting sugar from Sugar Beets, which mature in as few as 100 days in temperate climates, and processed it into white crystals. • In the 1800s, some vintners used Beet juice to color wine. • Beets can lower blood pressure naturally. If taking blood pressure medication, consult with your healthcare provider before adding Beets to your diet. • If a woman and a man eat the same Beet, they will fall in love. Use the juice to write words of love to a lover. • If you need blood for ink, use Beet juice instead.

No. 084

Betonica officinalis ☠☙

Wood Betony

Betaine | Betonie | Betony | Bishopwort | Lamb's Ear | Lousewort | Purple Betony | Stachys betonica | Stachys officinalis | Wild Hop

☀ SYMBOLIC MEANINGS
Emotion; Love; Protection; Spiritual borders; Surprise.

✹ POSSIBLE POWERS
Business; Effective against sorcery; Expansion; Fire element; Guard against harm; Honor; Jupiter; Leadership; Love; Masculine energy; Politics; Power; Protection; Protection against a ghost, snakebite, dog bite, drunkenness, sorcery, or witchcraft; Public acclaim; Purification; Responsibility; Royalty; Success; Ward off an evil spirit or evil magic; Wealth.

☙ FOLKLORE AND FACTS
Wood Betony is the original magical herb. • Wood Betony was believed to protect the body and the soul. • During the Middle Ages, Wood Betony was grown in monastery gardens to fend off many different types of evil. • Wood Betony is used in magic to purify one's body and soul before performing serious healing rituals. • The Druids believed that Wood Betony was magical enough to use it to be rid of evil spirits, bad dreams, and overwhelming sadness. • Wood Betony is believed to be the logical choice of being the unidentifiable "Atterlothe" in the Nine Sacred Herbs healing charm that was originally written in the dialect used in Wessex, England around the time of the tenth century. The other contender is believed to possibly be Cockspur Grass, but intuitively it seems to be the least likely of the two potential options. • Wood Betony leaves are velvety soft and shaped like a lamb's ear. • One superstition regarding Wood Betony is that a pair of serpents would kill each other if placed in a circle made of Wood Betony. • Wear an amulet of Wood Betony to help in the curing of a psychosomatic illness. • Wood Betony can be rubbed on all door and window frames to create a protection barrier that is impervious to evil. • A small pillow filled with Wood Betony leaves and placed under the bed pillow will hopefully help end a plague of nightmares. • Plant Wood Betony in a cemetery to deter ghostly activity. • Place Wood Betony under a pillow to block visions and dreams that plague the sleeper. • When Wood Betony is grown in the garden it will protect the home. • Make and then carry or wear a pink and red sachet of Wood Betony when ready to approach a potential love.

B

No. 085

Betula pendula ☠☙

Silver Birch

East Asian White Birch | European White Birch | Lady of the Woods | Warty Birch

✸ SYMBOLIC MEANINGS

Lady of the Woods.

❀ POSSIBLE POWERS

Cleansing; Feminine energy; Fertility; New beginnings;
Purifying the property; Thor; Venus; Water element.

❦ FOLKLORE AND FACTS

The Silver Birch is an ancient species that will easily reseed
burned-over land to help establish a woodland. • Mites or
fungus cause deformities, called "galls" or "witch's brooms,"
that resemble bird nests or tangles of twigs on a Silver Birch
branch. • A witch's broom, or besom, usually consists of a
bundle of Silver Birch twigs bound together. • The Silver
Birch is not a tree that lives much longer than seventy years
because too often dies from premature old age or a fungus.
Even so, during its lifetime, it will provide protection and
support for slower-growing plant species in the woodland
that may be growing beneath it in the light shade it
provides. • Depending on the fiber and the mordant used,
vegetable dye made from Silver Birch
can produce red, yellow, or brown
colors. • The Silver Birch wand is
a powerful symbol of fertility and
new beginnings, cleansing and
purification.

No. 086

Bistorta officinalis ☙

Bistort

Adderwort | Armstrong | Ars-Smerte | Bistort Root | *Bistorta abbreviata* | *Bistorta confusa* |
Bistorta ensigera | *Bistorta lapidosa* | *Bistorta major* | *Bistorta subauriculata* | Buckwheat |
Centinode | Common Bistort | Cowgrass | Dragonwort | Easter Giant | Easter Ledger | Easter
Ledges | Easter Magiant | Easter Man-Giant | European Bistort | Gentle Dock | Great Bistort |
Hogweed | Knotgrass | Knotweed | Meadow Bistort | Mile-a-Minute | Nine Joints | Ninety Knot |
Osterick | Oysterloit | Passion Dock | Patience Dock | Patient Dock | *Persicaria bistorta* |
Pigrush | Pigweed | Pink Pokers | *Polygonon bistortum* | *Polygonum abbreviatum* | *Polygonum
alpestre* | *Polygonum amoenum* | *Polygonum ampliusculum* | *Polygonum bistorta* | *Polygonum
bistortoides* | *Polygonum bistortum* | *Polygonum bourdinii* | *Polygonum carthusianorum* |
Polygonum confusum | *Polygonum ensigerum* | *Polygonum lapidosum* | *Polygonum paleaceum* |
Polygonum pilatense | *Polygonum subauriculatum* | Pudding Dock | Pudding Grass | Red Legs |
Red Robin | Snakeweed | Sparrow's Tongue | Swynel Grass | Tear-Thumb | Twice-Writhen |
Water Ledges

✸ SYMBOLIC MEANINGS

Arrow-shaped; Barbed; Horror.

❀ POSSIBLE POWERS

Binding; Binding spell; Clairvoyance; Colorize; Divination;
Earth element; Feminine energy; Fertility; Health;
Protection; Psychic power; Saturn; Trance.

❦ FOLKLORE AND FACTS

If you want to conceive, carry or wear a
Bistort amulet until you do. • If carried
close to the breast, Bistort is considered
to be a charm to help those suffering
from frenzy. • Bistort is also thought to
heal one of their unwanted desires.
• Another power of Bistort is that when
a person touches it, Bistort was believed
to give that person the special powers
offered by their astrological Sun sign.
• Bistort is good for attracting money.
• Make a Bistort sachet then carry
or wear it when you want to pull in
good fortune. • To rid a home of pesky
poltergeists, make an infusion of Bistort
and rainwater, natural spring water,
or distilled water, then sprinkle it all
around the house. • Bistort will produce
an attractive tan vegetable dye for
fibers. • Prior to the steady emigration
from England, Bistort was virtually
unknown in North America until it
was introduced into the newly planted
English gardens in the New World.

B

Bixa orellana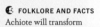

Achiote

Annatto | Bijol | Bixa acuminata | Bixa americana | Bixa katangensis | Bixa odorata | Bixa orleana | Bixa purpurea | Bixa tinctaria | Bixa upatensis | Orellana americana | Orellana orellana | Urucu | Urucum

✴ **SYMBOLIC MEANINGS**
Blood; Masculinity; the Sun.

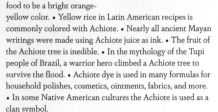

✺ **POSSIBLE POWERS**
Protect against snakebite; Ward off infection.

✿ **FOLKLORE AND FACTS**
Achiote will transform food to be a bright orange-yellow color. • Yellow rice in Latin American recipes is commonly colored with Achiote. • Nearly all ancient Mayan writings were made using Achiote juice as ink. • The fruit of the Achiote tree is inedible. • In the mythology of the Tupi people of Brazil, a warrior hero climbed a Achiote tree to survive the flood. • Achiote dye is used in many formulas for household polishes, cosmetics, ointments, fabrics, and more. • In some Native American cultures the Achiote is used as a clan symbol.

No. 088

Boesenbergia rotunda

Finger Root

Boesenbergia cochinchinensis | Boesenbergia pandurata | Chinese Ginger | Chinese Keys | Curcuma rotund | Fingerroot | Gastrochilus panduratus | Gastrochilus rotundus | Haran Kaha | K'Cheay | Kachai | Kaempferia cochinchinensis | Kaempferia ovata | Kaempferia pandurata | Kcheay | Krachai | Kuntji | Lesser Galangal | Nga Truật | Ngài BúnTemu | Temu Kunci | Yai-Macha

✴ **SYMBOLIC MEANINGS**
Keys.

✺ **POSSIBLE POWERS**
Aphrodisiac; Attract love; Calm anger; Fire element; Healing; Mars; Masculine energy; Promote a pleasant environment.

✿ **FOLKLORE AND FACTS**
Finger Root essential oil aromatherapy can help calm anger and promote a positive atmosphere in which to find ease. • Make and then tuck a red Finger Root sachet under the mattress to add a boost to lovemaking.

No. 089

Borago officinalis

Borage

Borago advena | Borago aspera | Borago hortesis | Borak | Borraja | Bugloss | Burrage | Flor de Borraja | Herb of Gladness | Lesan-El-Tour | Lisan Selvi | Starflower

✴ **SYMBOLIC MEANINGS**
Abruptness; Bluntness; Bravery; Rudeness.

✺ **POSSIBLE POWERS**
Air element; Courage; Jupiter; Masculine energy; Psychic power; Sense of well-being.

✿ **FOLKLORE AND FACTS**
The simple five-point bright blue Borage blossoms were a common subject carefully stitched into needlework designs. • To fortify your courage, carry or wear a Borage flower and leaf sachet. • Wear a Borage flower when walking outdoors for protection.

No. 090

Boswellia sacra ☠✿

Frankincense

Boswellia | Boswellia bhaw-dajiana | Boswellia carterii | Boswellia undulatocrenata | Frankincense Plant | Incense Plant | Indian Frankincense | Olibans | Olibanum | Olibanus | Sacred Boswellia

✴ **SYMBOLIC MEANINGS**
Sanctity.

✺ **POSSIBLE POWERS**
Abundance; Advancement; Baal; Blessings; Conscious will; Divine energy; Energy; Exorcism; Fire element; Friendship; Growth; Healing; Heavenly energy; Holy energy; Jesus; Joy; Leadership; Life; Light; Masculine energy; Natural power; Offerings; Petitions; Prayer; Protection; Purification; Ra; Spirituality; Success; the Sun.

✿ **FOLKLORE AND FACTS**
Frankincense is the aromatic resinous sap obtained from the Boswellia sacra tree. Although it is written into the Christian Bible's New Testament as one of the precious gifts given by one of the Three Magi to the newborn Jesus of Nazareth in the stable in Bethlehem, the earliest known written record referring to Frankincense is inscribed on ancient Egyptian tombs. • The charred remains of burned Frankincense is known as the eyeliner called kohl. • Incense has been used in the rituals of many different religions since ancient times, since it was believed that the smoke of the Boswellia sacra incense carried prayers and petitions directly upward to waft

B

into Heaven. • Frankincense was discovered within a sealed flask in Pharaoh Tutankhamun's tomb when it was opened in 1922. The Frankincense resin was still viable, releasing scent after being in the vial for 3,300 years. • Frankincense is vital for many different magical purposes such as the bestowing of blessings, and for various initiation rituals. • Frankincense has a very high and powerful vibration which makes it one of the best of all herbs used to drive away any kind of evil. • At one time, Frankincense was more valuable than gold. • Frankincense essential oil is particularly soothing and will help lift the downtrodden emotions of one who has been deeply saddened for any reason.

No. 091

Botrychium lunaria 🜍

Moonwort

Botrypus lunaria | Common Moonwort | Grapefern | Luan-Lus | Moon Fern | *Osmunda lunaria* | *Osmunda lunata* | Unshoe the Horse

☀ **SYMBOLIC MEANINGS**
Forgetfulness; Unfortunate.

❀ **POSSIBLE POWERS**
Feminine energy; Love; Money; the Moon; Moonlight passage into fairyland; Water element.

🜨 **FOLKLORE AND FACTS**
In Scotland, Moonwort has a long reputation for being able to provide a portal through which one can access the realm of Fairyland. • Moonwort is believed to have the alchemic power to create gold or silver from lead. • It is believed that the light of the Moon is collected in the leaves of Moonwort to capture and make the magical powers of the Moon available for use via the herb. • It is said that Moonwort will have the power to unlock a lock if placed in the keyhole as if it were a key. • Moonwort was believed to have such a strong alchemical power over metal it was rumored that if a horse were to step on the plant that the nails in the shoe would loosen and the shoe would fall right off.

No. 092

Brassica juncea 🜍🍴

Brown Mustard

American Mustard | Bamboo Mustard | *Brassica argyi* | *Brassica besseriana* | *Brassica chenopodiifolia* | *Brassica integrifolia* | *Brassica japonica* | *Brassica lanceolata* | *Brassica napiformis* | *Brassica richeri* | *Brassica rugosa* | *Brassica taquetii* | *Brassica urbaniana* | *Brassica willdenovii* | Chinese Mustard | *Crucifera juncea* | Curled Mustard | Curled-Leaf Mustard | Cut-Leaf Mustard | Dai Gai Choy | Giant-Leafed Mustard | Green-in-Snow Mustard | Head Mustard | Heart Mustard | Horned Mustard | Hsueh Li Hung | Indian Mustard | Japanese Giant Red Mustard | Korean Red Mustard | Large-Petiole Mustard | Leaf Mustard | Mustard Cabbage | Oriental Mustard | Rai | *Raphanus junceus* | Raya | Red-in-Snow Mustard | *Rhamphospermum volgense* | *Sinabraca juncea* | *Sinapis brassica* | *Sinapis cernua* | *Sinapis chinensis* | *Sinapis cuneifolia* | *Sinapis integrifolia* | *Sinapis juncea* | *Sinapis lanceolata* | *Sinapis oleracea* | *Sinapis patens* | *Sinapis ramosa* | *Sinapis rugosa* | *Sinapis sinensis* | *Sinapis tenella* | *Sinapis timoriana* | Small Gai Choy | Southern Curled Mustard | Southern Mustard | Swatow Mustard | Vegetable Mustard

☀ **SYMBOLIC MEANINGS**
Faith.

🜏 **COMPONENT MEANING**
Seed: Good luck charm; Indifference; Visible faith.

🜨 **POSSIBLE POWERS**
Confidence; Fire element; Mars; Mental clarity or power; Protection; Reassurance.

🜨 **FOLKLORE AND FACTS**
Carry Brown Mustard seed in a red cloth pouch to increase your mental powers. • Brown Mustard provides the "mustard" element to the Moutarde de Dijon, which is more commonly known as Dijon mustard, an iconic recipe that originated in Dijon, France and was presented on the dining table of King Philip VI of France in 1336.

B

No. 093
Brassica nigra 🥣🍽

Black Mustard

Brassica brachycarpa | Brassica bracteolata | Brassica persoonii | Brassica sinapioides | Brassica sinapis | Brassica turgida | California Wild Mustard | Crucifera sinapis | Erysimum glabrum | Melanosinapis communis | Melanosinapis nigra | Mostaza | Mutarda nigra | Raphanus sinapis-officinalis | Sinapis bracteolata | Sinapis erysimoides | Sinapis gorraea | Sinapis nigra | Sinapis orgyalis | Sinapis persoonii | Sinapis torulosa | Sinapis turgida | Sisymbrium nigrum | Wild Mustard

☀ SYMBOLIC MEANINGS
Charity; Indifference.

🌿 COMPONENT MEANING
Seed: Aesculapius; Fire element; Good luck charm; Indifference; Mars; Masculine energy; Visible faith.

🌀 POSSIBLE POWERS
Banish negativity; Ending a relationship; Endings; Fertility; Fire element; Mental clarity or power; Protection.

🜂 FOLKLORE AND FACTS
The golden-yellow Black Mustard flowers blossom in the summer to color vacant lots and wilderness hiking trails. • People have eaten and used Black Mustard for more than 2,000 years. • Black Mustard appears in the work of Columella, a first century CE Roman author. • Biblical experts consider Black Mustard to be the reference point for "having faith" as in the "grain of a mustard seed" in the Gospel of Matthew in the New Testament. • Put ground Black Mustard seeds on thresholds for protection. • Bury Black Mustard seeds under or near your doorstep to keep supernatural beings from entering your home. • Carry or wear a sachet of Black Mustard seeds to travel through the air by plane or otherwise. • Make and carry or wear a red sachet filled with Black Mustard seeds to increase your mental powers.

No. 094
Brassica oleracea 🥣

Wild Cabbage

Colewort | Collet | Crambe | Jersey Cabbage | Tree Cabbage | True Colewort

☀ SYMBOLIC MEANINGS
Destiny; Grace.

🌀 POSSIBLE POWERS
Calming; Cleansing; Correctness; Drive away drunkenness; Luck; Money; Psychic ability; Relaxation; Shrewdness.

🜂 FOLKLORE AND FACTS
Wild Cabbage can only rarely still be found growing on the seaside cliffs on both sides of the English Channel. • Wild Cabbage that is still growing on the Channel Island of Jersey is sometimes known as a Jersey Cabbage and is also known as a Tree Cabbage. Its leaves are harvested throughout the year, without destroying the plant itself. • By stripping the leaves off the stalk, eventually the stalk of the Wild Cabbage will grow up to ten feet tall, plenty tall enough to harvest, dry, cut into appropriate lengths and then fashion to be used as a sturdy Jersey walking stick. • Wild Cabbage was the only internal remedy for digestive illnesses used by the Romans for at least 600 years. • The Wild Cabbage or True Colewort is the plant from which all of the Brassica varieties evolved. • It is thought that the looming height of the Wild Cabbage stalks may have inspired the story of Jack and the Bean Stalk. • In Great Britain, it was a common practice when cutting any Cabbage to leave the stalk in the ground to continue to grow table greens. At that time, it was an occasional practice to carve an "x" on the flat cut end of the remaining stalk to fend off garden sprites and demons. • There was a time when blood-letting cuts were practiced by medical apprentices on the raised veins of the Wild Cabbage leaf.

B

No. 095

Brassica rapa var. *rapa* ♀🍶

Turnip

Barbarea derchiensis | Brassica amplexicaulis | Brassica antiquorum | Brassica arvensis | Brassica asperifolia | Brassica brassicata | Brassica briggsii | Brassica campestris | Brassica celerifolia | Brassica chinensis | Brassica colza | Brassica cyrenaica | Brassica dubiosa | Brassica japonica | Brassica lutea | Brassica musifolia | Brassica napella | Brassica narinosa | Brassica nipposinica | Brassica oleronensis | Brassica parachinensis | Brassica perfoliata | Brassica perviridis | Brassica polymorpha | Brassica pseudocolza | Brassica saruna | Brassica sativa | Brassica septiceps | Brassica sphaerorhiza | Brassica trilocularis | Brassica trimestris | Brassica tuberosa | Caulanthus sulfureus | Crucifera rapa | Gongÿla | Nabos | Napus campestris | Napus rapa | Rapa oblonga | Raphanus amplexicaulis | Raphanus campestris | Raphanus chinensis | Raphanus rapa | Sinapis auriculata | Sinapis campestris | Sinapis communis | Sinapis dichotoma | Sinapis pekinensis | Sinapis rapa | Sinapis trilocularis | Sinapis tuberosa | White Turnip

☀ SYMBOLIC MEANINGS
Charity; Indifference.

🌼 POSSIBLE POWERS
Banish negativity; Earth element; Ending relationships; Feminine energy; Fertility; Mental clarity or power; The Moon; Protection.

⬥ FOLKLORE & FACTS
Put a hollowed and candlelit Turnip at the window on Halloween night to scare away malicious spirits. • Place a Turnip in the home to turn away every kind of negativity. • Turnips grow best in cool weather. • Turnips are biennial, meaning seeds planted one year will yield a ripe Turnip at the end of the following year's growing season. • The brainchild of Trevor Prideaux in Wedmore, England, the Turnip Prize began in 1999, satirizing the London's Tate Museum's prestigious but sometimes controversial annual Turner Prize. First prize for the Turnip Prize is a Turnip nailed to a block of wood.

No. 096

Bryonia alba ☠♀

White Bryony

Bryonia dioica | Bryonia monoeca | Bryonia nigra | Bryonia vulgaris | Bryonie | Devil's Turnip | English Mandrake | False Mandrake | Kua-Lou | Kudzu of the Northwest | Ladies' Seal | Tamus | Tetterbury | White Briony | White Hop | Wild Hops | Wild Nep | Wild Vine | Wood Vine

☀ SYMBOLIC MEANINGS
Grow luxuriantly; Here then gone.

🌼 POSSIBLE POWERS
Aphrodisiac; Attract love; Fire element; Healing; Image magic; Mars; Masculine energy; Money; Protection.

⬥ FOLKLORE AND FACTS
All parts of White Bryony are deadly poisonous, so you should avoid the plant completely in every way. • Witches used to soak White Bryony in milk to maliciously draw the milk from a cow. • Long ago, peasants in Poland sometimes used it to fumigate their non-producing milk cows with White Bryony if they believed a witch's curse had caused the problem. • Like Mandrake, people believe that White Bryony screams when pulled from the ground, but the similarities end there. • Hung in the garden, the White Bryony root will protect it from bad weather. • Place money near the White Bryony plant and leave it there. An increase in money will cease when the offering is removed.

No. 097

Bupleurum falcatum ♀

Sickle Hare's Ear

Bupleurum antiochium | Bupleurum chlorocarpum | Bupleurum corsicum | Bupleurum dilatatum | Bupleurum flexuosum | Bupleurum occidentale | Bupleurum oppositifolium | Bupleurum parnassicum | Bupleurum petiolare | Bupleurum petrogenes | Bupleurum rossicum | Bupleurum sibthorpianum | Bupleurum souliaei | Bupleurum woronowii | Chái Hú | Chai-Hu | Chinese Thoroughwax | Isophyllum falcatum | Pei Cha'ai | Selinum bupleurum | Sickle-Leaf Hare's Ear | Sickle-Leaved Hare's-Ear | Tenoria falcata

☀ SYMBOLIC MEANINGS
Flow.

🌼 POSSIBLE POWERS
Anti-depressant; Balance internal energies or organs; Chi stagnation; Cleansing; Harmonize the body; Healing; Old-age stagnation of life energy.

⬥ FOLKLORE AND FACTS
Traditional Chinese medicine has used it for more than 2,000 years. • Make a sachet of Sickle Hare's Ear leaf to carry or wear to balance and harmonize your internal energies.

B

No. 098

Bursera graveolens ⚗

Palo Santo

Alii A | *Amyris caranifera* | *Amyris graveolens* | *Amyris pubescens* | Bijá | Bursera | *Bursera anderssonii* | *Bursera pubescens* | *Bursera tatamaco* | Caraño | Chachique | Crispín | *Elaphrium graveolens* | *Elaphrium pubescens* | *Elaphrium tatamaco* | Holy Stick | Holy Wood | Sasafrás | Tamagaco | Tatamaco | *Terebinthus graveolens* | *Terebinthus pubescens* | West Indian Sandalwood

✺ SYMBOLIC MEANINGS
Cleanliness.

✺ POSSIBLE POWERS
Cleanliness; Clear misfortune; Dispel evil spirits or negative thoughts; Fire element; Good luck; Masculine energy; Purification; Relaxation; Soothe nervousness; Spiritual purification; the Sun.

✺ FOLKLORE AND FACTS
Palo Santo is a sacred tree that grows wild in parts of South America and is in the same *Burseraceae* family as Frankincense and Myrrh. • Palo Santo essential oil is often used for its ability to remove and ward off negative energy. • Dating back to the Inca era, according to some local Ecuadorian customs, Palo Santo is burned, like incense, to eliminate malevolent energy. • Palo Santo charcoal is occasionally used for smudging during some South American ritual customs. • Palo Santo essential oil is useful in aromatherapy to help ease insomnia, stress, and center the mind for meditation and prayer. • Palo Santo helps promote compassion whenever it is needed. • Palo Santo is helpful in encouraging inner peace.

No. 099

Buxus sempervirens ☠⚗

Boxwood

American Boxwood | Box | Box Tree | *Buxus angustifolia* | *Buxus arborescens* | *Buxus argentea* | *Buxus aurea* | *Buxus caucasica* | *Buxus colchica* | *Buxus crispa* | *Buxus cucullata* | *Buxus elegantissima* | *Buxus fruticosa* | *Buxus handsworthii* | *Buxus hyrcana* | *Buxus marginata* | *Buxus mucronata* | *Buxus myrtifolia* | *Buxus rosmarinifolia* | *Buxus salicifolia* | *Buxus tenuifolia* | *Buxus variegata* | *Buxus vulgaris* | Common Box | European Box | Evergreen Boxwood

✺ SYMBOLIC MEANINGS
Constancy; Constancy in friendship; Determination; Immortality; Indifference; Longevity; More than enough; Stature; Stoicism.

✺ POSSIBLE POWERS
Confusion; Distractions; Frustration; Interference; Longevity; Plenty; Protection; Protective.

✺ FOLKLORE AND FACTS
More than 4,000 years ago, the ancient Egyptians first formally trimmed Boxwood in their gardens. • For centuries, Mediterranean woodworkers made small, finely-carved boxes and musical instruments from Boxwood's fine-grained wood. • A Boxwood hedge is said to be a distraction to a witch wanting to steal flowers from a garden. • Boxwood leaves are so small and dense that a challenged witch cannot count the leaves, losing count and forced to futilely start over and over again. • To have a Boxwood hedge surrounding the home is a very powerful protection of the property and all that is within its boundaries.

B

No. 100
Calamintha grandiflora
Large-Flowered Calamint
Clinopodium grandiflorum | Drymosiphon grandiflorus | Faucibarba grandiflora | Melissa grandiflora | Mint Savory | Satureja grandiflora | Showy Calamint | Thymus grandiflorus

✳ **SYMBOLIC MEANINGS**
Joy.

🌀 **POSSIBLE POWERS**
Ease emotional pain; Flavoring; Increase joy; Recovery from emotional suffering; Restore optimism; Soothe sorrow.

☙ **FOLKLORE AND FACTS**
Fragrant Large-Flowered Calamint is a showy variety of mint with profuse lilac-pink tubular flowers that attract hummingbirds, bees, and butterflies throughout the summer.
• Make then carry or wear a sachet of Large-Flowered Calamint to boost a feeling of joyfulness.

No. 101
Calendula officinalis ⚗
Calendula
Caléndula | Calendula aurantiaca | Calendula eriocarpa | Calendula hydruntina | Calendula prolifera | Calendula ranunculodes | Calendula santamariae | Calendula sinuata | Caltha officinalis | Common Marigold | Drunkard | English Marigold | Garden Marigold | Husbandman's Dial | Marigold | Mary's Gold | Marybud | Pot Marigold | Prophetic Marigold | Prophetic Marygold | Ruddles | Scottish Marigold | Summer's Bride | Throughout-the-Months

✳ **SYMBOLIC MEANINGS**
Affection; Anxiety; Constructive loss; Cruelty; Despair; Fidelity; Grace; Grief; Health; Jealousy; Joy; Longevity; Pain; Sacred affection; Trouble.

🌀 **POSSIBLE POWERS**
Amorousness; Dream magic; Evil thoughts; Helps with seeing fairies; Legal matters; Prediction; Prophetic dreams; Protection; Psychic power; Rebirth; Sleep.

☙ **FOLKLORE AND FACTS**
The Calendula plant is considered one of the most sacred herbs of ancient India. Its flower heads were commonly strung into garlands and used in temples and at weddings.
• Calendula flower heads follow the sun like Sunflowers do. • Carry or wear a sachet of Calendula petals along with a Bay Laurel leaf to quell gossip. • Early Christians would place its bright yellow flowers by statues of the Virgin Mary.
• Pass a prepared Calendula amulet, talisman, or sachet through its smoke to entirely imbue it with magical powers.
• It may be possible to see visions upon Calendula smoke.

No. 102
Calluna vulgaris ⚗
Heather
Calluna | Calluna atlantica | Calluna beleziana | Calluna ciliaris | Calluna elegantissima | Calluna erica | Calluna genuina | Calluna sagittifolia | Common Heather | Erica | Erica ciliaris | Erica confusa | Erica glabra | Erica herbacea | Erica lutescens | Erica nana | Erica prostrata | Erica reginae | Erica sagittifolia | Erica vulgaris | Ericoides vulgaris | Heath | Heath Heather | Ling | Scottish Heather

✳ **SYMBOLIC MEANINGS**
Admiration; Attraction; Beauty; Good luck; Healing from within; Increases physical beauty; Luck; Mystery; Protection from danger; Purity; Refinement; Reveal the inner self; Romance; Secret longings; Solitude; Wishes.

🌸 **COLOR MEANINGS**
Pink: Good luck.
Purple: Admiration; Beauty; Solitude.
White: Protection from danger.

🌀 **POSSIBLE POWERS**
Cleansing; Colorize; Feminine energy; Ghost conjuring; Good luck; Healing; Immortality; Initiation; Intoxication; Mystery; Protection; Protection against rape, theft, or violent crime; Rainmaking; Secret longing; Venus; Warding off an inappropriate suitor; Water element; Weather-working; Wish magic.

☙ **FOLKLORE AND FACTS**
Wearing an amulet made of a Heather twig will help facilitate awareness of your own true immortal soul. • Heather twigs were once gathered up together to be used as brooms. • A sprig of it is carried as a protection charm against violent crime, most specifically as protection against rape. • Wear or carry a sprig of white Heather as a good luck charm.

C

No. 103
Camellia sinensis ☙

Black Tea

Assam Tea | Bird's Tongue | Camellia angustifolia | Camellia arborescens | Camellia assamica | Camellia dehungensis | Camellia dishiensis | Camellia longlingensis | Camellia multisepala | Camellia oleosa | Camellia parvisepala | Camellia parvisepaloides | Camellia polyneura | Camellia tea | Camellia waldeniae | Ceylon | Cha | China Tea | Congou | Darjeeling | Dianhong | Green Tea | Jaekseol | Jiu Qu Hong Mei | Kangra | Keemun | Kukicha | Lahijan | Lapsang | Munnar | Nepali | Nilgiri | Nine Winding Red Plum Tea | Oolong | Orange Pekoe Tea | Pinyin | Puerh Tea | Rize | Sun Moon Lake Tea | Tea Plant | Tea Shrub | Thea assamica | Thea bohea | Thea cantonensis | Thea chinensis | Thea cochinchinensis | Thea grandifolia | Thea olearia | Thea oleosa | Thea parvifolia | Thea sinensis | Thea viridis | Theaphylla cantonensis | White Tea | Yingdehong

❋ SYMBOLIC MEANINGS
Change; Constancy; Contentment; Courage; Fire element; Harmony; Mars; Masculine energy; Peace; Refreshment; Rejuvenation; Riches; Spiritual awakening, connection, or enlightenment; Steadfastness; Strength; Young sons and daughters.

❀ POSSIBLE POWERS
Courage; Feminine energy; Healing; the Moon; Peace; Prosperity; Rejuvenation; Riches; Spiritual connection; Stress relief; Water element.

☙ FOLKLORE AND FACTS
Wear a sachet or pouch of Black Tea as a talisman to increase your strength and give yourself a boost of courage. A premade store-bought tea bag is not the proper kind of sachet. Even so, the dried tea within it is acceptable, but it should be emptied into the handmade sachet packet. The ideal tea leaves are those which are hand-picked from the bush itself. • Green Tea or White Tea is the new stem tip growth of Black Tea leaves. • The word "tea" in the common names for *Camellia sinensis* Tea Shrub, *Melaleuca alternifolia* Tea Tree, and *Leptospermum scoparium* New Zealand Teatree imply they are similar plants. However, they're not related to each other and are not a substitute for each other in any way for any reason. • A hot cup of Black Tea has been the go-to cure-all for nearly every sudden impairment small or great, lightheadedness, swooning, sadness, or gloomily slumping spirit for hundreds, perhaps thousands of years. Who knows? Maybe even millions of years.

No. 104
Campanula rotundifolia ☙

Harebell

Bluebell of Scotland | Campanula allophylla | Campanula angustifolia | Campanula antirrhina | Campanula asturica | Campanula bielzii | Campanula bocconei | Campanula caballeroi | Campanula chinganensis | Campanula cinerea | Campanula decloetiana | Campanula delicatula | Campanula diversifolia | Campanula filiformis | Campanula grammosepala | Campanula heterodoxa | Campanula heterophylla | Campanula hostii | Campanula inconcessa | Campanula juncea | Campanula lanceolata | Campanula lancifolia | Campanula langsdorffiana | Campanula legionensis | Campanula linifolia | Campanula lobata | Campanula lostrittii | Campanula minor | Campanula minuta | Campanula paenina | Campanula pennica | Campanula pennina | Campanula pseudovaldensis | Campanula pubescens | Campanula racemosa | Campanula reboudiana | Campanula rotunda | Campanula sarmentosa | Campanula solstitialis | Campanula tenuifolia | Campanula tracheliifolia | Campanula urbionensis | Campanula variifolia | Campanula wiedmannii | Depierrea campanuloides | Rapunculus esculentus | Scottish Bluebell

❋ SYMBOLIC MEANINGS
Gratitude; Grief; Humility; Retirement; Submission; Thinking of you.

❀ POSSIBLE POWERS
Luck; Truth.

☙ FOLKLORE AND FACTS
If you wear a Harebell flower, you will feel the need to tell the truth. • If you can turn a Harebell blossom inside out without damaging it, the one you love will love you in return someday.

No. 105
Cananga odorata

Ylang-Ylang

Cananga scortechinii | Cananga Tree | Canangium mitrastigma | Canangium odoratum | Canangium scortechinii | Climbing Ylang-Ylang | Fitzgeraldia mitrastigma | Flower of Flowers | Fragrant Cananga | Ilang-Ilang | Kenanga | Mata'oi | Mohokoi | Mokasoi | Mokohoi | Mokosoi | Moso'oi | Moto'oi | Unona fitzgeraldii | Unona leptopetala | Unona odorata | Unona ossea | Uvaria axillaris | Uvaria farcta | Uvaria hortensis | Uvaria javanica | Uvaria odorata | Uvaria ossea | Uvaria trifoliata | Uvaria undulata | Ylang-Ylang Vine

❋ SYMBOLIC MEANINGS
Wilderness flower.

C

POSSIBLE POWERS

Aphrodisiac; Elevate mood; Help alleviate sexual dysfunction; Relieve anxiety and stress.

FOLKLORE AND FACTS

The Ylang-Ylang tree has an unusual, beautifully fragrant blossom, leading to the mistranslation of its common name as "flower of flowers." The name correctly derives from *ilang*, the Tagalog word for "wilderness." • In aromatherapy, Ylang-Ylang's exotically scented essential oil encourages closing your eyes and smelling the air as a means of transporting your imagination to the South Pacific. This helps ease a worried mind, releases nervous tension, and relaxes the body. • In aromatherapy, there are three grades of Ylang-Ylang essential oils. The first and earliest oil extracted is called "extra" and is the most potent and expensive version (it's used in upscale perfumery. "First through third" is a distillate that continues for several hours after the first "extra" distillate has been completed. This will be a more subtle version. The final distillate is called "complete" and is the most commonly available essential oil. The distillate of the blossoms is processed through each of these steps for ten to twenty hours to fully complete the process. The result is a milder, but still quite fragrant, essential oil. Although it's not used to make high-end perfume, it's still exotically fragrant on its own.

No. 106

Canarium luzonicum

Elemi

Canarium carapifolium | Canarium oliganthum | Canarium polyanthum | Canarium triandrum | Elemi Canary Tree | Java Almond | Pimela luzonica

SYMBOLIC MEANINGS

Above and below; Calm; New beginning; Peace; Quiet.

POSSIBLE POWERS

Balance; Emotional plane; Grounding; Healing; Honor the spirits of nature; Initiation; Magic; Rejuvenation; Rights of passage; Spiritual calm; Spiritual plane; Strengthen mental or psychic capacity.

FOLKLORE AND FACTS

The Elemi essential oil has a Dill-like minty, lemony fragrance that can be helpful in aromatherapy for balancing and grounding during meditation. • Elemi essential oil's viscosity is similar to Myrrh. • The ancient Egyptians used Elemi essential oil as one of the ingredients that was used to mummify a body. • Put a single drop of Elemi essential oil on a sachet to calm your inner spirit enough to enter the spiritual plane during meditation.

No. 107

Cannabis sativa ♂

Marijuana

Bud | Cannabis | *Cannabis americana* | *Cannabis chinensis* | *Cannabis erratica* | *Cannabis foetens* | *Cannabis generalis* | *Cannabis gigantea* | *Cannabis indica* | *Cannabis intersita* | *Cannabis kafiristanica* | *Cannabis lupulus* | *Cannabis macrosperma* | *Cannabis ruderalis* | Chanvre | Doodle | Gallow Grass | Ganeb | Ganja | Grass | Green | Hanf | Hemp | Hempseed Plant | Herb | Industrial Hemp Plant | Kif | Mary Jane | Neckweed | *Polygonum viridiflorum* | Pot Weed | Reefer | Scratch Weed | Tekrouri | Wacky Weed | Weed

SYMBOLIC MEANINGS

Fate; Hardiness; Roughness.

POSSIBLE POWERS

Contemplation; Feminine energy; Healing; Love; Meditation; Saturn; Sleep; Visions; Water element.

FOLKLORE AND FACTS

Since ancient times in China, Marijuana ropes were made from *Cannabis sativa* fiber, commonly called "hemp rope." • People used Marijuana hemp rope as a proxy snake to beat a "sickbed" in an attempt to drive out any demons that caused the patient's illness. • There is a "hemp seed divination" that takes place at a churchyard at midnight at the start of midsummer. With a handful of *Cannabis sativa* seeds, you walk around the church nine times, sprinkling them as you go and repeating, "Hemp seed I sow. Hemp seed I sow. Who will come after me and mow?" At this point, you might see a vision of your future mate mowing the area using an old-fashioned sickle. • Controversy has surrounded the criminalization and decriminalization of Marijuana in the United States for over a century. Some states have decriminalized and eventually legalized the sale, the possession, and the use of *Cannabis sativa* dried herb and its derivatives for medicinal and recreational purposes.

No. 108

Capparis spinosa

Caper

Abiyyonah | Abiyyonot | *Blumea grandiflora* | Caper Bush | Caperberry Bush | *Capparis aculeata* | *Capparis microphylla* | *Capparis murrayi* | *Capparis ovalis* | *Capparis ovata* | *Capparis peduncularis* | *Capparis sativa* | Fakouha | Flinders Rose | Kabar | Kápparis | Kebre | Kypros | Lasafa | Shaffallah | Zalef

SYMBOLIC MEANINGS

Escapade.

POSSIBLE POWERS

Aphrodisiac; Attract love; Feminine energy; Love; Lust; Potency; Venus; Water element.

FOLKLORE AND FACTS

It was once believed that an impotent man just needs to eat Capers to be miraculously cured. • The Caper flower is beautifully unusual. • Make two love-and-lust red sachets, with each containing a Caper flower and a leaf or just the buds if you don't have flowers and leaves. Tuck the sachets under your mattress with one on each side of your bed.

No. 109

Capsicum annuum

Aleppo Pepper

Halaby Pepper | Haleb Biber | Pul Biber | Syrian Chili

SYMBOLIC MEANINGS

Beauty; Culture; Perseverance; Resilience.

POSSIBLE POWERS

Fire element; Hope; Mars; Masculine energy.

FOLKLORE AND FACTS

Capsicum annuum encompasses many different peppers, from the sweetest to some of the hottest varieties. The Aleppo Pepper is one of them. • People have occupied the site of Aleppo in northern Syria for more than 6,000 years, making it one of the oldest cities in the world. • Aleppo lies on the Silk Road, the route that spice traders traveled heavily from around 114 BCE to 1450 CE. • People have used it as a spicy (around 10,000 Scovilles) culinary herb for millennia. • Aleppo Peppers are traditionally processed by cutting them in half and removing the seeds and inner flesh. The flesh is wiped with a white cloth and given a light coating of oil and salt, then dried on a rooftop. They are then coarsely ground to produce a mild peppery flaky spice with a natural touch of sweetness that is beloved and liberally used in many Middle Eastern and Mediterranean dishes.

No. 110

Capsicum annuum

Banana Pepper

Armenian Banana Pepper | Banana Chili | Hungarian Wax Pepper | Yellow Wax Pepper

SYMBOLIC MEANINGS

Hidden desires or feelings.

POSSIBLE POWERS

Banishing; Creativity; Energy; Fire element; Healing; Love; Mars; Masculine energy; Mental ability; Prosperity; Protection; Strength; Things missing in life; Ward off evil or the evil eye; Wealth.

FOLKLORE AND FACTS

Capsicum annuum encompasses many different peppers, from the sweetest to some of the hottest varieties. The Banana Pepper (around 250 Scovilles) is one of them. • The Banana Pepper has a bright yellow color like a banana and can be found in the produce department or pickled in a jar. As it ripens, the color of the Banana Pepper eventually changes to orange and then red. The riper the pepper becomes, the sweeter it will be.

No. 111

Capsicum annuum

Bell Pepper

Capsicum | Sweet Pepper

SYMBOLIC MEANINGS

Beneficial change; Consumerism; Deception; Desire to gain freedom; Dishonesty; Fairness; Greed; Healing; Hidden desires or feelings; Hope; Maturity; Peace; Productivity; Selfishness; Things missing in life; Well-being.

POSSIBLE POWERS

Creativity; Energy; Fire element; Healing; Love; Mars; Masculine energy; Mental ability; Prosperity; Protection; Strength; Ward off the evil eye; Wealth.

FOLKLORE AND FACTS

Capsicum annuum encompasses many different peppers, from the sweetest to some of the hottest varieties. The Bell Pepper—mildest, heat-free (0 Scovilles), and flavorful—is one of them. • The wide range of mild sweet Bell Pepper colors are green, red, orange, yellow, lavender, dark purple, brown, and white. • The thick fleshed and sweet Bell Pepper is enjoyed as a vegetable, but it is botanically a berry.

No. 112

Capsicum annuum 🌱🍴

Bird's Eye Chili

Bird Eye Chili | Bird's Chili | Thai Chili

✳ SYMBOLIC MEANINGS

Overview; Spice in your life.

🌀 POSSIBLE POWERS

Aphrodisiac; Attract love; Break a hex; Fidelity; Fire element; Love; Mars; Masculine energy; Ward off evil spirits or the evil eye.

🜨 FOLKLORE AND FACTS

If you believe that you've been cursed, you can encircle your house with these small, bright red peppers to break the curse. • The little Bird's Eye Chili doesn't look like it would be very hot, but at around 5,000 Scovilles, it's much hotter than a Jalapeño Pepper. • Make a red sachet using one whole small Bird's Eye Chili. Put the sachet under your mattress to encourage spicy romance.

No. 113

Capsicum annuum 🌱🍴

Cayenne Pepper

Red Hot Pepper

✳ SYMBOLIC MEANINGS

Hidden desires or feelings; Things missing in life.

🌀 POSSIBLE POWERS

Banishing; Creativity; Energy; Fire element; Healing; Love; Mars; Masculine energy; Mental ability; Prosperity; Protection; Strength; Ward off evil or the evil eye; Wealth.

🜨 FOLKLORE AND FACTS

Capsicum annuum encompasses many different peppers, from the sweetest to some of the hottest varieties. The Cayenne Pepper (40,000 Scovilles) is one of them. • Its usual bright red color resembles what we recognize as the iconic chili pepper, but the Cayenne comes in orange, yellow, or green varieties as well. • Manufacturers usually dry and grind it into a powder, but packaged "Cayenne Pepper powder" might not include any actual Cayenne Pepper at all.

No. 114

Capsicum annuum 🌱🍴

Friggitello

Golden Greek Pepper | Greek Golden Pepperoncini Pepper | Mild Golden Salonika Pepper | Sweet Italian Chili Pepper | Sweet Italian Pepper | Tuscan Pepper

✳ SYMBOLIC MEANINGS

Hidden desires or feelings; Things missing in life.

🌀 POSSIBLE POWERS

Banishing; Creativity; Energy; Fire element; Healing; Love; Mars; Masculine energy; Mental ability; Prosperity; Protection; Strength; Ward off evil or the evil eye; Wealth.

🜨 FOLKLORE AND FACTS

Capsicum annuum encompasses many different peppers, from the sweetest to some of the hottest varieties. The mild and flavorful Friggitello pepper (around 300 Scovilles) is one of them. • Pickled when green or greenish-yellow, the Friggitello is often mistaken for the Banana Pepper.

No. 115

Capsicum annuum 🌱🍴

Jalapeño Pepper

Chili Gordo | Chipotle Chili | Cuaresmeño | Fat Chili Pepper | Huachinango | Jalapa

✳ SYMBOLIC MEANINGS

Hidden desires or feelings; Things missing in life.

🌀 POSSIBLE POWERS

Banishing; Creativity; Energy; Fire element; Healing; Love; Mars; Masculine energy; Mental ability; Prosperity; Protection; Strength; Ward off evil or the evil eye; Wealth.

🜨 FOLKLORE AND FACTS

Capsicum annuum encompasses many different peppers, from the sweetest to some of the hottest varieties. The spicy hot Jalapeño Pepper (around 5,000 Scovilles) is one of them. • In the marketplace, the most familiar version is the unripe green pepper, but fully ripe Jalapeño Peppers appear yellow, orange, or red. Due to the development of capsaicin in the fruit, the brighter the color, the hotter the pepper becomes, making the red Jalapeño one of the hottest of the color variations. • A chipotle chili is a smoke-dried Jalapeño Pepper. • Although it's a Mexican chili, the beloved Jalapeño Pepper was declared the "state pepper of Texas" in 1995. • Texans' abiding love and utter devotion for the pepper is evident in their recipes. They almost always include it in at least one dish at every celebration meal of every year. • The Jalapeño Pepper takes its name from Xalapa (also spelled "Jalapa"), the capital city of Veracruz State in Mexico.

No. 116

Capsicum annuum 🗡️🍴

Paprika

Paparka | Peperke | Pimentón | Pimentón de Murcia | Piperi | Piperke | Pippali

🌟 **SYMBOLIC MEANINGS**
Hidden desires or feelings; Things missing in life.

🌼 **POSSIBLE POWERS**
Banishing; Creativity; Energy; Fire element; Healing; Love; Mars; Masculine energy; Mental ability; Prosperity; Protection; Strength; Ward off evil or the evil eye; Wealth.

🜨 **FOLKLORE AND FACTS**
Capsicum annuum encompasses many different peppers, from the sweetest to some of the hottest varieties. The mild Paprika pepper (250–1,000 Scovilles) is one of them. • Ranging from mild to hot, it comes in different grades, depending on pungency and heat. • The word "paprika" means pepper in Hungarian. • Farmers first cultivated Paprika peppers in Budapest in 1569. At that time, it tasted very hot. In the 1920s, growers grafted the plant on to other rootstock, and the resulting peppers tasted much sweeter. • Peppers used to make the ground spice usually have thin skins. • The Spanish version of Paprika has a smokiness to it because it's dried using oak-wood smoke.

No. 117

Capsicum annuum 🗡️🍴

Pimiento

Cherry Pepper | Pimento | Portuguese Pimento | Red Cherry Pepper | Spanish Pimiento

🌟 **SYMBOLIC MEANINGS**
Hidden desires or feelings; Things missing in life.

🌼 **POSSIBLE POWERS**
Banishing; Creativity; Energy; Fire element; Healing; Love; Mars; Masculine energy; Mental ability; Prosperity; Protection; Strength; Ward off evil or the evil eye; Wealth.

🜨 **FOLKLORE AND FACTS**
Capsicum annuum encompasses many different peppers, from the sweetest to some of the hottest varieties. The mild Pimiento pepper (around 300 Scovilles) is one of them. • The proverbial "pickled pepper" Peter Piper picked was a Pimiento. • Food producers routinely stuff bits of Pimento into the hollows of pickled, pitted green Olives.

No. 118

Capsicum baccatum 🗡️🍴

Aji Cito Pepper

Aji Amarillo Chili | Aji Chili | Aji Cito | Aji Cristal Pepper | Aji Dulce Pepper | Aji Escabeche | Aji Fantasy | Aji Habanero | Aji Norteño | Aji Panca | Aji Pineapple | Amarillo Chili | Bishop's Crown | Brazilian Starfish Pepper | *Capsicum angustifolium* | *Capsicum baccatum* | *Capsicum cerasiflorum* | *Capsicum cerasiforme* | *Capsicum chamaecerasus* | *Capsicum ciliare* | *Capsicum conicum* | *Capsicum microcarpum* | *Capsicum microphyllum* | *Capsicum pulchellum* | *Capsicum umbilicatum* | Hot Lemon | Kellu Uchu | Lemon Drop Pepper | Locoto | Northern Aji | Peppadew | Peruvian Hot Pepper | Piquanté Pepper

🌟 **SYMBOLIC MEANINGS**
Enchanted; Holy; Magical.

🌼 **POSSIBLE POWERS**
Break a hex; Fidelity; Fire element; Love; Love charms; Mars; Masculine energy; Protection against vampires or werewolves.

🜨 **FOLKLORE AND FACTS**
The literal translation of Baccatum is "berry-like." The Ají Cito Pepper looks like a berry. It's small, squat, and comes in colors of bright orange, red, and yellow. • At around 100,000 Scovilles, it's the hottest of the *Capsicum baccatum* peppers.

No. 119

Capsicum chinense 🗡️🍴

Habanero Chili

La Habana

🌟 **SYMBOLIC MEANINGS**
Spice in your life.

🌼 **POSSIBLE POWERS**
Break a hex; Fidelity; Fire element; Love; Mars; Masculine energy; Ward off an evil spirit or the evil eye.

🜨 **FOLKLORE AND FACTS**
The *Capsicum chinense* species contains the hottest peppers in the world. • The Habanero Chili comes in green, yellow, orange, red, purple, or brown varieties. • Habanero Chili peppers are red when ripe and extremely hot (around 225,000 Scovilles). • Most Habanero Chili peppers are grown and exported from Mexico's Yucatán Peninsula.

C

No. 120

Capsicum chinense 🌶️🍴

Hot Pepper

Adjuma Pepper | Aji chombo | Aji dulce | Arriba Saia | Bhut Jolokia | Cabik Gronong Pepper | *Capsicum sinense* | *Capsicum toxicarium* | Datil | Fatalii | Ghost Pepper | Habanero Chili | Hainan Yellow Lantern Chili | Kambuzi Pepper | Madame Jeanette Pepper | Malawian Pepper | Scotch Bonnet | Trinidad Scorpion Pepper

✴️ SYMBOLIC MEANINGS
Spice in your life.

🌐 POSSIBLE POWERS
Break a hex; Fidelity; Fire element; Love; Mars; Masculine energy; Ward off an evil spirit or the evil eye.

🜨 FOLKLORE AND FACTS
The *Capsicum chinense* species contains the hottest peppers in the world. • In Mexico, archaeologists have found *Capsicum chinense* seeds in burial sites dating to 7000 BCE. • In 2017, Guinness World Records certified the "Carolina Reaper," grown by Ed Currie, as the world's hottest pepper. It has an average of 1,641,183 Scovilles, exceeding the heat of the Ghost Pepper in 2007 and the Trinidad Scorpion Butch T Pepper in 2011. • With the ongoing competition of new Hot Pepper hybrids, the Hot Pepper seems to be getting hotter and hotter. • Because a *Capsicum chinense* Hot Pepper contributes considerable heat to food, cooks primarily use it in salsas, sauces, and stews. • Encircle your house with red Hot Peppers to break a curse.

No. 121

Capsicum frutescens var. *tabasco* 🌶️🍴

Tabasco Pepper

Capsicum assamicum | Capsicum conoides | Capsicum fastigiatum | Capsicum minimum | Capsicum pendulum | Piman | Tabasco Chili

✴️ SYMBOLIC MEANINGS
Hidden desires or feelings; Things missing in life.

🌐 POSSIBLE POWERS
Banishing; Creativity; Energy; Fire element; Healing; Love; Mars; Masculine energy; Mental ability; Prosperity; Protection; Strength; Ward off evil or the evil eye; Wealth.

🜨 FOLKLORE AND FACTS
The state of Tabasco, Mexico is the original location of the Tabasco Pepper. • The iconic sauce made from this pepper is very spicy and so pleasantly hot enough (around 40,000 Scovilles) it seems to have birthed a cadre of hot-sauce connoisseurs who amass large hot pepper sauce collections to discuss and compare.

Capsicum pubescens 🌿🍴

Rocoto Pepper

Apple Pepper | Apple-Shaped Pepper | Locoto | Luqutu | Manzano Pepper | Rukutu | Ruqutu | Tree Pepper

✹ SYMBOLIC MEANINGS
Hidden desires or feelings;
Things missing in life.

✹ POSSIBLE POWERS
Banishing; Creativity; Energy;
Fire element; Healing; Love;
Mars; Masculine energy; Mental
ability; Prosperity; Protection;
Strength; Ward off evil or the
evil eye; Wealth.

✹ FOLKLORE AND FACTS
Unlike other *Capsicum* peppers, the Rocoto
Pepper cannot survive tropical heat. The plant requires
the cool temperature of higher elevations to thrive well
enough to fruit. • Rocoto Pepper is a vital ingredient in many
Bolivian and Peruvian recipes.

Cardamine hirsuta 🌿

Hairy Bittercress

Arabis heterophylla | Bitter Cress | Cardamine angulata | Cardamine borbonica | Cardamine fagetina | Cardamine hirsuta lasiocarpa | Cardamine humilis | Cardamine micrantha | Cardamine multicaulis | Cardamine parviflora | Cardamine praecox | Cardamine simensis | Cardamine tenella | Cardamine tetrandra | Cardamine virginica | Crucifera cardamine | Ghinia hirsuta | Ghinia sylvatica | Hairy Bitter Cress | Stune Lamb's Cress

✹ SYMBOLIC MEANINGS
Paternal error.

✹ POSSIBLE POWERS
Protection; Spiritual warfare.

✹ FOLKLORE AND FACTS
Hairy Bittercress is one of the magical ingredients in the
"Nine Herbs Charm" of tenth century England. Soldiers in
holy battle used the ancient charm to fend off the Serpent's
perceived power against them.

Cardamine pratensis 🌿

Cuckoo Flower

Cardamine acaulis | Cardamine buchtormensis | Cardamine fontinalis | Cardamine fossicola | Cardamine grandiflora | Cardamine herbivaga | Cardamine iliciana | Cardamine integrifolia | Cardamine monticola | Cardamine nasturtii | Cardamine nasturtiifolia | Cardamine nasturtioides | Cardamine orophila | Cardamine praticola | Cardamine pseudopratensis | Cardamine scaturiginosa | Cardamine stolonifera | Cardamine sylvatica | Crucifera pratensis | Dracamine pratensis | Ghinia pratensis | Lady's Smock | Mayflower | Milkmaids

✹ SYMBOLIC MEANINGS
Ardor; Sacred to fairies.

✹ POSSIBLE POWERS
Feminine energy; Fertility; Love;
Venus; Water element.

✹ FOLKLORE AND FACTS
The Cuckoo Flower is considered
to be a very sacred fairy flower.
They're not used in May Day
wreaths and garlands to prevent
offending the fairies. • If you offend
a fairy by disrespecting their sacred
Cuckoo Flower, it is believed that
the fairy will drag you underground into Fairyland as an
insufferable consequence. • It's bad luck to bring a Cuckoo
Flower into your home.

Carphephorus odoratissimus

Vanillaleaf

Anonymos odoratissima | Chaff Heads | Chrysocoma odoratissima | Deer's Tongue | Eupatorium glastifolium | Liatris amplexicaulis | Liatris odoratissima | Serratula odoratissima | Sweet After Death | Trilisa odoratissima | Vanilla Leaf

✹ SYMBOLIC MEANINGS
Eloquence; Good luck in a court case, love affair, or
promoting love with marriage; Pleasing speech.

✹ POSSIBLE POWERS
The Arts; Attraction; Beauty; Eloquence; Friendship; Gifts;
Harmony; Joy; Love; Pleasures; Sensuality.

✹ FOLKLORE AND FACTS
For a positive response to a marriage proposal, place
Vanillaleaf inside a pink and red sachet made especially for
the occasion and wear it over your heart. • Wear or carry
a Vanillaleaf sachet for the power to speak eloquently in a
public setting or courtroom.

C

No. 126
Carum carvi 🌿🍴

Caraway

Aegopodium carum | Alcaravea | al-Karawya | *Apium carvi* | *Bunium carvi* | Caro | Carum | *Carum decussatum* | *Carum gracile* | *Carum officinale* | *Carum rosellum* | *Carum velenovskyi* | *Carvi careum* | Cumino Tedesco | *Falcaria carvifolia* | Finocchio Meridionale | *Foeniculum carvi* | Kamoon | Karavi | *Karos carvi* | Karve | Kreuzkümmel | Kümmel | *Lagoecia cuminoidesl* | *Ligusticum carvi* | Meridian Fennel | Persian Cumin | *Pimpinella carvi* | *Pimpinella involucrata* | *Selinum carvi* | *Seseli carum* | *Seseli carvi* | *Sium carvi*

✳ SYMBOLIC MEANINGS
Faithfulness.

✿ POSSIBLE POWERS
Air element; Anti-theft; Business transactions; Caution; Cleverness; Communication; Creativity; Faith; Faithfulness; Health; Illumination; Initiation; Intelligence; Keeps lovers true; Learning; Love; Lust; Masculine energy; Memory; Mental power; Mercury; Passion; Protection; Protection against Lilith; Prudence; Repel negativity; Science; Self-preservation; Sound judgment; Thievery; Wisdom.

✾ FOLKLORE AND FACTS
What people commonly call the seed is actually the tiny fruit of the *Carum carvi* plant. • In the Middle Ages, people often used Caraway in love potions to prevent lovers from turning and wandering away from each other. • Use Caraway, along with other herbs, to increase protection. • Sprinkle some Caraway seeds over and around your most prized possessions to fend off a burglary. A thief who makes it into the protected house will be held transfixed until arrested. • Wear an amulet of Caraway seeds to improve your memory. • Tuck a small pouch of Caraway seeds in a hidden place in a child's room as protection against illness. • Caraway has the power to consecrate magical tools. • Wearing an amulet of Caraway seeds will improve your memory.

No. 127
Catha edulis ☠🌿

Khat

African Tea | Arabian Tea | Cat | *Catha forsskalii* | *Catha glauca* | *Catha inermis* | *Celastrus edulis* | *Celastrus tsaad* | *Dillonia abyssinica* | *Hartogia thea* | *Methyscophyllum glaucum* | Qat | Quat | *Trigonotheca serrata*

✳ SYMBOLIC MEANINGS
Contrariness.

✿ POSSIBLE POWERS
Additive stimulation; Heavy depression.

✾ FOLKLORE AND FACTS
For centuries, people have chewed Khat as a euphoric stimulant that leads almost immediately to a decrease in depression. • Europe, Britain, and American metropolis cities import large quantities of fresh Khat leaves from Kenya and Ethiopia. However, many countries have banned it.

No. 128
Catharanthus roseus ☠🌿

Madagascar Periwinkle

Ammocallis rosea | Bright Eyes | Cape Periwinkle | Cayenne Jasmine | Graveyard Plant | *Lochnera rosea* | Old Maid | *Pervinca rosea* | Pink Periwinkle | Rose Periwinkle | *Vinca rosea* | *Vinca speciosa*

✳ SYMBOLIC MEANINGS
Peace; Pleasures of memories.

✿ POSSIBLE POWERS
Feminine energy; Healing; Venus; Water element.

✾ FOLKLORE AND FACTS
The Madagascar Periwinkle has been used medicinally since around 2600 BCE. • Madagascar Periwinkle is an extremely common sight growing wild in the southern United States and other subtropical gardens. • The Madagascar Periwinkle is the source of vital extracts used to make two modern drugs that are frequently used to treat a variety of cancers.

C

No. 129
Ceanothus americanus 🦪
Red Root

Buckbrush | *Ceanothus decumbens* | *Ceanothus dillenianus* | *Ceanothus ellipticus* | *Ceanothus glomeratus* | *Ceanothus hybridus* | *Ceanothus intermedius* | *Ceanothus latifolius* | *Ceanothus levigatus* | *Ceanothus macrocarpus* | *Ceanothus macrophyllus* | *Ceanothus milleri* | *Ceanothus multiflorus* | *Ceanothus officinalis* | *Ceanothus ovalifolius* | *Ceanothus perennis* | *Ceanothus pitcheri* | *Ceanothus procumbens* | *Ceanothus reclinatus* | *Ceanothus sanguineus* | *Ceanothus tardiflorus* | *Ceanothus trinervus* | *Ceanothus virgatus* | Desert Buckthorn | Jersey Tea Ceanothus | Mountain Lilac | Mountain Sweet | New Jersey Tea | Red Shank | Redroot | Wild Snowball

✹ **SYMBOLIC MEANINGS**
Spiny.

❀ **POSSIBLE POWERS**
Healing; Rebellion.

🜂 **FOLKLORE AND FACTS**
During the American Revolution, Red Root leaf was used as a tea substitute when imported Black Tea was difficult to get. During that time, Red Root obtained the common name of "New Jersey Tea." • The enormous, deep roots of the Red Root plant can grow to up to eight inches in diameter. • Red Root flowers can produce a light green vegetable dye.

No. 130
Ceanothus velutinus 🦪
Mountain Balm
Ceanothus grandis | Sticky Laurel

✹ **SYMBOLIC MEANINGS**
Delay.

❀ **POSSIBLE POWERS**
Healing.

🜂 **FOLKLORE AND FACTS**
The seed of Mountain Balm can remain in the soil for over 200 years before it germinates. • Indigenous people of the Northwest Plateaus used an infusion of Mountain Balm leaves as a treatment to help prevent dandruff.

No. 131
Ceiba pentandra
Kapok Tree

Balso | *Bombax cumanense* | *Bombax mompoxense* | *Bombax occidentale* | *Bombax orientale* | *Bombax pentandrum* | *Bombax plumosum* | Bonga | Bongo | Ceiba | Ceiba Bonga | Ceiba Bruja | *Ceiba caribaea* | *Ceiba casearia* | Ceiba de Lana | *Ceiba guineensis* | *Ceiba occidentalis* | *Ceiba thonningii* | Ceiba Tree | Ceibo | Chivecha | Cumaca | *Eriodendron anfractuosum* | *Eriodendron caribaeum* | *Eriodendron occidentale* | *Eriodendron orientale* | *Eriodendron pentandrum* | *Gossampinus alba* | *Gossampinus rumphii* | Jabillolano | Java Cotton Tree | Java Kapok | Samauma | Silk Cotton Tree | Silk-Cotton | Toborachi | *Xylon pentandrum* | Yuque

✹ **SYMBOLIC MEANINGS**
Stay afloat.

❀ **POSSIBLE POWERS**
Protection.

🜂 **FOLKLORE AND FACTS**
Kapok Tree seeds contain an exceptionally buoyant fluff that was once used to stuff life jackets. • Indigenous tribes along the Amazon use the Kapok seed fluff to wrap around their blowgun darts. This helps thicken the dart's diameter for a better fit in the blowgun and more forceful reactive ejection under pressure.

C

No. 132

Celastrus scandens

Bittersweet

American Bittersweet | Bitter Nightshade | Bittersweet Nightshade | *Celastrus bullatus* | Climbing Bittersweet | Climbing Nightshade | *Euonymus scandens* | European Bittersweet | *Evonymoides scandens* | Fellenwort | Felonwood | Poisonberry | Poisonflower | Scarlet Berry | Snakeberry | Staff Tree | Staff Vine | Trailing Bittersweet | Trailing Nightshade | Woody Nightshade

✹ SYMBOLIC MEANINGS
Honesty; Truth.

✸ POSSIBLE POWERS
Air element; Air magic; Death; Forget a heartbreak; Healing; Lunar activity; Masculine energy; Mercury; Protection; Protection from a witch's harmful magic or evil magic; Rebirth; Truth; Ward off witches.

✦ FOLKLORE AND FACTS
The woody Bittersweet vine stems are around thirty feet long, twining upward. It blooms attractive clusters of vivid orange fruits that are no larger than a pea-sized berry. As pretty as it is, Bittersweet is highly poisonous. • Bittersweet was once commonly used to push away any malevolent magic from the home, along with the witches who may have been practicing it. • Put a small piece of Bittersweet in a little pouch or sachet and tie it anywhere on your body to banish persistent evil.

No. 133

Celosia argentea var. *cristata* ✿

Cockscomb Celosia

Cockscomb Amaranth | Common Cockscomb | Coxcomb | Feather Cockscomb | Lagos Spinach | Mfungu | Rooster Comb | Soko Yokoto | Velvet Flower | Woolflower

✹ SYMBOLIC MEANINGS
Affection; Constancy; Fidelity; Foppery; Friendship; Humor; Immortality; Love; Partnerships; Silliness; Singularity; Warmth.

✸ POSSIBLE POWERS
Love; Partnerships.

✦ FOLKLORE AND FACTS
Cockscomb Celosia plants have interesting looking velvety or fluffy plumed flowers that encourage children to have fun growing plants in the garden.

No. 134

Centaurea cyanus ✿

Bachelor Button

Bachelor's Button | Bluebottle | Bluet | Boutonniere Flower | *Centaurea cyaneum* | *Centaurea cyanocephala* | *Centaurea lanata* | *Centaurea pulcherrima* | *Centaurea pulchra* | *Centaurea rhizocephala* | *Centaurea segetalis* | *Centaurea umbrosa* | Common Cornflower | Cornflower | Cyani Flower | *Cyanus arvensis* | *Cyanus cyaneus* | *Cyanus dentato-folius* | *Cyanus segetum* | *Cyanus vulgaris* | Devil's Flower | Hurtsickle | *Jacea segetalis* | *Jacea segetum* | *Leucacantha cyanus* | *Setachna cyanus*

✹ SYMBOLIC MEANINGS
Celibacy; Clearness; Delicacy; Elegance; Endless love; Hope; Hope in love; Immortal love; Immortality; Light; Love; Patience; Refinement; Single blessedness; Single wretchedness; Unchangeable.

✸ POSSIBLE POWERS
Colorize; Feminine energy; Healing; Love; Protection; Snake deterrent; Venus; Water element.

✦ FOLKLORE AND FACTS
There was a time when men wore Bachelor Button flowers to indicate that they were in love. If the flower faded too fast it was a sign that his love would not be returned. • A wash of Bachelor Button water, also known as "cornflower water," was supposedly a treatment for the plague in the Middle Ages. • Bachelor Button flowers are sometimes used in long-lasting Hawaiian leis because they hold their shape and color long after the flowers have dried. • There was a time when the sure cure for a nosebleed was to gather Batchelor Button flowers on Corpus Christi Sunday, which was sixty days after Easter, and hold the flowers in your hands until they were warm to the touch. By then, your nose should have stopped bleeding!

C

Centaurium erythraea

Centaury

Centaurella dichotoma | Centaurium capitatum | Centaurium corymbosum | Centaurium latifolium | Centaurium lomae | Centaurium minus | Centaurium vulgare | Chironia centaurium | Chironia erythraea | Christ's Ladder | Common Centaury | Erythraea capitata | Erythraea centaurium | Erythraea corymbosa | Erythraea germanica | Erythraea latifolia | Erythraea lomae | Erythraea vulgaris | European Centaury | Gentiana centaurium | Gentiana gerardii | Gentiana palustris | Gonipia linearis | Hippocentaurea centaurium | Libadion variabile | Xolemia palustris

✳ SYMBOLIC MEANINGS
Delicacy.

✿ POSSIBLE POWERS
Boosts power in working magic; Colorize; Counter magic; Fire element; Masculine energy; Reduces anger; Repels cruel energy; Snake repellent; Sun; Vanishing.

✦ FOLKLORE AND FACTS
Centaury is an ancient herb that is mentioned several times in medieval writings as being a bitter herb effective against wicked spirits.

Chamaelirium luteum ✿

Fairywand

Abalon albiflorum | Blazing Star | Chamaelirium Carolinian | Chamaelirium carolinianum | Chionographis lutea | Dasurus luteus | Diclinotrys lutes | False Unicorn | Helonias | Helonias dioica | Helonias lutes | Helonias pumilalis | Melanthium | Melanthium dioicum | Ophiostachys virginica | Siraitos luteus | Veratrum flavum | Veratrum luteum

✳ SYMBOLIC MEANINGS
Angel's fishing rod.

✿ POSSIBLE POWERS
Balance; Inner peace; Protection.

✦ FOLKLORE AND FACTS
Make a Fairywand sachet to carry or wear for protection and restore inner peace and balance. • In the past, this herb was used for medicinal purposes. • Wear or carry a Fairywand sachet to promote inner peace and balance. • A pregnant woman can wear or carry a Fairywand sachet for protection.

Chamaemelum nobile

English Chamomile

Anacyclus aureus | Anacyclus nobilis | Anthemis apiifolia | Anthemis aurea | Anthemis chamomilla-romana | Anthemis nobilis | Anthemis odorata | Anthemis parthenioides | Anthemis santolinoides | Camomile | Camomyle | Chamaemelum romanum | Chamaimelon | Chamomile | Chamomilla nobilis | Chrysanthemum partheniodes | Dendranthema parthenioides | Garden Camomile | Ground Apple | Heermannchen | Lawn Chamomile | Low Chamomile | Lyonnetia abrotanifolia | Manzanilla | Marcelia aurea | Matricaria nobilis | Matricaria parthenioides | Maythen | Ormenis aurea | Ormenis nobilis | Perennial Chamomile | Whig Plant | Wild Chamomile

✳ SYMBOLIC MEANINGS
All who know you will love you; Attracts wealth; Energy in action or adversity; Ingenuity; Initiative; Love in adversity; Patience; Sleep; Sleepiness; Sleepy; Wisdom.

✿ POSSIBLE POWERS
Abundance; Advancement; Calming; Conscious will; Energy; Friendship; Growth; Healing; Joy; Leadership; Life; Light; Love; Luck; Meditation; Money; Natural power; Purification; Sleep; Success; Sun; Tranquility; Water element.

✦ FOLKLORE AND FACTS
English Chamomile was considered a "plant doctor," so it was planted near weaker plants to strengthen them. • Some gamblers wash their hands with an English Chamomile infusion made with the herb mixed with rainwater, natural spring water, or distilled water to increase their chances of winning. • You can also bathe in this English Chamomile infusion to increase your chances of attracting love. • Wear or carry a sachet of English Chamomile to attract money. For the best result, place it in your wallet. • Sprinkle the English Chamomile infusion around the perimeter of your property to remove curses and spells that may have been cast upon those who live there. • English Chamomile is believed to be Mathen in the Nine Sacred Herbs healing charm, originally written in the dialect used in Wessex, England in the tenth century. • English Chamomile might interfere with the absorption of some medications.

C

No. 138
Chamaemelum nobile ☙
Roman Chamomile
Anacyclus aureus | Anacyclus nobil | Anthemis apiifolia | Anthemis aurea | Anthemis chamomilla-romana | Anthemis nobilis | Anthemis odorata | Anthemis parthenioides | Anthemis santolinoides | Camomile | Camomyle | Chamaemelum romanum | Chamaimelon | Chamomilla nobilis | Chrysanthemum parthenioides | Dendranthema parthenioides | Lyonnetia abrotanifolia | Marcelia aurea | Matricaria nobilis | Matricaria parthenioides | Roman Camomile

✷ SYMBOLIC MEANINGS
All who know you will love you; Attracts wealth; Energy in action or adversity; Ingenuity; Initiative; Love in adversity; Patience; Sleep; Sleepiness; Sleepy; Wisdom.

⊛ POSSIBLE POWERS
Abundance; Advancement; Calming; Conscious will; Deity dedication; Energy; Friendship; Growth; Healing; Joy; Leadership; Life; Light; Love; Luck; Masculine energy; Meditation; Money; Natural power; Noble offering; Offering; Purification; Sleep; Success; Sun; Tranquility; Water element.

☘ FOLKLORE AND FACTS
Roman Chamomile was considered a "plant doctor," so it was planted near weaker plants to strengthen them. • Sprinkle an infusion of rainwater, natural spring water, or distilled water and Roman Chamomile around your home to purify it from negative energy that has disrupted calm and peacefulness. • Some gamblers wash their hands with the Roman Chamomile-infused water before gambling with hopes of increasing their chances of winning. • You can also bathe in the same Roman chamomile infused water to increase your chances of attracting love. • Sprinkle Roman Chamomile around the perimeter of your property to remove curses and spells cast upon those who live there. • Egyptians would dedicate Roman Chamomile to their gods. • Aromatherapy using Roman Chamomile essential oil can soothe restlessness and promote sleep. • Roman Chamomile might interfere with the absorption of some medications.

No. 139
Chelidonium majus ☠☙
Greater Celandine
Celydoyne | Chelidonium haematodes | Chelidonium laciniatum | Chelidonium luteum | Chelidonium murale | Chelidonium quercifolium | Chelidonium ruderale | Chelidonium umbelliferum | Devil's Milk | Garden Celandine | Kenning Wort | Swallow Herb | Swallow-Wort | Tetterwort

✷ SYMBOLIC MEANINGS
Deceptive hopes.

⊛ POSSIBLE POWERS
Escape; Fire element; Happiness; Joy; Legal matters; Masculine energy; Protection; Sun; Vision.

☘ FOLKLORE AND FACTS
The ancient Greeks observed sparrows applying Greater Celandine leaves to the eyes of their young in the nest. If you wear it, Greater Celandine will impart joy, good spirits and possibly lift depression. • Wear or carry a small pouch or sachet of Greater Celandine to thwart unwarranted psychological, emotional, or psychic imprisonments or entrapments. Replace it every three days • Wear or carry a small pouch or sachet of Greater Celandine to a court hearing as protection and to garner the favor of the judge and jury.

No. 140
Chelone glabra ☙
Balmony
Bitter Herb | Chelone alba | Chelone chlorantha | Chelone linifolia | Chelone montana | Chelone purpurea | Chlonanthes montana | Chlonanthes tomentosa | Dysosmon amoenum | Hummingbird Tree | Snakehead | Turtle Bloom | White Turtlehead

✷ SYMBOLIC MEANINGS
Patient; Persevering; Steadfast.

⊛ POSSIBLE POWERS
Patience; Perseverance; Steadfastness.

☘ FOLKLORE AND FACTS
Long ago, Native American Abenaki tribal women used Balmony as birth control. • Wear or carry a sachet of Balmony to stay on task when you're working on anything that requires focus and unwavering perseverance.

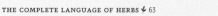

C

No. 141
Chenopodium album ☠
Fat-Hen

Atriplex alba | Atriplex viridis | Bathua | Blitum viride | Botrys albus | Botrys ferulatus | Botrys pagana | Chenopodium agreste | Chenopodium bicolor | Chenopodium browneanum | Chenopodium candicans | Chenopodium catenulatum | Chenopodium concatenatum | Chenopodium densifoliatum | Chenopodium divaricatum | Chenopodium elatum | Chenopodium ferulatum | Chenopodium glomerulosum | Chenopodium laciniatum | Chenopodium lanceolatum | Chenopodium leiospermum | Chenopodium lobatum | Chenopodium neglectum | Chenopodium neoalbum | Chenopodium opulaceum | Chenopodium ovalifolium | Chenopodium paganum | Chenopodium paucidentatum | Chenopodium pedunculare | Chenopodium probstii | Chenopodium riparium | Chenopodium strictum | Chenopodium subaphyllum | Chenopodium superalbum | Chenopodium viride | Chenopodium viridescens | Chenopodium vulgare | Chenopodium vulpinum | Chenopodium zobelii | Goosefoot | Lamb's Quarters | Melde | Salsola stricta | Vulvaria albescens | White Goosefoot | Wild Spinach

✹ SYMBOLIC MEANINGS
Goodness; Insult.

✹ POSSIBLE POWERS
Call on ancestors.

✸ FOLKLORE AND FACTS
Fat-Hen's fragrant flowers supposedly repel moths.
• According to ancient Sanskrit writing, the juice of the Fat-Hen plant is vital for making wall plaster.
• Archaeologists have found *Chenopodium album* seed grain in the stomachs of ancient bodies uncovered from Danish bogs. • Napoléon Bonaparte supposedly depended on Fat-Hen seeds to feed his troops when other food was difficult to obtain. It's best to consume it in moderation and avoid eating the leaves raw due to oxalic acid toxicity. • Young Fat-Hen shoots can produce a green dye.

No. 142
Chrysanthemum × morifolium ☙
Chrysanthemum

Chrysanth | Florist's Daisy | Flower of Happiness | Flower of Life | Flower of the East | Hardy Garden Mum | Juhua | Mum

✹ SYMBOLIC MEANINGS
Abundance; Cheerfulness; Cheerfulness and rest; Cheerfulness in adversity; Fidelity; Happiness; A heart left to desolation; Loveliness; Optimism; Promotes mental health; Wealth; You're a wonderful friend.

❀ COLOR MEANINGS
Rose: In love.
Red: I love; I love you; Love;
    Slighted love.
White: Truth.
Yellow: Imperial; Scorned in love;
    Slighted love.

✹ POSSIBLE POWERS
Fire element; Immortality; Masculine energy; Protection; Sun.

✸ FOLKLORE AND FACTS
Grow Chrysanthemums in your garden to fend off evil spirits. • Chrysanthemum is the oldest ingredient in Chinese medicine. It appears in the oldest of Chinese medical writings for an elixir of immortality. • In Asia, Chrysanthemums are considered a sacred flower. • Chinese Feng Shui suggests that Chrysanthemums bring happiness into your home. • During the years of Imperial Reign in China, common people were not permitted to grow Chrysanthemums, only the nobility had that privilege. • The Chrysanthemum is the second national flower of Japan. The other is the Cherry blossom. • The Chrysanthemum is the symbol of the Japanese emperor and the imperial family. • In Malta and Italy, it's unlucky to have a Chrysanthemum in your house. • The Chrysanthemum flower—both fresh and artificially stylized and constructed using mixed materials such as ribbons, rhinestones, small stuffed animals, and a wide variety of little plastic and metallic trinkets—is the somewhat adopted official flower of all middle and high school homecoming events in the state of Texas, USA.

C

No. 143
Chrysanthemum coronarium 🌿🍴

Edible Chrysanthemum

Buphthalmum oleraceum | Chamaemelum coronarium | Chop-Suey Greens | Chrysanthemum breviradiatum | Chrysanthemum coronarium | Chrysanthemum Greens | Chrysanthemum matricariodes | Chrysanthemum roxburghii | Chrysanthemum senecioides | Chrysanthemum speciosum | Crown Daisy | Crown Daisy Chrysanthemum | Dendranthema coronarium | Garland Chrysanthemum | Garland Daisy | Glebionis coronaria | Glebionis discolor | Glebionis roxburghii | Japanese Greens | Matricaria coronaria | Matricaria oleracea | Pinardia coronaria | Pyrethrum indicum | Spring Chrysanthemum | Tong Ho | Tónghāo | Xantophtalmum coronarium

✳ SYMBOLIC MEANINGS
Cheerfulness; Cheerfulness and rest; Cheerfulness in adversity; Fidelity; Happiness.

✸ POSSIBLE POWERS
Cheerfulness; Fire element; Immortality; Masculine energy; Protection; Sun.

✦ FOLKLORE AND FACTS
The Edible Chrysanthemum is a sacred flower in Asia. • The flower of the young Edible Chrysanthemum has a mustard-like flavor that is used in Asian cuisine as a vegetable and as a culinary herb.

No. 144
Chrysanthemum leucanthemum 🌿

Oxeye Daisy

Bull Daisy | Butter Daisy | Button Daisy | Dog Blow | Dog Daisy | Dun Daisy | Dutch Morgan | Field Daisy | Golden Marguertes | Herb Margaret | Horse Daisy | Horse Gowan | Leucanthemum ageratifolium | Marguerite | Maudlinwort | Midsummer Daisy | Moon Daisy | Moon Flower | Moon Penny | Ox-Eye | Pontia vulgaris | Poorland Daisy | Poverty Weed | White Man's Weed

✳ SYMBOLIC MEANINGS
Cheer; Disappointment; Faith; Innocence; Loyal love; Patience; Purity; Simplicity; Token.

✸ POSSIBLE POWERS
Divination; Divination for love.

✦ FOLKLORE AND FACTS
The Oxeye Daisy has been used for a divination of love for many generations, by plucking the petals to the chant of "he loves me, he loves me not." The last petal remaining is the answer to the question. • Oxeye Daisy is depicted on many ancient ornaments, decorations, paintings, and ceramics in the Middle East. • The ancient Celts believed that Oxeye Daisy was the spirit of a baby who died at birth. • If you dream about an Oxeye Daisy in the spring, good luck will come to you. It's bad luck to dream about it in the autumn or winter.

No. 145
Chrysopogon zizanioides

Vetiver

Agrostis verticillata | Anatherum muricatum | Anatherum zizanioides | Andropogon muricatus | Andropogon odoratus | Andropogon zizanioides | Chamaeraphis muricat | Khus | Khus-Khus | Moras | Oplismenus abortivus | Phalaris zizanioides | Rhaphis zizanioides | Vetiveria arundinacea | Vetiveria muricata | Vetiveria odorata | Vetiveria odoratissima | Vetiveria zizanioides | Vetivert

✳ SYMBOLIC MEANINGS
Harmony; Justice; Righteousness; Tree of life.

✸ POSSIBLE POWERS
Anti-theft; Arts; Attraction; Beauty; Break a hex; Earth element; Feminine energy; Friendship; Gifts; Harmony; Joy; Love; Luck; Money; Pleasure; Sensuality; Venus.

✦ FOLKLORE AND FACTS
In aromatherapy, Vetiver essential oil calms, balances, and relaxes. • Place a sprig or sachet of Vetiver in a cash register, in your pocket, under a computer, or under a desk to encourage more business. • Add Vetiver to your bath to attract the opposite sex. • Carry Vetiver for good luck.

No. 146
Cichorium endivia

Endive

Barbe de Capucin | Belgian Endive | Chicory | Cichorium crispum | Cichorium esculentum | French Endive | Succory | White Gold | Witloof Chicory

✳ SYMBOLIC MEANINGS
Frugal.

✸ POSSIBLE POWERS
Air element; Frugality; Jupiter; Love; Lust; Masculine energy; Money.

C

FOLKLORE AND FACTS

Carry or wear a pink and red sachet of Endive seeds to attract love. If Endive is worn fresh as a talisman to attract love, replace it every third day. • *Cichorium endivia* is not found in the wild. • Interestingly, after returning from the Belgian War of Independence in 1831, Jan Lammers discovered the Chicory roots he had stored in his cellar for several months, thinking they would have dried out. But while in that damp dark space, the roots had sprouted leafy, nearly white shoots at the top. Bravely, he tasted them, finding them pleasantly crunchy and mildly bitter. As a result of this surprise, a new vegetable was discovered, with Endive now commonly farmed on shelves in dark damp rooms with the roots planted just beneath the soil.

No. 147

Cichorium intybus ☘🍴🍸

Chicory

Blue Daisy | Blue Dandelion | Blue Sailors | Blue Weed | Bunk | *Cichorium balearicum* | *Cichorium byzanthinum* | *Cichorium caeruleum* | *Cichorium callosum* | *Cichorium casnia* | *Cichorium cicorea* | *Cichorium commune* | *Cichorium cosnia* | *Cichorium divaricatum* | *Cichorium glabratum* | *Cichorium glaucum* | *Cichorium hirsutum* | *Cichorium officinale* | *Cichorium perenne* | *Cichorium rigidum* | *Cichorium sylvestre* | *Cichorium sylvestre* | Coffeeweed | Common Chickory | Cornflower | Hendibeh | *Hieracium cichorium* | Horseweed | Intybus | Ragged Sailors | Succory | Wild Bachelor's Buttons | Wild Cherry | Wild Succory

☀ SYMBOLIC MEANINGS

Delicacy; Economy; Endless waiting; Rigidity; Perseverance.

⚙ POSSIBLE POWERS

Air element; Cursing; Emotional barriers; Favors; Fire element; Frigidity; Frugality; Humor; Invisibility; Luck; Masculine energy; Optimism; Protection; Removing obstacles; Sun.

☘ FOLKLORE AND FACTS

There's an interesting Chicory legend that supposedly transpired on July 25th, Saint James' Day. As the legend goes, if a lock picker holds Chicory leaves and a gold knife against a lock, it will magically open—but only if the task is done in total silence. If even a single word is spoken, the lock picker will die. • Early American European settlers would carry Chicory for good luck. • Wear a Chicory flower to attract a man. • Carry a sprig of Chicory to magically remove the obstacles that stand between you and your goals. • Carry a sprig of Chicory to promote frugality. • If you bless yourself with chicory juice, great people will pay attention to you

and offer you favors. • During the Middle Ages, the Chicory flower was considered a protector of Christian martyrs.

No. 148

Cinchona officinalis ☘

Cinchona

Bark of Barks Tree | Cargua Cargua | Cascarilla | *Cascarilla officinalis* | Chinhona Bark | *Cinchona condaminea* | *Cinchona crispa Tafalla* | *Cinchona cucumifolia* | *Cinchona josephiana* | *Cinchona legitima* | *Cinchona obtusifolia* | *Cinchona peruviana* | *Cinchona suberosa* | *Cinchona uritusinga* | *Cinchona vritusino* | Corteza Coja | Countess Powder | Ecorce du Pérou | Fever Tree | Holy Bark Tree | Ioxa Bark | Jesuit's Bark Tree | Jesuit's Powder Tree | Peruvian Bark Tree | Quinà | Quina Quina | Quinine Bark Bush | Quinine Tree | Quinquina | *Quinquina officinalis* | *Quinquina palton* | Red Cinchona | Wild Quinine

☀ SYMBOLIC MEANINGS

Aspiring; Fever breaker.

⚙ POSSIBLE POWERS

Boost power to magic working; Break a fever; Healing; Health; Luck; Protection; Repel anger or malicious energy; Resist a spell.

☘ FOLKLORE AND FACTS

Dr. Samuel Hahnemann tested Cinchona bark, which marked the start of a form of alternative medicine known as homeopathy around the turn of the nineteenth century. • Carry a small piece of Cinchona bark to protect yourself against evil and bodily harm. • *Cinchona officinalis* bark provides quinine, the medicinal treatment for malaria.

No. 149

Cinnamomum camphora ☠☘

White Camphor

Camphire | Camphor Laurel | Camphor Tree | *Camphora camelliifolia* | *Camphora camphora* | *Camphora hahnemannii* | *Camphora hippocratei* | *Camphora vera* | *Camphorina camphora* | Camphorwood | Chang Nao | *Cinnamomum camphoriferum* | *Cinnamomum camphoroides* | *Cinnamomum henricii* | *Cinnamomum nominale* | *Cinnamomum officinarum* | *Cinnamomum simondii* | *Cinnamomum taquetii* | Harathi Karpuram | Ho Wood | Kafoor | Kafrovnik Lékarsky | Kapoor | Kapura-gaha | Karpooram | Karpuuram | Kusu No Ki | *Laurus calycina* | *Laurus camphora* | *Laurus camphorifera* | *Laurus gracilis* | Nok Na Mu | Paccha Karpoora | Paccha Karpooramu | Pacchaik Karpooram | Pachai Karpuram | Ravintsara | Shajarol-kafoor | Trees of Kafoor | Zhang Shu | Zhangshù

C

❋ SYMBOLIC MEANINGS

Chastity; Divination.

❀ POSSIBLE POWERS

Chastity; Divination; Emotions; Feminine energy; Fertility; Generation; Health; Inspiration; Intuition; Moon; Psychic ability; Sea; Subconscious mind; Tides; Travel by water; Water element.

☘ FOLKLORE AND FACTS

During the times of the Black Death in the 1300s, White Camphor was valued as a fumigant. • During the fourteenth century, people made infusions of White Camphor with Roses and sprinkled them over a corpse before wrapping it within its burial shroud. • White Camphor has been and still is used as an insect repellant to fend off cloth-eating insects from stored clothing.

No. 150

Cinnamomum cassia 🍴

Cassia

Camphorina cassia | Chinese Cassia |
Chinese Cinnamon | *Cinnamomum aromaticum* |
Cinnamomum longifolium | *Cinnamomum medium* |
Cinnamomum nitidum | *Laurus cassia* | *Persea cassia*

❋ SYMBOLIC MEANINGS

Sweet love.

❀ POSSIBLE POWERS

Encourage self-worth; Healing; Love; Luck; Money; Passion; Power; Prosperity; Protection; Psychic power; Spirituality; Strength; Success.

☘ FOLKLORE AND FACTS

The warm fragrance of Cassia essential oil can encourage healthy feelings of self-worth. • Carry or wear a Cassia sachet to increase spiritual vibrations when meditating. • A Cassia sachet in a gambler's pocket might increase luck at the casino. • A Cassia sachet in a salesperson's pocket can help increase sales. • Carry or wear a Cassia sachet to focus concentration and stimulate psychic abilities. • Place a pink and red Cassia sachet that you have lovingly made under your mattress to encourage spiritually romantic intimacy and an increase in passionate affection.

No. 151

Cinnamomum verum ☠🦪🍴

Cinnamon

Baker's Cinnamon | Camphorina cinnamomum | Ceylon Cinnamon | Cinnamomum alexei |
Cinnamomum aromaticum | Cinnamomum barthii | Cinnamomum bengalense |
Cinnamomum biafranum | Cinnamomum bonplandii | Cinnamomum boutonii |
Cinnamomum capense | Cinnamomum cayennense | Cinnamomum cinnamomum |
Cinnamomum commersonii | Cinnamomum cordifolium | Cinnamomum decandollei |
Cinnamomum delessertii | Cinnamomum ellipticum | Cinnamomum erectum |
Cinnamomum humboldtii | Cinnamomum iners | Cinnamomum karrouwa | Cinnamomum
leptopus | Cinnamomum leschenaultii | Cinnamomum madrassicum | Cinnamomum
maheanum | Cinnamomum mauritianum | Cinnamomum meissneri | Cinnamomum
ovatum | Cinnamomum pallasii | Cinnamomum pleei | Cinnamomum pourretii |
Cinnamomum regelii | Cinnamomum roxburghii | Cinnamomum sieberi | Cinnamomum
sonneratii | Cinnamomum vaillantii | Cinnamomum variabile | Cinnamomum wolkensteinii |
Cinnamomum zeylanicum | Cinnamomum zollingeri | Cinnamon Tree | Laurus
cinnamomum | Sri Lanka Cinnamon | Sweet Wood | True Cinnamon

❋ SYMBOLIC MEANINGS

Forgiveness of injuries; Logic; Temptress.

❀ POSSIBLE POWERS

Abundance; Advancement; Aphrodite; Beauty; Business; Conscious will; Energy; Fire element; Friendship; Growth; Healing; Joy; Leadership; Life; Light; Love; Lust; Masculine energy; Natural power; Passion; Power; Protection; Psychic power; Spirituality; Success; Sun; Venus.

☘ FOLKLORE AND FACTS

Ancient Hebrew high priests used Cinnamon oil as a vital ingredient of a holy anointing oil. • The ancient Egyptians used Cinnamon as one of their mummification spices. • When used as an incense or in a sachet, Cinnamon provides the power to increase spiritual vibrations. This will help heal, bring in money, stimulate psychic powers, and provide protection. • The ancient Chinese and Egyptians used Cinnamon to purify their temples. • Cinnamon essential oil can be used for aromatherapy to reduce depression and improve sleeping.

C

No. 152
Circaea lutetiana 🐛⚗️

Enchanter's Nightshade
Broad-Leaved Enchanter's Nightshade | Carlostephania major | Circaea erecta | Circaea major | Circaea nemoralis | Circaea ovatifolia | Circaea pubescens | Circaea vulgaris | Regmus lutetianus

🌑 **SYMBOLIC MEANINGS**
Death; Doom; Treachery; Trickery.

✷ **POSSIBLE POWERS**
Sorcery; Spell; Witchcraft.

🜨 **FOLKLORE AND FACTS**
Circaea lutetiana was named in honor of Circe, the daughter of the Greek god, Helios. According to the tale in Homer's epic, the *Odyssey*, Circe was notably an exceedingly cruel and terribly evil sorceress who commonly enticed then graciously welcomed shipwrecked sailors and other unfortunates, including her own enemies, to her island. That was before she drugged them. Next, she magically transformed them into pigs and other animals, which she would kill in one way or another before she ate them. • Over time, the story of Circe gained embellishments, to finally be included in some tellings of the tale to include that a plant was once used in Circe's potions. That plant was given the name *Circaea lutetiana*, and its most common name of Enchanter's Nightshade.

No. 153
Cirsium vulgare ⚗️

Common Thistle
Brushes and Combs | Bull Thistle | Carduus chinensis | Carduus firmus | Carduus spinosissimus | Carduus vulgaris | Cnicus firmus | Cnicus misilmerensis | Epitrachys vulgaris | Flower of the Sun | Herb of the Witches | Lady's Thistle | Spear Thistle | Thistle | Thrissles

🌑 **SYMBOLIC MEANINGS**
Aggressiveness; Austerity; Harshness; Independence; Nobility; Pain; Pride; Retaliation; Sternness.

🌱 **COMPONENT MEANING**
Seed head: Depart.

✷ **POSSIBLE POWERS**
Assistance; Break a hex; Exorcism; Fertility; Fire element; Harmony;

Healing; Independence; Mars; Masculine energy; Material gain; Minerva; Persistence; Protection; Stability; Strength; Tenacity; Thor.

🜨 **FOLKLORE AND FACTS**
There was a time in England when wizards would select the tallest Common Thistle they could find to use as a magic wand. • In the Bible, the Common Thistle refers to a desolate wilderness. Nowadays, the Common Thistle is a top provider of nectar for pollinating bees, butterflies, and some small birds. • Grow Common Thistle in your garden to fend off thieves. • Wear or carry a Common Thistle blossom to get rid of melancholic feelings. • Put a vase of freshly cut flowered Common Thistle stems in a room to renew the vitality of everyone in the room. • Carry a Common Thistle blossom for protection against evil. • A man can carry a Common Thistle blossom to improve his lovemaking skills. • Carry or wear a Common Thistle on a white cotton cord around your neck as a protective amulet to fend off witches and witchery. • Tuck Common Thistle under both sides of your mattress to boost fertility.

No. 154
Cistus ladanifer ⚗️

Cistus
Brown-Eyed Rockrose | Cistus grandiflorus | Cistus ladanosma | Cistus viscosus | Common Gum Cistus | Gum Ladanum | Gum Rockrose | Jara Pringosa | Labdanum | Ladanum officinarum | Ladanum | Ladanum verum

🌑 **SYMBOLIC MEANINGS**
I shall die tomorrow.

✷ **POSSIBLE POWERS**
Premonitions.

🜨 **FOLKLORE AND FACTS**
The entire Cistus plant is covered with a dark, sticky balsam-like fragrant resinous sap that has been used as a fixative to make perfumes since ancient times. • Cistus essential oil for aromatherapy can help draw energy inward to open a stagnant state of mind and warm any icy thoughts.

C

No. 155
Citrus × *aurantiifolia* 🌿🍴
Key Lime
Bartender's Lime | Bilolo | *Citrus amblycarpa* | Dayap | *Limonia acidissima* | Mexican Lime | Omani Lime | West Indian Lime

✳ SYMBOLIC MEANINGS
Fidelity; Love; Justice.

🌸 POSSIBLE POWERS
Fire element; Love; Luck;
Marital affection or love; Marriage;
Matrimony; Sun.

🐛 FOLKLORE AND FACTS
Long before there were other cultivated
Citrus varieties being raised in South Florida, the Key Lime
fulfilled the need for something that was "tart, but not too
tart" in cooking. • The Key Lime is the key ingredient in
the iconic Key Lime pie. • The Key Lime was used for the
same "tart, but not too tart" desired flavor in beverages. This
balanced tartness shines in the zingy, thirst-quenching Lime
Rickey cocktail that became a South Florida favorite among
the upper-crust elite in the late 1800s. • Hot Key Lime tea
with honey is a worthy home remedy for the sniffles. • A
ripened to yellow Key Lime is still tart but sweeter than a
Persian Lime. • The Key Lime originated in Malaysia and
is believed to have been carried to the Caribbean, where it
became naturalized by the Spanish around 1500 CE.

No. 156
Citrus × *aurantium* 🌿🍴
Bitter Orange
Bigarade Orange | Bitter Orange | Daidai | Laraha | Marmalade Orange | Narthangai | Neroli Oil
Orange | Raranj | Seville Orange | Sour Orange

✳ SYMBOLIC MEANINGS
Sensual love.

🌸 POSSIBLE POWERS
Aphrodisiac; Attract love; Cleansing;
Fire element; Freshening; Sun.

🐛 FOLKLORE AND FACTS
Bitter Orange is considered a sacred spiritual tree.
• Although it's not eaten raw, Bitter Orange fruit is used
as a flavoring in liqueurs, in cooking, and for making
traditional marmalade due to its high level of pectin. • Dried,
powdered Bitter Orange peel is also known as pomeranssi
and pomerans. • The wood from a Bitter Orange tree is often
made into Cuban baseball bats. • Bitter Orange essential

oil is useful in deodorizing. • Sweet Orange tree cuttings
are often grafted to the stronger more durable *Citrus* ×
aurantium rootstock. • Bitter Orange fruit and leaves will
lather enough to be used like a soap. • Bitter Orange health
food supplements are believed to have been linked to serious
cardiovascular side effects.

No. 157
Citrus bergamia 🌿🍴
Bergamot Orange
Bergamot | Orange Bergamot | Orange Mint

✳ SYMBOLIC MEANINGS
Enchantment; Irresistibility.

🌸 POSSIBLE POWERS
Air element; Eliminating interference;
Improved memory; Irresistible; Masculine
energy; Mercury; Money; Prosperity;
Protection from evil or illness; Restful
sleep; Success.

🐛 FOLKLORE AND FACTS
Bergamot Orange is also known
simply as Bergamot. This is not to be
confused with *Monarda didyma* Bee Balm, which is also
known as Bergamot. • Rub Bergamot Orange leaves on
money before spending it to ensure that it comes back to
you. • Put a few Bergamot Orange leaves wherever you
carry your money, preferably within a wallet, to attract
more money to that location. • Make a good luck sachet of
Bergamot Orange leaves or rind and carry it in your pocket
to attract money while gambling at a casino. • Use Bergamot
Orange to increase success. • In aromatherapy, Bergamot
Orange essential oil helps lighten a dark mood, especially in
times of grief or sadness.

No. 158
Citrus hystrix 🌿🍴
Makrut Lime
Caffre | *Citrus auraria* | *Citrus boholensis* | *Citrus cambria* | *Citrus celebica* | *Citrus combara* |
Citrus kerrii | *Citrus latipes* | *Citrus macroptera* | *Citrus micrantha* | *Citrus papeda* | *Citrus
papuana* | *Citrus southwickii* | *Citrus torosa* | *Citrus tuberoides* | *Citrus ventricosa* | *Citrus
vitiensis* | *Citrus westeri* | *Fortunella sagittifolia* | Leech Lime | Mauritius Papeda | *Papeda
rumphii* | Thai Lime

✳ SYMBOLIC MEANINGS
Prosperity.

C

POSSIBLE POWERS

Leech repellant; Water element.

FOLKLORE AND FACTS

The Makrut Lime's leaves, extremely bumpy rind, as well as the grated zest of the rind are frequently used as a culinary herb. • Makrut Lime juice is often used in Asian recipes whenever acid is needed. • Makrut Lime leaves are shaped like an hourglass. • The Makrut Lime's intensely fragrant rind produces an essential oil that is extensively used in perfumery.

• There are texts from Sri Lanka that date back to 1868 indicating that the Makrut Lime's juice was often used as a leech repellant by rubbing it on a person's legs.

No. 159

Citrus × *latifolia* 🌿🍴

Persian Lime

Bearss Lime | Page Lime | Pond's Lime | Tahiti Lime

SYMBOLIC MEANINGS

Fornication.

POSSIBLE POWERS

Aphrodisiac; Attract love; Fire element; Healing; Immortality; Love; Luck; Lust; Protection; Refresh; Refreshment; Sun.

FOLKLORE AND FACTS

The Persian Lime will turn yellow as it ripens on the tree, but it is harvested and sold as fresh produce while still dark green. • Carry a Persian Lime tree twig to protect yourself against the evil eye. • The Persian Lime's leaf and flower can be used in a love spell. • Hang a Persian Lime branch over a door for protection. • A folk cure for a sore throat was to wrap and tie a string around a whole Persian Lime then wear it as necklace. • Carve a good luck charm out of Persian Lime tree wood. • Citrusy Persian Lime essential oil is used as aromatherapy for invigoration and to uplift a broody mood. Be aware that its essential oil on bare skin could possibly cause severe dermatitis.

No. 160

Citrus × *limon* 🌿🍴

Lemon

Bonnie Brae Lemon | Eureka Lemon | Flat Lemon | Four Seasons Lemon | Lemon Tree | Lisbon Lemon | Meyer Lemon | Ponderosa Lemon | Quatre Saisons | Rough Lemon | Sweet Lemon | Ulamula | Variegata Lemon | Volkamer Lemon | Yen Ben Lemon

SYMBOLIC MEANINGS

Long-suffering; Patience; Pleasant thoughts; Zest.

COMPONENT MEANING

Blossom: Discretion; Fidelity; Fidelity in love; I promise to be true; Prudence.

POSSIBLE POWERS

Feminine energy; Friendship; Longevity; Love; Moon; Protection; Purification; Refresh; Refreshment; Uplift; Water element.

FOLKLORE AND FACTS

Lemon was first referenced in writing regarding Arabic farming in the tenth century. • Christopher Columbus brought Lemon seeds to Hispaniola. • During a full moon, add Lemon juice to your bath for purification. • For a lasting friendship, place a Lemon slice under your friend's chair when they visit your home. • Lemon essential oil has been used for centuries to uplift, energize, and refresh a slumped mood.

No. 161

Citrus maxima 🌿🍴

Pomelo

Aurantium decumana | Aurantium maximum | Bhogate | Citrus costata | Citrus grandis | Citrus obovoidea | Citrus sabon | Citrus yamabuki | Jabong | Jambola | Pampelmuse | Pampleousse | Pomélo | Pommelo | Pompelmo | Pompelmoes | Pumelo | Pummelo | Sarcodactilis helicteroides | Shaddock | Suha

SYMBOLIC MEANINGS

Biggest; Largest.

POSSIBLE POWERS

Healing; Healthy; Refresh; Uplifting.

FOLKLORE AND FACTS

The Pomelo is the largest *Citrus* fruit and is very much like a sweet Grapefruit. • Like a Grapefruit, the Pomelo can affect medication absorption. • Pomelo is a favorite fruit to serve at Asian celebrations. • One Pomelo can provide several days' worth of vitamin C. • You don't eat the Pomelo membrane along with its juicy segments like

C

you do when you eat a Grapefruit or Orange. • The Pomelo's very large size does not particularly affect the acidity of the juice, but it certainly does provide much more of it. • Pomelo essential oil is helpful in aromatherapy for soothing the flustered mind, relieving stress, and helping to alleviate depression.

No. 162

Citrus medica 🦷🍴

Citron

Cederat | Cédrat | Cedro | Citron | *Citrus acida* | *Citrus alata* | *Citrus balotina* | *Citrus bicolor* | *Citrus bigena* | *Citrus cedra* | *Citrus cedrata* | *Citrus crassa* | *Citrus fragrans* | *Citrus gaoganensis* | *Citrus gongra* | *Citrus hassaku* | *Citrus hiroshimana* | *Citrus kizu* | *Citrus kwangsiensis* | *Citrus limonimedica* | *Citrus lumia* | *Citrus nana* | *Citrus odorata* | *Citrus pyriformis* | *Citrus sarcodactylis* | *Citrus tuberosa* | Etrog | Forbidden Fruit | Hadar | *Limon racemosum* | *Limon spinosum* | *Limon vulgare* | Median | Persian Apple | Rough Lemon | Sukake | Turunj | Youzi Cha | Yuzucha

✳ SYMBOLIC MEANINGS
Estrangement; Ill-natured beauty; Tradition.

⦿ POSSIBLE POWERS
Air element; Healing; Masculine energy; Psychic power; Sun.

❦ FOLKLORE AND FACTS
Citron is an original species of three *Citrus* trees from which all other *Citrus* was eventually developed. The other are the Pomelo and the Mandarin Orange. Its acidic fruit is edible, and the peel is often candied. However, the fruit is primarily used as a flavoring. • *Citrus medica* is the most tender of all the *Citrus* species, and it is primarily cultivated in tropical and subtropical home gardens. • Citron is one of the fruits required for rituals during the Jewish Feast of Tabernacles, or Sukkot.

No. 163

Citrus × paradisi 🦷🍴

Grapefruit

Aranja | Grapefrugt | Grapefrukt | Greibipuu | Greip-Frout | Greipfrut | Greipfrüts | Greippi | Grejp | Grejpfrut | Grenivka | Grep | Grepfrut | Grépfrüt | Greyfurt | Toranja | Toronja

✳ SYMBOLIC MEANINGS
Bitterness; Mental problems; Successful independence.

⦿ POSSIBLE POWERS
Independence from a person or thing; Moon; Refresh; Refreshment; Sun; Uplifting; Water element.

❦ FOLKLORE AND FACTS
Grapefruit grows in white, pink, or red varieties. • In 1750, Griffith Hughes, a Welsh reverend, first referenced a Grapefruit hybrid called "forbidden fruit" in his book about Barbados. • The fragrance of Grapefruit essential oil in aromatherapy is uplifting. • Grapefruit juice is known to adversely affect the proper absorption of some medications by increasing or decreasing its effect within the body.

No. 164

Citrus × reticulata 🦷🍴

Mandarin Orange

Citrus × clementina | Clementine | Daoxian Mandarines | Kid Glove Orange | Mandarine | Mangshan Wild Mandarins | Suanpangan | Tachibana

✳ SYMBOLIC MEANINGS
Abundance; Gold; Good fortune; Life; New beginning; Potential for better experiences; Prayers; Wishes for good fortune.

⦿ POSSIBLE POWERS
Abundance; Cheer; Fire element; Good fortune; Improvement; Prosperity; Sun; Warmth.

❦ FOLKLORE AND FACTS
Mandarin Oranges have been cultivated in China for over 3,000 years. • The Mandarin Orange was carefully cultivated with cross-pollinations between other *Citrus* varieties to ultimately be what we think of today as the Mandarin Orange. • The Mandarin Orange is a sacred plant in China. • The Mandarin Orange's dried peel is used in traditional Chinese medicine to regulate the flow of qi, or vital energy. • The dried peel of the Mandarin Orange is also used as a spice called chenpi. • Mandarin Oranges from Japan have become a traditional Christmastime gift in America, Great Britain, Canada, and Russia. • It became a tradition to put three Mandarin Oranges in a Christmas stocking instead of the earlier tradition of three gold coins. • In China during the Chinese New Year celebrations, Mandarin Oranges are traditional decorations and gifts. • Mandarin Orange essential oil can be used for aromatherapy to help reduce nervousness and clear the mind.

C

No. 165
Citrus × *sinensis* 🌿🍴

Sweet Orange

Apelsin | Apelsinas | Apelsinipuu | Apelsins | Apfelsine | Appelsien | Appelsiini | Appelsin | Appelsina | Arancia | Arancia Dolce | Arancio | China Dulce | Golden Fruit | Laranja | Laranjeira | Larinč | Lariñg | Love Fruit | Naranča | Narancs | Naranja | Naranja de China | Naranjo | Navel Orange | Orange | Orange Douce | Oranger | Oranža | Pomaranč | Pomarančа | Pomarańcza | Pomarańcza Chińska | Pomarańcza Słodka | Pomeranč | Portakal | Portocal | Portocală | Portocalul Dulce | Portokali | Portokalia | Portokalli | Sinaasappel | Sladka Pomaranča | Taronger | Taronja | Valencia

✸ SYMBOLIC MEANINGS
Eternal Love; Generosity; Innocence; Virginity.

☙ COMPONENT MEANING
Blossom: Bridal festivities; Brings wisdom; Chastity; Eternal love; Fruitfulness; Good fortune; Innocence; Marriage; Your purity equals your loveliness.

❀ POSSIBLE POWERS
Divination; Fire element; Good fortune; Health; Healthy; Leo; Love; Luck; Masculine energy; Money; Protection; Sun.

☘ FOLKLORE AND FACTS
The Sweet Orange is the most cultivated fruit in the world. • The Sweet Orange tree was never wild. • During the Victorian era, brides carried fresh Sweet Orange blossoms whenever possible. It was common for a bride to wear a crowning wreath of the flowers, on which her bridal veil was attached. • The Chinese consider the Sweet Orange to be a symbol of good luck and good fortune. • Chinese writings referenced the Sweet Orange in 314 BCE. • France's Louis XIV adored Sweet Oranges and had a fabulous orangery cultivated in the beautiful gardens at his Château de Versailles where potted Sweet Orange trees grew indoors throughout the entire palace. • The Spanish explorers introduced Sweet Oranges to North America. • Beehives placed in fruit groves produce the delicate and orangey delicious orange blossom honey that is sold in just about every souvenir gift shop and grocery store throughout Florida and California. • The Sweet Orange is the state flower of Florida, USA. • Sweet Orange blossom petals are mixed with water to make orange blossom water or orange flower water, which is a Sweet Orange version of rosewater. • In Spain, the fallen petals of Sweet Orange blossoms are gathered, dried, and used to brew an herbal tea. • The orangewood sticks that manicurists use are made from wood taken from the Sweet Orange tree. • Sadly, at least ninety percent of the beloved, iconic Sweet Orange groves that grew prolifically in South Florida are now either dead or dying from a devastating plague brought on by a lethal and incurable bacterium called *huanglongbing* which means "yellow dragon sickness", citrus greening disease, and yellow shoot disease. All *Citrus* trees are affected by this bacterium. *Huanglongbing* was first discovered in China. The disease was introduced to South Florida where it was spread from tree to tree by another invasive species: a tiny insect known as the Asian citrus psyllid which draws the bacteria into its body as it feeds. The bacteria is then carried from tree to tree, leaf to leaf. There has been an intense, concerted effort to find a way to battle this crisis, but sadly, the bacteria and the insect appear to still be winning the war. This crisis with the Sweet Orange trees is not only happening in Florida, but anywhere Sweet Orange and other *Citrus* trees are cultivated, such as California, Brazil, Cuba, Mexico, and Belize. • In Florida, grove owners were dealt a terrible blow when they lost their *Citrus* trees to *Huanglongbing*. In an effort to recover, many of the devastated *Citrus* groves have been replanted with Mango trees.

No. 166
Citrus sphaerocarpa 🌿🍴

Kabosu Papeda
Papeda Kabosu

✸ SYMBOLIC MEANINGS
Coveted.

❀ POSSIBLE POWERS
Fire element; Flavoring; Sun.

☘ FOLKLORE AND FACTS
Kabosu is a Chinese Citrus that was brought into Japan at least 300 years ago. There are some 200-year-old trees that are still producing its fruit. • Kabosu Papeda is an evergreen Citrus with fruit that is used in Japanese cuisine as an acidic herb. • Some farm-raised fish food mixes have Kabosu Papeda blended into it.

C

No. 167
Citrus sudachi

Sudachi
Sudashi

🌸 **SYMBOLIC MEANINGS**
Vinegar citrus.

🌐 **POSSIBLE POWERS**
Fire element; Flavor; Sun.

🜂 **FOLKLORE AND FACTS**
The Sudachi fruit is green like a Lime and just as tart.
• Sudachi has been used as a Japanese condiment for
hundreds of years.

No. 168
Citrus tangerina

Tangerine
Citrus × reticulata

🌸 **SYMBOLIC MEANINGS**
Abundant happiness; Life; New beginning; Potential for
better experiences; Prayers; Wishes for good fortune.

🌐 **POSSIBLE POWERS**
Air element; Calm nervousness; Cheer; Fire element;
Improvement; Prosperity; Sun; Warmth.

🜂 **FOLKLORE AND FACTS**
The Tangerine has been cultivated in China for over 3,000
years. • The child-friendly, easy-to-peel sweet Tangerines are
closely related to the Mandarin Orange. • Tangerine essential
oil is used in aromatherapy to help calm nervousness and
clear the mind of cluttering, nerve-wracking thoughts.

No. 169
Claytonia perfoliata 🜨

Miner's Lettuce
Claytonia | Claytone de Cuba | Cuba Lettuce | Indian Lettuce | Kubaspinat | Lahchumeek |
Limnia angustifolia | Limnia carnosa | Limnia perfoliata | Montia perfoliata | Palsingat | Spring
Beauty | Tellerkraut | Winter Purslane

🌸 **SYMBOLIC MEANINGS**
New beginning; Survival.

🌐 **POSSIBLE POWERS**
Feminine energy; Happiness; Heals; Love; Luck; Mercury;
Moon; Protection; Sleep; Soothes; Water element.

🜂 **FOLKLORE AND FACTS**
Miner's Lettuce easily takes over an area where the ground
has been broken. • It was knowledge that came down
from the Native Americans that saved the ailing and too
often nearly starving miners who had flocked to the hills of
California. The miners discovered that to fend off scurvy and
hunger they should eat the *Claytonia perfoliata* plant. The
hungry gold miners readily consumed the Miner's Lettuce
that prolifically covered so much ground near their camps
during the California Gold Rush. The high levels of vitamin
C in the plants greatly improved their health and staved off
their growling hunger.

No. 170
Clematis vitalba 🜨

Traveler's Joy
*Anemone vitalba | Clematis bannatica | Clematis bellojocensis | Clematis crenata | Clematis
dumosa | Clematis odontophylla | Clematis pilosa | Clematis scandens | Clematis sepium |
Clematis taurica | Clematis transiens | Clematis vitalba | Old Man's Beard | Viorna clematis*

🌸 **SYMBOLIC MEANINGS**
Artfulness; Artifice; Beauty of the
mind; Ingenuity; Love; Mental
beauty; Poverty; Soul mates; Want.

🌐 **POSSIBLE POWERS**
Healing; Protection.

🜂 **FOLKLORE AND FACTS**
In Switzerland during the Stone Age, it was believed that
Traveler's Joy was used to make a serviceable rope. • It has
been used to weave baskets. • Since mice will not chew
on *Clematis vitalba*, sheaves of harvested grain stalks were
securely tied with it. • Carry or wear a sachet of Traveler's
Joy when challenged to find an ingenious method of doing
something not done before or finding a better way of doing it.

C

Clinopodium menthifolium 🍴

Calamint

Ascending Wild Basil | Calamintha ascendens | Calamintha menthaefolia | Calamintha menthifolia | Calamintha sylvatica | Common Calamint | Satureja menthifolia | Satureja sylvatica | Wood Calamint | Woodland Calamint

☀ SYMBOLIC MEANINGS
More joy.

✿ POSSIBLE POWERS
Drives off the basilisk; Earth element; Eases emotional pain; Fire element; Increases joy; Mercury; Recovery from emotional suffering; Restores optimism; Soothes sorrow.

✦ FOLKLORE AND FACTS
According to legends, Calamint drives away a snake if the herb is burned or scattered. If that fails, the next legend is that it could heal a snake bite. It seems best to entirely avoid the snake. • Fresh Calamint is said to heal bruises after being in a fight. • Calamint in a warm bath can do much to soothe sorrows brought on by emotional pain. • Make, then carry or wear a sachet of Calamint to boost a feeling of joy from good to better to best. • Calamint is a necessary ingredient in the popular Middle Eastern spice blend known as Za'atar.

Cnicus benedicta

Holy Thistle

Benedicta officinalis | Blessed Thistle | Calcitrapa benedicta | Calcitrapa lanuginosa | Carbeni benedicta | Carbenia benedicta | Cardosanctus officinalis | Carduus benedictus | Carduus horridus | Centaurea centriflora | Centaurea pseudobenedicta | Cirsium horridum | Cirsium munitum | Cnicus benedictus | Cnicus bulgaricus | Cnicus kotschyi | Cnicus microcephalus | Cnicus pseudobenedictus | Epitrachys microcephala | Hierapicra benedicta | St. Benedict's Thistle | Spotted Thistle

☀ SYMBOLIC MEANINGS
Bravery; Determination; Devotion; Durability; Strength.

✿ POSSIBLE POWERS
Animal healing; Assistance; Breaks a hex; Fertility; Fire element; Harmony; Independence; Mars; Masculine energy; Material gain; Persistence; Protection; Purification; Stability; Strength; Tenacity.

✦ FOLKLORE AND FACTS
Wear or carry a piece of Holy Thistle as protection from evil. • If Holy Thistle is grown anywhere on the property, it will help attract peace, love and harmony around the home.

Coccoloba uvifera ⚱

Sea Grape

Bay Grape | Baygrape | Coccolobis uvifera | Guaiabara uvifera | Polygonum uviferum

☀ SYMBOLIC MEANINGS
Grape bearer of the shore.

✿ POSSIBLE POWERS
Sea magic; Wishing.

✦ FOLKLORE AND FACTS
The highly salt-tolerant and wind-tolerant Sea Grape can withstand the trials and tribulations of an extreme seaside existence in South Florida, but barely a shiver of frost, since the plant cannot survive below 35.6°F. • The male and the female Sea Grape flowers are on completely separate trees. Pollination is achieved with the help of bees. • Unable to withstand storage, the ripened, purplish-red seeds of the Sea Grape must be planted immediately. • Wherever turtles hatch, all of the taller Sea Grape trees and shrubs along populated coastlines can do much to help block some of the lights that buildings cast onto the sandy beaches. The lights easily confuse baby turtles who are instinctively responding to the full moon's light that has guided newly hatched turtles to the saltwater for millions of years. • The Sea Grape plays an integral part in preventing coastal soil erosion and dune stabilization. • Sea Grape wood can make a reddish vegetable dye. • On a day when the sea is calm, wishes can be scratched on Sea Grape leaves and floated off into the ocean. The wishing leaves can also be sent out from a boat. • Sea Grape plant sap has been used in leather tanning and dying.

C

No. 174

Coffea arabica

Coffee

Arabian Coffee | Buna | Bünn | Café Coffee Tree |
Coffea bourbonica | Coffea corymbulosa | Coffea
launifolia | Coffea moka | Coffea sundana | Coffea
vulgaris | Coffee Bean Tree | Coffee Shrub of Arabia

✺ **SYMBOLIC MEANINGS**
Alertness; Camaraderie; Friendship; Sociability.

✺ **POSSIBLE POWERS**
Change; Clearing; Courage; Dispels negative thinking;
Fluctuation; Grounding; Helps keep away a nightmare;
Liberation; Make a new friend; Mercy; Overcomes a thought
blockade; Peace of mind; Sociability; Victory.

✺ **FOLKLORE AND FACTS**
Coffee arabica is believed to be the first species of Coffee ever
cultivated. • In the twelfth century Coffee was discovered
in Yemen, where scholars wrote of how it was made into a
beverage brewed from roasted Coffee beans that helped them
work longer. From there Coffee was introduced to Egypt and
Turkey, then all around the world. • When feeling under the
weather, the fragrance of Coffee essential oil can be uplifting.
• A magical-seeming method of immediately clearing a scent
from the nose is to sniff Coffee—whole beans or ground.

No. 175

Coix lacryma-jobi

Job's Tears

Adlai | Adlay | Bali | Bo Bo | Chinese Pearl Barley | Christ's Tears | Chuan Gu | Coix | Coix
lacryma | Coix ovata | Coix pendula | Coix Seed | Coixseed | Croix Seed | Curom Gao | David's
Tears | Hanjeli | Hatomugi | Hot Bo Bo | Jali | Jobs Tears | Juzudama | Lacryma Christi |
Lithagrostis lacryma-jobi | Luk Dueai | St. Mary's Tears | Sphaerium lacryma | Tear Drops |
Tear Grass | Vyjanti Beads | Y Di | Yi Yi | Yulmu

✺ **SYMBOLIC MEANINGS**
Survived great suffering.

✺ **POSSIBLE POWERS**
Healing; Luck; Wishing.

✺ **FOLKLORE AND FACTS**
Job's Tears is a wild grass with seeds that are perfect beads,
as they have natural holes so they can be easily strung and
worn as jewelry. • Job's Tears can be used inside hollow
dried gourds to create shaker instruments. • To make a wish,
concentrate on your wish while counting out seven Job's
Tears seeds, then carry them with you everywhere for seven
days. At the end of seven days, make your wish once more,
then throw the seven seeds into naturally running water,
such as a river or stream.

No. 176

Cola acuminata ✿

Kola Nut

Bichea acuminata | Bichea solitaria | Bichea
sulcata | Bissy Nut | Braxipis grandiflora |
Clompanus longifolia | Cola Nut | Cola
grandiflora | Cola ledermannii | Cola
macrocarpa | Cola pseudoacuminata | Colaria
acuminata | Edwardia acuminata | Edwardia
lurida | Helicteres paniculata | Icosinia paniculata |
Kola | Lunanea bichy | Siphoniopsis monoica |
Southwellia longifolia | Sterculia acuminata | Sterculia
grandiflora | Sterculia macrocarpa

✺ **SYMBOLIC MEANINGS**
Hospitality; Friendship; Respect.

✺ **POSSIBLE POWERS**
Alertness; Diminish fatigue; Increase stamina.

✺ **FOLKLORE AND FACTS**
Kola can produce a caffeinated extract that is used as a natural
food flavoring for some soft drinks and energy beverages.
• The Kola Nut is not a true nut, but the seed removed from
the center of the Kola fruit. • The seed nut is sacred to the
Igbo people of southeastern Nigeria. The Kola Nut has many
rituals surrounding it. It forms an integral part at the center
of important Igbo social ceremonies, such as weddings,
baby naming, and funerals. These events always include the
important plate of Kola Nuts, where visitors receive a nut
that is blessed with a charm spell. The nut is broken open and
the number of the seed's pieces reveal the level of prosperity
in the charm. However, if the nut breaks into two pieces,
something sinister will happen. • The Kola seeds originally
gave Coca-Cola its unique flavor and caffeine kick.

C

No. 177

Coleus amboinicus

Indian Mint

Coleus aromaticus | Coleus carnosus | Coleus crassifolius | Coleus subfrutectosus | Coleus suborbicularis | Coleus suganda | Coleus vaalae | Country Borage | French Thyme | Indian Borage | Majana amboinica | Majana carnosa | Majana suganda | Mexican Mint | Ocimum vaalae | Plectranthus amboinicus | Soup Mint | Spanish Thyme

☀ SYMBOLIC MEANINGS
Soothing.

❁ POSSIBLE POWERS
Courage; Good luck; Protection; Psychic power; Sense of well-being.

❦ FOLKLORE AND FACTS
An infusion of fresh Indian Mint in water can be used as herbal rinse to add fragrance to hair. • To impart a sense of well-being, pin a sprig of Indian Mint on the lapel.

No. 178

Commiphora gileadensis ✿

Balm of Gilead

Amyris gileadensis | Amyris opobalsamum | Arabian Balsam Tree | Balm of Gilead Tree | Balm of Mecca Tree | Balsam of Gilead Tree | Balsam of Mecca Tree | Balsamea gileadensis | Balsamea meccanensis | Balsamea opobalsamum | Balsamodendrum ehrenbergianum | Balsamodendron gileadense | Balsamodendron opobalsamum | Balsamus libanotus | Balsamus meccanensis | Balsamus theophrasti | Beshem | Commiphora albiflora | Commiphora ancistrophora | Commiphora anfractuosa | Commiphora cassan | Commiphora gillettii | Commiphora microcarpa | Commiphora opobalsamum | Commiphora suckertiana | Commiphora velutina

☀ SYMBOLIC MEANINGS
Healing perfume; Impatience; Rare perfume.

❧ COMPONENT MEANINGS
Resin: Cure; Healing; I am cured; Love; Manifestations; Protection; Relief; Universal cure.

❁ POSSIBLE POWERS
Binding; Building; Death; Feminine energy; Healing; History; Knowledge; Limitations; Love; Manifestations; Obstacles; Protection; Relief from distress after losing a loved one; Time; Venus; Water element.

❦ FOLKLORE AND FACTS
Commiphora gileadensis is a sacred holy tree that dates back to Biblical times. • The name of the Balm of Gilead tree is a term that implies a universal cure. • Balm of Gilead is a rare perfume that was first referenced in the Bible's Old Testament Book of Genesis that is believed to be *Commiphora gileadensis* but may not be. Until proven otherwise, it is believed that the Arabian Balsam Tree is what produces the Balm of Gilead. • The Queen of Sheba gifted King Solomon with many fantastic things, with one of them being a Balm of Gilead root that King Solomon supposedly personally planted in his Jericho garden. • Cleopatra brought Balm of Gilead to Egypt and planted it in a Cairo district known as Ain-Shams, where there in a garden it is believed to have flourished. The legend about that particular tree and that particular garden continues, when after taking refuge in Egypt, Jesus' mother, Mary, washed baby Jesus' swaddling clothes in an Ain-Shams village spring before returning to Palestine. The legend is that, from then onward, the Balm of Gilead trees of Cairo would only produce secretions if they were growing on land watered by that spring. • The soldiers of Rome brought Balm of Gilead trees home as exotic gifts given to Emperor Vespasian in 79 BCE. The Emperor considered them a magnificent prize, which they surely were. When two groves of the Balm of Gilead trees were threatened by an invasion, fearing their destruction, he placed them both under armed guard to protect them from damage. • The best-quality sap from the trees is gathered from slow trickles bleeding from carefully made cuts in the bark before the Balm of Gilead tree comes into its fruits. • In ancient times, Balm of Gilead was also used by young women as a fragrance because it had the proven power to seduce men. • In the Catholic Church's Confirmation ritual, the anointing oil called chrism is a combination of Olive oil and the sacred holy Balm of Gilead. • Balm of Gilead tears, or drops of dried resin, can be used to help de-stress and heal from the trauma of losing a loved one. • Currently, the Balm of Gilead tree, *Commiphora gileadensis* grows wild in certain areas of Saudi Arabia. • Wear or carry a sachet of Balm of Gilead tree buds to help mend a broken heart.

C

No. 179

Commiphora myrrha 🏺

Myrrh

African Myrrh | *Balsamea myrrha* | *Balsamea myrrha* | *Balsamea playfairii* | *Balsamodendrum myrrha* | *Balsamodendrum simplicifolium* | *Commiphora coriacea* | *Commiphora cuspidata* | *Commiphora molmol* | *Commiphora rivae* | *Commiphora simplicifolia* | Common Myrrh | Gum Myrrh | Herabol Myrrh | Somali Myrrhor

✻ SYMBOLIC MEANING
Gladness.

✹ POSSIBLE POWERS
Abundance; Adonis; Advancement; Binding; Building; Conscious will; Death; Energy; Exorcism; Feminine energy; Friendship; Growth; Healing; History; Isis; Joy; Knowledge; Leadership; Life; Light; Limitations; Marian; Moon; Natural power; Obstacles; Protection; Purification; Ra; Spirituality; Success; Time; Water element.

☘ FOLKLORE AND FACTS
Throughout history, Myrrh has been treasured as a medicine, an incense, and a perfume. It is harvested as a sap that is bled from the *Commiphora myrrha* tree by making multiple cuts into the bark to weep the waxy gum. After it is all collected, the gum hardens to a glossy resin that is further processed to extract the essential oils. • According to the Gospel of Matthew in the New Testament, Myrrh was one of the three precious gifts presented to the newborn Jesus of Nazareth by the magi who, it was written, had traveled there from some unnamed land far to the east of Bethlehem. One of the other two gifts is written to have been gold, with the other being Frankincense. Considering that two of the three tributes were spices, there is a thought that perhaps the gold might have been a bright golden-colored spice, like Turmeric. • The name Myrrh is also applied to *Myrrhis odorata*, which is commonly known Sweet Cicely. The two herbs are completely unrelated to each other. • In aromatherapy, Myrrh essential oil creates a relaxing, uplifting atmosphere for meditation and prayer.

No. 180

Convallaria majalis ☠🏺

Lily of the Valley

Convall Lily | Convall-lily | Convallaria | *Convallaria bracteata* | *Convallaria fragrans* | *Convallaria latifolia* | *Convallaria mappii* | *Convallaria scaposa* | *Convallaria transcaucasica* | Ladder to Heaven | *Lilium convallium* | *Lilium-convallium majale* | Lily Constancy | Lily-of-the-Valley | Male Lily | May Bells | May Lily | Muguet | Our Lady's Tears | *Polygonatum majale*

✻ SYMBOLIC MEANINGS
Christ's second coming; Forever love; Fortune in love; Good luck; Happiness; Humility; Joy; Purity of heart; Return of happiness; Returning happiness; Sociability; Sweet; Sweetness; Tears of the Virgin Mary; Trustworthy; Unconscious sweetness; You've made my life complete.

✹ POSSIBLE POWERS
Air element; Apollo; Asclepius; Colorize; Happiness; Healing; Making the right choice; Masculine energy; Mental clarity or power; Mercury; Power to visualize a better world.

☘ FOLKLORE AND FACTS
Put fragrant Lily of the Valley flowers in a room to uplift and cheer all the people in it. • Wear a sprig of the flower to feel uplifted by its fragrance. A Lily of the Valley scented cologne or perfume can be as uplifting as if wearing a fresh sprig of the flower. • As an essential oil, the aroma of Lily of the Valley can induce thoughts of dreamy, somewhat delicate, elegant romantic love. • Lily of the Valley is the national flower of Finland. • The leaves make a green vegetable dye for fabric.

C

Coriandrum sativum 🥣🍴

Cilantro

Bifora loureiroi | Chinese Parsley | Cilentro | Coreander | Coriander | Coriandre | *Coriandropsis syriaca* | Coriandrum | *Coriandrum diversifolium* | *Coriandrum globosum* | *Coriandrum majus* | *Coriandrum majus* | *Coriandrum melphitense* | Culantro | Dhania | Hu-Sui | Koriadnon | Koriandron | Koriannon | Ko-ri-ja-da-na | *Selinum coriandrum* | *Sium coriandrum* | Stinkdillsamen | Uran-Suy

☀ SYMBOLIC MEANINGS
Good cheer; Hidden merit or worth; Luck; Peace between those who don't get along.

🌿 COMPONENT MEANINGS
Seed: Peace between those who don't get along.

🌀 POSSIBLE POWERS
Aphrodisiac; Attracts love; Fire element; Healing; Health; Helps to find romance; Immortality; Intelligence; Love; Lust; Mars; Masculine energy; Protection; Protects gardeners and their households; Virility.

🜨 FOLKLORE AND FACTS
Resembling the look of Parsley, Cilantro has a uniquely tangy and somewhat citrusy flavor. Most people who have tasted it will like it. However, there are some who detest it, vehemently complaining Cilantro tastes unpleasantly soapy to them. • Hang a small bunch of Cilantro in the home for protection. • In the Middle Ages, Cilantro was used in love potions and spells. • Make and wear a sachet of Cilantro seeds to wear as an amulet to help ease a headache. • As a seed or as a ground herb the most common name used is its proper name, Coriander. But, particularly in Central, South, and North America it is much more well known as Cilantro. • In the Middle Ages, Cilantro was frequently used in magic spells and witchcraft. Hanging Cilantro at a door offers protections against harm and will keep out anyone who is envious of you, or who you consider to be unpleasant in nature. • A sprinkle of the dry powdered herb in a glass of warm wine may make an inspiring aphrodisiac. • A sprig of Cilantro tucked atop a baby's cradle offers its protection to the baby in it.

Coriandrum sativum 🥣🍴

Coriander

Bifora loureiroi | Chinese Parsley | Cilentro | *Coriandropsis syriaca* | *Coriandrum diversifolium* | *Coriandrum globosum* | *Coriandrum majus* | *Coriandrum melphitense* | Culantro | Daisy Corn | Dizzy Corn | Hu-Sui | *Selinum coriandrum* | *Sium coriandrum* | Stinkdillsamen | Uran-Suy

☀ SYMBOLIC MEANINGS
Good cheer; Luck; Romance.

🌀 POSSIBLE POWERS
Aphrodisiac; Attracts love; Love; Lust; Money; Protection; Romance; Soothing; Survival; Wards off evil.

🜨 FOLKLORE AND FACTS
As a ground herb and as a seed spice, the most common name used is its proper name, Coriander. But, in Central, South, and North America it is much more well known as Cilantro due to the extensive use of this herb in Mexican cuisine, and with the Spanish word for the herb being Cilantro. • In the Middle Ages, Coriander seed was frequently used in magic spells and witchcraft. • Hanging a pouch filled with Coriander seed on a door offers protections against harm and will keep out anyone who is envious or unpleasant. • A sprinkle of dry powdered Coriander seed in a glass of warm wine may make an inspiring aphrodisiac. • The hard, sweet confection known as a jawbreaker, sugar ball, or comfit, used to have a tasty Coriander seed at its center. • A pink and red colored sachet of Coriander seeds that has been made with love to be worn or carried will invite romance to enter into an otherwise platonic relationship. • The name Coriander is rooted in the Greek word *korianon*, meaning bug, which is reminiscent of the odor of the unripe seeds.

Corylus avellana 🥣

Hazel

Coll | Common Hazel | *Corylus sylvetris* | Filbert | Hazelnut | Hazelnut Tree

☀ SYMBOLIC MEANINGS
Communication; Creative inspiration; Epiphanies; Reconciliation.

🌀 POSSIBLE POWERS
Air element; Anti-lightning; Artemis; Diana; Divination; Fertility; Heightened awareness; Luck; Masculine energy; Meditation; Mercury; Protection; Sun visions; Thor; Wisdom; Wishing.

C

FOLKLORE AND FACTS

Give a Hazelnut to a bride to wish her good fortune, fertility, and wisdom. • Make a wishing crown by weaving Hazel tree twigs together. Wear this crown when making wishes. • A forked Hazel tree branch is the diviner's dowsing rod of first choice. • The Hazel tree's nut is believed to have been given the common name of Filbert because the tree's nuts matured on August 20th, which is the Feast Day of Saint Philibert of Jumièges. • Eat one Hazelnut before attempting a divination. • For the most opportune effect to be imbued into a brand new divining rod, the cutting must be done after the sun sets on one of the following nights: on the eve of a new moon, on the first night of a new moon, Good Friday, Shrove Tuesday, Epiphany, or Saint John's Day. The one who is severing the branch from the tree should be the intended diviner, who would best be the seventh son of a seventh son. He must face east to cut the first branch, which will be the one to catch the first of the morning sunlight. In this way the divining rod would be prepared to perform particularly well for the magically destined operator.

No. 184

Cota tinctoria

Dyer's Chamomile

Anacyclus tinctorius | Anthemis tinctoria | Boston Daisy | Chamaemelum tinctorium | Golden Marguerite | Oxeye Chamomile | Paris Daisy | Yellow Chamomile

SYMBOLIC MEANINGS
Golden color.

POSSIBLE POWERS
Colorize; Money.

FOLKLORE AND FACTS
With nary another purposeful use, as a vegetable dye plant, Dyer's Chamomile does what it does exceptionally well by imbuing lovely colors into wool and other fibers. Depending on the fabric and mordants used, it can produce very beautiful buffs, warm yellows, and bright yellow-orange colors. In addition to the warm tones, some very lovely green colors can be produced by using Woad to add in some blue. • Make, then wear or carry, preferably in a wallet or pocket, a sachet of Dyer's Chamomile to draw money to it and increase what money is there.

No. 185

Crataegus laevigata ☙

English Hawthorn

Crataegus coriacea | Crataegus cuneatotrifida | Crataegus oxyacanthoides | Crataegus palmstruchii | Crataegus sorbifolia | Crataegus spinosa | Crataegus subinermis | Crataegus walokochiana | Mayflower | Mespilus digyna | Mespilus intermedia | Mespilus laevigata | Mespilus oxyacanthoides | Midland Hawthorn | Oxyacantha matthioli | Oxyacantha obtusata | Oxyacantha vulgaris | Fairy Tree | Woodland Hawthorn

SYMBOLIC MEANINGS
Fairy tree; Sweet hope.

POSSIBLE POWERS
Cardea; Caution; Chastity; Fairies; Fend off negative energies; Fend off negative magic; Fend off witches and witchcraft; Fertility; Fire element; Fishing magic; Flora; Happiness; Hymen; Love; Mars; Masculine energy; Relaxation.

FOLKLORE AND FACTS
The English Hawthorn is the most common small tree or shrub in the British Isles and also one of the most sacred trees on Earth. It is also known as the Fairy Tree, with the fairies of the area living under it as its guardians, dedicated to treating the tree with love, respect, and care, as all mortal humans should do too. • Respectfully collecting English Hawthorn sprigs and flower blossoms for brides to wear in their hair, or to pin up their veils is permitted by the fairies because the act is associated too much with love to deny this pleasure to a mortal human on her wedding day. • The English Hawthorn was a medicinal tree favored by the Druids for use in a strengthening tonic. • It is said that Cardea, the Roman goddess of door hinges and handles, who thwarted evil spirits from crossing thresholds, used an English Hawthorn branch as a magical wand for her enchantments. • It is believed that one will be able to see fairies where the English Hawthorn, Oak, and Ash trees are growing together in a cluster. • The association of the English Hawthorn to the crown of thorns has given the tree special magical powers to fend off negative energies. • Because of its power to fend off negative forces, English Hawthorn twigs were put in, on, or near baby cradles. • English Hawthorn branches were placed over doors and windows of homes and barns to keep witches from entering the building. • An English Hawthorn twig was often tucked into the sock of the dead or placed atop the body in the coffin. • An English Hawthorn stake was considered a highly effective instrument to use to impale a vampire. • The Hawthorn is the state flower of Missouri, USA.

No. 186

Cratoxylum formosum

Pink Mempat

Ancistrolobus formosus | Derum | Elodes formosa | Entemu | Geronggang Biabas | Gerunggung | Kemutul | Kemutun | Mempat | Mempitis | Phak Tiu | Tew | Thành Nganh Dep | Thành Nganh Vàng | Tridesmis formosa | Tridesmis jackii

✹ SYMBOLIC MEANINGS
Strong wood.

✺ POSSIBLE POWERS
Colorize; Healing.

☢ FOLKLORE AND FACTS
Pink Mempat is a tropical tree with orchid-like bright pink flowers that will typically grow to be around thirty-two feet tall. However, growing out it the wild, the tree can grow up to 147 feet tall. • Pink Mempat wood is primarily used for making charcoal. • A brown vegetable dye can be obtained from the bark of the Pink Mempat tree. • The resin of the Pink Mempat tree is used in folk medicine as a remedy for scabies.

No. 187

Crithmum maritimum ✿

Sea Fennel

Cachrys maritima | Crest Marine | Crithmum canariense | Herbe du St. Pierre | Rock Fennel | Rock Samphire | St. Peter's Herb | Samphire

✹ SYMBOLIC MEANINGS
Down to earth.

✺ POSSIBLE POWERS
Grounding; Healing; Regeneration; Renewing; Seasoning.

☢ FOLKLORE AND FACTS
Due to over-harvesting, succulent, salty, and wild Sea Fennel has become rare in its natural environment. Any effort to domestically cultivate the herb is highly encouraged. • It was believed by some that Sea Fennel essential oil supposedly has skin regenerative properties that combats the issues plaguing aging skin. • Because of Sea Fennel's sea-saltiness, in coastal areas where it grows, the dried herb is often used to add a salty, carroty-lemony aspect to some foods. • Sea Fennel abides on sea-sprayed, slippery, rocky coastal spots. It grows in the clefts of rocks, which makes gathering Sea Fennel a treacherous endeavor. • Referenced as *samphire*, the Sea Fennel was written into Shakespeare's play, *King Lear*.

No. 188

Crocus sativus ✿🍴

Saffron

Crocus autumnalis | Crocus officinalis | Crocus orsinii | Crocus pendulus | Crocus setifolius | Geanthus autumnalis | Kashmiri Saffron | Kesar | Krokos | Krokos Kozanis | Kunkuma | Saffer | Saffron Crocus | Safran officinarum | Spanish Saffron

✹ SYMBOLIC MEANINGS
Ancient symbol of the Sun; Beware of excess; Cheerfulness; Do not abuse; Excess is dangerous; Happiness; Mirth.

✺ POSSIBLE POWERS
Abuse; Aphrodisiac; Ashtoreth; Attracts love; Eros; Euphoria; Fire element; Happiness; Healing; Laughter; Love; Lust; Magic; Masculine energy; Psychic power; Raises up a spirit; Singing; Spirituality; Strength; Sun; Uplifting; Wind raising.

☢ FOLKLORE AND FACTS
In India, Saffron flowers are often scattered on the marriage bed of newlyweds. • During the Bronze Age, Saffron was used in Minoan religious rituals to later be adopted, over time, by other religions for their own religious rituals. • Once, a *Crocus sativus* bulb was successfully smuggled from the Middle East into England, then throughout Europe when it was hidden inside a walking stick. By the time the Saffron bulb reached its final destination, its value was considered priceless. • Be sure to plant Saffron in a garden that is intended to please the fairies. • When Saffron reached India, it was discovered there that a beautiful golden-colored vegetable dye could be rendered from it for fabrics. The rich, golden yellow-orange color was used for royal garments in many different countries and cultures. • During the Middle Ages, inks made from Saffron were used by the poorer illuminators to replace gold leaf in their religious art renderings. • There was a time in Ireland when the bed linen was rinsed with an infusion of Saffron with the belief that the arms and legs would be made stronger while sleeping upon them. • Ancient Persians would toss Saffron into the air as an attempt to raise the wind. • The lucrative lure of turning nothing into something entices spice counterfeiters to fake Saffron and trade it off to unsuspecting retailers as genuine. Thus, using Beet and Pomegranate to dye faked threads of such things as horsehair, corn silk, and even finely shredded paper, have forced counterfeit Saffron into the legitimately high-priced Saffron spice market, most especially on the internet.

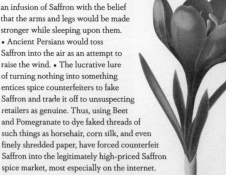

- Powdered Saffron has been even easier to fake with the addition of powdered Turmeric or Paprika. • During medieval times in the Middle East, changing Saffron by adding to it anything of a lesser value in an effort to increase its quantity, but lower the quality, was punishable by some horrible means of death, which included being buried alive! It has been the higher-quality Kashmiri Saffron growers who have suffered at the hands of Saffron spice counterfeiters the most. • One pound of Saffron contains seventy to 200,000 stigma threads that will wholesale for between 500 to 5,000 dollars, depending on the quality of the Saffron. This same pound of Saffron will retail for 5,000 to 10,000 dollars. • By weight, Saffron is worth more than gold. This is due to the fact it takes approximately a football field's worth of flowers to produce one pound of Saffron stigmas. • The visible difference between the Saffron crocus, *Crocus sativus*, and the deadly poisonous *Colchicum autumnale*, which is also known as Autumn Crocus or Meadow Saffron, is that the Saffron *Crocus sativus* flower blossom never has any more than three stigmas. • The fragrance of Saffron is especially exotic while harvesting. It is also somewhat mood-altering due to its natural anti-depressant properties. • After a while of harvesting the stigmas, medieval nuns would break into song, being somewhat euphoric under the stimulating influence of Saffron.

No. 189

Croton tiglium ☠🝆

Purging Croton

Alchornea vaniotii | Bā Dòu | Croton | *Croton acutus* | *Croton arboreus* | *Croton birmanicus* | *Croton camaza* | *Croton himalaicus* | *Croton jamalgota* | *Croton muricatus* | *Croton officinalis* | *Croton pavana* | *Croton xiaopadou* | *Halecus verus* | Jamaal Gota | Jamālgoṭa | Japaala | Jayapala | Kurkas tiglium | *Oxydectes birmanica* | *Oxydectes blancoana* | *Oxydectes tiglium* | *Tiglium officinale*

✴ **SYMBOLIC MEANINGS**
Change.

🌀 **POSSIBLE POWERS**
Emotions; Fertility; Generation; Inspiration; Intuition; Psychic ability; Sea; Subconscious mind; Tides; Travel on water.

🜍 **FOLKLORE AND FACTS**
The Purging Croton is one of the fifty herbs depended upon in Chinese medicine, where it is known by the name of Bā Dòu. • Purging Croton is extremely poisonous, enough for whole seeds to be able to stun fish by simply tossing the seeds into the water of ponds and streams. • Himalayan tribes used poisonous arrows that were tipped with the toxins extracted from the Purging Croton plant bark.

No. 190

Cucumis sativus 🝆

Cucumber

Belt Alpha Cucumber | *Cucumis esculentus* | *Cucumis hardwickii* | *Cucumis muricatus* | *Cucumis rumphii* | Cuke | Dosakaya | East Asian Cucumber | European Cucumber | Kekiri | Kheera Cucumber | Lebanese Cucumber | Persian Cucumber | Schälgurkens | Schmorgurken | Telegraph Cucumber

✴ **SYMBOLIC MEANINGS**
Chastity; Criticism.

🌀 **POSSIBLE POWERS**
Chastity; Feminine energy; Fertility; Healing; Moon; Water element.

🜍 **FOLKLORE AND FACTS**
Roman midwives would carry a Cucumber then throw it away when they delivered a baby. • Roman wives, desiring a baby, would wear a Cucumber tied around the waist as a talisman. • Roman households would use a Cucumber to frighten away mice that would enter into their homes.

C

No. 191

Cucurbita pepo ⚱

Pumpkin

Citrullus variegatus | Cucumis pepo | Cucumis zapallo | Cucurbita aurantia | Cucurbita ceratoceras | Cucurbita clodiensis | Cucurbita courgero | Cucurbita elongata | Cucurbita esculenta | Cucurbita fastuosa | Cucurbita hybrida | Cucurbita lignosa | Cucurbita mammeata | Cucurbita mammosa | Cucurbita marsupiiformis | Cucurbita oblonga | Cucurbita polymorpha | Cucurbita pomiformis | Cucurbita pyridaris | Cucurbita pyxidaris | Cucurbita succado | Cucurbita succedo | Cucurbita tuberculosa | Cucurbita urnigera | Cucurbita variegata | Cucurbita venosa | Field Pumpkin | Pepo aurantius | Pepo citrullus | Pepo clypeiformis | Pepo oblongus | Pepo potiron | Pepo vulgaris | Pompion | Squash | Winter Squash

✹ SYMBOLIC MEANINGS
Bounty; Coarseness; Grossness; Plenty.

✹ POSSIBLE POWERS
Earth element; Fertility; Grant a wish; Health; Love; Moon; Prosperity; Sustenance.

🌿 COMPONENT MEANINGS
Carved: Protection.

✷ FOLKLORE AND FACTS
The iconic Halloween jack-o'-lantern never seems quite the same unless it has been carved using a Pumpkin. • Jack-o'-lanterns originally were made in Ireland to put out on the front step to scare away the Devil and any other sinister spirits that may come near. • In 2016, Mathias Willemijns of Belgium set the current world record for the heaviest gourd, at 2,624 pounds • On October 31st, illuminate a carved, hollowed-out Pumpkin using a white candle for additional protection from intrusive or pesky negative spirits.

No. 192

Cuminum cyminum ⚱🍴

Cumin

Cumino | Cumino Aigro | Cuminum aegyptiacum | Cuminum hispanicum | Cuminum odorum | Cuminum officinale | Cuminum sativum | Cummin | Cymen | Cyminon longeinvolucellatum | Gamun | Geerah | Kammon | Kammun | Kimoon | Ku-mi-no | Kuminon | Ligusticum cuminum | Luerssenia cyminum | Sanoot | Selinum cuminum

✹ SYMBOLIC MEANINGS
Faithfulness; Fidelity.

✹ POSSIBLE POWERS
Anti-theft; Cleansing; Constancy in love; Exorcism; Fidelity; Fire element; Mars; Masculine energy; Memory; Peace of mind; Protection; Retention.

✷ FOLKLORE AND FACTS
Cumin will supposedly prevent the theft of anything that has this spice on it or in it. • Mixed with salt and scattered on the floor, Cumin will supposedly drive out evil. • A sprig of the Cumin plant is sometimes worn by a bride to keep any negativity away from her on her wedding day. • To gain peace of mind when it is needed the most, make, then carry or wear a Cumin sachet using a sprig of the plant or ground Cumin from a spice bottle. • Cumin's ability to possess the power of retention has given it a rightful place in love potions and love charms to help maintain love as being constant and faithful.

C

No. 193
Cupressus sempervirens ☠♻🗡
Cypress

Chamaecyparis thujiformis | Cupressus conoidea | Cupressus elongata | Cupressus expansa |
Cupressus fastigiata | Cupressus foemina | Cupressus globulifera | Cupressus horizontalis |
Cupressus lugubris | Cupressus mariae | Cupressus mas | Cupressus orientalis | Cupressus
patula | Cupressus pyramidalis | Cupressus roylei | Cupressus sphaerocarpa | Cupressus
stricta | Cupressus thujifolia | Cupressus thujiformis | Cupressus umbilicata | Cupressus
whitleyana | Italian Cypress | Juniperus whitleyana | Tree of Death

✸ **SYMBOLIC MEANINGS**
Death; Despair; Grief; Mourning; Sorrow.

🌀 **POSSIBLE POWERS**
Aphrodite; Apollo; Artemis; Ashtoreth; Comfort; Cupid;
Earth element; Eternity; Feminine energy; Healing; Hebe;
Heqet; Immortality; Jupiter; Longevity; Mithras; Pluto;
Protection; Saturn; Zoroaster.

🜨 **FOLKLORE AND FACTS**
Wear a sprig of Cypress for comfort to ease the suffering
mind of the grief experienced upon the death of a
friend or relative. • Since it is such a strong symbol of
immortality, growing a Cypress tree provides blessings
and protection. • Using Cypress essential oil for
aromatherapy can provide emotional strength, especially
during times of extreme sadness.

No. 194
Curcuma longa
🗡🍴
Turmeric

Amomum curcuma | Curcuma brog |
Curcuma domestica | Curcuma
ochrorhiza | Curcuma soloensis |
Haldi | Haridra | Harldar | Indian Saffron |
Kua domestica | Manjal

✸ **SYMBOLIC MEANINGS**
Fertility; Luck; Sun.

🌀 **POSSIBLE POWERS**
Air element; Luck;
Mercury; Power;
Purification.

🜨 **FOLKLORE AND FACTS**
In every part of India, Turmeric is considered to be
very lucky and has been used in weddings and religious
ceremonies for thousands of years. • Occasionally in Hawaii,
for the purpose of purification, powdered Turmeric is mixed
with salt and water to be sprinkled with a Ti leaf over the
affected area. • Traces of Turmeric has been identified in
an Israeli tomb that dates back to 2600 BCE. • Turmeric is
believed to be greatly beneficial in reducing inflammation.

No. 195
Curcuma zedoaria
Zedoary

Amomum latifolium | Amomum zedoaria | Costus luteus | Curcuma malabarica | Curcuma
pallida | Curcuma raktakanta | Curcuma speciosa | Erndlia zerumbet | Kentjur | Roscoea lutea |
Roscoea nigrociliata | Tempu Putih | White Turmeric

✸ **SYMBOLIC MEANINGS**
Confidence.

🌀 **POSSIBLE POWERS**
Air element; Aphrodisiac; Attracts love; Confidence;
Courage; Healing; Magic; Mercury; Passion; Protection;
Purification; Spell-breaking; Stimulation; Strength.

🜨 **FOLKLORE AND FACTS**
Zedoary is an ancient spice consumed by the ancient
Austronesian people. • Since the plant itself is very showy,
Zedoary is sometimes a houseplant. • The essential oil
of the fragrant Zedoary rhizome is used in soap making
and perfumery.

C

No. 196

Cuscuta campestris

Dodder

Amar Bail | Angel Hair | Beggarweed | Devil's Guts | Devil's Hair | Devil's Ringlet | *Epithymum arvense* | Field Dodder | Fireweed | Golden Dodder | Goldthread | *Grammica campestris* | Hailweed | Hairweed | Hellbine | Hellweed | Lady's Laces | Large-Seeded Alfalfa Dodder | Love Vine | Prairie Dodder | Pull-Down | Scaldweed | Strangle Tare | Strangleweed | Witch's Hair | Wizard's Net | Yellow Dodder

☀ SYMBOLIC MEANINGS
Baseness; Meanness; Parasite.

☸ POSSIBLE POWERS
Feminine energy; Knot magic; Love divination; Saturn; Water element.

☙ FOLKLORE AND FACTS
Dodder starts growing in the ground from seed. As its long thin tendrils grow out, they parasitically attach to other plants with tiny suckers that puncture the host plant, drawing nutrients from it. Once Dodder has attached to a plant, its own roots die and it completely overwhelms the host plant by existing off of it to even prolifically bloom. Eventually, Dodder will not show signs of the chlorophyll it originally had, because it no longer needs any of its own.
• An interesting love divination is to pluck a large sprig of Dodder then throw it over the shoulder at the plant you picked it from, while asking if the person you love loves you in return. Leave. Return the next day and examine the sprig. If it has not reattached itself, your answer is No. If the sprig has reattached, then the answer is yes.

No. 197

Cyclamen hederifolium ☠☗

Cyclamen

Cyclamen albiflorum | *Cyclamen angulare* | *Cyclamen autumnale* | *Cyclamen crassifolium* | *Cyclamen cyclaminus* | *Cyclamen insulare* | *Cyclamen linearifolium* | *Cyclamen neapolitanum* | *Cyclamen oedirrhizum* | *Cyclamen poli* | *Cyclamen romanum* | *Cyclamen sabaudum* | *Cyclamen subhastatum* | *Cyclaminum vernum* | *Cyclaminus neapolitana* | Groundbread | Ivy-Leaved Cyclamen | Pain de Pourceau | Pan Porcino | Sowbread | Swinebread | Varkensbrood

☀ SYMBOLIC MEANINGS
Diffidence; Goodbye; Resignation.

☸ POSSIBLE POWERS
Aphrodisiac; Attracts love; Fertility; Happiness; Lust; Protection.

☙ FOLKLORE AND FACTS
A pot of Cyclamen growing with Saint John's Wort in a bedroom is believed by some to offer protection against any evil spirits trying to take unfair advantage of those in the room who are vulnerable while they're sleeping. No negative spells can have any power there.

No. 198

Cydonia oblonga ☠☗

Quince

Apple Quince | Aromatnaya Quince | Bereczki Quince | Champion Quince | Cooke's Jumbo | *Crataegus serotina* | *Cydonia communis* | *Cydonia cydonia* | *Cydonia europaea* | *Cydonia lusitanica* | *Cydonia maliformis* | *Cydonia silvestris* | *Cydonia sumboshia* | Cydonian Pome | Dwarf Orange Quince | Gamboa | Iranian Quince | Isfahan | Jumbo Quince | Kashmiri Bummtchoont | Le Bourgeaut | Lescovacz | Ludovic | Lusitanica | Maliformis | Meeches Prolific | Morava | Orange Quince | Perfume Quince | Perishin | Pineapple Quince | Prish | *Pyrus cydonia* | *Pyrus lusitanica* | *Pyrus maliformis* | *Pyrus oblonga* | *Pyrus sumboshia* | Safarjal | Shams Quince | Siebosa | Smyrna Quince | *Sorbus cydonia* | Supurgillu | Van Deman | Vranja

☀ SYMBOLIC MEANINGS
Excellence; Fairies' fire; Fertility; Fidelity; Happiness; Life; Love; Scornful beauty; Temptation.

☸ POSSIBLE POWERS
Earth element; Happiness; Love; Protection; Protection from evil; Saturn; Venus.

C

FOLKLORE AND FACTS

Art seen in the excavated remains of Pompeii have revealed images of bears carrying Quince fruit in their paws. • To carry even one Quince seed is supposed to provide protection against accidents, evil, and harm to the body. • The Quince is sacredly associated with the goddesses Aphrodite and Venus. • In ancient Rome, to guarantee their happiness together as a married couple, a Quince fruit was shared between the bride and groom. • The Quince is yet another fruit that is considered to be the forbidden fruit found in the Garden of Eden. • In many parts of the Balkans, when a baby is born a Quince tree is planted to wish the child a long life, love, and future fertility. • A mother-to-be eating a Quince along with a Coriander seed would assure that her child in the womb would be born to be clever and witty.

No. 199

Cymbopogon citratus 🐾☑🍴

Lemongrass

Andropogon cerifer | Andropogon ceriferus | Andropogon citratus | Andropogon citriodorus | Andropogon fragrans | Andropogon roxburghii | Balioko | Lemon Grass | Salai | Serai | Serai Dapur | Sereh | Takhrai | Tanglad | West Indian Lemon Grass

✸ SYMBOLIC MEANINGS

Open communication.

⊛ POSSIBLE POWERS

Air element; Aphrodisiac; Attracts love; Communication; Fosters openness; Lust; Masculine energy; Mercury; Psychic cleansing; Psychic opening; Psychic power; Repels insects; Repels a snake.

FOLKLORE AND FACTS

Lemongrass planted around the home is believed to repel snakes. • Lemongrass is good for psychic cleansing and opening, which allows for the development of one's psychic ability. • Lemongrass essential oil can be used for aromatherapy to uplift a sagging spirit.

No. 200

Cymbopogon martinii

Palmarosa

Andropogon calamus-aromaticus | Andropogon martini | Andropogon pachnodes | Cymbopogon martini | Cymbopogon martinianus | Gingergrass | Gymnanthelia martini | Indian geranium | Palm Rose | Rosha | Rosha Grass

✸ SYMBOLIC MEANINGS

Gentle; Loyal; Powerful.

⊛ POSSIBLE POWERS

Gentleness; Loyalty; Repels mosquitos.

FOLKLORE AND FACTS

Palmarosa essential oil sweetly smells very much like roses. It is commonly used to add a rosy fragrance to cosmetics and soaps. • Palmarosa oil is often used as an effective mosquito repellent or air sanitizer.

No. 201

Cymbopogon nardus ☠

Citronella

Andropogon citrosus | Andropogon confertiflorus | Andropogon grandis | Andropogon hamulatus | Andropogon nardus | Andropogon pseudohirtus | Andropogon thwaitesii | Barbed Wire Grass | Cha de Dartigalongue | Citronella Grass | Cymbopogon afronardus | Cymbopogon claessensii | Cymbopogon confertiflorus | Cymbopogon prolixus | Cymbopogon thwaitesii | Cymbopogon validus | Cymbopogon virgatus | Cymbopogon winterianus | Fever Grass | Gavati Chaha | Hierba Luisa | Lagurus paniculatus | Silky Heads | Sorghum nardu | Tanglad

✴ SYMBOLIC MEANING
Open communication.

❀ POSSIBLE POWERS
Communication; Fosters openness; Lust; Psychic power; Repels flying insects; Repels snakes.

☙ FOLKLORE AND FACTS
Citronella planted around the home is believed to repel snakes. • The Citronella plant's essential oil can be used in candle making to produce a highly effective flying insect-repellent candle. A Citronella candle has a grass-like, herbal-floral fragrance that has a citrusy edge to it. It's very pleasant. This type of scented candle has been a longtime favorite for use outside since 1948, when Citronella was registered for use as an insect-repellent in the United States. Candles of this type are marketed as small as tealight size up to a large favorite available in a seven- or eight-inch galvanized bucket capable of burning multiple wicks. • The diameter of insect repellence around an average-sized Citronella candle is around four feet.

No. 202

Cynoglossum officinale ⚗

Hound's Tongue

Cynoglossum bicolor | Cynoglossum foetens | Cynoglossum hybridum | Cynoglossum paucisetum | Cynoglossum punctatum | Cynoglossum ruderale | Dog's Tongue | Gypsy Flower | Houndstongue | Houndstooth | Rats and Mice

✴ SYMBOLIC MEANING
Healing.

❀ POSSIBLE POWERS
Cure madness; Fire element; Healing; Mars; Masculine energy.

☙ FOLKLORE AND FACTS
Hound's Tongue received the common name Rats and Mice because it smells like them. • An unpleasant-sounding concoction and absurd process used in the mid-1700s for curing a madness that seemed to follow after suffering a head cold involved a freshly shaven head, a mix of flowers and herbs that included Hound's Tongue, and a live pigeon to rub that blend of herbal goop onto. More herbs went into a pot of honey water mixed with Absinthe Wormwood, the ashes of a dead tortoise, and a pinch of Rosemary at the end for a touch of seasoning. After twenty-five days of having some of that fancy homemade cure concoction mixed into their breakfast broth, the mad individual was expected to make a full recovery.

No. 203

Cyperus papyrus

Papyrus

Bulrush | *Chlorocyperus papyrus* | Indian Matting Plant | Nile Grass | Paper Plant | Paper Reed | Papyrus Sedge

✳ **SYMBOLIC MEANINGS**
History; Written communication.

✸ **POSSIBLE POWERS**
Air element; Communication; Masculine energy; Mercury; Messages; Protection.

☙ **FOLKLORE AND FACTS**
The Papyrus plant has immense historical fame as it is the plant that the ancient Egyptians used to make Papyrus paper. • It was believed that Papyrus inside a boat will protect it from attack by crocodiles. • The Papyrus plants played a critically empirical role in ancient Biblical history. During a murderous drowning purge of all male Hebrew children at the command of her father the Pharaoh, the Egyptian Princess Bithiah discovered the Hebrew infant, Moses, in a floating reed basket that has since been reasonably determined could have been made of Papyrus. Bithiah then raised Moses to be an Egyptian prince.

No. 204

Cytisus scoparius ☠️🏺

Broom

Banal | Basam | Besom | Bisom | Bizzon | Breeam | Broom Topos | Brum | Common Broom | English Broom | Genista Green Broom | *Genista scoparius* | Hog Weed | Irish Broom | Irish Tops | Link | *Sarothamnus bourgaei* | *Sarothamnus oxyphyllus* | *Sarothamnus scoparius* | Scot's Broom | Scotch Broom | *Spartium scoparium*

✳ **SYMBOLIC MEANINGS**
Sweep; Tidy up.

✸ **POSSIBLE POWERS**
Collect; Colorize; Divination; Gather up; Protection; Purification; Remove; Union; Wind spell.

☙ **FOLKLORE AND FACTS**
Hang Broom outside the home to keep evil from entering into it. • Broom will produce a vegetable dye color that ranges from very pale yellow to beige. • There is an unproven belief that by holding a nosegay of self-gathered sprigs of Rue, Broom, Maidenhair Fern, Agrimony, and Ground Ivy that one can gain profound intuition of who is and who is not a practicing witch. • Make an infusion of rainwater, natural spring water, or distilled water mixed with the flowering tops from a stem of Broom. To make a clean sweep-out of all the evil that may be lurking around the home, sprinkle this infusion everywhere inside and all around the entire house.

C

No. 205

Daphne bholua ☠

Nepali Paper Plant

Baruwa | Chu Chu | *Daphne emeiensis* | Kagatpate | Lokta Paper Plant

✳ **SYMBOLIC MEANINGS**
Coquetry; Desire to please; a Flirt; Flirt; Glory; I desire to please; I would not have you otherwise; Immortality; Make beautiful that which is beautiful.

✵ **POSSIBLE POWERS**
Art; Communication.

✿ **FOLKLORE AND FACTS**
In the traditional manner handed down through the ages, the Nepalese use the bark from the Nepali Paper Plant to make beautiful handmade paper, known as Lokta paper. Artists use the high-quality paper for drawing, painting, and paper crafting. • The paper that is made using the Nepali Paper Plant is durable, being highly resistant to mildew, insects, and tearing. This makes the paper the preference for religious sacred writings and official Nepalese government documents.

No. 206

Datura stramonium ☠☗

Datura

Angel's Trumpet | Carda | Chamico | Datira | *Datura bernhardii* | *Datura bertolonii* | *Datura cabanesii* | *Datura capensis* | *Datura ferocissima* | *Datura ferox* | *Datura hybrida* | *Datura inermis* | *Datura laevis* | *Datura loricata* | *Datura lurida* | *Datura microcarpa* | *Datura muricata* | *Datura parviflora* | *Datura praecox* | *Datura pseudostramonium* | *Datura tatula* | *Datura wallichii* | Devil's Apple | Devil's Cucumber | Devil's Trumpet | Devil's Weed | Espinoso | Estramonio | Floripondio Tree | Ghost Flower | Hell's Bells | Herb of the Devil | Hierba Hedionda | Indian Apple | Indian Whiskey | Jamestown Weed | Love-Will | Mad Apple | Mad Herb | Mad Seeds | Madherb | Malpitte | Manicon | Manzano | Nana-honua | Nongué | Pedro Noche | Prickly Burr | Sorcerer's Herb | Stinkweed | *Stramonium foetidum* | *Stramonium globosum* | *Stramonium laeve* | *Stramonium spinosum* | *Stramonium tatula* | *Stramonium vulgare* | *Stramonium vulgatum* | Thorn Apple | Thornapple | Tolache | Tolguacha | Witches' Thimble | Yerbe del Diablo

✳ **SYMBOLIC MEANINGS**
Deceitful charms; Deceitfulness; Disguise; Suspicion.

✵ **POSSIBLE POWERS**
Breaks a hex; Death; Feminine energy; Gross mental and physical disturbances; Protection; Saturn; Sleep; Water element.

✿ **FOLKLORE AND FACTS**
All parts of the Datura plant are extremely poisonous. • Datura has been part of ritualistic coming-of-age ceremonies by indigenous tribes in northern Mexico for thousands of years. Some shamans of northern Mexico and southern Texas, USA use it to cross over the border between life and death on their quest to communicate with deceased spirits. • Depending exactly where it is growing, Datura has the ability to change the size of plant, leaf, and flowers.

No. 207

Daucus carota ☠☗

Queen Anne's Lace

Bee's-nest | Bird's-nest | Bird's-nest Root | Bishop's Flower | Carota | *Carota sylvestris* | Carotte | Carrot | *Caucalis carnosa* | *Caucalis carota* | *Caucalis daucus* | Common Carrot | Crow's-nest | Daucon | *Daucus agrestis* | *Daucus alatus* | *Daucus allionii* | *Daucus australis* | *Daucus blanchei* | *Daucus brevicaulis* | *Daucus dentatus* | *Daucus esculentus* | *Daucus exiguus* | *Daucus foliosus* | *Daucus gibbosus* | *Daucus gingidium* | *Daucus heterophylus* | *Daucus kotovii* | *Daucus levis* | *Daucus marcidus* | *Daucus maritimus* | *Daucus martellii* | *Daucus montanus* | *Daucus neglectus* | *Daucus nudicaulis* | *Daucus officinalis* | *Daucus polygamus* | *Daucus scariosus* | *Daucus sciadophylus* | *Daucus strigosus* | *Daucus sylvestris* | *Daucus vulgaris* | Dawke | Devil's-plague | Fiddle | Gallicam | Garden Carrot | Gelbe Rübe | Gingidium | Gizri | Hill-trot | Laceflower | Mirrot | Möhre | Philtron | *Platyspermum alatum* | Rantipole | Staphylinos | *Tiricta daucoides* | Wild Carrot | Zanahoria

✳ **SYMBOLIC MEANINGS**
Do not refuse me; Fantasy; Haven; Sanctuary.

✵ **POSSIBLE POWERS**
Fertility; Good intentions; Lust; Rebellion.

✿ **FOLKLORE AND FACTS**
Daucus carota appears on a list of aromatic herbal plants grown in a royal Babylonian garden in the eighth century BCE—not as a vegetable, but for its fragrant seeds and leaves. • Brought over to North America with the first colonists, the Queen Anne's Lace plant was eventually developed into the Common Carrot that has been cultivated ever since. • Queen Anne's Lace takes its common name from the flowers resembling the fine lace that was popular during the reign of Queen Anne of England between 1702 and 1707. • Superstition holds that, if someone picks Queen Anne's Lace then brings it into the home, his or her mother will die. • When enacting a spell, Queen Anne's Lace symbolizes good intentions. • If a woman true to herself plants Queen Anne's Lace in her garden, the plant will thrive. • Because of its prolific growth, Queen Anne's Lace is good to use in fertility magic. To encourage fertility that leads to conception, make, then carry or wear a pink sachet using the full flower cluster until pregnancy is confirmed. • Legend has it that while making lace as beautiful as the wild white flowers in the fields at the edge of her garden, Queen Anne pricked her

D

finger. A drop of blood fell on the lacework, which the red stamen of the Queen Anne's Lace flower represents. Because of the red stamen, the plant can substitute for blood in a spell that requires it. • Be aware that there are several deadly wild plants that have very similar flowers to that of Queen Anne's Lace and Carrot, both wild and cultivated. One example is *Conium maculatum*, which is poison hemlock. Another wild plant, *Heracleum mantegazzianum*, which is commonly known as giant hogweed, also has the same type of flower, and is so poisonous you cannot touch it without suffering scaring and blistering burns. For these reasons, for safety's sake, it is always best to avoid them all.

No. 208

Daucus carota subsp. *sativus* 🍞🍴

Carrot

Carota | *Carota sativa* | Carotte | Cantenay Carrot | Common Carrot | Danvers Carrot | Daucon | *Daucus sativus* | Imperator Carrot | Nantes Carrot

✳ SYMBOLIC MEANINGS
Do not refuse me; Fantasy; Good character; Haven; Sanctuary.

🌸 POSSIBLE POWERS
Aphrodisiac; Attracts love; Fertility; Fire element; Lifts worry; Lust; Mars; Masculine energy; Relaxation.

🜨 FOLKLORE AND FACTS
Although a commonly enjoyed root vegetable, the Carrot is very often used as an aromatic culinary herb. The Carrot is one part of the three essential chopped herbs combination that is known as mirepoix, the three fundamental flavors that are at the base of many soups, stews, and sauces. The other two of the three chopped herbs ratio are one part Celery and two parts Onion. • Carrots will have a bitter taste if grown near an apple tree. • There is a superstition that if a woman who is true to herself plants Carrot in her garden, the plant will thrive. • When the Carrot was first cultivated it was only for the fragrant leaves and seeds. • Carrot essential oil is useful in aromatherapy for relieving worry and helping to promote relaxation prior to sleep. • Although the orange-colored root vegetable is iconic and the most commonly available, there are easily obtained Carrot seeds for yellow, white, red, purple, and even black taproots. • Be aware that there are several deadly wild plants that have very similar flowers to that of Carrot, both wild or cultivated, and Queen Anne's Lace. One example of that is *Conium maculatum*, which is poison hemlock. Another wild plant, *Heracleum mantegazzianum*, which is commonly known as

giant hogweed, also has the same type of flower, and is so poisonous you cannot touch it without suffering scarring and blistering burns. For these reasons, for safety's sake, it is always best to avoid them all.

No. 209

Dianthus carthusianorum ☠

Carthusian Pink

Betónica Silvestre | Blutnelke | Blutströpfchen | Carthusian Carnation | *Caryophyllus carthusianorum* | Clavel | Clavel Silvestre | Clavelillo | Clavelina | Clavelina de los Cartujos | *Dianthus ceretanicus* | *Dianthus chloaephyllus* | *Dianthus clavatus* | *Dianthus congestus* | *Dianthus fasciculatus* | *Dianthus ferrugineus* | *Dianthus gramineus* | *Dianthus montanus* | *Dianthus nanus* | *Dianthus rupicola* | *Dianthus semperflorens* | *Dianthus subneglectus* | Donnernelke | Garofanino dei Certosini | Karthäusernelke | Oeillet des Chartreux | St. Hugh's Flower | *Silene carthusianorum* | Steinnelke | *Tunica carthusianorum*

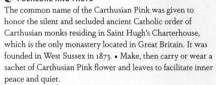

✳ SYMBOLIC MEANINGS
Perfection.

🌸 POSSIBLE POWERS
Quietude.

🜨 FOLKLORE AND FACTS
The common name of the Carthusian Pink was given to honor the silent and secluded ancient Catholic order of Carthusian monks residing in Saint Hugh's Charterhouse, which is the only monastery located in Great Britain. It was founded in West Sussex in 1873. • Make, then carry or wear a sachet of Carthusian Pink flower and leaves to facilitate inner peace and quiet.

No. 210

Dianthus caryophyllus ☠🍞

Carnation

Caryophyllus tunica | Clove Carnation | Clove Pink | *Dianthus acinifolius* | *Dianthus arbuscula* | *Dianthus arrectus* | *Dianthus binatus* | *Dianthus coronarius* | *Dianthus corsicus* | *Dianthus kayserianus* | *Dianthus longicaulis* | *Dianthus miniatus* | *Dianthus morrisii* | *Dianthus moschatus* | *Dianthus multinervis* | Divine Flower | Flower of God | Flower of the Gods | Gillies | Gilliflower | Jove's Flower | Nelka | Pinks | Scaffold Flower | *Silene caryophylla* | Sops-in-Wine | *Tunica caryophyllus* | *Tunica morrisii*

✳ SYMBOLIC MEANINGS
Admiration; Bad luck; Bonds of affection; Deep love; Dignity; Disappointed; Disdain; Distinction; Fascination; Good fortune; Good luck; Gratitude; Health and energy; Heavenly; Joy and commitment; Love; Marriage; Misfortune; Pride; Pride and beauty; Pure love; Self-esteem; Strength; True love; Woman's love.

🎨 COLOR MEANINGS

Green: Gay devotion; Gay love; Gay romance; St. Patrick's Day.

Pink: Always on my mind; Deep love; I'll never forget you; Mother's Day; Mother's love; Sentimental love; Woman's love.

Light red: Admiration.

Red: Admiration; Admiration from afar; Affection; Alas, for my poor heart; Ardent love; Deep romantic love; Desire; Desires that never come to pass; Forlorn; My heart aches for you; Poor heart; Pure love; Pure.

Dark red: Affection; Alas, for my poor heart; Deep love.

Mauve: Dreams of fantasy.

Purple: Antipathy; Capriciousness; Changeability; Changeable; Condolences; Unreliability; Whimsical.

White: Disdain; Faithfulness; Good luck; Innocence; Pure love; Purity; Sweet and lovely; Sweet love.

Yellow: Disappointment; Disdain; Rejection; Unreasonableness; You have disappointed me

Solid: Acceptance; Affirmative; I want to be with you; Yes.

Striped: No; Refusal; Regret that love cannot be reciprocated; Rejection; Sorry, I can't be with you.

🌀 POSSIBLE POWERS

Divination; Fire element; Healing; Jupiter; Luck; Masculine energy; Protection; Strength; Sun.

🜂 FOLKLORE AND FACTS

In ancient Greece, the Carnation was the most loved of all flowers. • A corsage or nosegay made up of a Carnation, a sprig of Rosemary, and a Geranium flower means Love, Fidelity, and Hope. • Fresh Carnation flowers in the room of a convalescing patient will promote strength and energy. • The red Carnation is the state flower of Ohio, USA, and the national flower of Spain. • Wearing a Carnation flower was popular during Elizabethan times because it was believed that the flower helped prevent someone being executed on the scaffold. • The name Carnation is believed to originate from the flesh-like natural shades of the flower petals.

No. 211

Dianthus deltoides 💀🏺

Maiden Pink

Caryophyllus deltoides | Caryophyllus glaucus | Cylichnanthus deltoides | Dianthus albus | Dianthus crenatus | Dianthus endressii | Dianthus glaucus | Dianthus supinus | Dianthus volgensis | Lady's Cushion | Silene deltoides

✴ SYMBOLIC MEANINGS

Vigorous.

🌀 POSSIBLE POWERS

Groundcover; Healing.

🜂 FOLKLORE AND FACTS

Although the profusely blossoming, fragrant Maiden Pink is usually pink, the flowers can be white, pink marked, or spotted with white. • The Maiden Pink is an important herb that has been in regular use in Chinese medicine. • In the wild, should you happen upon a fairy ring or fairy circle of mushrooms and see any flowers growing within it, especially if any one of them is a Maiden Pink, take special care to not step into the ring itself. Take absolute care that none of the flowers within the circle are disturbed in any way, as they are the personal property of a fairy, fairy family, or community of fairies. Do not trespass into that circular space they have claimed to be their own. The fairy circle is a place where fairies carry out their own magical ceremonies and celebrations. The mushrooms are there to provide a seat for the elder fairies and those others who may need to sit and rest. They are also used as circular seating for a group gathering. According to English and Celtic legends, the consequences of disregarding that circle of sacred private fairy property can be dire. One of those unpleasant punishments is being forced to uncontrollably dance until driven to madness by it, or until collapsing to die from complete exhaustion. Whichever comes first. Another threat is to be tempted to step into the ring then coaxed to dance for at least twenty minutes. During that specific span of time, all will seem and look the same, as if the two realms were melted together to be as one. But, shortly thereafter, twenty or so minutes later, upon stepping outside of the circle, it would be discovered that years had actually passed in the original realm of one's own home. It would be stunning when you arrived, since you had disappeared so long ago to have miraculously returned at last. If you were so lucky to get that far with it. So it is that it stands to reason, to simply and safely avoid going too close to any fairy ring. Most especially if even just one Meadow Pink flower is growing within it.

No. 212

Dianthus plumarius 💀🏺

Pink

Caryophyllus plumarius | Common Pink | Cylichnanthus plumarius | Dianthus blandus | Dianthus dubius | Dianthus hortensis | Dianthus odoratus | Dianthus portensis | Garden Pink | Plumaria vulgaris | Silene plumaria | Tunica plumaria | Wild Pink

✴ SYMBOLIC MEANINGS

Ardent love; Aversion; Boldness; Make haste; Pure affection; Pure love.

D

COLOR MEANINGS

Pink: Pure love.
Red: Ardent love; Pure love.
White: Ingeniousness; You are fair; Talent.
Yellow: Disdain; Unreasonableness.
Variegated: Refusal.

POSSIBLE POWERS

Admiration; Affection; Capriciousness; Divination;
Gratitude; Healing; Love; Luck; Passion; Protection;
Strength.

FOLKLORE AND FACTS

Because of their sweet, clove-like fragrance and being so easy
to grow, the Pink is one of the oldest flowers ever cultivated.
• Dried Pink flowers can be added to potpourri mixes and
sachets. • The legend is that serrated pinking shears might
have been named after the Pink's serrated petals' edges. • It
is quite likely that the color pink was named after the Pink.
Not the other way around. • There are churchyards in parts
of Germany and Switzerland where the practice of planting
Pinks on the graves is common. The overall effect of them all
blooming is quite lovely and peaceful.

No. 213

Digitalis lanata 🕱☣

Grecian Foxglove

*Digitalis epiglottidea | Digitalis eriostachya | Digitalis nova |
Digitalis orientalis | Digitalis winterii | Woolly Foxglove*

SYMBOLIC MEANINGS

Adulation; to Heal; to Hurt; Work.

POSSIBLE POWERS

Attracts fairies; Communicate with
fairies; Death; Feminine energy;
Healing; Life; Magic; Protection;
Venus; Water element.

FOLKLORE AND FACTS

As it is with all other foxgloves, every part
of the Grecian Foxglove plant is highly
poisonous. • As with other foxgloves, the
powerful drug digoxin is extracted from Grecian
Foxglove. Digoxin has been used as a modern medicine to
treat heart conditions such as congestive heart failure and
atrial arrhythmia. • In the nineteenth century mental asylums
used Grecian Foxglove's *Digitalis* extracts as a sedative to
control in-patient behavior. • A medical book written in 1785
referred to the potential of *Digitalis* extracted from Grecian
Foxglove as being a possible treatment for the painful swelling
caused by excessive fluid retention. Back then, the condition

was called dropsy. Today it is commonly referred to as edema.
• As with other foxgloves, fairies like to use the Grecian
Foxglove flowers as hats.

No. 214

Digitalis purpurea 🕱☣

Foxglove

Common Foxglove | Cow Flop | Dead Man's Bells | Digitalis | Dog's Finger | Fairy
Fingers | Fairy Petticoats | Fairy Thimbles | Fairy Weed | Fairy-caps |
Fingerhut | Floppy-Dock | Floptop | Folk's Gloves | Fox Bells | Foxes Glofa |
Foxglove | Fox-Glove | Gant de Notre Dame | Goblin's
Gloves | The Great Herb | Lady's Glove | Lion's Mouth |
Lus Na Mbau Side | Lusmore | Our Lady's Glove |
Purple Foxglove | Purpur | Witches' Bells | Witches'
Thimbles | Witch's Bells | Witch's Thimble

SYMBOLIC MEANINGS

Adulation; Deception; I
am ambitious only for
you; Insincerity; Mystery;
Occupation; Stateliness; a Wish;
Work; Youth.

POSSIBLE POWERS

Attracts fairies; Communicate with fairies; Death; Feminine
energy; Fends off evil; Healing; Life; Magic; Protection;
Venus; Water element.

FOLKLORE AND FACTS

Every part of the Foxglove is highly poisonous. • Be sure
to plant Foxglove in a garden that is intended to please the
fairies. • It's well known that the fairies love their favorite
Foxglove blossom hats, but the fairies love Foxglove blossoms
mittens too! • There is a superstition that if you pick a
Foxglove, the fairies will be offended. It is wise to never
vex a fairy. • Medieval witches kept Foxglove growing in
their gardens because each part of the plant was a regular
ingredient in several different spells. • At one time Welsh
housewives would make a black vegetable dye using the
Foxglove leaves. They would use the black dye like ink to
paint crossed lines on the outside of their houses to be a
charm to fend off evil.

D

No. 215

Diospyros ebenum

Ebony

Ceylon Ebony Tree | *Diospyros assimilis* | *Diospyros glaberrima* | *Diospyros laurifolia* | *Diospyros melanoxylon* | *Diospyros membranacea* | *Diospyros timoriana* | India Ebony

✴ **SYMBOLIC MEANINGS**
Blackness; Hypocrisy.

✾ **POSSIBLE POWERS**
Power; Protection; Venus; Water element.

🜊 **FOLKLORE AND FACTS**
A magic wand made from the wood of any *Diospyros* genus tree, such as the Ebony, can provide undiluted pure power. An amulet of it offers powerful protection to the wearer. • Ebony wood is black and it is so dense that it will not float. • It's illegal to cut or sell Ebony wood in Sri Lanka. • Polished Ebony wood will feel cold, while its ability to transmit heat is so high that it can cause the metal containers in which the wood is burnt to melt. • Between the sixteenth and the nineteenth centuries, the best furniture was made of Ceylon Ebony. • Ebony wood has been used to fashion all manners of handles, from those on doors to shanks for cutlery and tableware. • Grand piano keys and fingerboards for string instruments such as guitars, violins, and cellos are frequently made using Ebony wood. • High-quality, lathe-turned pieces such as for chopsticks and chess pieces have been fashioned from beautiful black Ebony wood.

No. 216

Dipteryx odorata ☠

Tonka Bean Plant

Baryosma tongo | *Coumaria Nut* | *Coumarouna odorata* | *Cumaru* | *Heinzia peregrina* | Kumaru | Kumarú | Tonka | Tonqua | Tonquin Bean

✴ **SYMBOLIC MEANINGS**
Wishing for love.

✾ **POSSIBLE POWERS**
Courage; Feminine energy; Love; Money; Venus; Water element; Wishing.

🜊 **FOLKLORE AND FACTS**
Some believe that the Tonka Bean Plant can grant wishes by holding one in the hand while whispering the wish to it. Then, carrying the bean until the wish comes true. Then, burying or stomping on the bean after the wish is granted. • Another method for wishing upon a Tonka Bean is to bury the bean in a fertile, hospitable location and the wish will come true during the time that the plant is growing. • Astonishingly, radio-carbon dating of large Tonka Bean Plant stumps left behind by loggers in the Amazon proved that the Tonka Bean Plant is definitely a species of tree that could live to a great age of over 1,000 years.

No. 217

Dracaena cinnabari

Dragon's Blood

Draco cinnabari | Dragon Blood Tree | Dragon's Blood Tree | Socotra Dragon Tree

✴ **SYMBOLIC MEANINGS**
Dragon's blood.

✾ **POSSIBLE POWERS**
Accidents; Aggression; Anger; Carnal desire; Conflict; Exorcism; Fire element; Love; Lust; Machinery; Mars; Masculine energy; Potency; Power; Protection; Purification; Rock music; Strength; Struggle; War.

🜊 **FOLKLORE AND FACTS**
Being that the resinous sap of the *Dracaena cinnabari* tree is crimson red, it was highly prized in the ancient world as being the actual blood of a dragon. • Dragon's Blood was, and still is, commonly used in ritual magic and alchemy. • *Dracaena cinnabari* Dragon's Blood resin is added to ink to create Dragon's Blood Ink, which is used to officially inscribe magical talismans and seals. • Dragon's Blood is used for religious purposes in American hoodoo, New Orleans voodoo, and African-American folk magic. • Like all good things magical, bottled Dragon's Blood may not be all it's hyped up to be. Take care that a purchase isn't sap from another type of tree, as that is too often the case. • To quiet a boisterous home and impose peace and quiet, put equal parts of powered Dragon's Blood, salt, and sugar in a small, tight-fitting jar and then hide it in the house where it cannot be found.

D

No. 218
Echinacea purpurea 🜍

Echinacea

Black Sampson | Bush's Purple Coneflower | Coneflower | Eastern Purple
Coneflower | *Echinacea angustifolia* | *Echinacea atrorubens* | *Echinacea
laevigata* | *Echinacea pallida* | *Echinacea paradoxa* | *Echinacea sanguinea* |
Echinacea serotina | *Echinacea simulata* | *Echinacea tennesseensis* | Narrow-
Leaved Purple Coneflower | Pale Purple Coneflower | Purple Coneflower | Red
Sunflower | Sacred Plant | Sampson Root | Sanguine Purple Coneflower |
Smooth Coneflower | Smooth Purple Coneflower | Tennessee Coneflower |
Topeka Purple Coneflower | Wavyleaf Purple Coneflower | Yellow Coneflower

✹ SYMBOLIC MEANINGS
Shielded; Spiritual warfare; Spiritual warrior.

⚜ POSSIBLE POWERS
Healing; Health; Immunity; Inner strength; Prosperity;
Spiritual warfare; Strength; Strengthening spells.

☙ FOLKLORE AND FACTS
The Native American people of the North American plains
relied on the medicinal benefits of Echinacea more than any
other herb available to them. • Echinacea growing in the
garden will attract small birds, butterflies, and bees. • Carry
or wear a sachet or amulet of Echinacea to help provide inner
strength during the most difficult of times. • Fill a vase with
Echinacea flowers to pull prosperity into the home, most
especially if the household has been spiritually crippled due
to any sweeping domestic destruction brought on by sudden
poverty. • Add in a bit of Echinacea with the other elements
of a magical charm to increase the charm's ultimate effect.

No. 219
Echium vulgare ☠

Viper's Bugloss

Blueweed | *Echium anglicum* | *Echium elegans* | *Echium
hispanicum* | *Echium lacaitae* | *Echium laetum* | *Echium
monstrosum* | *Echium parviflorum* | *Echium schifferi* | *Echium
spinescens* | *Echium tenoreanum* | *Echium tuberculatum* |
Echium vaudense | *Echium violaceum* | *Echium wierzbickii*

✹ SYMBOLIC MEANINGS
Courage.

⚜ POSSIBLE POWERS
Courageousness; Fends off snakes; Prejudices.

☙ FOLKLORE AND FACTS
In ancient times, Viper's Bugloss was used as a treatment for
snakebite. • Wear a sachet of Viper's Bugloss flower when
walking outdoors for a possible protection against snakes.

• There is a legend that if a song is sung to a Viper's Bugloss
that describes an ailment, the plant will remove the malady
in gratitude for the thoughtful entertainment. It's certainly
worth a try.

No. 220
Elaeis guineensis

Oil Palm

African Oil Palm | *Elaeis dybowskii* | *Elaeis macrophylla* |
Elaeis madagascariensis | *Elaeis melanococca* | Magical Palm
Tree Oil | *Palma oleosa*

✹ SYMBOLIC MEANINGS
Hope.

⚜ POSSIBLE POWERS
Drives off evil spirits; Healing; Hopefulness;
Invulnerability.

☙ FOLKLORE AND FACTS
The Oil Palm fruit seed oil is an integral ingredient in most
West African rituals. • During certain Liberian initiation
rites calling for scarification cutting, the healing oil from Oil
Palm is applied to the initiate's wounds with an owl feather.
• In Liberia, the Mano people have been known to use the
Oil Palm oil to try to awaken someone who was comatose
by massaging the unconscious person's cheeks with the oil in
an attempt to force them to speak. Any other use of the oil in
the same Liberian society might be taboo, because it could
be considered a magical method devised by using witchcraft
as a means to protect against the negative effect of malicious
witchcraft. • Throughout coastal Benin, the oil from the
Oil Palm tree is used daily in personal sacrifices, offerings,
and divinations. • One method of being rid of a problem
has been to use the power of the magical oil to drive off evil
spirits by combining it with something else, like a Kola Nut,
then leaving the nut in the road to be run down by vehicles
throughout the day, thus destroying whatever problem was
attached to it. • The seeds of the Oil Palm tree are regarded
as sacred ritual objects when used for divination involving
an oracle, such as when it was used in secret Benin oracle
divinations from Fa, the Benin god of oracles. • In Malaysia
and Indonesia, Oil Palm tree leaves are sometimes woven
to make nests for chickens and to create effective barriers
to keep chickens confined to a particular area. • In parts
of Benin and Togo, woven shields of Oil Palm leaves were
worn on the arms or around the neck to provide a sense
of invulnerability to the wearer. • In Ghana, the flowering
branches of the Oil Palm tree have been burned by the Akan
people for the smoke to force evil spirits away.

E

No. 221

Elettaria cardamomum 🍴

Cardamom

Alpinia cardamomum | Amomum cardamomum | Amomum ensal | Amomum racemosum | Amomum repens | Amomum uncinatum | Cardamomum elletari | Cardamomum malabaricum | Cardamomum officinale | Cardamomum verum | Cardamon | Ceylon Cardamom | Ela | Elachi | Elaichi | Elakkaai | Elam | Elettaria repens | Green Cardamom | Matonia cardamomum | True Cardamom | Truti | Zingiber minus

🌸 **SYMBOLIC MEANINGS**
Brings peaceful thoughts.

✤ **POSSIBLE POWERS**
Aphrodisiac; Attracts love; Erzulie; Feminine energy; Love; Lust; Peacefulness; Venus; Water element.

☙ **FOLKLORE AND FACTS**
Cardamom is said to be "the Queen of Spice." • Cardamom is one of the oldest spices, having been used since the fourth century BCE. • Cardamom is the third most expensive spice in the world. • The fragrance of Cardamom essential oil in aromatherapy supposedly improves the body's ability to utilize oxygen during exercise. • Use Cardamom to add a delicious flavor to coffee and tea. • Add Cardamom seed powder to warm wine for an aphrodisiac.

No. 222

Elsholtzia ciliata 🌿

Xiang Ru

Aromatic Madder | Crested Late Summer Mint | Elsholtzia cristata | Elsholtzia formosana | Elsholtzia hallasanensis | Elsholtzia interrupta | Elsholtzia patrinii | Elsholtzia pseudocristata | Elsholtzia serotina | Elsholtzia springia | Hyssopus bracteatus | Hyssopus ocymifolius | Kinh Giới | Mentha baikalensis | Mentha cristata | Mentha ovata | Mentha patrinii | Perilla polystachya | Sideritis ciliata | Vietnamese Balm | Vietnamese Lemon Balm | Vietnamese Lemon Mint

🌸 **SYMBOLIC MEANINGS**
Crested

✤ **POSSIBLE POWERS**
Healing; Flavoring; Soothes.

☙ **FOLKLORE AND FACTS**
Xiang Ru has been used in traditional Chinese medicine for thousands of years. • Xiang Ru was first recognized in America in 1889, to later be classified as a noxious weed and actually banned in the state of Connecticut, USA. • Where there are large Vietnamese communities, Xiang Ru citrus-scented mint herb is available fresh in markets nearby.

No. 223

Epilobium angustifolium 🌿

Willow Herb

Asperge | Boisduvalia | Chamaenerion angustifolium | Chamaenerion denticulatum | Chamaenerion spicatum | Chamerion angustifolium | Epilobium antonianum | Epilobium brachycarpum | Epilobium difforme | Epilobium elatum | Epilobium gesneri | Epilobium gracile | Epilobium latifolium | Epilobium leiostylon | Epilobium macrocarpum | Epilobium montanum | Epilobium neriifolium | Epilobium persicifolium | Epilobium rubrum | Epilobium salicifolium | Epilobium spicatum | Epilobium variabile | Epilobium verticillatum | Feuerkraut | Fireweed | French Willow | Great Willowherb | Pyrogennema angustifolium | Rosebay Willowherb | St. Anthony's Laurel | Spiked Willowherb | Spike-Primrose | Willowherb

🌸 **SYMBOLIC MEANINGS**
Beauty returns; Bravery; Constancy; Humanity; Pretension; Production; Renewal.

✤ **POSSIBLE POWERS**
Communication; Courage; Earth element; Feminine energy; Grounding; Potential for newness; Rebirth; Release; Strength; Transformation; Venus; Vitality.

☙ **FOLKLORE AND FACTS**
Willow Herb can establish itself rapidly upon burnt ground, such as at abandoned bomb sites, which are very quickly covered over with this prolific purple-flowering plant as long as there is enough room and light for it to grow. • In London, England, when WWII ended, there was much devastation that the bombings had wrought upon the city. Willow Herbs growing and blooming on the bomb sites became a symbol and visible promise that newness was imminent. That there could be a recovery from much that had been suffered was real enough to believe in.

No. 224
Equisetum arvense ☠♨

Horsetail

Allostelites arvensis | Bottlebrush | Common Horsetail |
Dutch Rushes | Equisetum alpestre | Equisetum
boreale | Equisetum calderi | Equisetum riparium |
Equisetum saxicola | Field Horsetail | Horsetail Rush |
Paddock Pipes | Pewterwort | Rough Horsetail |
Scouring Rush | Shavegrass | Snake Grass

☀ SYMBOLIC MEANINGS
Docility.

♨ POSSIBLE POWERS
Earth element; Feminine energy;
Fertility; Saturn; Snake charming.

☙ FOLKLORE AND FACTS
Horsetail is somewhat peculiar in the herbal world. It is reed-
like, also known as a rush. It reproduces by spores instead
of by seeds. It does not utilize the powers of photosynthesis
at all. And, as the only survivor of the *Equisetaceae* family,
it is closer to the nature of forest plants that grew during the
Paleozoic Era 300 million years ago.

No. 225
Erigeron annuus ♨

Fleabane

Annual Fleabane | Aster annuus | Aster stenactis | Cineraria
corymbosa | Daisy Fleabane | Diplopappus annuus |
Diplopappus dubius | Doronicum bellidiflorum | Eastern Daisy
Fleabane | Erigeron bellidioides | Erigeron diversifolius |
Erigeron heterophyllus | Erigeron strigosus | Phalacroloma
acutifolium | Phalacroloma annuum | Pulicaria annua | Pulicaria
bellidiflora | Stenactis annua | Stenactis dubia

☀ SYMBOLIC MEANINGS
Chastity.

♨ POSSIBLE POWERS
Chastity; Exorcism; Feminine energy;
Protection; Repels evil; Repels fleas;
Venus; Water element.

☙ FOLKLORE AND FACTS
Hang Fleabane over doors to keep evil from entering.
• Make an infusion of rainwater, natural spring water, or
distilled water and Fleabane to sprinkle over the thresholds
of all the doors to keep evil from entering. It is also
supposed to be a way to magically keep fleas from entering
the home.

No. 226
Eriobotrya japonica ♨

Loquat

Crataegus bibas | Mespilus japonica |
Pipa | Pyrus bibas

☀ SYMBOLIC MEANINGS
Gold; Wealth.

♨ POSSIBLE POWERS
Healing; Health; Luck;
Richness; Wealth.

☙ FOLKLORE AND FACTS
The tiny and tartly sweet Loquat fruit has been a trusted
favorite in Chinese gardens, where it is known to be enjoyed
fresh and in teas. • Loquat fruit is also used in delicious
Asian-inspired jams and sweet confections. • The Loquat
is also a favorite in Chinese and home folk medicine, being
a trusted thinner and dissolver of lung phlegm, as well as
an expectorant. • If your birthday should be on a Sunday,
there is a way to increase your good luck on that day that
must be carried out before sunset. First, tuck a Loquat leaf
into your wallet before going to the casino. Preferably go
to the one nearest to where you were when you woke up
that morning. When you enter the casino, look for a game
or a table that shows something gold on it or very near to it.
Intend to gamble no more than your age on that day. Not one
penny more. See what comes of it. It's worth a Loquat leaf,
a reasonable amount of money to wager, some genuine high
hopes, and a birthday wish to find out.

No. 227
Eriodictyon californicum ♨

Yerba Santa

Bear Weed | Consumptive's Weed | Eriodictyon californicum subsp. australe | Eriodictyon
californicum subsp. glutinosum | Eriodictyon californicum var. pubens | Eriodictyon glutinosum |
Eriodictyon glutinosum var. serratum | Gum Bush | Gum Plant | Herbe à Ourse | Herbe des
Montagnes | Herbe Sacrée | Holy Herb | Sacred Herb | Tarweed | Wigandia californica |
Yerba Santa

☀ SYMBOLIC MEANINGS
Holy herb; Spirituality.

♨ POSSIBLE POWERS
Beauty; Business; Expansion; Feminine energy; Healing;
Honor; Inner beauty; Leadership; Politics; Power; Protection;
Psychic power; Public acclaim; Responsibility; Reverance;
Royalty; Spirituality; Success; Wealth.

Carry a sprig of Yerba Santa to attain the inner beauty you desire. • Make a Yerba Santa sachet to wear or to carry while fulfilling your business responsibilities, which will bode positively to your honorable credit.

No. 228

Eruca vesicaria 🏺

Arugula

Aruka | Beharki | Borsmustár | Brassica eruca | Brassica erucoides | Brassica lativalvis | Brassica pinnatifida | Brassica turgida | Brassica uechtritziana | Brassica vesicaria | Crucifera eruca | Eruca | Eruca aurea | Eruca cappadocica | Eruca deserti | Eruca drepanensis | Eruca eruca | Eruca foetida | Eruca glabrescens | Eruca grandiflora | Eruca lanceolata | Eruca latirostris | Eruca longirostris | Eruca longistyla | Eruca oleracea | Eruca orthosepala | Eruca permixta | Eruca pinnatifida | Eruca ruchetta | Eruca sativa | Eruca stenocarpa | Eruca sylvestris | Eruca vesicaria | Euzomum sativum | Euzomum vesicarium | Garden Rocket | Gargeer | Jirjir | Oruga | Raphanus eruca | Raphanus vesicarius | Rauke | Rocket | Rocket Leaf | Rocket Salad | Roka | Rokka | Roquette | Ruca | Ruchetta | Rucola | Rucoli | Rúcula | Rughetta | Rugola | Rugula | Rukola | Sinapis eruca | Velleruca longistyla | Velleruca vesicaria

✷ SYMBOLIC MEANINGS
Rivalry.

✸ POSSIBLE POWERS
Aphrodisiac; Attracts love.

⚑ FOLKLORE AND FACTS
Arugula apparently didn't get the name of Rocket and be considered an effective aphrodisiac for no good reason. • Since back during

the days of ancient Rome, Arugula was considered an effective aphrodisiac for both men and women. It is for that reason alone that during the Middle Ages, Arugula was absolutely forbidden to be grown in any monastery garden. • In 802 CE, the Holy Roman Emperor, Charlemagne, decreed that Arugula could be planted in any garden.

No. 229

Erythroxylum coca ☠🏺

Coca

Cocaine Plant

✷ SYMBOLIC MEANINGS
Endure.

✸ POSSIBLE POWERS
Healing; Pain relief; Stimulation.

⚑ FOLKLORE AND FACTS
The Coca plant was considered to be sacred and divine by the ancient Inca people. • Although Coca has been outlawed in many countries, its daily use has played a role in South American religious rituals and communal life for thousands of years, particularly in the Andes region. • Evidence that there was communal chewing of Coca leaves in Peru dates back to 8,000 years ago. • Coca was utilized in feasts and religious rituals among the ancient Incas, who considered it vital to their culture. • The ancient Incas placed Coca leaves into the mouths of bodies they considered important enough to mummify. • Bags of Coca leaves were tied to the ancient Incan dead. • To this day, Peruvians living at high altitudes depend on chewing Coca to give them the endurance they require to manage whatever daily tasks their lifestyle demands. • Coca leaf tea is commonly offered to visitors to the Andes to help them acclimatize to the high altitude. • The cash potential of Coca and its primary narcotic derivative, cocaine, is at the source of its exploitation via dangerously unsavory international business dealings. • Between 1885 and 1903 the Coca-Cola beverage included Coca plant extract.

No. 230

Eucalyptus globulus ☠🏺

Tasmanian Blue Gum

Blue Gum | Eucalyptus globulus subsp. bicostata | Eucalyptus globulus subsp. globulus | Eucalyptus globulus subsp. maidenii | Eucalyptus globulus subsp. pseudoglobulus | Eukkie | Gum Tree | Maiden's Gum | Southern Blue Gum | Tasmanian Oak | Victorian Blue Gum | Victorian Eurabbie

✷ SYMBOLIC MEANINGS
I watch over you; Loftiness; Prudence; Quiet.

✸ POSSIBLE POWERS
Feminine energy; Healing; Moon; Protection; Purification; Water element.

FOLKLORE AND FACTS

There are 758 species of Eucalyptus, with the most common in California and all around the world being *Eucalyptus globulus*, the Tasmanian Blue Gum. • On November 27, 1962, the Tasmanian Blue Gum became Tasmania's official floral emblem. • To the Aboriginal people of Australia, Eucalyptus is sacred because it represents the division of Earth from Heaven above and the Underworld below. • The roots of all species of Eucalyptus trees excrete a toxic chemical that inhibits the growth of any plants that might be growing close by. • Eucalyptus has been used for magical purposes, medicines, antiseptics, aromatherapy, and some perfume blends for an uncounted length of time. The first mention of there being such a plant known with the properties of the Eucalyptus was not written down until 1642, when Abel Janszoon Tasman journaled his exploration of Tasmania. Later, in 1770, after Captain James Cook arrived in Botany Bay in New South Wales, Australia, he too made a note of Eucalyptus in his journal. • In 1800, the French botanist, Jacques Labillardière, described the Tasmanian Blue Gum specimens he had collected in 1792. He detailed his findings in his book, *Relation du Voyage à la Recherche de la Pérouse*. • Fresh Eucalyptus leaves are the primary diet of the particularly picky Australian marsupial, the iconically adorable koala. • Australia's *Eucalyptus regnans* is the tallest flowering plant in the entire world. • The gigantic Eucalyptus *Eucalyptus regnans* is the second-tallest tree in the world, with *Sequoia sempervirens* of North America being the tallest. • There are claims that the Tasmanian Blue Gum is known to have specimens that have grown between 298 and 331 feet tall, with the capability of growing to be 400 feet tall in the wild, given adequate space, light, and water. • There are some regions in some countries where Eucalyptus trees naturally grow where they were removed as a safety measure. This is due to the volatility of their natural oils making them excessively flammable and a constant fire threat to the safety of the surrounding area. • The steam from a shower can release the benefits of a small dried or fresh nosegay of Eucalyptus hanging in a thin fabric or net pouch from the shower head. • A drop of Eucalyptus essential oil in aromatherapy may help alleviate stress and anxiety when feeling under the weather. • Carry Eucalyptus leaves to maintain good health. • Hang a piece of Eucalyptus over a sick bed to encourage healing.

No. 231

Eupatorium maculatum

Joe Pye Weed

Eupatoriadelphus maculatus | Eupatorium maculatum | Gravelroot | Hempweed | Joe-Pie | Jopi Weed | Trumpet Weed

SYMBOLIC MEANINGS
Privileged; Purple.

POSSIBLE POWERS
Love; Respect.

FOLKLORE AND FACTS
The large, mounding flower heads of Joe Pye Weed have fragrant flowers full of nectar that attract bees and butterflies. In the autumn, the seeds attract songbirds. • To encourage those you meet to look upon you favorably and respectfully, make, then carry or wear a sachet of Joe Pye Weed flower blossoms and leaves.

No. 232

Euphrasia officinalis

Eyebright

Augentrostkrout | Bartsia imbricata | Euphrasia cantalensis | Euphrasia fennic | Euphrasia nebulosa | Euphrasia praerostkoviana | Euphrasia saxatilis | Eye Bright | Herba Euphrasiae | Herbe d'Euphraise | Odontites caucasicus

SYMBOLIC MEANINGS
Good cheer.

POSSIBLE POWERS
Air element; Joy; Masculine energy; Mental clarity or power; Psychic power; Sun.

FOLKLORE AND FACTS
Make, then carry or wear a sachet of Eyebright when it is necessary to see the truth in any matter. • The ancient Greeks were keen to observe birds, such as goldfinches, sparrows, and finches, applying Eyebright leaves to the eyes of their young that were still occupying the nest. • Make, then carry or wear a sachet of Eyebright to increase psychic powers.

No. 233

Fagopyrum esculentum 🜹

Buckwheat

Beechwheat | Bitter Buckwheat | Brank | Common Buckwheat | Fagopyrum cereale | Fagopyrum dryandrii | Fagopyrum emarginatum | Fagopyrum fagopyrum | Fagopyrum polygonum | Fagopyrum sagittatum | Fagopyrum sarracenicum | Fagopyrum vulgare | French Wheat | Helxine fagopyrum | Kunokale carneum | Phegopyrum emarginatum | Phegopyrum esculentum | Polygonum cereale | Polygonum dioicum | Polygonum elegans | Polygonum emarginatum | Polygonum fagopyrum | Polygonum gracile | Polygonum macropterum | Polygonum nepalense | Polygonum pyramidatum

🌸 **SYMBOLIC MEANINGS**
Peace of mind; Psychological peace.

🌐 **POSSIBLE POWERS**
Earth element; Feminine energy; Money; Peacefulness; Protection; Venus.

🜪 **FOLKLORE AND FACTS**
Buckwheat was among the very first seed crops planted in North America by colonists in the 1600s. • Convert Buckwheat grains into a powder, then sprinkle this flour around the entire perimeter outside your house to keep evil from it. • Buckwheat is not related to Wheat. • Because the tiny seeds of Buckwheat are triangular and resemble the Beechnut, it also became known as "Beechwheat." • Buckwheat pollen dating back to 4000 BCE has been found in Japan. • Buckwheat contains something called phototoxic fagopyrins, which can cause an inflamed reaction to skin when exposed to sunlight by susceptible people who consume a lot of Buckwheat sprouts, flowers, or extracts. The reactive condition, known as fagopyrism, can also cause a sensitivity to the cold, as well as numb and tingling hands.

No. 234

Fagus sylvatica 🜹

European Beech

Castanea fagus | Common Beech | Copper Beech | Faggio | Faggots | Fagos | Fagus cochleata | Fagus comptoniifolia | Fagus cuprea | Fagus echinata | Fagus incisa | Fagus laciniata | Fagus purpurea | Fagus sylvestris | Faya | Haya | Hetre | Queen of the Forest

🌸 **SYMBOLIC MEANINGS**
Ancient wisdom; Lovers' tryst; Personal finances.

🌐 **POSSIBLE POWERS**
Creativity; Divination; Feminine energy; Gambling; Happiness; Money; Prosperity; Saturn; Wishing; Writing.

🜪 **FOLKLORE AND FACTS**
The European Beech is considered native to southern England. In northern England the tree is removed from native woods. • Make, then carry or wear an amulet or sachet of Beech tree leaves or a piece of Beech bark to promote and increase creativity. • To make a wish, carve it on a Beechwood stick, then bury it. If the wish is meant to be, it will be. • Make, then wear or carry a Beech sachet to improve your writing skills. • To increase inspiration, put a Beech tree leaf within any two pages of your Book of Shadows. • Considered to be the Queen of the Forest, the Beech tree is the feminine matched to the masculine Oak tree, which is the King of the Forest. • The smoothed wood of the Beech tree was used for writing tablets. • The fruit of the Beech tree is the unusual triangular-shaped Beechnut, which is found inside the splitting burrs that drop from the tree in the autumn. Beechnuts are edible but should not be eaten raw. • European Beech wood is a favorite to use at the bottom of tanks used to ferment beer, and also for smoking meats and some cheeses. • European Beech tree wood is hard with a straight grain that is a favorite for cabinetry, furniture, tool handles, and even musical instruments, such as drums.

No. 235

Ferula assa-foetida 🜳

Asafoetida

Asafetida | Asant | Assyfetida | Devil's Dung | Ferula assafoetida | Ferula foetida | Food of the Gods | Giant Fennel | Hilteet | Hing | Ingu | Ingua | Kaayam | Narthex polakii | Narthex silphium | Perungayam | Peucedanum assa-foetida | Peucedanum hooshee | Scorodosma ass-foetida | Stinking Gum | Ting | Ungoozeh

🌸 **SYMBOLIC MEANINGS**
Chase away evil; Chase away the Devil; Luck; Positive energy; Stink.

🌐 **POSSIBLE POWERS**
Avoiding spirits; Banish negativity; Curses; Evokes demonic forces and binds them; Exorcism; Fire element; Fish bait; Mars; Masculine energy; Protection; Protection from demonic forces or illness; Purification; Repels spirits; Wolf bait.

🜪 **FOLKLORE AND FACTS**
Asafoetida is a very powerful herb that was believed to have the ability to destroy all manifestations of spirits. • Asafoetida didn't get the name Devil's Dung for nothing. It has one of the most horrible odors of all herbs. Merely the scent of it is known to induce vomiting. It is one herb that must be stored in an airtight container so the smell does not permeate herbs and spices near it. • In India, Asafoetida is one of the most

F

commonly used medicinal and culinary herbs. • In India the religious Brahmins and Jains substitute Asafoetida for the herbs Onion and Garlic, which are forbidden by their beliefs.

No. 236
Ferula gummosa 🜹

Galbanum

Ferula erubescens | Ferula galbaniflua | Férule Gommeuse | Gálbano | Galbanum Gum | Galbanum Gum Resin | Galbanum Oleogum Resin | Galbanum Oleoresin | Galbanum Resin | Oléorésine de Galbanum | Peucedanum galbanifluum | Résine de Galbanum

✻ SYMBOLIC MEANING
New beginnings.

🌼 POSSIBLE POWERS
Banishing negative energies; Change; Meditation; Protection; Psychological resolution; Purification; Transformation.

🜨 FOLKLORE AND FACTS
Galbanum's gum-like resin obtained from the stems has been used as a domestic incense and for medicinal purposes since Biblical times. • Galbanum resin is very often used in perfumery as a scent fixative agent. • In aromatherapy, the woody, intensely green, balsamic-like fragrance of Galbanum essential oil is very helpful in facing traumas from the past and working through them, over time, to an acceptably comfortable resolution. • Galbanum was an ingredient frequently used in ancient Egyptian religious ceremonial rituals, as well as for use in embalming.

No. 237
Ficus carica 🜹

Fig

Caprificus insectifera | Caprificus leucocarpa | Caprificus oblongata | Caprificus pedunculata | Caprificus rugosa | Caprificus sphaerocarpa | Chagareltin | Common Fig | Doomoor | Dumur | Fico | Ficus albescens | Ficus burdigalensis | Ficus caprificus | Ficus colchica | Ficus colómbra | Ficus communis | Ficus deliciosa | Ficus dottata | Ficus globosa | Ficus hypoleuca | Ficus hyrcana | Ficus kopetdagensis | Ficus latifolia | Ficus leucocarpa | Ficus macrocarpa | Ficus neapolitana | Ficus pachycarpa | Ficus pedunculata | Ficus polymorpha | Ficus praecox | Ficus rugosa | Ficus silvestris | Mhawa

✻ SYMBOLIC MEANINGS
Argument; Desire; Kiss; a Kiss; Longevity; Long-lived; Prolific.

🌼 POSSIBLE POWERS
Aphrodisiac; Attracts love; Dionysus; Divination; Fertility; Fire element; Isis; Juno; Jupiter; Love; Love charm; Masculine energy.

🜨 FOLKLORE AND FACTS
In the Jewish text known as the Aggadah, the Forbidden Fruit grown on the Tree of Knowledge in the Garden of Eden was a Fig. • Fig leaves from a Fig tree in the Garden of Eden were what Adam and Eve supposedly clothed themselves with in the Christian Bible's Book of Genesis. As a consequence, Fig leaves were often used to modestly cover the genitals of many other nude figures in artworks throughout the ages. • For a yes-or-no divination, write a question on a Fig leaf. If the leaf dries quickly the answer is no. If it dries slowly, then the answer is yes. • For both men and women to increase fertility and also to overcome any sexual impotency or sexual incompetence of any kind, whittle a small phallic carving from *Ficus carica* wood. Then tuck it under the mattress and leave it there. • The Fig tree has been cultivated since ancient times.

No. 238
Ficus religiosa

Bodhi

Bo Tree | Ficus caudata | Ficus peepul | Ficus rhynchophylla | Ficus superstitiosa | Peepal | Pippala | Pipul | Sacred Bo Tree | Sacred Fig | Sacred Tree | Urostigma affin | Urostigma religiosum

✻ SYMBOLIC MEANINGS
Awakening; Bright energy; Enlightenment; Fertility; Good luck; Happiness; Inspiration; Longevity; Meditation; Peace; Prosperity; Religiousness; Remembrance; Sacred tree; Sacredness; Ultimate potential; Wisdom.

🌼 POSSIBLE POWERS
Air element; Enlightenment; Fertility; Jupiter; Masculine energy; Meditation; Protection; Wisdom.

🜨 FOLKLORE AND FACTS
The Bodhi tree is believed by Hindu worshippers to be the mythic World Tree that is the god Brahma, himself, with

F

all other gods and goddesses as divine branches of that tree spread over the Universe. • Some Biblical scholars believe that the Tree of Life was actually a huge *Ficus religiosa*. There is some scripture that could support this idea, being that Adam and Eve were believed to have clothed themselves using Fig leaves. The *Ficus religiosa* tree is a Fig tree. The tree would have most likely been near to the center of the Garden of Eden, which might have been where Adam and Eve went to hide themselves from God's fury towards them after they went near the Tree of the Knowledge of Good and Evil, and actually handled and then ate of the forbidden fruit. A mature *Ficus religiosa* tree is certainly large enough to hide behind. • Legend tells that Siddhartha Gautama was sitting under the celestial blessed Bodhi tree at the time of his enlightening. He sat under it, continually, for six years. A direct descendant of this particular tree is enshrined within the Mahabodhi Temple in Bodh Gaya, India, and is a frequent destination for Buddhist pilgrims. • It takes at least one hundred years to up to 500 years for a Bodhi tree to be fully grown. • To simply look directly upon any Bodhi tree will bring exceptionally good luck and many blessings. • The Bodhi tree has a very distinctive heart-shaped leaf. • Highly detailed religious Buddhist art can be found painted on Bodhi leaves. • A Bodhi leaf is possessed as a sacred treasure. • Walk clockwise around a Bodhi tree several times to make evil flee. • The ritual known as Bodhi Puja means "veneration of the Bodhi tree." It is carried out by chanting a mantra to the tree and by offering the tree gifts such as milk, lamps, incense, cakes, sweets, and water. • Whenever a Bodhi tree dies, for whatever the reason, a sapling grown from another blessed Bodhi will be planted and consecrated to take its place.

No. 239
Ficus sycomorus

Sycamore Fig

Ficus chanas | Ficus cocculifolia | Ficus comorensis | Ficus damarensis | Ficus gnaphalocarpa | Ficus integrifolia | Ficus sakalavarum | Ficus scabra | Fig-Mulberry | Mugumo Tree | Sycomore | Sycomorus antiquorum | Sycomorus gnaphalocarpa | Sycomorus rigida | Sycomorus trachyphyllus

☀ SYMBOLIC MEANINGS
Curiosity; Grief.

⊛ POSSIBLE POWERS
Divination; Fertility; Love; Luck; Prosperity; Protection.

☘ FOLKLORE AND FACTS
Sycamore Fig trees were as sacred to ancient Egyptians and primitive nomadic tribes as the Oak was to ancient Druids.

• The ancient Egyptians considered the Sycamore Fig to be the Tree of Life. • Legend tells that Joseph and Mary rested under the shade of a Sycamore tree when they were fleeing to Egypt from Bethlehem with baby Jesus. • The Sycamore is one of the few trees mentioned in the Bible. It is referred to seven times in the Old Testament, and once in the New Testament. • To protect them, King David commissioned a careful watch over the Sycamore Fig trees. • The Sycamore Fig is a sacred tree to the Kikuyu people who live in the highlands near Mount Kenya. So much so, if a Sycamore Fig tree were to fall, it was a very bad omen requiring rituals to fend off the trouble that was coming. • Some Egyptian mummy caskets were made from Sycamore Fig wood. • In the Christian Bible, Zacchaeus had climbed up a Sycamore Fig to see Jesus over the heads in a crowd. Jesus called for Zacchaeus to climb back down because Jesus wanted to visit his house. The crowd was shocked by that, because they considered Zacchaeus too much of a sinner for someone like Jesus.

No. 240
Foeniculum vulgare ☕🍴

Sweet Fennel

Batatas butatas | Convolvulus batatas | Convolvulus esculentus | Fennel | Finocchio | Florence Fennel | Ipomoea chrysorrhiza | Orion Fennel | Solaris Fennel | Zefa Fino Fennel

☀ SYMBOLIC MEANINGS
Courage; Deceit; Endurance; Flattery; Force; Grief; Merit; Worthy of all praise.

⊛ POSSIBLE POWERS
Charm ingredient; Courage; Dionysus; Exorcism; Fire element; Healing; Immortality; Longevity; Masculine energy; Mercury; Prometheus; Protection; Purification; Repels a ghost; Repels an evil spirit; Strength; Virility.

☘ FOLKLORE AND FACTS
Be very cautious with all the herbs that have a flower that looks like Queen's Anne Lace, such as that of Sweet Fennel as well as poison hemlock or great hogweed. Sweet Fennel seeds will impart a delicious flavor to your food that tastes much like Anise, which happens to taste much like Licorice. Sweet Fennel seeds will also aid with digestion, ease flatulence, and freshen the breath. On the other hand, poison hemlock can kill you and great hogweed will burn your skin so bad from simply touching it, that huge liquid-filled blisters will wheal up then scar after they finally heal. • Sweet

F

Fennel essential oil for aromatherapy can ease worries and impart a feeling of inner calm without sleepiness because it is also uplifting. • Sweet Fennel is in the Nine Sacred Herbs healing charm that was originally written of in the dialect used in Wessex, England, around the tenth century.

No. 241
Forsythia suspensa

Forsythia

Forsythia fortunei | Forsythia sieboldii | Golden-Bell | Liánqiáo | Ligustrum suspensum | Lilac perpensa | Rangium suspensum | Syringa suspensa | Weeping Forsythia

✺ SYMBOLIC MEANING
Joyful anticipation.

✺ POSSIBLE POWERS
Calm energy; Spiritual warmth.

✺ FOLKLORE AND FACTS
The blooming of Forsythia at the start of spring presents the cheerful yellow-flowered branches as a welcome sight to see after a long, cold, gray winter. • To invite and welcome spring right into the home, fill a vase with long, fresh-cut Forsythia branches to bid winter a fond adieu for another year. • Forsythia is one of the fundamental herbs relied upon in Chinese medicine.

No. 242
Fortunella japonica ✹

Kumquat

Atalantia hindsii | Citrus hindsii | Citrus inermis | Citrus madurensis | Citrus margarita | Cumquat | Fortunella bawangica | Fortunella crassifolia | Fortunella hindsii | Fortunella margarita | Fortunella venosa | Gäm-Gwát | Golden Orange | Golden Tangerine | Jangsu Kumquat | Kim Quất | Kinkan | Marumi Kumquat | Meiwa Kumquat | Morgani Kumquat | Muntala | Nagami Kumquat | Round Kumquat | Sclerostylis hindsii | Sclerostylis venosa | Somchid

✺ SYMBOLIC MEANINGS
Fortunate; Good luck; Good luck of the best kind; Prosperity; Prosperous good luck; What glitters may not be gold.

✺ POSSIBLE POWERS
Air element; Prosperity; Sun; Wealth.

✺ FOLKLORE AND FACTS
The Kumquat fruit has an appealing sweet peel with a very tart interior that could imply, "that which appears golden may not truly be gold." • Kumquats are referenced in Imperial Chinese literature dating back to the twelfth century CE. • In 1846 a collector for the London Horticultural Society introduced the Western world to the Kumquat. • Kumquats and Kumquat trees are often given as much-appreciated gifts during the Lunar New Year celebration in Asian countries. • There is an annual Kumquat Festival that is held in Dade City, Florida. However, nearby Saint Joseph, Florida, claims to be the Kumquat capital of the world. • Kumquat trees are very adaptable to bonsai training. • There is one particular variety of the Kumquat that is found growing wild in Southern China. It is also known as the Hong Kong Kumquat, *Citrus hindsii*, or *Fortunella hindsii*. The fruit is not much larger than pea-size, has large seeds with very little pulp, and tastes very bitter. It is grown more as an attractive ornamental tree. But what is most interesting about it is that it is the most primitive of all the Kumquat varieties and the one that is considered the most primitive of all *Citrus*, from which all *Citrus* has evolved.

No. 243
Fragaria vesca ✹

Wild Strawberry

Allstar Strawberry | Alpine Strawberry | Cambridge Favorite Strawberry | Common Strawberry | Dactylophyllum fragaria | European Strawberry | Fragaria abnormis | Fragaria aliena | Fragaria alpina | Fragaria botryformis | Fragaria efflagellis | Fragaria elatior | Fragaria florentina | Fragaria gillmanii | Fragaria hortensis | Fragaria insularis | Fragaria minor | Fragaria multiplex | Fragaria muricata | Fragaria nemoralis | Fragaria nuda | Fragaria portentosa | Fragaria retrorsa | Fragaria roseiflora | Fragaria succulenta | Fragaria sylvestris | Fragaria unifolia | Fragaria vulgaris | Fraises des Bois | Fresa | Fressant | Frutilla | Garden Strawberry | Hapil Strawberry | Honeoye Strawberry | Jewel Strawberry | Jordboer | Ozark Beauty | Pegasus Strawberry | Potentilla vesca | Poziomki | Rhapsody Strawberry | Sparkle | Surecrop Strawberry | Symphony Strawberry | Tchilek | Tristar Strawberry | Wild European Strawberry | Woodland Strawberry | Wood Strawberry

✺ SYMBOLIC MEANINGS
Delight; Fertility; Intoxication; Perfect excellence; Perfect goodness; Perfection; Righteousness.

✺ COMPONENT MEANING
Blossom: Love; Luck.

✺ POSSIBLE POWERS
Aphrodisiac; Attracts love; Feminine energy; Freya; Love; Luck; Lust; Venus; Water element.

F

🌿 FOLKLORE AND FACTS

Carry or wear Wild Strawberry leaves in a sachet for good luck. • The ornamentations at the tops of many medieval church pillars and altars have depictions of a stylized Wild Strawberry carved into them. • To boost fertility, carry or wear a sachet of Wild Strawberry flowers and leaves • At one time, the Wild Strawberry represented the Virgin Mary. • The strawberries sold in the grocery store are all cultivars of the Wild Strawberry. The different cultivars of strawberries are delicious. Some are smallish. Some are very large. Each plant is differentiated by their growing season as being either day-neutral, june-bearing, or everbearing. • There have been archeological indications that Wild Strawberry fruit has been a delight to find since the Stone Age.

No. 244

Fraxinus excelsior ☙

Ash

Ash Tree | Ashe | Asktroed | Beli | Common Ash | European Ash | Fraxinus | Fraxinus americana | Freixo | Jasen

✴ SYMBOLIC MEANINGS

Expansion; Grandeur; Greatness; Growth; Higher perspective.

⚜ POSSIBLE POWERS

Colorize; Fire element; Good singing; Gwydion; Healing; Health; Image magic; Invincibility; Love; Luck; Mars; Masculine energy; Neptune; Poseidon; Prosperity; Protection; Protection from drowning; Sea magic; Sea ritual; Sea spells; Sun; Thor; Uranus; Woden.

🌿 FOLKLORE AND FACTS

The Ash can grow large and tall with a wide diameter. These trees supply strong wood used in woodworking for furniture, tool handles, and sports equipment such as tennis rackets and cue sticks. • The Ash is also a tree that was revered by the ancient Greeks, Romans, and Germanic people. The ancient Greeks once believed that the clouds were the canopy of a great mythical Ash tree that was the father of all the world. Oak trees were considered the first mothers. • In Norse mythology a mythical Ash tree is believed to be the greatest and best of all trees. It is called "Yggdrasil" and is considered to be the actual center of the world, with its roots in the Underworld watered by wisdom and faith. Its trunk supports the Earth. Its leafy canopy is touching the arch of Heaven. All that transpires on the Ash Yggdrasil is believed to affect all life, to everyone and everything, everywhere on the Earth. All that is what, where, when, why, or who can be identified by something that transpired on the Yggdrasil tree. It is an interesting legend that is well worth reading, about how Norse mythology all connects back to Yggdrasil in some way, if even remotely. • If going out to sea, for protection against drowning, carry a solar cross that has been carved from Ash wood. The solar cross symbol is a cross within a circle. • An Ash-wood staff placed over doors and windows is used as protection against sorcery. • Burn a Yule log of Ash wood for prosperity. • Carry Ash leaves to gain love from the opposite sex. • Placing Ash leaves under a pillow was believed to promote prophetic dreams. • Scatter Ash leaves in all four directions near the home to protect the house and the entire area around it. • Fresh Ash leaves in a bowl of clean water left beside the bed overnight is supposedly a preventative against illness. Empty it out in the morning. • It is believed by some that snakes are not particularly fond of Ash trees and Ash wood, in general. • If you wish for your baby to grow up to sing well, bury the child's first fingernail clippings at the base of an Ash tree. • Carry an Ash leaf when you travel for protection on your journey. • A rich olive-colored dye for wool and other fibers can be made from Fraxinus excelsior bark and leaves. • A Fraxinus excelsior Ash tree can be easily propagated from a seed.

No. 245

Fucus vesiculosus

Bladderwrack

Black Tang | Black Tany | Bladder Fucus | Bladder Wrack | Cut Weed | Cutweed | Dyers Fucus | Red Fucus | Rock Wrack | Rockweed | Sea Oak | Sea Spirit

✴ SYMBOLIC MEANING

Call on the winds over the sea for help.

⚜ POSSIBLE POWERS

Feminine energy; Money; Moon; Protection; Psychic power; Water element.

🌿 FOLKLORE AND FACTS

Bladderwrack is a seaweed most commonly found on the shores of the British Isles. It is also found on the beaches of the Western Baltic Sea and the North Sea, as well as the Atlantic and Pacific Oceans. • Bladderwrack was the original source of therapeutic iodine, discovered in 1811 by French chemist Bernard Courtois. • Carry a Bladderwrack amulet when traveling on or over the sea as protection for the sea-going traveler.

F

No. 246
Galium aparine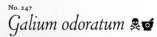
Cleavers
Aparine hispida | Aparine vulgaris | Asperula aparine | Asterophyllum aparine | Bobby Buttons | Catchweed | Catchweed Bedstraw | Clivers | Coachweed | Crucianella purpurea | Galion aparinum | Galium aculeatissimum | Galium adhaerens | Galium asperum | Galium charoides | Galium chilense | Galium chonosense | Galium hispidum | Galium horridum | Galium lappaceum | Galium larecajense | Galium parviflorum | Galium pseudoaparine | Galium segetum | Galium tenerrimum | Galium uliginosum | Galium uncinatum | Goosegrass | Grip Grass | Hedgeheriff | Hitchhikers | Robin-Run-the-Hedge | Rubia aparine | Sticklejack | Sticky Grass | Sticky Willow | Stickybob | Stickybud | Stickyjack | Stickyleaf | Stickyweed | Stickywilly | Whippysticks

☀ SYMBOLIC MEANINGS
Clinging; Do not let go; Hold on tight; Sticky.

🌱 COMPONENT MEANING
Burr: Cling to me.

⚜ POSSIBLE POWERS
Binding; Commitment; Feminine energy; Fire element; Protection; Relationships; Saturn; Tenacity.

🜚 FOLKLORE AND FACTS
The Cleavers' seed has fine, hook-like hairs all around it that make it possible to firmly attach to clothing and animal fur. • A love spell can be cast upon a Cleaver seed before attaching it to the object of love to bind its power to him or her. But be careful what and who is longingly wished for, as that may not be the right person for the long term.

No. 247
Galium odoratum ☠🜚
Sweet Woodruff
Asperula eugeniae | Asperula matrisylva | Asperula odora | Asperula odorata | Asterophyllum asperula | Asterophyllum sylvaticum | Chlorostemma odoratum | Herb Walter | Master of the Woods | Waldmeister | Wild Baby's Breath | Wood Rove | Woodruff | Wuderove

☀ SYMBOLIC MEANING
Humility.

⚜ POSSIBLE POWERS
Fire element; Mars; Masculine energy; Money; Protection; Victory.

🜚 FOLKLORE AND FACTS
Carry or wear a sachet of Sweet Woodruff to attract money. • Carry or wear a sachet of Sweet Woodruff as protection against harm. • Carry a sprig of Sweet Woodruff to be victorious in sports or battles of any kind. • The toxicity of Sweet Woodruff is due to the presence of coumarin that intensifies as the herb dries. Germany disallows its extract to be used in sweet confections, since children would be the most vulnerable due to their smaller size. It is still permitted in foods and beverages intended for consumption by adults. • Sweet Woodruff potpourri can be used as a moth repellent.

No. 248
Galium verum 🜚
Lady's Bedstraw
Asterophyllum galium | Bedstraw | Cheese Bedstraw | Cheese Rennet | Cudweed | Fragrant Bedstraw | Frigg's Grass | Galium floridum | Gul Snerre | Maid's Hair | Our Lady's Bedstraw | Petty Mugget | Renning | Rubia vera | Sweet-Scented Bedstraw | Yellow Bedstraw

☀ SYMBOLIC MEANINGS
Comfort; Love; Rejoicing; Rudeness; Sweet dreams.

⚜ POSSIBLE POWERS
Colorize; Feminine energy; Love; Sun; Venus; Water element.

🜚 FOLKLORE AND FACTS
The legend is that Lady's Bedstraw was the hay used in the makeshift cradle where Jesus was placed as a newborn in the Bethlehem manger. • In days of old, dried Lady's Bedstraw was often used as a mattress stuffing because it was thought to be a fairly effective flea killer. • Wear or carry a sprig of Lady's Bedstraw to attract love. • Lady's Bedstraw is called Sânziana in Romania because it is closely connected to the gentle and good Sânziene Fairies in their folk tales. The fairies are annually celebrated with a midsummer Sânziene festival each June 24th that also celebrates the Sun. This annual celebration is also called Dragaica. It is believed that the eve of Sânziene is the strongest night of the year for magical love spells. It is also the day when the herb is magically transformed into being medicinal. On the day after, the Lady's Bedstraw plants stop growing. On Sânziene Eve, the most beautiful girls in the village wear white and

𝒢

spend the entire day picking flowers. One of their choices absolutely must be Lady's Bedstraw, as those harvested on this day are extremely magical. That night they put flowers under their pillows with the hope of dreaming of their future lover. On Sânziene Eve night huge bonfires are ignited to scare away all evil spirits. The young men jump over the hot coals left by the bonfires to purify themselves and, more likely, to bravely show off, especially to the young ladies. On Sânziene Day the girls use the flowers to decorate their hair with floral wreaths they have fashioned themselves, which are later thrown over the houses. If the floral crown lands on a roof, it is decreed that the harvest will be great, wealth will benefit the household, and the young lady will be married within a year. • Lady's Bedstraw can be used to make a red vegetable dye for fabric.

No. 249
Gardenia jasminoides ☕
Gardenia
Cape Jasmine | Cape Jessamine | Common Gardenia | *Gardenia angustifolia* | *Gardenia augusta* | *Gardenia florida* | *Gardenia grandiflora* | *Gardenia longisepala* | *Gardenia pictorum* | *Gardenia radicans* | *Genipa florida* | *Genipa grandiflora* | *Genipa radicans* | *Jasminum capense* | Moon's Tears | *Mussaenda chinensis* | *Warneria augusta*

✺ SYMBOLIC MEANINGS
Ecstasy; Emotional support; Exhilarating emotions; Good luck; Healing; I am too happy; I love you in secret; Joy; Love; Peace; Purification; Purity; Refinement; Secret love; Spirituality; Sweet love; Transient joy; Transport; Transport of joy; You're lovely.

⚗ POSSIBLE POWERS
Aphrodisiac; Attracts love; Feminine energy; Healing; Love; Moon; Peace; Seduction; Spirituality; Water element.

☕ FOLKLORE AND FACTS
The exotic perfume of the Gardenia flower is irresistibly intoxicating and has an extremely high spiritual vibration. Used as aromatherapy, the fragrance of just one freshly picked Gardenia blossom floating in a bowl of fresh water will promote a sense of extreme inner peacefulness and increased spirituality.
• There is a legend that the Gardenia was a gift from a sea goddess to her earthly lover. • The fragrance of the Gardenia is believed to have the ability to attract angels that offer spiritual guidance. • It was once believed that engaged young women who died before they were married are very upset, viciously lusty, wandering ghosts looking for love,

leaving the scent of Gardenia behind wherever they go. They even seduce living men who would lust after the ghosts in their sleep. The men would wake up exhausted and sore with the vague recollection of a very weird dream. Most difficult for them to make sense of was a lingering scent of Gardenia in their bed.

No. 250
Gaultheria procumbens ☕
American Wintergreen
American Mountain Tea | Boxberry | *Brossaea procumbens* | Canada Tea | Canterberry | Checkerberry | Chickenberry | Creeping Wintergreen | Deerberry | Drunkards | Eastern Teaberry | *Gaultheria humilis* | *Gaultheria repens* | *Gautiera procumbens* | Gingerberry | Ground Berry | Ground Tea | Groundberry | Grouseberry | Hill Berry | Hillberry | Mountain Tea | One-Berry | Procalm | Red Polom | Spice Berry | Spicy Wintergreen | Spring Wintergreen | Teaberry | Wax Custer | Wintergreen | Youngsters

✺ SYMBOLIC MEANINGS
Harmony.

⚗ POSSIBLE POWERS
Breaks a hex; Feminine energy; Harmony; Healing; Moon; Protection; Water element.

☕ FOLKLORE AND FACTS
It is believed that a sprig of American Wintergreen tucked under a child's mattress offers protection and a life of good fortune. • American Wintergreen is the state herb of Maine, USA. • Sprinkle an infusion of American Wintergreen and rainwater, natural spring water, or distilled water to remove any hex or curse in the home. • American Wintergreen can inhibit blood clotting. • American Wintergreen essential oil is useful in aromatherapy to uplift the spirit and promote positive thinking. • Teaberry extract is used to flavor chewing gum, candy, and medicine.

G

No. 251

Gentiana cruciata 🜮

Gentian

Bitter Root | Bitterroot | Cross Gentian | Hochwurzel | Star Gentian | *Tretorhiza cruciata*

✳ **SYMBOLIC MEANINGS**

Loveliness.

💮 **POSSIBLE POWERS**

Applying knowledge;
Astral plane; Breaks a
hex; Controlling lower
principles; Finding lost
objects; Fire element; Love;
Luck; Mars; Masculine
energy; Overcoming evil;
Power; Regeneration;
Removing depression;
Sensuality; Truth; Uncovering secrets; Victory.

🜊 **FOLKLORE AND FACTS**

A stylized Gentian flower is the emblem of the Minamoto
clan, which was one of the four great and powerful Japanese
clans that dominated Japanese politics from 794 to 1185 CE.
• When seeking something that is lost and needs to be found,
carry or wear a sachet of Gentian to help find it. • When
trying to uncover a secret, carry or wear a sachet of Gentian
to help reveal the truth. • The state flower of Montana, USA, is
Bitterroot. • Make, then wear a Gentian sachet as a talisman
to help connect with the higher self to seek wisdom with
regard to sorting and countering the negative effect of an evil
spell that was intended to create a confusing reality.

No. 252

Gentiana lutea 🜮

Yellow Gentian

Asterias hybrida | *Asterias lutea* | *Coilantha biloba* | *Gentiana major* | *Gentianusa lutea* | Great
Yellow Gentian | *Lexipyretum luteum* | *Swertia lutea* | Yellow Mountain Gentian

✳ **SYMBOLIC MEANINGS**

Loveliness.

💮 **POSSIBLE POWERS**

Applying knowledge; Astral plane; Breaks a hex; Controlling
lower principles; Finding lost objects; Love; Overcoming
evil; Power; Regeneration; Removing depression; Sensuality;
Uncovering secrets; Victory.

🜊 **FOLKLORE AND FACTS**

Make and wear a Yellow Gentian sachet of a flower and a
leaf as a talisman to help connect with the higher self, in
order to seek wisdom with regard to sorting and countering
the negative effect of an evil spell that intended to create a
confusing reality. • When seeking something that was lost
and needs to be found, carry or wear a sachet of a Yellow
Gentian flower and leaf to help find it. • When trying to
uncover a secret, carry or wear a sachet of a Yellow Gentian
flower and leaf to help reveal the truth. • Yellow Gentian
requires ten years to mature before flowering. If the plant is
permitted to grow, it will do so for up to fifty years. However,
since wild-crafters are seeking the root, that is quite unlikely
to occur. As a consequence of over-harvesting, *Gentiana
lutea* is considered to be a threatened species, and wild
harvesting is prohibited.

No. 253

Geranium macrorrhizum 🜮

Bigroot Geranium

Bulgarian Geranium | *Geranium balkanum* | *Geranium lugubre* | *Robertium macrorrhizum* |
Rock Crane's-Bill

✳ **SYMBOLIC MEANINGS**

Health; Meeting; Unexpected meeting.

💮 **POSSIBLE POWERS**

Aphrodisiac; Attracts love; Feminine energy; Health;
Sensuality; Stimulation; Uplifting of the spirit; Venus; Water
element.

🜊 **FOLKLORE AND FACTS**

Bigroot Geranium essential oil is occasionally used in
aromatherapy. In perfume making it is widely used as a
fragrance fixative.

No. 254

Geranium maculatum 🜮

Wild Geranium

Alum Bloom | Alum Root | Crowbill |
Crowfoot | Crows-bill | Geranium |
Geranium album | *Geranium ludovicianum* |
Old Maid's Nightcap | Spotted Cranesbill

✳ **SYMBOLIC MEANINGS**

Envy; Gentility; Steadfast piety.

💮 **POSSIBLE POWERS**

Balances body or mind; Encourages conception; Feminine
energy; Happiness; Lifts the spirits; Overcome negative
attitudes or thoughts; Protection; Repels insects; Repels
unwanted love spells; Venus; Water element.

G

FOLKLORE AND FACTS

Wild Geranium petals and a leaf in a sachet can be made to be carried or worn when trying to become pregnant. • A bit of Wild Geranium root in a sachet to carry or wear can attract prosperity and happiness.

No. 255

Geranium pratense

Meadow Geranium

Geranium acknerianum | *Geranium aconitifolium* | *Geranium alpinum* | *Geranium batrachioides* | *Geranium caeruleum* | *Geranium coelestinum* | *Geranium kemulariae* | *Geranium mariae* | *Geranium napellifolium* | *Geranium neapolitanum* | *Geranium pinetophilum* | *Geranium rovirae* | *Geranium valde-pilosum* | Hardy Geranium | Meadow Crane's-Bill | Meadow Cranesbill | True Geranium

SYMBOLIC MEANINGS

Availability; Constancy; Deceit; Envy; Fertility; Folly; Friendship; Frustrations passing away; Gentility; Health; Joy; Preference; Protection; Returning joy; Stupidity; True friend.

POSSIBLE POWERS

Camaraderie; Coming together; Feminine energy; Healing; Love; Peace; Spirituality; Unity; Venus; Water element.

FOLKLORE AND FACTS

There are over 400 species of Cranesbill true *Geranium* plants. • There is a superstition that snakes and flies will not go near Cranesbill plants that have white flowers. • The Cranesbill may have the ability to bring the heart, mind, body, and spirit together to accomplish a greater purpose of goodness for self and others.

No. 256

Geranium robertianum

Herb Robert

Crow's Foot | Death-Come-Quickly | Fox Geranium | *Geranium eriophorum* | *Geranium foetidum* | *Geranium graveolens* | *Geranium inodorum* | *Geranium lebelii* | *Geranium lindleyanum* | *Geranium modestum* | *Geranium mosquense* | *Geranium neapolitanum* | *Geranium palmatisectum* | *Geranium pedunculatum* | *Geranium rubellum* | *Geranium scopulicola* | Jack Horner | Red Robert | Red Robin | *Robertiella robertianum* | *Robertium modestum* | *Robertium vulgare* | Roberts Geranium | Squinter Pip | Stinking Bob | Storksbill

SYMBOLIC MEANINGS

Amusement; Fun; Lovable; Power; Protector; Tease.

POSSIBLE POWERS

Arts; Beauty; Feminine energy; Love; Mirth; Power; Prankish; Protection; Venus; Water element.

FOLKLORE AND FACTS

Valued when discovered to be a miracle plant in the Pacific Northwest, Herb Robert has the powers of healing, magic, and comfort by also being an excellent mosquito repellent. • Herb Robert was an instrumental herbal treatment for cattle suffering from foot-and-mouth disease. • Herb Robert grows extremely well under power-line corridors, where the plant has the incredible power to be able to remove radiation from the soil and actually break it down. • As the Herb Robert plant ages, it will turn shades of red, hence the common names Red Robin and Red Robert • Mischievous and sometimes rudely prankish, the vivacious mythological fairy, Puck (also known as Robin Goodfellow), immortalized by William Shakespeare in his play *A Midsummer's Night Dream*, will not allow the plant Herb Robert to be taken into a home without first scaring the wits out of someone who might consider doing it. He has threatened certain death would come of it, so most people will wisely not. So, again, just to be on the safe side, don't vex any fairy, even if they are mythological! Fairies can react with such objection that they can make themselves be presentably unpleasant, to say the least. • Herb Robert will happily grow wherever it chooses. • Crushed Herb Robert leaves have the fragrance of burning tires. • Discovering Herb Robert growing on your property is lucky. Leave it there, undisturbed, nurturing it, and permitting it to spread as it will. It is good for the soil and the area around it.

No. 257

Geum urbanum

Wood Avens

Avens | Bennet | *Bernoullia media* | *Blessed Herb* | *Caryophyllata officinalis* | *Caryophyllata urbana* | *Caryophyllata vulgaris* | Clove Root | Cloveroot | *Geum ambiguum* | *Geum caryophyllata* | *Geum caucasicum* | *Geum hederifolium* | *Geum hirtum* | *Geum hyrcanum* | *Geum ibericum* | *Geum klettianum* | *Geum pseudomolle* | *Geum robustum* | *Geum roylei* | *Geum salvatoris* | *Geum sordidum* | *Geum umbrosum* | *Geum vicanum* | *Geum vidalii* | *Geum willdenowii* | Golden Star | Goldy Star | Harefoot | Herb Bennet | Minart | Minarta | Pesleporis | St. Benedict's Herb | Star of the Earth | *Streptilon odoratum* | Way Bennet | Yellow Avens

✳ SYMBOLIC MEANINGS

Work as a prayer.

🌀 POSSIBLE POWERS

Drives away an evil spirit; Exorcism; Fire element; Jupiter; Love; Masculine energy; Meaningful work; Purification.

✿ FOLKLORE AND FACTS

If worn as an amulet, Wood Avens protects against attacks by wild beasts, dogs, and venomous snakes. • In the past, this herb has been used for medicinal purposes. • The seed of the Wood Avens is distributed by the burred fruits that attach to the fur of small animals that brush up to it. • Since the leaves grow in threes and the petals in fives, the Wood Avens has been associated with Christianity's Holy Trinity and the five wounds that Jesus suffered during his crucifixion. • The Wood Avens root has been used to flavor ale and soup.

No. 258

Ginkgo biloba ☠☙

Ginkgo

Ginkgo macrophylla | Ginnan | Icho | In Xing | Maidenhair Tree | *Pterophyllus salisburiensis* | *Salisburia adiantifolia* | *Salisburia biloba* | *Salisburia ginkgo* | *Salisburia macrophylla* | Tree of Life

✳ SYMBOLIC MEANINGS

Age; Old age; Remembering; Survival; Thoughtfulness; True Tree of Life.

🌀 POSSIBLE POWERS

Aphrodisiac; Attracts love; Fertility; Healing; Intense concentration; Longevity; Love; Mental acuity; Survival under the most extreme of all circumstances.

✿ FOLKLORE AND FACTS

Ginkgo biloba is a large tree that can normally grow to be 115 feet tall. Some trees in China are over 165 feet tall. • *Ginkgo biloba* is considered a living fossil because it is the only member of its genus, which is also the only genus in its family, which is also the only family in its order, which is also the only order in its subclass. • Gingko dates from before the time that dinosaurs roamed the Earth. • Ginkgo leaf fossils are very commonly found in the rocks that date back to both the Jurassic and Cretaceous Eras. • Wild *Ginkgo biloba* is seriously rated as critically endangered, with only a few hundred trees remaining due to other species of trees planted much too close for use as timber, which forces competition for nutrients, water, and light. • Ginkgo has been used in Chinese medicine since the eleventh century CE.

G

No. 259

Glechoma hederacea ☠☢

Ground Ivy

Alehoof | *Calamintha hederacea* | Cat's Foot | Catsfoot | *Chamaecissos hederaceus* | *Chamaeclema hederacea* | Creeping Charley | Creeping Charlie | Creeping Jenny | Field Balm | Gill-Creep-by-Gound | Gill-Go-by-Ground | Gill-over-the-Ground | *Glechoma borealis* | *Glechoma bulgarica* | *Glechoma heterophylla* | *Glechoma intermedia* | *Glechoma lobulata* | *Glechoma longicaulis* | *Glechoma magna* | *Glechoma micrantha* | *Glechoma repens* | *Glechoma rigida* | *Glechoma rotundifolia* | *Glechoma serbica* | *Glechonion hederaceum* | Haymaids | *Hedera terrestris* | Hedgemaids | Lizzy-Run-up-the-Hedge | *Nepeta glechoma* | *Nepeta hederacea* | *Nepeta rigida* | Robin-Run-in-the-Hedge | Run-Away-Robin | Runaway Robin | Tunhoof | Turn-Hoof

☀ SYMBOLIC MEANINGS
Assertiveness; Attachment; Persistence.

⚘ POSSIBLE POWERS
Divination; Enduring friendship; Loving friendship.

☘ FOLKLORE AND FACTS
To find out who is working against you using negative magic, starting on a Tuesday encircle a yellow candle with Ground Ivy and then light the candle. The knowledge of who it is will come to mind. • European settlers eventually and successfully carried seeds and cuttings of Ground Ivy all around the world. • There is an unproven belief that by holding a nosegay of self-gathered sprigs of Rue, Broom, Maidenhair Fern, Agrimony, and Ground Ivy, one can gain profound intuition of who is and who is not a practicing witch. • There was a time when Ground Ivy was planted on a grave as a symbol of love and friendship.

No. 260

Glycine max ☠☢

Soybean

Cadelium nigrum | Cadelium viride | Daizu | *Glycine hispida* | Kadëlë | *Phaseolus max* | *Phaseolus sordidus* | Shōyu | Sihyáuh | *Soja angustifolia* | *Soja hispida* | *Soja japonica* | *Soja max* | *Soja viridis*'| *Sooja japonica* | Soy | Soya | Soya Bean | Tempeh

☀ SYMBOLIC MEANINGS
Salty sweetness.

⚘ POSSIBLE POWERS
Earth element; Moon; Sustain.

☘ FOLKLORE AND FACTS
The Soybean is considered to be a sacred plant in China, where it has been cultivated for more than 5,000 years. • The first Soybean crop that was grown in North America was on Skidaway Island, Georgia, in 1765. • Raw Soybeans are toxic and must be cooked with wet heat to make them safe to consume. • Soybeans are sometimes referred to as being magic beans due to the diversity of their use, which includes being a very popular edible legume known as edamame. Soybeans are also diverse as unfermented derivative foods, such as tofu and soy milk, and fermented foods, such as soy sauce and tempeh. In 1908 bottled soy sauce production began in Hawaii, USA. • Soybean oil is used in the manufacture of some cleaning products, for illumination as candles, has been utilized as a biodiesel fuel, as well as enlisted for use as an effective solvent to help remove industrial oil spills from shorelines.

No. 261

Glycyrrhiza glabra ☢🍴

Licorice

Gancao | *Glycyrrhiza alalensis* | *Glycyrrhiza alaschanica* | *Glycyrrhiza brachycarpa* | *Glycyrrhiza echinata* | *Glycyrrhiza glandulifera* | *Glycyrrhiza hirsuta* | *Glycyrrhiza laevis* | *Glycyrrhiza michajloviana* | *Glycyrrhiza nadezhinae* | *Glycyrrhiza officinalis* | *Glycyrrhiza pallida* | *Glycyrrhiza violacea* | *Glycyrrhiza vulgaris* | Lacris | Licourice | *Liquiritia officinalis* | *Liquiritia officinarum* | Liquorice | Lycorys | Mulaithi | Reglisse | Sweet Root | Sweet Wood | Zoethout

G

Domination; Love; Rejuvenation.

🌹 POSSIBLE POWERS
Business transactions; Caution; Cleverness; Communication; Creativity; Faith; Feminine energy; Fidelity; Illumination; Initiation; Intelligence; Learning; Love; Lust; Memory; Prudence; Science; Self-preservation; Sound judgment; Thievery; Venus; Water element; Wisdom.

🜍 FOLKLORE AND FACTS
Carry a piece of Licorice root to attract love. • A long, dried, woody stem of the Licorice plant is believed to make a good magic wand. • Licorice is used in both Chinese and Ayurvedic medicine • In the Netherlands, as in most other countries, Licorice drops and other forms of licorice-flavored candy are a favorite sweet confection. Licorice has been deemed edible by the United States Food and Drug Administration as long as it is not excessively consumed. Pregnant women should avoid it. • In Italy and France, Licorice is a popular breath freshener. • In Italy, pure Licorice extract is used to make a confection that is sold in small pieces, and also to flavor liqueurs.

No. 262

Gossypium barbadense 🐛⚗️
Cotton
Cotton Root | Cotton Shrub | Egyptian Cotton | Extra Long Staple Cotton | Gossypium acuminatum | Gossypium auritum | Gossypium calycotum | Gossypium cambayense | Gossypium evertum | Gossypium fruticulosum | Gossypium fuscum | Gossypium glabrum | Gossypium guyanense | Gossypium isabelum | Gossypium javanicum | Gossypium jumelianum | Gossypium maritimum | Gossypium microcarpum | Gossypium multiglandulosum | Gossypium nankin | Gossypium nigrum | Gossypium niveum | Gossypium pallens | Gossypium pedatum | Gossypium perenne | Gossypium peruvianum | Gossypium pubescens | Gossypium quinacre | Gossypium racemosum | Gossypium religiosum | Gossypium rohrianum | Gossypium rupestre | Gossypium sarmentosum | Gossypium speciosum | Gossypium suffruticosum | Gossypium teleium | Gossypium tenax | Gossypium trichospermum | Gossypium versicolor | Gossypium virens | Gossypium virgatum | Gossypium vitifolium | Hibiscus barbadensis | Hibiscus fruticulosus | Hibiscus racemosus | Lint Plant | Neogossypium barbadense | Pima Cotton | Sea Island Cotton | Upland Cotton

✻ SYMBOLIC MEANINGS
I feel my obligations; Obligations.

🌹 POSSIBLE POWERS
Earth element; Feminine energy; Fishing; Fulfill obligations; Healing; Luck; Moon; Protection; Rain.

🜍 FOLKLORE AND FACTS
The *Gossypium barbadense* Cotton has been cultivated since ancient times. It is now grown in most countries around the world. • In the 1800s, a long-fiber form was developed that made the species the most desirable; it is used for spinning threads for weaving cloth that is destined for fine-quality linens of all types. • As a member of the *Malvaceae* family, Cotton flowers are yellow and look very much like those of the *Hibiscus* genus. • Cotton that is either scattered or planted on your property will keep ghosts away. • Cotton cloth should be your first choice when you require cloth for magical purposes. • Burning a piece of Cotton supposedly will bring rain. • A piece of Cotton in the sugar bowl brings good luck. • Throw Cotton over your right shoulder at sunrise to bring good luck to that day. • Little balls of Cotton that have been soaked in white vinegar and placed on all the windowsills will keep evil from entering. • Cottonseed oil is higher in fat than other vegetable oils, which has made it useful in soap and candle making, as well as laundry detergents, insecticides, and even rubber. Cottonseed oil can be extracted from *Gossypium barbadense*, however, other species are preferred because they will produce significantly more of it.

No. 263

Grindelia ciliata ⚗️
Goldenweed
Aster ciliatus | Donia ciliata | Grindelia | Grindelia papposa | Gumweed | Haplopappus ciliatus | Prionopsis ciliata | Spanish Gold | Waxed Goldenweed

✻ SYMBOLIC MEANINGS
Sticky grin.

🌹 POSSIBLE POWERS
Healing; Stickiness.

🜍 FOLKLORE AND FACTS
All parts of the Goldenweed plant are sticky to the touch. • Some Native American tribes used Goldenweed to treat poison ivy rash and other skin conditions. The Crow and the Pawnee people used Goldenweed medicinally as tea, and also as poultices used to heal sore raw skin and saddle sores. • Some Native Americans used Goldenweed flowers as a chewing gum.

No. 264

Haematoxylum campechianum ✿

Logwood

Acosmium trichonema | Blackwood | Bloodwood Tree | Bluewood | Campeachy Tree | Campeachy Wood | Campeche Logwood | Campeche Wood | *Cymbosepalum baronii* | Jamaica Wood

✹ SYMBOLIC MEANINGS
Blood wood.

✿ POSSIBLE POWERS
Colorize; Healing.

✿ FOLKLORE AND FACTS
Logwood is a flowering tree that has been used for folk medicinal purposes but more so to make a versatile dye that was useful for paper and fabrics from the seventeenth through the nineteenth centuries. • During the seventeenth century, cut Logwood was highly desired and expensive. It was not uncommon for English, French, and Dutch ships crossing the sea with cargos of Logwood to be attacked by the Spanish, because most of the ships were sailing out of Logwood cutting camps in Central and South America. These were the lands that the Spanish had claimed as their own. The English, French, and Dutch knew they risked being attacked for harvesting where they should not have had a camp in the first place, but it was commonly believed that for the valuable Logwood, it was worth taking a chance. In addition to attacks by the Spanish were relentless, attacking pirates who had significantly multiplied when out-of-work Logwood cutters were forced off the land and joined in to become pirates, too. There were also some unemployed cutters who worked on the sly, cutting Logwood that the pirates also took. The bonus for iconic pirate captains, such as Blackbeard, Samuel Bellamy and others, was that they also gained the captured vessels to add to their pirating fleet. • An extract that is used to stain blood samples is obtained from Logwood.

No. 265

Hamamelis virginiana ✿

Witch Hazel

American Witch Hazel | Common Witch Hazel | *Hamamelis androgyna* | *Hamamelis caroliniana* | *Hamamelis communis* | *Hamamelis corylifolia* | *Hamamelis dentata* | *Hamamelis dioica* | *Hamamelis hyemalis* | *Hamamelis macrophylla* | *Hamamelis nigra* | *Hamamelis parvifolia* | *Hamamelis riparia* | *Hamamelis rotundifolia* | *Hamamelis virginica* | *Lomilis ciliata* | *Trilopus dentata* | *Trilopus hyemalis* | *Trilopus nigra* | *Trilopus parvifolia* | *Trilopus riparia* | *Trilopus rotundifolia* | Wice Hazel | Winterbloom | Wych Elm

✹ SYMBOLIC MEANINGS
Changeable; Chastity; a Magic spell; a Spell.

✿ POSSIBLE POWERS
Chastity; Divination; Fire element; Masculine energy; Protection; the Sun.

✿ FOLKLORE AND FACTS
A forked twig of Witch Hazel is the preferred and most commonly used divining rod because it is the most effective. • Carry a sprig of Witch Hazel to heal a broken heart. • Many water dowsers, which are also known as water finders, doodlebugs, or water witchers, depend on their Witch Hazel forked divining rod or their dual, L-shaped divining sticks to seek out where to start digging a water well. • Dowsing with a Witch Hazel divining rod is believed to have started in Germany during the fifteenth century in an effort to find ground ores, most particularly gold. • Witch Hazel has been used as a soothing antiseptic and astringent for skin for several hundred years. • The Native American Iroquois people would pour hot water over crushed Witch Hazel leaves to use in poultices that would be applied to reduce the swelling and pain caused by a sprain. • A very fine wand to use for fending off malignant influences and to demand full restoration of positive energy is one made of Witch Hazel wood.

H

No. 266
Helianthus tuberosus 🌿

Jerusalem Artichoke
Earth Apple | Helianthemum tuberosum | Helianthus doronicoides | Helianthus esculentus | Helianthus pubescens | Helianthus serotinus | Helianthus spathulatus | Helianthus squarrosus | Helianthus subcanescens | Helianthus tomentosus | Sunchoke | Sunroot | Topinambour

☀ SYMBOLIC MEANINGS
Sunny outlook on life.

⚘ POSSIBLE POWERS
Healing.

☙ FOLKLORE AND FACTS
Regardless of its most common name, Jerusalem Artichoke has no relationship to Jerusalem, although possibly with early North American settlers who carried roots with them to plant. Many of the settlers occasionally considered America to be a new world for all who braved such a dramatic change in the direction of their lives. At the time, they may have considered America to be a new Jerusalem.

No. 267
Helichrysum italicum 🌿

Immortelle
Curry Plant | Gnaphalium italicum | Immortal | Italian Starflower | Scaredy-Cat

☀ SYMBOLIC MEANINGS
Turn around.

⚘ POSSIBLE POWERS
Exorcism; Healing; Overcome an addiction; Overcome psychological bondage to a trauma; Protection; Summoning.

☙ FOLKLORE AND FACTS
Shamans burn Immortelle to summon ancestors and snake spirits. • The essential oil from the Immortelle plant is helpful in aromatherapy to support overcoming an addiction to such things as alcohol, nicotine, and anything else that has taken one into bondage. • Making an amulet of Immortelle is very useful to carry or wear when scrying or channeling a spirit. • Make a white sachet of Immortelle to carry or wear for use when considering immortality and self-regeneration by way of reincarnation. • An Immortelle plant's leaf is often used as a flavoring in some Mediterranean recipes before removing the leaf prior to serving.

No. 268
Helleborus foetidus ☠

Stinking Hellebore
Bear's Foot | Dungwort | Hellebore

☀ SYMBOLIC MEANINGS
Anxiety; Calumny; Relief; Relieve my anxiety; Scandal; Tranquilize my anxiety; Wit.

⚘ POSSIBLE POWERS
Astral projection; Exorcism; Feminine energy; Invisibility; Peace; Protection; Saturn; Tranquility; Water element.

☙ FOLKLORE AND FACTS
Every part of the Stinking Hellebore is deadly poisonous, and thus it is too dangerous to use for any reason whatsoever. • It is believed that Alexander the Great might have been treated for an illness with a Hellebore plant, only to subsequently violently and grotesquely die from the plant's poisoning.

No. 269
Hemerocallis fulva ☠

Orange Daylily
Ditch Lily | Giglio di San Giuseppe | Hemerocallis crocea | Outhouse Lily | Railroad Daylily | Roadside Daylily | Tawny Daylily | Washhouse Lily

☀ SYMBOLIC MEANINGS
Coquetry; Diversity; Tenacity.

⚘ POSSIBLE POWERS
Indifference; Jupiter; Moon; Nonchalance; Purity; St. Joseph; Tenderness.

☙ FOLKLORE AND FACTS
The Orange Daylily is not a true lily, but a member of the *Asphodel* family. • Introduced to North America by European immigrants, the Orange Daylily originated in China and Korea. • Because the *Hemerocallis fulva* bulb can survive for weeks unplanted, Orange Daylily bulbs were carried across the sea and all the way across North America by wagon trains, to now bloom wild along roadsides and railroad tracks where they are still prolifically growing. • Orange Daylily flowers last for one day. • The petals of *Hemerocallis fulva* flower can be found in several Chinese dishes, the best known in Chinese restaurants everywhere as Moo Shu Pork.

No. 270
Hepatica nobilis ☠☙

Liverwort

Anemone angulosa | Anemone hepatica | Anemone praecox | Anemone triloba | Common
Hepatica | Edellebere | Heart Leaf | Hepatica | *Hepatica anemonoides | Hepatica angulosa |
Hepatica hepatica |* Herb Trinity | Kidneywort | Liverleaf | Liverweed | Pennywort | Trefoil

✻ SYMBOLIC MEANINGS
Confidence; Constancy; Trust.

❀ POSSIBLE POWERS
Fire element; Jupiter; Love; Masculine energy; Protection;
Trust.

☙ FOLKLORE AND FACTS
For a woman to secure the love from a man she can trust, she
could make, then wear or carry a Liverwort sachet.

No. 271
Hibiscus rosa-sinensis ☙

Hibiscus

Astromelia | Bunga Raya | Cañeno | Chemparathy | Chijin | Chinese Hibiscus | Clavel Japonés |
Erhonghua | Escandalosa | Flor de Jamaica | Fosang | Fusang | Graxa | Gumamela | *Hibiscus
arnottii | Hibiscus festalis | Hibiscus fulgens | Hibiscus javanicus | Hibiscus metallicus |
Hibiscus rosiflorus | Hibiscus tricolor |* Hongfusang | Hongmujin | Huohonghua | Jaba |
Jaswand | Jiamudan | Kembang Sepatu | Kharkady | Mamdaram | Mondaro | Queen of Tropical
Flowers | Rijii Rosa de Cayena | Sangjin | Sembaruthi | Shoe Flower | Shoeflower | Songjin |
Tuhonghua | Tulipan | Wada Mal | Zhaodianhong | Zhongguoqiangwei

✻ SYMBOLIC MEANINGS
Beauty; Delicate; Delicate beauty; Peace and Happiness;
Rare beauty.

❀ POSSIBLE POWERS
Ambition; Attitude; Celebration of the simplest joy; Clear
thinking; Divination; Enjoying each step of life's journey;
Feminine energy; Harmony; Higher understanding; Logic;
Love; Lust; Manifestation in material form; Outward
expression of happiness or joy; Seeing hidden and obvious
beauty; Spiritual concepts; Thought processes; Venus; Water
element.

☙ FOLKLORE AND FACTS
The Hibiscus is called Shoe Flower because the crushed
petals can be used to shine shoes. • In the Pacific Islands,
a red Hibiscus flower is worn by women as a sign of their
interests. If worn behind the left ear, it signals that she desires
a lover. If behind the right ear, she already has a lover. If
a Hibiscus is worn behind both ears it signals that she has
one lover but would welcome another one. • In tropical
countries, Hibiscus flowers are tucked into marital wreaths
that are used as a marriage ceremony decoration. • In parts
of India, the Hibiscus flower is used
to venerate the Hindu goddess,
Kali. • The Hibiscus is the state
flower of Hawaii, USA and the
national flower of Malaysia.
• A Hibiscus flower will
bloom to live for only one
day. • Gifting the Hibiscus
is an invitation to vacation to
where they grow.

No. 272
Hierochloe odorata ☠☙

Sweetgrass

Batatas batatas | Bison Grass | Buffalo Grass | *Convolvulus
batatas | Convolvulus esculentus |* Holy Grass | *Ipomoea
chrysorrhiza |* Manna Grass | Mary's Grass | Seneca Grass |
Sweet Grass | Vanilla Grass

✻ SYMBOLIC MEANINGS
Healing; Mother Earth's hair; Peace; Poor
but happy; Spirituality.

❀ POSSIBLE POWERS
Calling in good spirits; Healing;
Meditation; Peace; Repels negative
energy; Protection; Purification.

☙ FOLKLORE AND FACTS
Native Americans consider Sweetgrass to be the oldest
of all plants and the hair of Mother Earth. • Sweetgrass
is considered a sacred plant that still holds significant
importance to Native Americans, who burn it as an incense.
It is often used for smudging to purify and protect the body,
mind, spirit, and living environment, as well as repel all
forms of negative energy. • Sweetgrass is often braided or left
in bundles at burial sites and other sacred sites as an offering.
• Basket-weavers will cut the Sweetgrass when it is green,
then sun-dry it. Before weaving, the long grass is soaked
in water to make it flexible. • The Native American Plains
tribes consider Sweetgrass to attract positive energy and

H

good spirits. It is also considered to be one of the four sacred medicines, symbolizing healing and peace. • In Poland, Sweetgrass extract has been used to flavor vodka. • In parts of Europe, Sweetgrass extract has been used to flavor some sweet confections and beverages, as well as a fragrance added to perfumes.

No. 273

Hordeum vulgare 🥣

Barley

Akitii | Cebada | *Frumentum hordeum* | *Frumentum sativum* | *Hordeum aestivum* | *Hordeum americanum* | *Hordeum bifarium* | *Hordeum brachyatherum* | *Hordeum caspicum* | *Hordeum coeleste* | *Hordeum daghestanicum* | *Hordeum defectoides* | *Hordeum durum* | *Hordeum elongatum* | *Hordeum gymnodistichum* | *Hordeum heterostychon* | *Hordeum hexastichon* | *Hordeum hibernaculum* | *Hordeum hibernans* | *Hordeum himalayense* | *Hordeum hirtiusculum* | *Hordeum horsfordianum* | *Hordeum ircutianum* | *Hordeum jarenskianum* | *Hordeum juliae* | *Hordeum kalugense* | *Hordeum karzinianum* | *Hordeum kiarchanum* | *Hordeum laevipaleatum* | *Hordeum lapponicum* | *Hordeum leptostachys* | *Hordeum macrolepis* | *Hordeum mandshuricum* | *Hordeum mandshuroidcs* | *Hordeum mlchalkowii* | *Hordeum nekludowii* | *Hordeum nigrum* | *Hordeum pamiricum* | *Hordeum parvum* | *Hordeum pensanum* | *Hordeum polystichon* | *Hordeum praecox* | *Hordeum pyramidatum* | *Hordeum revelatum* | *Hordeum sativum* | *Hordeum scabriusculum* | *Hordeum septentrionale* | *Hordeum stassewitschii* | *Hordeum strobelense* | *Hordeum taganrocense* | *Hordeum tanaiticum* | *Hordeum tetrastichum* | *Hordeum transcaucasicum* | *Hordeum violaceum* | *Hordeum vulgare* | *Hordeum walpersii* | Hulless Barley | Jt | Naked Barley | *Secale orientale* | Sma | Vavilov

☀ SYMBOLIC MEANINGS
Love; Grain of life.

⚙ POSSIBLE POWERS
Demeter; Earth element; Feminine energy; Fertility; Harvest; Healing; Love; Love spell; Male sexual potency; Pain relief; Protection; Venus.

☘ FOLKLORE AND FACTS
Evidence of wild Barley dates to approximately 8500 BCE. • Ancient growers domesticated Barley between approximately 1500 and 891 BCE. • Barley has important significance in religious rituals of various Middle Eastern, Egyptian, and Greek cultures in antiquity. • In the Middle Ages, one type of divination, called alphitomancy, used Barley cakes to determine guilt or innocence. Suspected criminals ate the Barley bread or cake. The first person to get indigestion was guilty. • The word barn means "Barley house." • To cast away pain, wrap Barley straw around a rock and visualize the pain as you throw the rock into the moving water of a river or a stream. • Scatter Barley on the ground near your home to keep evil and negativity from approaching.

No. 274

Humulus lupulus 🥣

Hop

Beer Flower | Common Hop | European Hop | Flores de Cerveza | *Humulus volubilis* | *Humulus vulgaris* | *Lupulus amarus* | *Lupulus communis* | *Lupulus humulus* | *Lupulus scandens* | *Waldensia lupulina*

☀ SYMBOLIC MEANINGS
Injustice; Mirth; Passion; Pride.

⚙ POSSIBLE POWERS
Air element; Colorize; Healing; Mars; Masculine energy; Sleep.

☘ FOLKLORE AND FACTS
Ingesting Hops in any other way than using it in the brewing of beer is definitely not recommended. • In the brewing of beer, the female cone-shaped Hop fruits add an aromatic bitter note and natural preservative. • Sleep on a pillow that has been stuffed with dried Hops for improved rest. • Hops can be used to make a yellow dye for fabric.

No. 275

Hyacinthoides non-scripta ☠🥣

Bluebell

Agraphis nutans | Common Bluebell | *Endymion cernuus* | *Endymion non-scriptus* | *Endymion nutans* | English Bluebell | *Hyacinthus cernuus* | *Hyacinthus non-scriptus* | *Scilla cernua* | *Scilla festalis* | *Scilla non-scripta* | *Scilla nutans*

☀ SYMBOLIC MEANINGS
Constancy; Delicacy; Grateful; Gratitude; Grief; Humility; Kindness; Luck; Retirement; Solitude; Sorrowful regret; Submission; Thinking of you; Truth.

⚙ POSSIBLE POWERS
Friendship; Luck; Truth.

☘ FOLKLORE AND FACTS
In Britain, many colognes and toiletries make use of Bluebells' pleasing fragrance. • Whoever wears a Bluebell flower will feel the need to tell the truth about anything. • If you can turn a Bluebell blossom inside out without damaging it, the one you love someday will return that love. • Fairies ring the Bluebell to call other fairies to gather. If a human hears the bell ringing, he or she will die or suffer a fairy enchantment. • If a human steps within a circle of Bluebells, he or she risks the ire of displeased fairies.

No. 276

Hyacinthus orientalis

Hyacinth

Common Hyacinth | Dutch Hyacinth | Garden Hyacinth | *Scilla coronaria*

SYMBOLIC MEANINGS

Amenity; Benevolence; Constancy; Faith; Forgiveness; Game; Games and sports; Gentleness of nature; Happiness; Impulsiveness; Jealousy; Love; Overcoming grief; Play; Protection; Rashness; Sport.

COLOR MEANINGS

Blue: Consistency.
Pink: Harmless mischief; Play; Playful joy.
Purple: I'm sorry; Jealousy; Please forgive me; Regret; Sadness; Sorrow; Sorrowful.
Red: Harmless mischief; Play; Playful joy.
White: I'll pray for you; Loveliness; Prayers for those in need; Unobtrusive loveliness.
Yellow: Jealousy.

POSSIBLE POWERS

Death and revival; Delays sexual maturity; Feminine energy; Happiness; Love; Protection; Venus; Water element.

FOLKLORE AND FACTS

The sweet perfume of fresh Hyacinth flowers is excellent aromatherapy that can help ease depression and grief. • The fragrance of a Hyacinth is believed to have the ability to call upon the soul's angels, who will illuminate the mind with clarity and instill wisdom within. • Grown in a pot in the bedroom, the Hyacinth can help prevent nightmares. • The Hyacinth is the ultimate flower of personal compassion and forgiveness. • The spirit of the Hyacinth is to let the past be past and to let bygones be bygones. In that way, it becomes possible to proceed forward with the past behind and not ahead to create blockades and unnecessary detours required to bypass them. • The Hyacinth can help motivate one to inspire the effort required to create the type of life that one is meant to be living.

No. 277

Hydrangea arborescens

Wild Hydrangea

Hydrangea acuta | *Hydrangea amplifolia* | *Hydrangea cordata* | *Hydrangea frutescens* | *Hydrangea glauca* | *Hydrangea heterophylla* | *Hydrangea laevigata* | *Hydrangea paniculata* | *Hydrangea rotundifolia* | *Hydrangea urticifolia* | *Hydrangea viburnifolia* | *Hydrangea vulgaris* | Sevenbarks | Sheep Flower | Smooth Hydrangea | *Viburnum alnifolium* | *Viburnum americanum*

SYMBOLIC MEANINGS

Coolness; Thank you for understanding; Understanding.

POSSIBLE POWERS

Attracts love; Breaks a hex; Draws a straying lover to return; Fidelity; Helps identify and repel a psychic attack; Helps identify karmic patterns; Helps rebuild protective energy fields; Helps redirect a curse; Intuition; Protects boundaries; Psychic awareness; Understanding.

FOLKLORE AND FACTS

The stem of the Wild Hydrangea can be peeled off in multiple layers to reveal several underlying layers of different colors. • Fossilized Wild Hydrangea seeds have been discovered in Alaska, USA and Poland. • Make, then carry or wear a sachet of Wild Hydrangea petals and leaves to increase psychic awareness. • Make, then carry or wear a sachet of Wild Hydrangea petals and leaves to encourage goodness to come forward from without and within.

Hydrastis canadensis ☠☙

Goldenseal

Eye Balm | Eye Root | Golden Seal | Ground Raspberry | *Hydrastis trifolia* | Indian Dye | Indian Paint | Jaundice Root | Orange Root | Orangeroot | Turmeric Root | Warnera | *Warneria canadensis* | Wild Curcurma | Yellow Puccoon | Yellow Root

✸ SYMBOLIC MEANINGS

Cleanse.

❁ POSSIBLE POWERS

Cleansing; Fire element; Healing; Masculine energy; Money; the Sun.

❦ FOLKLORE AND FACTS

Since the mid-1980s, Goldenseal has been utilized by many marijuana users with the hopes it would efficiently detoxify their urine enough to pass a mandatory drug test. The Goldenseal apparently did such a good job of cleansing that nowadays anywhere that requires their employees to be consistently drug free, regardless of marijuana's increasing legality, will tend to administer random drug tests immediately, allowing no time for a cleansing. • Wild Goldenseal is an endangered species due to rampant over-harvesting. • Pregnant and nursing mothers must absolutely avoid ingesting Goldenseal. There is evidence that brain damage has developed in newborn babies that were exposed to the Goldenseal herb either directly or through breastfeeding.

Hyoscyamus niger ☠

Henbane

Apollinaris | Belinuntia | Black Nightshade | Cassilago | Cassilata | Deus Caballinus | Devil's Eye | Hebenon | Henbells | Hogsbean | *Hyoscarpus niger* | *Hyoscyamus agrestis* | *Hyoscyamus auriculatus* | *Hyoscyamus bohemicus* | *Hyoscyamus lethalis* | *Hyoscyamus officinarum* | *Hyoscyamus pallidus* | *Hyoscyamus persicus* | *Hyoscyamus pictus* | *Hyoscyamus syspirensis* | *Hyoscyamus verviensis* | *Hyoscyamus vulgaris* | Hyoskyamos | Isana | Jupiter's Bean | Jusquiame | Pig Bean | Poison Tobacco | Stinking Nightshade | Symphonica | White Henbane

✸ SYMBOLIC MEANINGS

Blemish; Defect; Fault; Imperfection.

❁ POSSIBLE POWERS

Death; Lust; Saturn; Water element; Witchcraft.

❦ FOLKLORE AND FACTS

Every part of the Henbane plant is deadly poisonous, and thus it is too dangerous to use for any reason

whatsoever. Even touching the plant can be extremely toxic. • Henbane has a gross, putrid odor to it. • To gain the lusting love of a woman, Henbane would need to be gathered in the early morning by a solitary naked man who is standing on only one foot. • To the ancient Celts, Henbane was dedicated to the sun god, Bel. • Henbane was used as a deadly paint for the tips of the spears and arrows used by the ancient Gauls. • Henbane was used in sorcery and necromancy to call up demons along with the long-suffering souls of the dead. • During the late Middle Ages, Henbane seeds were toasted over coals in bathhouses to arouse lusty sensations. • In ancient Greece, Henbane was considered to be sacred and holy, dedicated to the god Apollo, and known by the name Apollinaris. • At the Oracle of Delphi, the high priestess, Pythia, was believed to be under the poisonous influence of Henbane when she gave her prophetic predictions. • The myths of Henbane being an ingredient in a medieval witch's flying ointment can easily be associated with the delirious hallucinations induced by the dreadful toxicity of the plant. There are much easier ways to astrally travel that will never involve poisonous plants. • Ancient German tribes used Henbane in their sacred rituals. • The smell of Henbane has been described to be that of death. • For whatever ritualistic purposes it was thought to contribute to, it is logically believed that all uses of the deadly poisonous Henbane never ended well or as it was believed it would be.

No. 280

Hypericum perforatum ☠☙▱

St. John's Wort

Amber | Chase Devil | Chase-devil | Common St. John's Wort | Fuga Daemonum | Goat Weed | Herba John | Hypericum officinale | Hypericum officinarum | Hypericum vulgare | John's Wort | Klamath Weed | Scare Devil | Sol Terrestis | Tipton Weed | Tipton's Weed

☀ **SYMBOLIC MEANINGS**
Animosity; Simplicity; Superstition.

❀ **POSSIBLE POWERS**
Baldur; Courage; Divination; Exorcism; Expels negative energy; Fire element; Happiness; Health; Love divination; Masculine energy; Money spells; Power; Protection; Repels evil spirits; Strength; the Sun.

✦ **FOLKLORE AND FACTS**
St. John's Wort was said to be so offensive to evil spirits that one sniff of it would force them to fly away. • St. John's Wort has the power to drive away negative spirits and their negative energies. • It was once thought that if girls slept with St. John's Wort under the pillow, the herb would chase away evil spirits so they could dream of who their husbands would someday be. • It was once believed that if St. John's Wort did not bloom, someone would die.
• Worn as an amulet, St. John's Wort is supposed to protect the wearer against evil. • St. John's Wort was believed to protect a house against such calamities as fire, lightning, and storms. • St. John's Wort can make a yellow dye for fabrics. • A pot of St. John's Wort growing with Cyclamen in a bedroom was believed by some to offer protection to those vulnerable and sleeping against any evil spirits trying to take unfair advantage. • Witches are believed to be quite offended by St. John's Wort whenever it is nearby.

No. 281

Hyssopus officinalis ☙🍴

Hyssop

Herb Hyssop | Holy Herb | Hyssop Herb | Isopo | Thyme hyssopus | Ysopo | Yssop

☀ **SYMBOLIC MEANINGS**
Cleanliness; Holiness.

❀ **POSSIBLE POWERS**
Fire element; Healing; Jupiter; Masculine energy; Protection; Purification; Spiritual cleansing; Wards off an evil spirit.

✦ **FOLKLORE AND FACTS**
Referred to many times in the Bible and having been used since ancient times, Hyssop is considered to be especially sacred and is the herb that is most often used for holy purification. • Hang Hyssop in the home to force out evil and negativity.
• The sponge, wet with vinegar, that was brought to Jesus to drink from when he was suffering on the cross, was held up to his mouth on a Hyssop branch.
• Hyssop essential oil can be used for aromatherapy to help stimulate creativity and aid concentration when meditating.
• Hyssop is a mint that is used in the popular Middle Eastern spice blend known as Za'atar. It is also used to flavor some liqueurs, with it being part of the official recipe for the distilling of Chartreuse as well as absinthe. • Hyssop nectar will produce a fragrant honey, making it a favorite plant of beekeepers.

H

No. 282

Ilex aquifolium ☠☙

English Holly

Aquifolium croceum | Aquifolium
ferox | Aquifolium heterophyllum |
Aquifolium ilex | Aquifolium
lanceolatum | Aquifolium
planifolium | Aquifolium
spinosum | Aquifolium
undulatum | Aquifolium
vulgare | Aquifolius | Bat's
Wings | Christ's Thorn | Christmas
Holly | Common Holly | European Holly | Holly |
Holly Bush | Holly Herb | Holly Tree | Holm Chaste |
Hulm | Hulver Bush | Ilex | Ilex balearica | Ilex camelliifolia | Ilex chrysocarpa | Ilex ciliata | Ilex
citriocarpa | Ilex crassifolia | Ilex echinata | Ilex ferox | Ilex fischeri | Ilex heterophylla | Ilex
maderensis | Ilex nigricans | Ilex platyphylla | Ilex sempervirens | Ilex vulgaris | Tinne

❋ SYMBOLIC MEANINGS

Am I forgotten?; Courage; Defense; Difficult victory attained;
Domestic happiness; Dreams; Enchantment; Eternal Life;
Fire element; Forecast; Foresight; Good cheer; Good luck;
Goodwill; Looking; Mars; Masculine energy; Protection;
Questioning; Subconscious; Symbol of a Human Being;
Symbol of Man; Vigilance; Wisdom.

❦ COMPONENT MEANING

Berries: Christmas joy.

❀ POSSIBLE POWERS

Anti-lightning; Attracts and repels energy; Dream;
Immortality; Luck; Protection; Protection against harm in
a dream; Protection against the evil eye; Protection against
witchcraft.

☙ FOLKLORE AND FACTS

An English Holly leaf will bring good luck to any person
who carries or wears it. • The ancient Druids believed that
English Holly kept the Earth beautiful during the time when
Oak trees had no leaves. During that period, the Druids wore
English Holly leaves in their hair when it was time to watch
their priests cut Mistletoe from White Oak trees, which were
(and still are) sacred to them. • In medieval Europe, English
Holly was planted near homes to protect them from lightning
and to bring good fortune. • In England, it was thought that a
sprig of English Holly on a bedpost would bring about sweet
dreams. • In Wales, it was thought that if English Holly
were brought into the home before it was Christmastime, it
would instigate family arguments. • It was also believed that
if English Holly was left around the home as a decoration
past Twelfth Night, misfortune would occur for each and
every one of the English Holly leaves and branches that were

not removed in time. • It was thought that bringing English
Holly into the home of a friend could cause death. • Another
belief is that keeping a piece of English Holly that was used
in a church for a Christmas decoration will bring about good
fortune throughout the year. • If English Holly is picked on
Christmas Day, it will be very good protection against evil
spirits and witches. • One divination that can be used is to
place tiny candles on English Holly leaves and float them on
water. If the leaves stay afloat, an endeavor that the seeker
has in mind will prosper. However, if any of the leaves sink
to extinguish a candle, it is a sign that it is best to not do it.
• It is believed that throwing English Holly at wild animals
will make them leave you alone even if they are not actually
touched by any part of the plant. • A weather divination
that was once frequently taken very seriously is that if the
English Holly shrub had an overabundance of berries, it was
an ominous sign that winter would be harsh. • The Druids
believed that it was an important safety measure to bring
English Holly into their dwellings in the winter to give
shelter to the elves and fairies who would dare to house with
humans to escape the bitter cold. • In parts of England, it is
still believed that it is very bad luck to cut down an English
Holly tree because the tree represents Eternal Life. • In some
parts of Hampshire, England, it was believed that a child
suffering from whooping cough would be cured by drinking
milk from a wooden English Holly bowl. • English Holly
wood makes a fine protective magic wand for the impetuous
practitioner. It has the strong protective quality of all the
various magical woods and will especially bring luck to men.

No. 283

Ilex guayusa ☙

Guayusa

Illex utilis | Wais | Waisa | Wayus

❋ SYMBOLIC MEANINGS

Night watchman.

❀ POSSIBLE POWERS

Dream interpretation; Dreams; Healing; Insect repellent;
Lucid dreaming; Ritual use; Snake repellent; Stimulation;
Wakefulness.

☙ FOLKLORE AND FACTS

The dried leaves of the Amazonian Guayusa tree have been
used to make a caffeinated tea by indigenous people who
live in the rainforest. • A bundle of Guayusa leaves was
found in the fifteen-hundred-year-old tomb of a Bolivian
shaman that was far from where the Guayusa tree grows. • A
ritual practiced by the head-hunting, head-shrinking, upper
Amazonian tribe known as the Jivaroans would involve

I

drinking large quantities of a Guayusa leaf infusion just to forcibly vomit it back out. • Another indigenous Amazonian people known as the Kichua would drink a Guayusa leaf infusion to provoke lucid dreams to seek clues before going on a hunt. • That Guayusa leaf tea is a snake repellent comes from the idea that a snake is too afraid to bite anyone with the tea within them. • Tena, Ecuador, is thought to be the Guayusa capital of the world. • Beyond the Amazonian jungle, Guayusa leaf tea bags can be found in many supermarkets. • A pre-Columbian plantation of Guayusa trees was discovered in Baños, Ecuador, by British botanist, Richard Spruce, in 1857.

No. 284

Ilex paraguariensis ☠⛾

Yerba Mate

Erva Mate | *Ilex bonplandiana* | *Ilex congonhas* | *Ilex curitibensis* | *Ilex domestica* | *Ilex mate* | *Ilex paraguayensis* | *Ilex sorbilis* | *Ilex theaezans* | Mate | Paraguay Tea | *Rhamnus quitensis* | Yerba | Yerba Maté | Yerva Mate

☀ **SYMBOLIC MEANINGS**
Love; Mate; Romance.

🌼 **POSSIBLE POWERS**
Binding; Building; Death; Fidelity; History; Knowledge; Limitations; Love; Lust; Masculine energy; Obstacles; Time.

🜨 **FOLKLORE AND FACTS**
A popular tea-like caffeinated infusion that is brewed with the leaves of the Yerba Mate plant and water is known as "mate." Mate was first consumed by the early indigenous Guaraní people of Paraguay, to spread far and wide from there. • The Yerba Mate herb and the drinking of mate are particularly popular in Paraguay and Uruguay, where it is a social experience. People are commonly seen carrying around containers of the tea. • The type of container that the mate is drunk from has traditionally been a hollowed-out Calabash gourd. Although hollowed gourds are still used to drink mate, nowadays the symbolic "mate cup" might be made of ceramic, carved wood, a bull's horn, or even plastic. • Wear a sprig of Yerba Mate to attract the opposite sex. • Spill an infusion of Yerba Mate to break off what was once a romantic relationship.

No. 285

Ilex vomitoria ☠⛾

Yaupon Holly

Cassina | *Ilex ligustrina* | Yaupon

☀ **SYMBOLIC MEANINGS**
Expel; Put out.

🌼 **POSSIBLE POWERS**
Alert togetherness; Energy booster; Laxative; Purgative.

🜨 **FOLKLORE AND FACTS**
The botanical species *vomitoria* originated when Native Americans included the poisonous Yaupon Holly stems and leaves with other ingredients to make a ritualistic, male-only drink for unity ceremonies, which included profuse group vomiting somewhere along the progression of the male-bonding festivities. • Yaupon Holly is the only wild, naturally caffeinated plant that grows in the United States that has been brewed by Native Americans to be a ceremonial, tea-like beverage they called "Asi," "Black Drink," and "Big Magic."

No. 286

Illicium verum ☠⛾🍴

Star Anise

Ba Jiao Hui Xian | Badian | Badian Khatai | Badiana | Badiane | Bunga Lawang | Chinese Anise | Chinese Star Anise | Eight-Horn | *Illicium stellatum* | Khata | Star Aniseed | Staranise | Thakolam

☀ **SYMBOLIC MEANINGS**
Good luck; Luck.

🌼 **POSSIBLE POWERS**
Air element; Divination; Good luck charm; Healing; Jupiter; Masculine energy; Psychic ability; Psychic awareness; Psychic power.

🜨 **FOLKLORE AND FACTS**
Carry one whole, star-shaped Star Anise seed in a pocket for luck. • Make a Star Anise seed necklace then wear it to increase your psychic power. • A powerful pendulum can be made using a Star Anise seed tied on a string. • In aromatherapy, Star Anise essential oil may help calm

I

unexplainable feelings and sensations resulting from stress.
• A Star Anise seed can be burned like incense to increase
one's psychic awareness. • An enormous percentage of the
world's crops of the *Illicium verum* Star Anise plant have
been dedicated to making the urgent anti-viral medication
oseltamivir, which is more commonly known as Tamiflu.

No. 287

Imperata cylindrica ⚱

Cogongrass

Alang-Alang | *Arundo epigeios* | Blady Grass | *Calamagrostis lagurus* | Cogón | Cogon Grass |
Cotton Wool | *Imperata allang* | *Imperata angolensis* | *Imperata arundinacea* | *Imperata
dinteri* | *Imperata filifolia* | *Imperata koenigii* | *Imperata laguroides* | *Imperata latifolia* |
Imperata pedicellata | *Imperata praecoquis* | *Imperata ramosa* | *Imperata robustior* | *Imperata
sieberi* | *Imperata sisca* | Japanese Blood Grass | Kunai Grass | Kura-Kura | *Lagurus cylindricus* |
Langlang Grass | Pai Mao-Ken | *Saccharum alopecurus* | *Saccharum cylindricum* | *Saccharum
diandrum* | *Saccharum europaeum* | *Saccharum indum* | *Saccharum koenigii* | *Saccharum
laguroides* | *Saccharum negrosense* | *Saccharum sisca* | *Saccharum spicatum* | *Saccharum
thunbergii* | Satintail | Spear Grass | Sword Grass | Thatch Grass | Wooly Grass

☀ SYMBOLIC MEANINGS
Fire maker.

⚘ POSSIBLE POWERS
Erosion prevention; Paper-making; Procrastination;
Protection; Thatching.

☘ FOLKLORE AND FACTS
The deeply rooted and highly flammable Cogongrass can
grow up to ten feet tall. After a fire that burns it to the
ground, it will grow right back again and then spread to
cover an even wider area. • Traditional houses throughout
Southeast Asia may have roofs thatched with Cogongrass.
• The Aboriginal peoples of Australia are known to use
Cogongrass as a salt-like seasoning due to its saltiness.
• Congongrass is, by far, one of the world's most invasive
plants. Even from plants deemed to be sterile, there will be
more than enough viable seeds that develop to rapidly choke
out one's garden and the gardens of one's neighbors.

No. 288

Indigofera tinctoria

True Indigo

Anil tinctoria | Indigo | Nil-Awari

☀ SYMBOLIC MEANINGS
Great devotion.

⚘ POSSIBLE POWERS
Colorize; Fairness; Impartiality; Integrity; Intuition; Justice;
Opening of the Third Eye; Wisdom.

☘ FOLKLORE AND FACTS
The blue color produced by fermented True Indigo stems
and leaves has been greatly valued as a dye for more than
4,000 years. • The report that True Indigo was used in
India to make a blue-colored dye was made by Marco Polo.
• Natural True Indigo blue fabric dye that has been obtained
by processing the plant's leaves can still be obtained. In some
markets, True Indigo may be sold by the name of tarum, nila,
or basma.

No. 289

Inula helenium ⚱

Elecampane

Alantwurzel | Alycompaine | *Aster helenium* |
Aster officinalis | Aunee | *Corvisartia helenium* |
Elf Dock | Elfwort | *Helenium grandiflorum* |
Horse-Heal | Marchalan | Nurse Heal | Scabwort |
Velvet Dock | Wild Sunflower

☀ SYMBOLIC MEANINGS
Tears.

⚘ POSSIBLE POWERS
Air element; Love; Masculine
energy; Mercury; Protection;
Psychic power.

☘ FOLKLORE AND FACTS
Elecampane was sacred to the
ancient Celts. • Make an Elecampane sachet to wear or carry
to attract love. • Make an Elecampane sachet to place in
the home for protection. • Elecampane is a favorite flower
of fairies and elves. • In France, Elecampane was one of the
herbs used in the making of absinthe liqueur. • The legend
is that wherever Helen of Troy's tears fell to the ground,
Elecampane grew.

I

No. 290

Ipomoea hederacea ☠

Morning Glory

Bindweed | Cleiemera hederacea | Cleiemera hirsuta | Convolvulus | Convolvulus caeruleus | Flying Saucers | Glory Flower | Heavenly Blue | Indian Jasmine | Ipomoea avicularis | Ipomoea barbata | Ipomoea barbigera | Ipomoea desertorum | Ipomoea hirsutula | Ipomoea limbata | Ipomoea phymatodes | Ipomoea scabra | Ipomoea scabrida | Mina | Ornithosperma autumnalis | Pharbitis barbata | Pharbitis barbigera | Pharbitis caerulescens | Pharbitis hederacea | Pharbitis polymorpha | Pharbitis purshii | Pharbitis scabrida | Pharbitis triloba | Piule | Tliliitzin | Wormweed

✹ SYMBOLIC MEANINGS

Affection; Attachment; Bonds; Coquetry; Death; Death and rebirth; Deference; Embrace; Glorious beauty; Humility; I attach myself to you; Love in vain; Night; Obstinacy; Repose; She loves you; Spontaneity; Uncertainty; Willful promises.

🌰 COLOR MEANINGS

Blue: Happiness; Peacefulness.
Pink: Worth sustained by judicious and tender affection.

🌑 POSSIBLE POWERS

Happiness; Love; Masculine energy; Peace; Saturn; Water element.

☾ FOLKLORE AND FACTS

The Morning Glory is believed to have the power to attract an angel who will coax peace, love, and happiness into one's life. • Blue Morning Glory will give a special boost of peacefulness and happiness to whoever sees it in bloom first thing in the morning. • A sachet of Morning Glory seeds under the pillow will supposedly stop all nightmares. • In magical times past, a powerful spell could be cast by fully winding a Morning Glory vine around a person three complete times without breaking the continuous stem, dropping a flower, dropping a bud, or dropping a leaf from anywhere along the full length of the vine, from beginning to end.

No. 291

Ipomoea jalapa ☠⚗

High John the Conqueror

Batatas jalapa | Convolvulus jalapa | Convolvulus jatiauca | Convolvulus lividus | Exogonium jalapa | Ipomoea carrizalia | Ipomoea mechoacan | Ipomoea michauxii | Ipomoea perichnoa | Ipomoea robertsii | Jalap | John de Conquer | John the Conker | John the Conquer | John the Conquer Root | John the Conqueroo | John the Conqueror

✹ SYMBOLIC MEANINGS

Accomplishment; Conquer; Perseverance; Prevail.

🌑 POSSIBLE POWERS

Breaks a hex; Confidence; Fire element; Happiness; Health; Love; Mars; Masculine energy; Money; Sex; Strength; Success.

☾ FOLKLORE AND FACTS

Carry or wear a sachet of High John the Conqueror to stop depression, bring love, be protected against all hexes and curses that aren't already upon you, and to break and drive away all spells, curses, and hexes that you do happen to unfortunately have upon you. As well as all that, High John the Conqueror offers mystical protection against getting them back again. It's like having your own knight in shining armor's full-on power compactly stuffed into the discreet size of a tea bag.

No. 292

Iris florentina ☠☢

Orris Root Iris

Bearded Iris | Fleur de Lis | Fleur-de-Lis Iris | Florentine Iris | German Iris | *Iris albicans* | *Iris madonna* | *Iris officinalis* | Queen Elizabeth Root Iris | Yellow Flag

✻ **SYMBOLIC MEANINGS**

Courage; Faith; Fire element; Flame; Friendly; Good news; Graceful; Hope; I am burning with love; I burn; I have a message for you; Idea; Indifference; a Message; Message; My compliments; Pleasant message; Promise; Promise in love; Pure heart; Purity; a Rainbow; Travel; Valor; Victory and conquest but also pain; Wisdom; Your friendship means so much to me.

❂ **POSSIBLE POWERS**

Authority; Faith; Feminine energy; Healing; Iris; Juno; Magic; Magic and energy for a pure aim; Power; Protection from an evil spirit; Purification; Reincarnation; Venus; Water element; Wisdom.

☙ **FOLKLORE AND FACTS**

All *Iris* plants, including the Orris Root Iris, *Iris florentina*, have been a sacred symbol of divine protection and royalty all around the world, since around the fifth century CE. • In Japan, Orris Root was considered protection against evil spirits, with the Orris Root Iris plant's roots and leaves being hung from the eaves of homes. • The fragrance of the processed Iris's root is strong and like that of a Violet. • The most valued part of the Orris Root Iris is the essential oil that is known as Oil of Orris. • It can take up to five years to sufficiently dry the Iris's roots before grinding it to a powder for use. • Pleasantly scented Orris Root powder is very often used as a fixative when making homemade herbal blends for potpourri. • An interesting and unusual Orris Root divination pendulum can be created using a whole root suspended by a cord from a yam. Not a Sweet Potato. • To increase psychic power, burn an incense of powdered Orris Root sprinkled with a pinch of Celery seeds. • Place a vase of fresh *Iris florentina* flowers in an area that requires energy cleansing. • The three points of the Orris Root Iris flower symbolize faith, wisdom, and valor. • A pink and red sachet of Orris Root Iris powder or piece of root with or without a bit of leaf, will make a potentially effective love charm to carry or wear. • Among other uses, Orris Root is added to perfumes, soap, and laundry detergent.

No. 293

Iris versicolor ☠☢

Blue Flag

American Blue Flag | Blue Flag Iris | Blueflag | Blueflag Iris | Dagger Flower | Flag Lily | Fleur de Lis | Harlequin Blueflag | Iris | *Iris boltoniana* | *Iris caurina* | *Iris dierinckii* | *Iris flaccida* | *Iris picta* | *Iris pulchella* | Larger Blue Flag | *Limniris versicolor* | Liver Lily | Multi-Colored Blue Flag | Northern Blue Flag | Poison Flag | Poison Lily | Purple Iris | Snake Lily | Water Flag | Water Iris | *Xiphion flaccidum* | *Xiphion versicolor*

✻ **SYMBOLIC MEANINGS**

Courage; Faith; Grace; Indifference; Timeless eloquence; Valor; Wisdom.

❂ **POSSIBLE POWERS**

Attracts money; Feminine energy; Money; Success in business; Venus; Water element; Wealth.

☙ **FOLKLORE AND FACTS**

Make, then place a sachet of Blue Flag in a cash register, in a pocket, tucked under a computer, on or even under a desk to encourage more business. • The Blue Flag is the official flower of Quebec. • The three petals of the Blue Flag's blossom represent faith, valor, and wisdom.

No. 294

Isatis tinctoria ☠☢

Woad

Asp of Jerusalem | *Crucifera isatis* | Dyer's Woad | Glastum | *Isatis alpina* | *Isatis apiculata* | *Isatis bannatica* | *Isatis canescens* | *Isatis ciesielskii* | *Isatis funebris* | *Isatis glauca* | *Isatis indigotica* | *Isatis japonica* | *Isatis kamienskii* | *Isatis koelzii* | *Isatis maeotica* | *Isatis maritima* | *Isatis sibirica* | *Isatis transsilvanica* | *Isatis vermia* | *Isatis villarsii* | *Isatis virens* | *Isatis yezoensis*

✻ **SYMBOLIC MEANINGS**

Modest merit; Sky clad.

❂ **POSSIBLE POWERS**

Colorize.

☙ **FOLKLORE AND FACTS**

Woad is known to have been used by the ancient Egyptians to dye cloth blue. • Woad is believed to be what the Picts of ancient Scotland used to paint their bodies the particular shades of blue that made it possible for them to stand on the top of a hill and strategically blend in with the color of the sky, disappearing into the blue as an advantage over their aggressors. • Woad was used in ancient Egypt to dye cotton cloth blue that was intended for use as a mummy wrapping.

I

No. 295

Jacobaea vulgaris ☠

Ragwort

Benweed | Cankerwort | Common Ragwort | Cushag | Dog Standard | Fairies' Horses | Ground Glutton | Groundeswelge | Groundsel | Ground-Swallower | Grundy Swallow | Satyrion | St. James' Wort | *Senecio jacobaea* | *Senecio laciniatus* | Sention | Simson | Staggerwort | Stammerwort | Stinking Nanny | Stinking Willie | Tansy Ragwort | Welsh Groundsel | Welsh Ragwort

✸ SYMBOLIC MEANINGS

Swallow; Swallow the ground.

✸ POSSIBLE POWERS

Aphrodisiac; Attracts love; Feminine energy; Fends off a spell or a charm; Healing; Health; Lust; Passion; Teeth; Venus; Water element.

✿ FOLKLORE AND FACTS

Wearing a Ragwort amulet is believed to have the power to prevent toothaches. • The ancient Greeks used Ragwort as an amulet of choice to fend off spells and charms that had been cast upon the wearer. • The ancient Greeks and Romans made an aphrodisiac from Ragwort. • Ragwort, by its common name of Cushag, is the national flower of the Isle of Man. • During the dark days of witch persecution, it was claimed that witches rode out at midnight not upon broomsticks but on stalks of Ragwort. • Ragwort has the ability to incite passion by just being near to it, which once made using it to make love charms a somewhat profitable endeavor. • Prior to the steady emigration of people moving from England, Ragwort was virtually unknown in North America until it was introduced into the newly planted English gardens in the New World.

No. 296

Jasminum officinale ⚱

Jasmine

Jasminum officinale var. *piliferum* | *Jasminum officinale* var. *tibeticum* | *Jasminum officinale* var. *viminale* | *Jasminum officinale* var. *vulgatius* | Jessamine | Jessamine | Poet's Jasmine | Summer Jasmine | True Jasmine | White Jasmine | Yasmin

✸ SYMBOLIC MEANINGS

Amiability; Demure beauty; Gift from God; Sensuality; Unspoken elegance.

✸ POSSIBLE POWERS

Aphrodisiac; Attracts love; Comfort to the soul; Enchantment; Encourages the magic of the evening; Feminine energy; Love; Moon; Mystery; Psychic dreams; Vishnu; Water element.

✿ FOLKLORE AND FACTS

Jasmine flowers attract spiritual love. • The fragrance of Jasmine flowers helps to promote sleep. • Make a Jasmine flower sachet to tuck under the pillow to encourage psychic dreams. • Make two red sachets of Jasmine flowers and leaves to tuck under both sides of the mattress to encourage sensuous lovemaking. • Jasmine is the national flower of Syria and Pakistan.

No. 297

Jasminum sambac

Arabian Jasmine

Asian Jasmine | Asiatic Jasmine | *Jasminum bicorollatum* | *Jasminum blancoi* | *Jasminum fragrans* | *Jasminum odoratum* | *Jasminum pubescens* | *Jasminum quadrifolium* | *Jasminum quinqueflorum* | *Jasminum sambac* var. *heyneanum* | *Jasminum sanjurium* | *Jasminum undulatum* | *Jasminum zambac* | Jessamine | Melati Putih | *Mogorium gimea* | *Mogorium goaense* | *Mogorium sambac* | *Mogorium undulatum* | *Nyctanthes goa* | *Nyctanthes sambac* | *Nyctanthes undulata* | Sacred Jasmine | Sambac Jasmine | Sampaguita | Yeh Hsi Ming

✸ SYMBOLIC MEANINGS

Amiability; Cheerfulness; Folly; Glee; Material wealth; Modesty; Sensuality; Timidity; Wealth.

✸ POSSIBLE POWERS

Aphrodisiac; Attracts love; Business; Comfort to the soul; Divination; Dream magic; Emotions; Expansion; Fertility; Generation; Honor; Inspiration; Intuition; Leadership; Love; Money; Moon; Politics; Power; Prophetic dreams; Psychic ability; Public acclaim; Responsibility; Royalty; Sea; Subconscious mind; Success; Tides; Travel by water; Wealth.

✿ FOLKLORE AND FACTS

Arabian Jasmine has been made the national flower of Indonesia because it has been revered as a sacred flower and an integral part of Indonesian traditions since ancient times. • Arabian Jasmine flowers attract spiritual love. • The fragrance of Arabian Jasmine flowers helps to promote sleep. • Some traditional Javanese brides and grooms will deck themselves with exquisite, intricately designed Arabian Jasmine flower bud garlands known as "ronce melati" that look like they were woven of pearls or plump grains of rice. • Arabian Jasmine is presented, with reverence, at many Indonesian funerals. • It is believed by many that the aromatherapeutic fragrance of Arabian Jasmine essential oil is as effective as Lavender in calming anxiety to promote sleep.

J

No. 298

Juglans nigra ☠☕🍴

Black Walnut
Eastern American Black Walnut | *Juglans pitteursii* | *Juglans rugosa* | *Wallia nigra*

✳ SYMBOLIC MEANINGS
Infertility; Intellect; Presentiment; Stratagem.

⚜ POSSIBLE POWERS
Access divine energy; Brings forth blessings; Colorize; Fertility; Fire element; Health; Infertility; Masculine energy; Mental clarity or power; Strong mental power; Sun; Wishing.

❧ FOLKLORE AND FACTS
Given the space, a Black Walnut tree can live to an old age of several hundred years. It can grow tall to around 110 feet, with a trunk circumference of twenty feet, and with a canopy that can stretch out widely to approximately forty feet of leafy shade. The tree's fruit is a drupe, like an Almond or Peach. • Other plants will usually not grow under or anywhere in close proximity to the Black Walnut tree. The chemical juglone acts as a natural herbicide in the fallen leaves and husks, causing other plants to not grow under the tree. The Black Walnut is all about its own self, creating its own best advantage for a substantial establishment that is optimal for maximum growth potential. It accomplishes this by dominating the area where it is growing, by exuding overpowering chemicals that comes out from its roots. This biological chemical process is known as allelopathy. The chemicals will not allow anything but that tree to grow there. • Black Walnut can produce a brown-colored vegetable dye for fabric. • Once Black Walnut kernels have been laboriously removed from their sticky husks, then roasted, they are edible and used for flavoring. • Ground Black Walnut shells have been used for grit in sandblasting. • Black Walnut lumber is prized for furniture making and cabinetry. • For those persons suffering serious infertility issues, make four Black Walnut sachets or amulets by tucking the leaves into small, white cotton pouches that you, yourself, have made. In your best handwriting, write out your array of prayers, hopes, and dreams for a child on four pieces of paper. Fold each note small enough to tuck into each of the sachets. Hang the first over the head of the bed. Tuck the second under the foot of the mattress. Tuck the remaining two on each side of the mattress. Relax.

No. 299

Juglans regia ☠☕

English Walnut
Allegheny Walnut | Bedoo Walnut | Broadview Walnut | Carpathian Walnut | Carya | Circassian Walnut | Common Walnut Tree | Dió | Echter Walnussbaum | Europaische Walnuss | European Walnut | Gewone Walnoot | Hetao Shu | *Juglans asplenifolia* | *Juglans dissecta* | *Juglans duclouxiana* | *Juglans fallax* | *Juglans fertilis* | *Juglans frutescens* | *Juglans fruticosa* | *Juglans heterophylla* | *Juglans kamaonia* | *Juglans longirostris* | *Juglans orientis* | *Juglans quercifolia* | *Juglans regia var. laciniata* | *Juglans regia subsp. sinensis* | *Juglans salicifolia* | *Juglans sinensis* | Karydia | Kkernoot | Madeira Walnut | Noce | Noce Commune | Nogal | Nogal Común | Nogal de Castilla | Nogal Inglés | Noghera | Nogueira-Comum | Nos | Noyer | Noyer Commun | Noz | Nuc | Nuez | Nus | Nut fit for a God | Orech | Oresak Vlassky | Persian Nut | Persian Walnut | Valnød | Valnoettraed | Walnoot | Walnuss | Walnussbaum

✳ SYMBOLIC MEANINGS
Infertility; Intellect; Presentiment; Stratagem.

⚜ POSSIBLE POWERS
Attracts lightning; Colorize; Fertility; Fire element; Health; Infertility; Mental clarity or power; Strong mental power; Sun; Wishing.

❧ FOLKLORE AND FACTS
The English Walnut is a very large tree that can live for 200 years; it can grow up to 120 feet tall, with a six-foot circumference and a wide-reaching canopy. It is a tree that demands space and full sun to grow to its full potential. The fruit is a drupe with a seriously difficult hull to remove to reach the hard-shelled seed with its edible kernel within it. The kernel is edible after it has been roasted. English Walnut wood is prized for its strength and lustrous beauty. It is used to make furniture, guitars, flooring, gunstocks, and cabinetry. • The English Walnut is all about its own self, creating its own best advantage for a substantial establishment that is optimal for maximum growth potential. It accomplishes this by dominating the area where it is growing, by exuding overpowering chemicals that come out from its roots. This biological chemical process is known as allelopathy. The chemicals will not allow anything but that tree to grow there. The chemical juglone acts as a natural herbicide in the fallen leaves and husks, causing other plants to not grow under the tree. • All wishes will be granted if someone is luckily gifted a bag of English Walnuts. • Italian witches supposedly ritually danced under English Walnut trees. • An English Walnut supposedly attracts lightning, so don't carry one in a storm. • Gifting a bag of English Walnuts should be with

the hope that the recipient's wishes will come true. • If a bride wishes to delay conception for a while, she should tuck a number of roasted English Walnuts into the bodice of her wedding gown equal to the number of years she wishes to wait before having children. • For those persons suffering serious infertility issues, make four English Walnut sachets or amulets by tucking the leaves into small, white cotton pouches that you, yourself, have made. In your best handwriting, write out your array of prayers, hopes, and dreams for a child on four pieces of paper. Fold each note small enough to tuck into each of the sachets. Hang the first over the head of the bed. Tuck the second under the foot of the mattress. Tuck the remaining two on each side of the mattress. Relax. • It is believed that Alexander the Great introduced the *Juglans regia* to Macedonia and Greece, garnering one of the tree's first common names of Persian Nut and Persian Walnut. • English Walnut will create a brown dye. To get the black color, do the dying in an iron pot.

No. 300
Juniperus communis 🐦🍴
Juniper
Enebro | Gemeiner Wachholder | Geneva | Gin Berry | Gin Plant | Ginepro | Jenever | Juniper Berry | *Juniperus communis* var. *charlottensis* | *Juniperus communis* var. *communis* | *Juniperus communis* var. *depressa* | *Juniperus communis* var. *hemisphaerica* | *Juniperus communis* var. *kelleyi* | *Juniperus communis* var. *megistocarpa* | *Juniperus communis* var. *nipponica* | *Juniperus communis* var. *saxatilis*

✺ SYMBOLIC MEANINGS
Cleanse; Bless; Protect.

⟐ POSSIBLE POWERS
Abundance; Advancement; Anti-theft; Aphrodisiac; Binding; Blessing; Breaks a hex; Building; Cleanse; Conscious will; Curse breaking; Death; Drive off snakes; Energy; Exorcism; Fire element; Friendship; Growth; Healing; Health; History; Joy; Knowledge; Leadership; Life; Light; Limitations; Male sexual potency; Masculine energy; Natural power; Obstacles; Protection; Psychic power; Purification; Success; Sun; Time.

☙ FOLKLORE AND FACTS
Juniper berries can be strung together and hung over a door to help protect the home from evil forces, evil people, intruding ghosts, sickness, snakes, and theft. • Men can make,

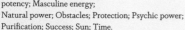

then carry or wear a red sachet or amulet of a Juniper sprig to hopefully increase their sexual potency. • Juniper berries can enhance psychic power. • Juniper essential oil can create a peaceful atmosphere for aromatherapy. • Juniper essential oil can also increase prosperity. • Make an amulet of Juniper to keep near the center of the home to continually help banish anything that will harm the health of those who live there. • Juniper berries from the *Juniperus communis* bush are of the type used in several Scandinavian and Northern European dishes, most particularly as a flavoring for wild game and wild birds. Juniper is also used to give gin and some other beverages their flavor. Take care which type of Juniper berries you eat. Some species of Juniper will produce inedible, toxic berries. • Using only brands of gin that use genuine Juniper berries for flavor, there is a gin-soaked raisin remedy that some arthritis sufferers swear by, though others find the remedy useless. At any rate, it might be worth giving it a try to discover if it provides any degree of relief. The remedy requires soaking golden raisins in gin for a few weeks. Then, eat approximately nine of these raisins a day. • The ancient Greeks believed that Juniper berries gave the Olympian athletes their stamina.

No. 301
Juniperus virginiana 🐦
Virginian Juniper
Aromatic Cedar | Baton Rouge | Eastern Juniper | Eastern Red Cedar | *Juniperus foetida* var. *virginiana* | *Sabina virginiana* | Pencil Cedar | Red Cedar | Red Juniper | Savin | Virginia Juniper | Virginian Cedarwood Tree

✺ SYMBOLIC MEANINGS
Constancy.

⟐ POSSIBLE POWERS
Art; Colorize; Communication; Fire element; Masculine energy; the Sun.

☙ FOLKLORE AND FACTS
The Virginian Juniper tree got the name Pencil Cedar because, up until the 1940s, it was used to make pencils. • Even though Virginian Juniper is also known as Virginian Cedarwood, the tree is in the *Juniperus* genus, rather than the *Cedrus*. • The essential oil is usually marketed as Virginian Cedarwood, which is useful for aromatherapy to promote a sense of oneness with woodsy nature. • The Virginian Juniper tree can live for 300 years. • When in need to dig bait worms to go fishing, you will most likely find all you need under a Virginian Juniper tree. • Virginian Juniper heartwood can be used to make a lovely dark-red dye.

No. 302
Kaempferia galanga 🝆
Resurrection Lily

Alpinia sessilis | Aromatic Ginger |
Camphor Root | Cekur | Cutcherry |
Galanga | Galangal | Galgant-Spice Lily |
Gisol | Kaempferia humilis | Kaempferia
latifolia | Kaempferia plantaginifolia |
Kaempferia procumbens | Kaempferia
rotunda | Kencur | Kuunkuun | Maraba |
Prăh | Prăh Krâ-oup | Proh Horm | Sand
Ginger | Sha Jiang | Shajiang | Shan Nai | Shannai | Waan Horm

☀ **SYMBOLIC MEANINGS**
Relive.

🌼 **POSSIBLE POWERS**
Aphrodisiac; Attracts love; Awareness; Breaks a hex; Clarity
of thought; Creates internal peacefulness; Euphoria; Healing;
Health; Hex breaking; Insecticide; Legal aid; Lust; Money;
Mosquito preventative; Overcomes exhaustion; Prophetic
dreams; Protection; Psychic powers; Seasoning.

🜍 **FOLKLORE AND FACTS**
The name Resurrection Lily comes from the fact that, even
after the root had been used to brew a medicinal tea, it
could be removed and allowed to dry and be reused again
several more times. • *Kaempferia galanga* is an aromatic
herb that has been used to flavor vodka and liqueurs. It is
also commonly used in Southeast Asian recipes where it is
known as Kencur, in a similar way as *Zingiber officinale*,
which is Common Ginger. However, the Resurrection Lily is
uniquely different from Common Ginger and the other three
of the four Galangals. The other three Galangals are *Alpinia
galanga*, *Alpinia officinarum*, and *Boesenbergia rotunda*,
which is also known as Fingerroot. • Chewing on a piece
of *Kaempferia galanga* while thinking of one's heart's desire
is supposed to be undertaken until the piece is reduced to a
mush. Spitting out all the mush fully determined that your
wish would come true. That can also be done to break a hex.
It was once believed that spitting it out onto a courtroom
floor would win the favor of the judge. Trust in the sage
advice that this absolutely will not bode well for the spitter.
It would be much better to do the chewing and spitting
charm before going into the court, or instead tucking a small
piece of the root into a pocket as an amulet before entering.
• Powdered *Kaempferia galanga* is used in Chinese medicine.

No. 303
Kigelia africana ☠🝆
Sausage Tree

Bignonia africana | Cucumber Tree | Kigeli-Keia | Modukguhlu | Muvevha | Tecoma africana |
UmFongothi | Um Vunguta | Worsboom

☀ **SYMBOLIC MEANINGS**
A lost loved one; Ingenuity.

🌼 **POSSIBLE POWERS**
Handicrafts; Healing; Hide tanning; Portability; Usefulness.

🜍 **FOLKLORE AND FACTS**
The sacred Sausage Tree flowers are huge, dark red, trumpet-
shaped, and dripping with nectar. • The unusual fruits of
the Sausage Tree look like long sausages hanging all over
the tree, with each one weighing up to fifteen pounds. • The
huge fruit of the Sausage Tree can be dried, hollowed out,
and converted into sturdy containers, cups, ladles, and even
mouse traps. • Considering the size and overall weight of the
Sausage Tree fruit, it is easy to imagine the extent of damage
that the fruit can cause to vehicles and people who may
happen to be under a tree when a "sausage" falls. • The green
fruits of the Sausage Tree are highly toxic, but during times
of extreme famine the seeds were roasted and consumed
anyway, at the risk of illness. •
Sausage Tree bark has been used
for tanning hides. • The Luo and
Luhya people in Kenya will bury a
Sausage Tree fruit as a proxy body
for someone who has been lost
and is believed dead. • A black
dye can be made from the Sausage
Tree fruit. A yellow dye can be
made from the roots.

K

No. 304
Lamium album ⚰

White Archangel
Archangel | Bee Nettle | Blind Nettle | Death Nettle | Dumb Nettle | *Lamium vulgatum* | White Dead Nettle | White Nettle

✳ SYMBOLIC MEANINGS
White light.

❀ POSSIBLE POWERS
Eases deep depression following emotional upheaval; Emotional healing following sexually related trauma; Healing; Health; Joy; Purity; Youth.

❦ FOLKLORE AND FACTS
White Archangel is especially attractive to bumblebees that depend on it as an early source of pollen and nectar after a long winter. • White Archangel has been used for medicinal purposes in Europe for centuries. • St. Hildegard of Bingen, the renowned German herbalist, Catholic abbess, mystique, and prolific writer, was also known as the Sibyl of the Rhine, and most importantly as Doctor of the Church. She wrote of White Archangel's healing properties in her nine-volume medieval masterwork on medicinal healings titled *Physica*.

No. 305
Lantana camara ☠

Lantana
Baho-Baho | Big-Sage | Coronet | Coronitas | Fart Flower | Gu Phool | Korsoe Wiwiri | Korsu Wiri | *Lantana camara* subsp. *aculeata* | *Lantana camara* subsp. *camara* | *Lantana camara* subsp. *glandulosissima* | *Lantana camara* subsp. *moldenkei* | *Lantana camara* subsp. *moritiana* | *Lantana camara* subsp. *portoricensis* | Putus | Red Sage | Shrub Verbena | Smelly Flower | Spanish Flag | Tickberry | Tutti-Frutti Flower | Umbelanterna | Utot-Utot | West Indian Lantana | Wild Sage | Yellow Sage

✳ SYMBOLIC MEANINGS
Severity; Rigor.

❀ POSSIBLE POWERS
Generosity; Helps to release emotional anguish; Helps to heal sadness; Openness.

❦ FOLKLORE AND FACTS
Lantana is a familiar native wild plant in the tropics and subtropics that profusely blooms round clusters of very small, mixed-color flowers per pretty cluster. • Lantana is very fragrant but not sweet-smelling. • Used in parts of India for some furniture making that is much like the more expensive cane and bamboo, items woven from Lantana are resistant to rain, sunshine, and termites.

No. 306
Lathyrus odoratus ☠

Sweetpea
Doncenón | *Lathyrus cyprius* | *Lathyrus maccaguenii* | *Lathyrus odoratus-zeylanicus* | *Pisum odoratum* | Sweet Pea | Tacones

✳ SYMBOLIC MEANINGS
Blissful pleasure; Chastity; Delicacy; Departure; Goodbye; I think of you; Meeting; a Meeting; Thank you for a lovely time.

❀ POSSIBLE POWERS
Chastity; Courage; Feminine energy; Friendship; Strength; Venus; Water element.

❦ FOLKLORE AND FACTS
Wear a sprig of Sweetpea for strength. • To help keep someone chaste, place a nosegay of Sweetpea flowers in a vase in their bedroom. • Fresh Sweetpea flowers forge friendships. • Hold a Sweetpea flower in your hand to encourage the truth to be told to you. • Make, then wear or carry a Sweetpea sachet for strength and courage.

No. 307
Laurus nobilis ⚕🍴

Bay Laurel
Bai | Bay | Bay Tree | Grecian Laurel | Laurel | Laurel Tree | Laurus | *Laurus angusta* | *Laurus tenuifolia* | *Laurus undulata* | Moon Laurel | Roman Laurel | Sweet Bay | True Laurel

✳ SYMBOLIC MEANINGS
Fadeless affection; Fame; Glory; Health; I change but in death; Immortality; Love; No change till death; Notability; Poets; Praise; Prosperity; Renown; Resurrection of Christ; Strength; Success; Victory.

🌱 COMPONENT MEANINGS
Leaf: I change but in death.
Wreath: Fame; Glory; Reward of merit.

❀ POSSIBLE POWERS
Abundance; Advancement; Apollo; Asclepius; Attract romance; Ceres; Clairvoyance; Cleansing; Conscious will; Energy; Eros; Faunus; Fire element; Friendship; Good fortune; Good luck; Growth; Healing; Induces prophetic dreams; Joy; Leadership; Life; Light; Masculine energy; Natural power; Physical and moral cleansing; prosperity; Protection; Protection against black magic; Protection

L

against evil spirits; or during an electrical storm; Psychic power; Purification; Ritual purification; Strength; Success; Sun; Wards off evil, evil magic, lightning, or negativity; Wisdom.

☘ FOLKLORE AND FACTS

In ancient Greece, the poets, heroes, winning athletes, and esteemed leaders were crowned with wreaths made from Bay Laurel leaves. • Prophets used to hold Bay Laurel boughs when foretelling the future. • Bay Laurel leaves were especially used to protect emperors and warriors going off into battle. • Put a whole undamaged Bay Laurel leaf in every corner of every room of the home to protect all who live there. • To ensure lasting love, a couple would break off a twig of Bay Laurel and then break it in half, with each retaining a piece. • Wishes written on Bay Laurel leaves, then buried in a sunny spot will help make them come true. • Bay Laurel leaves placed under a pillow can induce prophetic dreams. • According to legend, if you stood by a Bay Laurel tree you could not be struck by lightning or be affected by the evil of witches. • The dried berry-like fruit that is harvested from a *Laurus nobilis* tree and marketed as Laurel Berry is used as a spice. • One long-ago divination that encouraged dreaming of a future mate was only to be done on one's birthday, by arising between 3 and 4 A.M. in total secrecy, then make way to wherever one must go to pluck one perfect green Magic Laurel leaf before bringing it back to the bedroom. There, it must be held over lighted sulphur brimstone for five minutes carefully timed with a watch. Place the Bay Laurel leaf remnants within a white cotton cloth along with one's own name and that of one's lover or lovers, all written out in one's own best penmanship. Written, too, needs to be the day of the week, the date of the year, and the exact age of the Moon phase at the time of the writing. Fold the cloth over neatly then quickly bury it in the ground, where it is sure to not be disturbed for three days and three nights. On the early morning of the fourth day, lift the bundle up from the ground, bringing it forth to be placed under the pillow to sleep upon it for the first of three consecutive nights. All that to hopefully dream prophetically of one's own true destiny. Keep a notebook and pen by the bedside to write down as much of the dream as can be remembered upon first waking.

No. 308

Lavandula angustifolia ☙❶

English Lavender

Common Lavender | Elf | Elf Leaf | *Lavandula officinalis* | Nard | Nardus | Narrow-leaved Lavender | Official Lavender | Spike | True Lavender

✴ SYMBOLIC MEANINGS

Constancy; Devotion; Distrust; Faith; Faithful; Humility; Love; Mistrust; Silence.

⊛ POSSIBLE POWERS

Air element; Aphrodisiac; Attracts love; Business transactions; Business; Calls in Good Spirits; Caution; Charms against the Evil Eye; Chastity; Cleverness; Communication; Creativity; Deodorize; Expansion; Faith; Happiness; Healing; Honor; Illumination; Induces sleep; Initiation; Inner sight; Intelligence; Leadership; Learning; Longevity; Love; Magic; Masculine energy; Memory; Mercury; Peace; Politics; Power; Protection; Prudence; Public acclaim; Purification; Responsibility; Royalty; Science; Self-preservation; Sleep; Sound judgment; Success; Thievery; Wealth; Wisdom.

☘ FOLKLORE AND FACTS

Since ancient times, *Lavandula* herbs have been used to freshen rooms, linens, and one's own self. Other *Lavandula* species can be used for magical, strewing, and ornamental purposes. But it is the *Lavandula angustifolia* English Lavender plant that is used in foods. • *Lavandula angustifolia* English Lavender is the best choice for use in aromatherapy, in a diffusing mister, and in products intended for children and pets. • Sprigs of English Lavender were once given to women in labor to hold, as squeezing their hands upon it would release the calming fragrance to help ease their suffering. • English Lavender in the home is considered to bring peacefulness into it. • When combined with citrus fragrances, English Lavender will acquire a lovely

L

but different sweet scent. • During ancient Roman times, English Lavender was a luxury priced at almost equal to a month's wages. • English Lavender is one of the herbs in the spice blend *Herbes de Provence*. • Dried English Lavender buds make lovely confetti to toss toward newlyweds following their wedding ceremony. • English Lavender sprigs given to newlyweds are thought to bring them good luck. • It is thought that sniffing English Lavender fragrance will enable one to see ghosts. • Wearing clothes that have been scented with English Lavender flowers will attract love. • Writing a love note on paper that has been scented with the fragrance of English Lavender flowers will attract love. • Scatter English Lavender flowers around the home to induce peacefulness and lift a sense of depression from your environment. • English Lavender is an herb that can be used for nearly all positive purposes. • Aromatherapy using English Lavender essential oil is widely known to produce a calm, tranquil, and peaceful environment for relaxation, meditation, and restful sleep. • If one can possess only a small bottle of just one essential oil, it should be the immensely versatile English lavender, *Lavandula angustifolia*. • Put eight ounces of distilled water into a spray bottle before adding six to twelve drops of English Lavender essential oil for use as a shake-and-spray room deodorizer.

fingernails, fabrics, and leather. A Henna rinse over shades of blonde hair will transform it to be red-orange. • In Europe during the 1800s, Henna-colored red hair became popular with the Aesthetic and the Pre-Raphaelite artists who fancied painting red-haired women with flowing hair into their artistic visions. This, in itself, inspired bohemian young European women to color their own hair red, popularizing personal beautification via Henna all the more. • In India, it is often believed that the person with Henna on the palms can receive and offer blessings. • The Henna symbolism painted on the tops of the hands is placed there for protection. • Every culture that includes the use of Henna does so in its own way. In Morocco, Henna is used to paint symbols to fend off the evil eye. In India, a bride's hands are covered with intricate Henna tattoos as a blessing to her on her wedding day to grant her joy, the beauty of love, the commitment of marriage, and as an offering of herself to be spiritually awakened into her future as a wife and mother. • The dye products that are marketed as "neutral henna" are neither Henna, nor are they a derivative of any Henna species, instead from a *Senna* or *Cassia* species. • The dye products that are marketed as "black henna" are neither Henna, nor are they a derivative of any Henna species. They can be quite harmful, and should be entirely avoided.

No. 309

Lawsonia inermis ☠

Henna

Alcanna spinosa | Alkanna spinosa | Camphire | Casearia multiflora | Hina | Henna | Lawsonia alba | Lawsonia coccinea | Lawsonia falcifolia | Lawsonia purpurea | Lawsonia spinosa | Rotantha combretoides

✿ SYMBOLIC MEANINGS
Artifice; Fragrance; You are better than handsome.

🌀 POSSIBLE POWERS
Blessings; Emotions; Fertility; Generation; Headache relief; Healing; Health; Inspiration; Intuition; Love; Moon; Protection from the evil eye; Protection from illness; Psychic ability; Romance; Romantic love; Sea; Sea magic; Subconscious mind; Tides; Travel by water; Water element.

🜂 FOLKLORE AND FACTS
Wear a sprig of Henna leaves near your heart to attract romantic love to you. • Henna is used as a dye for skin,

No. 310

Lepidium meyenii ⚗

Maca

Ayak Chichira | Ayak Willku | Lepidium affine | Lepidium gelidum | Lepidium peruvianum | Lepidium weddellii | Maca-Maca | Maino | Peruvian Ginseng | Root of Life | Yellow Maca

✿ SYMBOLIC MEANINGS
Endure.

🌀 POSSIBLE POWERS
Adapt to stress; Anti-depressant; Aphrodisiac; Attracts love; Cope with a challenge or stress; Endurance; Energy; Fertility; Health; Improves stamina; Increases libido; Longevity; Memory booster; Sex magic; Sexual performance.

🜂 FOLKLORE AND FACTS
The overall shape of the Maca plant taproot is inconsistent, being large, small, flattened, rectangular, triangular, or an overall surprise when it is uprooted. • One Maca plant has the capacity to produce approximately 1,000 tiny seeds. • A crop of Maca needs to be heavily fertilized, most especially after harvesting, to replenish the nutrients in the soil that the plant will utterly exhaust. • The primary use of Maca is to dry and grind it into a flour, which has been used for baking, gruel, and a beer-like beverage in the Andes for more than 3,000 years. • Maca is heavily marketed for its unproven,

L

traditional, medicinal health benefits. • Maca-root powder has been heavily touted for its "curve-ability," that is, for the imbiber to grow a larger butt. The advertisements neglect to mention that Maca is believed to possibly produce too much testosterone in the body, causing voice deepening, excessive body hair growth, and a resistance to insulin. • It is believed that the ancient Inca warriors would carry Maca with them for endurance when they went out warring. • In contrast to what superfood herb marketers and herbal advisors have been recklessly recommending to naïve athletes in training, beware! The increase in testosterone that Maca will provide can appear on a drug test in direct violation of World Anti-Doping Code, which can result in dire consequences for any competitive athlete.

No. 311
Lepidium sativum ⚶

Cress

Arabis chinensis | *Cardamon sativum* | Chandrashoor | *Crucifera nasturtium* | Garden Cress | Garden Pepper Cress | *Lepia sativa* | *Lepidium spinescens* | Mustard and Cress | *Nasturtium crispum* | *Nasturtium hortense* | *Nasturtium sativum* | *Nasturtium spinescens* | *Nasturtium spinosum* | Pepper Cress | Pepper Grass | Pepperwort | Poor Man's Pepper | *Thlaspi nasturtium* | *Thlaspi sativum* | *Thlaspidium sativum*

☀ **SYMBOLIC MEANINGS**
Always reliable; Power; Roving; Stability.

🌎 **POSSIBLE POWERS**
Aphrodisiac; Attracts love; Courage; Daring; Invisibility; Power; Saturn.

🜍 **FOLKLORE AND FACTS**
Magically, Cress is considered a Saturn and Taurus herb that is used in combination with other magically designated plants in sex magic, among other things. • Due to its ability to draw up toxins from the ground, take extra care when selecting a spot to plant Cress so as not to unwittingly contaminate it.

No. 312
Leptospermum scoparium ⚶

Mānuka Myrtle

Broom Tea-Tree | Jelly Bush | Kāhikatoa | *Leptospermum bullatum* | *Leptospermum floribundum* | *Leptospermum humifusum* | *Leptospermum linifolium* | *Leptospermum multiflorum* | *Leptospermum nicholsii* | *Leptospermum obliquum* | *Leptospermum oxycedrus* | *Leptospermum pungens* | Manuka | Mānuka | *Melaleuca scoparia* | *Melaleuca tenuifolia* | New Zealand Teatree | Tea Tree

☀ **SYMBOLIC MEANINGS**
Tenacity.

🌎 **POSSIBLE POWERS**
Adaptation; Health.

🜍 **FOLKLORE AND FACTS**
In the twentieth century, the Mānuka Myrtle was considered a despised weed. Today, the sentiment is completely opposite, now that its function is a contribution to conservation and the economy. • Honeybees love Mānuka Myrtle and make delicious mānuka honey using its nectar and pollen. • New Zealand's wild parakeets, the kākāriki, eat the Mānuka Myrtle leaves to purge their parasites. • Although the Mānuka Myrtle is called Tea Tree, and it is somewhat related to the *Melaleuca alternifolia* Tea Tree, from which the Tea Tree essential oil is extracted, the two plants are not at all the same.

No. 313
Levisticum officinale ⚶🍴

Lovage

Angelica levisticum | *Angelica paludapifolia* | Chinese Lovage | Deveseel | Devesil | Helsvé | *Hipposelinum levisticum* | Italian Lovage | Italian Parsley | Lavose | Lestyán | Leustean | Levistico | *Levisticum caucasicum* | *Levisticum levisticum* | *Levisticum paludapifolium* | *Levisticum persicum* | *Levisticum vulgare* | Libbsticka | Libeček | Liebstöckel | Ligurček | Ligusticum | *Ligusticum levisticum* | Liperi | Lipstikka | Livèche | Løpstikke | Lovage Leaf | Love Herb | Love Parsley | Love Rod | Love Root | Love Sticklet | Løvstikke | Loving Herbs | Lubczyk | Lubestico | Luštrek | Lyubistok | Maggikraut | Maggiplant | Sea Parsley | Sedano di Monte | *Selinum levisticum* | Yaban Kerevizi

☀ **SYMBOLIC MEANINGS**
Bring love; Love.

🌎 **POSSIBLE POWERS**
Aphrodisiac; Attraction; Attracts trustworthy friends; Courage in love; Love; Permanent love; Protection against negative spirits; Removes sexual blockages; Sexual love; Success; Wealth.

🜍 **FOLKLORE AND FACTS**
People are believed to fall in love with someone who has been made magically attractive with Lovage. Due to that

L

particular magical property, Lovage has been used in love potions and charms for hundreds of years. • During medieval times, a bride would sometimes tuck a sprig of Lovage in her hair. • It is believed that adding Lovage to the bath water before going out to meet new people will increase one's attractiveness.

No. 314

Ligusticum scothicum

Scots Lovage

Angelica scothica | Apium ternatum | Haloscias scothicum | Ligusticum biternatum | Ligusticum boreale | Meum scothicum | Petroselinum ternatum | Scotch Wild Lovage | Scottish Licorice-Root | Sea Celery | Sea Lovage | Sea Parsley

☀ SYMBOLIC MEANINGS
Inspired love.

🌼 POSSIBLE POWERS
Enhances attractiveness; Fire element; Flavoring; Healing; Health; Love; Masculine energy; Prophetic dreams; Psychic cleansing; Purification; Romance; Sun.

✿ FOLKLORE AND FACTS
Scots Lovage is commonly found growing on cliff tops and in the crevices between rocks. • The flavor of Scots Lovage leaves is similar to Celery or Parsley. The seeds are similar to Cumin or Fenugreek. Young shoots are sometimes candied. • Scots Lovage will not continue to grow where it would be grazed upon. • Sailors returning from long voyages relied on Scots Lovage as a remedy for the scurvy they suffered. • A sachet to attract love is all the more effective with an herb that has the word "love" in its name, as Scots Lovage does. • Make, then carry or wear a pink and red sachet of Scots Lovage to attract romance and love.

No. 315

Lilium × asiatica ☠☕

Asiatic Lily

Asiatic Hybrid Lily

☀ SYMBOLIC MEANINGS
Beauty; Birth; Devotion; Divinity; Exalted and unapproachable; Holy Spirit; Honor; Humility; Magnificence; Majesty; Marriage; Modesty; Pride; Purity; Purity of Heart; Religious; Supreme; Sweetness and humility; Unity of heart.

🎨 COLOR MEANINGS
Gold: Purity; Surrender to the grace of God.
Lavender: Passion; Privilege; Royalty.
Orange: Desire; Dislike; Hatred; Passion; Revenge.
Pink: Admiration; Femininity; Love.
Rose: Love; Unity.
Scarlet: High-bred; High-souled; High-souled aspirations.
White: Celebration; It's heavenly to be with you; Majesty; Modesty; Purity; Sociability; Sweetness; Virginity; Youth.
Yellow: False; Falsehood; Gaiety; Gay; Gratitude; Happiness; I'm walking on air; Lies; Playful beauty.

🌼 POSSIBLE POWERS
Afterlife; Breaking a love spell; Exorcism; Feminine energy; Fends off a ghost; Juno; Keeps an unwanted visitor away; Kwan Yin; Moon; Nepthys; Protection; Purification; Repels negativity; Truth; Venus; Water element.

✿ FOLKLORE AND FACTS
The Asiatic Lily is a hybrid of multiple crossings between multiple *Lilium* species that are most common in Asia. They are a favorite with florists because of their smaller, fragrance-free blossoms, which are approximately four inches in diameter. The flowers are gorgeous and are available in every color. • Plant Asiatic Lilies in the garden to fend off ghosts. • Plant Asiatic Lilies in the garden to fend off evil. • Make a sachet with Asiatic Lily petals within it to wear or carry to break a love spell that has been cast upon you by a specific person. • Bury an old piece of leather in a bed of Asiatic Lily plants to bring forth clues from a crime committed in the past year. • Put a bouquet of Asiatic Lilies on a table in the house that can be seen from the front door to repel negativity.

L

No. 316
Lilium auratum ☠🝳

Goldband Lily
Goldenband Lily | Golden-Rayed Lily | Golden-Rayed Lily of Japan | Lilium auratum var. auratum | Lilium auratum var. platyphyllum | Mountain Lily | Yamayuri

🌸 **SYMBOLIC MEANINGS**
Pure of heart.

🌸 **POSSIBLE POWERS**
Repels a malicious spirit; Repels any malicious entity; Repels dark magic; Repels negative energy; Resists negative influences.

🌙 **FOLKLORE AND FACTS**
The Goldband Lily is one of the true lilies, strongly scented and considered to be the tallest, reaching up to eight feet, and most abundantly blooming of all the various species of *Lilium* plants. • By simply planting it in the garden, the Goldband Lily exudes positive energy that can protect the garden, the property, the home, and all who reside in it against dark magic, negative energy, malicious spirits, and unpleasant entities, as well as help resist pestering negative influences.

No. 317
Limnophila aromatica

Rice Paddy Herb
Ma Om | Ngổ | Ngò | Ngò Om | Ngò Ôm

🌸 **SYMBOLIC MEANINGS**
Submerged.

🌸 **POSSIBLE POWERS**
Fertility; Water element; Water magic.

🌙 **FOLKLORE AND FACTS**
Rice Paddy Herb is aquatic and is often cultivated and harvested for use in fish aquariums. • Rice Paddy Herb is harvested during the dry season after the Rice harvest. After drying it on the rooftop, Rice Paddy Herb is saved for use as a condiment for seafood or as a flavoring in soup.

No. 318
Lindera benzoin 🝳

Spicebush
Benjamin Bush | Benzoin aestivale | Benzoin benzoin | Benzoin geniculatum | Benzoin odoriferum | Calosmon acstivale | Calosmon benzoin | Common Spicebush | Euosmus aestivalis | Euosmus benzoin | Laurus aestivalis | Laurus axillaris | Laurus benzoin | Laurus fragrans | Laurus glomerata | Laurus pseudobenzoin | Malapoenna geniculata | Malapoenna glomerata | Northern Spicebush | Ozanthes benzoin | Tetranthera aestivalis | Tetranthera floridana | Wild Allspice

🌸 **SYMBOLIC MEANINGS**
Arable land; Growth potential.

🌸 **POSSIBLE POWERS**
Air element; Crop worthy; Masculine energy; Success in the field; the Sun.

🌙 **FOLKLORE AND FACTS**
During the pioneer years in North America, land surveyors used Spicebush as a sign that the land could sustain cultivated crops. • The *Papilio troilus* butterfly favors the Spicebush so much as a host plant to feed its developing caterpillars, that one of its common names is Spicebush Swallowtail. • A tea can be made from the buds and leaves. The fruits are dried for use like Allspice.

No. 319
Linum usitatissimum 🝳

Flax
Aazhi Vidhai | Agasi | Akshi | Alashi | Avisalu | Common Flax | Javas | Jawas | Linaza | Lino | Linseed | Linum arvense | Linum crepitans | Linum grandiflorum | Linum humile | Linum indehiscens | Linum monadelphum | Linum moroderorum | Linum mucronatum | Linum reuteri | Linum sativum | Linum trinervium | Linum utile | Sib Muma | Tisi

🌸 **SYMBOLIC MEANINGS**
Beauty; Benefactor; Domestic industry; Fate; Genius; Healing; I feel your benefits; I feel your kindness; Kindness; Money.

🌿 **COMPONENT MEANING**
Dried: Utility.

🌸 **POSSIBLE POWERS**
Beauty; Cloth; Clothe; Draws in money; Fends off poverty; Fire element; Healing; Health; Hulda; Luck; Masculine energy; Mercury; Money; Polishing; Preserves wood; Protection; Protection against sorcery; Psychic power; Purification.

L

FOLKLORE AND FACTS

Dyed wild Flax fibers found in the prehistoric Dzudzuana Cave were scientifically determined to be at least 34,000 years old. • Smooth, straight Flax fiber is up to three times as strong as Cotton fiber and is one of the oldest fiber plants in history, being grown and methodically processed since the times of ancient Egypt. • Using Flax fiber to create cloth in northern Europe goes back as far as Neolithic times. • Bundles of soft, lustrous Flax fiber inspired the term "flaxen blonde hair." • Starting with two small squares of woven linen, prepare the Flax plant materials for use as a natural vegetable dye to color the cloth whatever color they end up being. It might be anywhere from a blue to a tan color. It will not matter what. Dry them. Fashion the squares into sachets to hold each one silver coin each. Put one in the pocket, purse, or wallet to draw money to it. Hang the second one on the front door to pull money into the home. • Make, then wear or carry a Flax-flower sachet as protection against sorcery. • Mix Flax seeds with crushed Red Pepper to keep in a small, wooden keepsake box that was made from one of the several protective woods. Place the box in a position of honor in the home for luck and protection. • Place Flax seed in a sachet to wear for protection against malicious magic. • Place Flax seeds in a shoe, pocket, wallet, or purse to fend off poverty. • Place Flax on a home altar with shiny coins to fend off poverty. • The oil pressed from the *Linum usitatissimum* Flax seeds is known as linseed oil that is used as a pigment binder in oil paint, as a hardener in putty, as a varnish for finishing woods, and in the manufacture of linoleum flooring. • Ground Flax seed is often used in breads and cereals. • Flax fiber is also used for something as fine as lacemaking and as coarse as rope-making. It is also used in the manufacture of canvas, tea bags, cigarette rolling paper, blotting and filter papers, and the paper used for printing money.

No. 320

Lippia abyssinica

Koseret

A-Kimbo | African Verbena | Brégué Balenté | Butter Clarifying Herb | Dutmutzuri | Gambey Tea Bush | Gambia Tea Bush | Gambia Tea Shrub | Gambia-Teestrauch | Kasey | Kesenet | Kesse | Kessie | Kisiniti | Kosearut Koserēti | Kusaayee | Kusay | Kusaye | *Lantana abyssinica* | *Lantana polycephala* | Lemon Herb | *Lippia adoensis* var. *koseret* | *Lippia grandifolia* | *Lippia schimperi* | Mousso et Mâle | Ngadi | Quereret | Verveine d'Afrique

SYMBOLIC MEANINGS
Stay.

POSSIBLE POWERS
Longevity; Preservation; Protection.

FOLKLORE AND FACTS
Koseret is used as a potherb and seasoning, especially in Ethiopian cuisine. But Koseret's most notable use is for the preservation of oil and butter that can resist spoiling for as long as fifteen years.

No. 321

Lophophora williamsii

Peyote Cactus

Anhalonium lewinii | Anhalonium williamsii | Ariocarpus williamsii | Echinocactus lewisii | Lophophora echinata | Lophophora jourdaniana | Lophophora lewinii | Lophophora lutea | Lophophora pentagona | Lophophora pluricostata | Mammillaria lewinii | Mammillaria williamsii | Mescal Cactus | Peyotl xochimilcensis | Peyotl zacatensis

SYMBOLIC MEANINGS
Delusion; Glistening delusion.

POSSIBLE POWERS
Delusions; Dreams; Hallucinations.

FOLKLORE AND FACTS
In Southwest Texas, the spineless and very slow-growing Peyote Cactus has been so over-harvested since the onset of the psychedelic 1960s that it is now considered to be an endangered species. • The Peyote Cactus has been religiously, ritualistically, and ceremonially used by Native Americans for more than 2,000 years.

L

No. 322
Lunaria annua

Honesty
Crucifera lunaria | Flower of Io | Flower of the Cow | Lunaria biennis | Lunaria inodora | Lunary | Mondveilchen | Money Plant | Moonwort | Satin Flower | Silver Dollar Plant | Viola lunaria | Violet of the Moon

☀ SYMBOLIC MEANINGS
Am I forgotten?; Bad payment; Fascination; Forgetfulness; Honesty; Secret love.

🜨 POSSIBLE POWERS
Earth element; Feminine energy; Money; Moon; Prosperity; Protection; Repelling monsters; Sincerity.

🜨 FOLKLORE AND FACTS
One way to pull money toward you is to place one silvery, flat, papery Honesty seed pod in the socket of a candlestick then top it with a green candle. Burn the candle down to the socket. • Another way to pull money toward you is to carry one Honesty seed pod in the purse or wallet. Or, make, then carry or wear a green sachet with an Honesty seed pod within it. • Grow Honesty in the garden. When the plants produce the silvery seed pods, cut the stems on a Monday during a full Moon. Arrange the stems of seed pods in a vase, then place in a prominent position near the front door of the home to symbolize wealth and pull money towards it.

No. 323
Lycium barbarum 🗡

Goji Berry
Barbary Matrimony Vine | Boberella halimifolia | Box Thorn | Chinese Boxthorn | Chinese Wolfberry | Dretsherma | Duke of Argyll's Tea Plant | Duke of Argyll's Tea Tree | Himalayan Goji | Lycium barbatumis | Lycium cochinchinensis | Lycium dunalianumis | Lycium floridum | Lycium halimifolium | Lycium thunbergii | Lycium trewianum | Lycium vulgare | Matrimony Vine | Mede Berry | Murali | Ningxia Oõuuj | Red Medlar | Teremis vulgarities | Tibetan Goji

☀ SYMBOLIC MEANINGS
Ghost thorn.

🜨 POSSIBLE POWERS
Attracts love; Beauty; Sexual attraction.

🜨 FOLKLORE & FACTS
The ripe Goji Berry fruit is edible and the shrub has been used in England as a hedging plant since the eighteenth century. • Dried Goji Berries have been extensively marketed as a health food since the beginning of the twenty-first century, and they quickly showed up in snack foods and food supplements. The berries were marketed as a "superfruit" based on various false and unverifiable claims that the berries had anti-cancer properties. In addition, there was an unverifiable story that a Chinese man who had died in 1933 had eaten Goji Berries daily and lived to be over 256 years old. Grossly exaggerated false claims such as that were more than enough to have the U.S. Food and Drug Administration issue warnings that the berries were not at all capable of healing anything or extending life in any of the ways they were claimed to be. • Due to the possibility of unwittingly carrying in diseases or insects that will precipitate a devastating blight upon potato or tomato crops, it is illegal to import a Goji Berry plant into anywhere in the United Kingdom. • The Goji Berry fruit has been used in traditional Chinese medicine.

No. 324
Lycopodium clavatum 💀🗡

Club Moss
Cacho de Venado | Cacho de Yenao | Caminadera | Colchón de Pobre | Common Club Moss | Ground Pine | Lepidotis ciliata | Lepidotis clavata | Lepidotis inflexa | Licopodio | Lycopod | Lycopodium aristatum | Lycopodium ciliatum | Lycopodium eriostachys | Lycopodium inflexum | Lycopodium piliferum | Lycopodium preslii | Lycopodium serpens | Lycopodium torridum | Lycopodium trichiatum | Lycopodium trichophyllum | Moririr-Wa-Mafika | Princess Pine | Running Ground Pine | Running Moss | Running Pine | Selago | Stag's Horn Clubmoss | Urostachys plutonis | Vegetable Sulfur | Wolf Claw | Wolf's Claw | Wolf's Foot | Wolf's Paw Clubmoss

☀ SYMBOLIC MEANINGS
Protection.

🜨 POSSIBLE POWERS
Business transactions; Cleverness; Communication; Creativity; Feminine energy; Intelligence; Memory; Moon; Power; Protection; Science; Thievery; Water element.

🜨 FOLKLORE AND FACTS
The ability for Club Moss spores to be explosive when airborne and highly dense made it useful in the early years of photography. At that time, it was used as the lycopodium flash powder needed for the lighting those cameras required. That same unusual and very interesting property was taken

L

advantage of by magicians who could pretend astonishing fire magic tricks by tossing the oily Club Moss spore dust over a flame. It is still used to create theatrical special effects for stage performances and films. It is used in fireworks, fingerprint powder, and as an ice cream stabilizer. • During the Middle Ages, Club Moss was used for protection against a sorcerer's malignant spells. • The Druids had a ceremony for the gathering of Club Moss, which they considered to be the gift of God. The Druid doing the cutting was to wear white and be barefoot. The blade could not be iron. The Club Moss could not be touched by a bare hand.

No. 325

Lycopus europaeus 🥣

Gypsywort

Egyptian's Herb | European Bugleweed | Gipsywort | Lycopus alboroseus | Lycopus albus | Lycopus aquaticus | Lycopus decrescens | Lycopus menthifolius | Lycopus mollis | Lycopus niger | Lycopus palustris | Lycopus riparius | Lycopus solanifolius | Lycopus souliei | Lycopus vulgaris | Water Horehound

✴ SYMBOLIC MEANINGS
Wet wolf's feet.

🌐 POSSIBLE POWERS
Healing; Health; Protection.

🜂 FOLKLORE & FACTS
The straggly herb Gypsywort grows in freshwater wetlands around lakes, ponds, canals, streams, and rivers. • It is believed that there was a time when the Romani people would use a dye made from the Gypsywort plant roots to color linens brown, gray, and black. • An infusion of Gypsywort and rainwater, natural spring water, or distilled water can be sprinkled across doorways and windowsills to keep trouble away.

No. 326

Lythrum salicaria 🥣

Loosestrife

Chabraea vulgaris | Lythrum alternifolium | Lythrum altissimum | Lythrum anceps | Lythrum argyi | Lythrum cashmerianum | Lythrum cinereum | Lythrum coronense | Lythrum diffusum | Lythrum dubium | Lythrum gracile | Lythrum hexagonum | Lythrum nummulariifolium | Lythrum palustre | Lythrum propinquum | Lythrum pubescens | Lythrum purshianum | Lythrum spicatum | Lythrum spiciforme | Lythrum tomentosum | Purple Loosestrife | Purple Lythrum | Qian Qu Cai | Salicaire | Spiked Loosestrife

✴ SYMBOLIC MEANINGS
Pretension.

🌐 POSSIBLE POWERS
Earth element; Feminine energy; Friendship; Harmony; Moon; Peace; Protection; Protection against a witch.

🜂 FOLKLORE & FACTS
To promote harmony, place Loosestrife in each corner of a room. • Give Loosestrife to a friend to settle any argument that you have had. • Loosestrife strewn around the home will provide vibrations of peacefulness and hold back evil. • Beekeepers have liberally introduced Loosestrife all around North America because it will provide an abundance of nectar. • Although it has provided so much for bees, Loosestrife is still considered an invasive species because it just is. • Because they did not like its potential effect upon them, long ago Russian witches would set out on St. John's Day to search high and low for Loosestrife so they could destroy it wherever it grew.

L

No. 327
Magnolia officinalis ☠♀

Houpu Magnolia

Chinese Magnolia | Hou Po | *Houpoea officinalis* | Magnolia-Bark Tree

✿ **SYMBOLIC MEANINGS**
Love of nature; Natural; Purification.

✿ **POSSIBLE POWERS**
Control over addiction; Earth element; Faithfulness; Feminine energy; Loyalty; Reduces obsessive behavior; Venus.

✿ **FOLKLORE AND FACTS**
Some believe that a magic wand fashioned from the wood of Houpu Magnolia will bring its user closer to working the core magic and the spirits of ancient earth. At any rate, a Houpu Magnolia wood wand is good for psychic development. • Fashion a useful pendulum out of a small piece of Houpu Magnolia wood. • Houpu Magnolia bark is used in traditional Chinese medicine.

No. 328
Mahonia aquifolium ☠♀

Oregon Grape

Berberis brevipes | *Berberis wagneri* | California Barberry | *Mahonia brevipes* | *Mahonia diversifolia* | *Mahonia latifolia* | *Mahonia moseri* | *Mahonia moseriana* | *Mahonia murrayana* | *Mahonia undulata* | Mountain Grape | *Odostemon aquifolius* | *Odostemon brevipes* | *Odostemon nutkanus* | Oregon Grape-holly | Oregon Holly-grape | Oregon Grape Root | Oregon Grape-holly | Oregon Holly-Grape | Oregongrape | Oregon-Grape | Rocky Mountain Grape | Tall Oregon-grape | Trailing Grape | Wild Oregon Grape

✿ **SYMBOLIC MEANINGS**
Sharp-tempered beauty.

✿ **POSSIBLE POWERS**
Earth element; Feminine energy; Money; Prosperity.

✿ **FOLKLORE AND FACTS**
Make, then carry or wear an Oregon Grape sachet to attract money and assure financial security. • Oregon Grape is the state flower of Oregon, USA. • The Oregon Grape leaves resemble Holly and are very often used by florists for greenery in arrangements closer to Christmas. • Make, then carry or wear an Oregon Grape sachet to gain popularity. • After there has been a frost, the Oregon Grape fruit can be gathered and then eaten raw, or it can be brewed into a folk-style home-made wine using the same type of method as for the Barberry wine made in parts of Europe. • Oregon Grape berries can be used to make a purple vegetable dye for cloth. The inner bark will create a yellow dye.

No. 329
Malva sylvestris ♀

Common Mallow

Almindelig Katost | *Althaea godronii* | *Althaea mauritiana* | *Althaea vulgaris* | Amarutza | Apotekerkattost | Blue Mallow | Cheese-Cake | Cheeses | Country-Mallow | Crni Slez | Ebegümeci | Erdei Mályva | Gozdni Slezenovec | Grande Mauve | Groot | Groot Kaasjeskruid | High Mallow | Hobbejza Tar-Raba | Hocysen Gyffredin | Kaasjeskruid | Kiiltomalva | Kultur-Käsepappel | Malba | Malva | *Malva acutiloba* | *Malva albiflora* | *Malva altissima* | *Malva ambigua* | *Malva aragonensis* | *Malva ciliata* | *Malva Común* | *Malva de Cementiri* | *Malva elata* | *Malva equina* | *Malva erecta* | *Malva erevaniana* | *Malva glabra* | *Malva grossheimii* | *Malva gymnocarpa* | *Malva hirsuta* | *Malva longilobata* | *Malva lucida* | *Malva major* | *Malva martrinii* | *Malva mauritanica* | *Malva mauritiana* | *Malva obtusa* | *Malva orientalis* | *Malva plebeia* | *Malva polymorpha* | *Malva pumila* | *Malva racemosa* | *Malva recta* | *Malva rotundifolia* | *Malva ruderalis* | *Malva tomentella* | *Malva vivianiana* | *Malva vulgaris* | Mályva | Mamarutza | Marmaredda | Marva | Mauve des Bois | Mauve Sylvestre | Méiba | Mets-Kassinaeris | Nalba | Nalba de Cultură | Nalba de Padure | Narbedda | Papsajt | Pick-Cheese | Riondella | Rödmalva | Round Dock | Slaz Dziki | Sléz Lesni | Slez Lesny | Sljez Crni | Sljez Divlji | Sotsal | Tall Mallow | Vauma | Wild Mallow | Wood Mallow | Ziga | Zigiña

✿ **SYMBOLIC MEANINGS**
Consumed by love; Persuasion.

✿ **POSSIBLE POWERS**
Althea; Beltaine; Comfort; Communication; Exorcism; Fertility; Healing; Love; Lust; Moon; Protection; Softens a hard heart; Softens inflexible thinking; Soothes; Venus; Water element.

✿ **FOLKLORE AND FACTS**
Since medieval times, Common Mallow flowers were woven into garlands and wreaths for celebrating May Day on May 1. • Prior to the steady emigration from England, Common Mallow was virtually unknown in North America until it was introduced into the newly planted English gardens in the New World. • To soften a stubbornly hard heart that became numb due to inflexible thinking, make, to wear or carry, a Common Mallow sachet with both flower and leaves. • Make a Common Mallow sachet with flower, leaves, and root to tuck under the mattress to encourage fertility. • Common Mallow can be used to consecrate ritual implements.

M

No. 330

Mandragora officinarum ☠

Mandrake

Atropa acaulis | Atropa humilis | Atropa mandragora | Autumn Mandrake | European Mandrake | Herb of Circe | Mandragora acaulis | Mandragora mas | Mandragora praecox | Mandragora vernalis | Mandrake Root | Mediterranean Mandrake | Sorcerer's Root | Wild Lemon | Witch's Mannikin | Witches Mannikin

☀ SYMBOLIC MEANINGS

Horror; Rarity; Scarcity; Screaming; Uncommon thing; Wickedness replacing love.

◉ POSSIBLE POWERS

Aphrodisiac; Attracts love; Black magic; Caution; Conception by way of spell-casting; Death; Exorcism; Faith; Fertility; Fire element; Hathor; Health; Hecate; Illumination; Initiation; Learning; Love; Lust; Magical power; Masculine energy; Mercury; Money; Potency; Promotes conception, passion, or sterility; Protection; Prudence; Self-preservation; Sorcery; Sound judgment; Sudden death; Wisdom; Witchcraft; Witchery.

✦ FOLKLORE AND FACTS

The likeness of the Mandrake root to a human figure is why it was once feared that it was embodying a demon. • It was said that when the Mandrake plant was pulled out of the ground, its terrible shriek could be heard. • Witches often used the Mandrake root in spell-casting. • Many superstitions surround the possession of a Mandrake root, such as, if you had one, it was fortunate. But it had to be sold before dying, at a lower price than what was paid for it. Also, a person who received one for free would never be free, because the recipient would be in the grip of the Devil. • A book from 1870 gives instructions on how to make a homunculus, which was believed to be a tiny little man held as a magical slave to contribute power to its master's sorcery. The primary ingredient needed to start the first of many steps

in its diabolical creation was a Mandrake root. The root had to be removed from the ground on a Monday, just after the vernal equinox. • Over time, the shape of the root naturally imbued the Mandrake with different abilities. If the root was shaped like a female, to put it under the pillow would help a bachelor find a wife. A baby-shaped root would be used for wishing for a pregnancy. • During the Middle Ages, along with a growing demand for Mandrake root charms, came the scammers who passed off home-whittled, easier-to-obtain, customizable Bryony root to the unsuspecting, making counterfeiting Mandrake root a profitable endeavor.

No. 331

Maranta arundinacea 🍴

Arrowroot

Ararao | Araru | Araruta | Bermuda Arrowroot | Curcuma caulina | Hulankeeriya | Maranta | Maranta indica | Maranta minor | Maranta ramosissima | Maranta sylvatica | Obedience Plant | Phrynium variegatum | West Indian Arrowroot

☀ SYMBOLIC MEANINGS

Obedience; Prayer.

◉ POSSIBLE POWERS

Energy cleansing; Energy healing; Good fortune; Graveyard dust; Luck; Opportunities; Petition; Protection; Purification.

✦ FOLKLORE AND FACTS

Arrowroot has been cultivated by indigenous cultures around the world for over 8,000 years. • Dust hands with powdered Arrowroot before choosing specific lottery numbers. • Sprinkle Arrowroot at the doors of the home to help keep unwanted people's negative energy from crossing over the threshold. • Sprinkle a little Arrowroot at the doorways and along the windowsills to keep positive energy inside the home. • When in need of graveyard dust for a spell, Arrowroot powder makes an acceptable substitute. • Sprinkle Arrowroot powder around a child's room to help protect them from harm. • Powdered Arrowroot is often used as a substitute for cornstarch in thickening sauces.

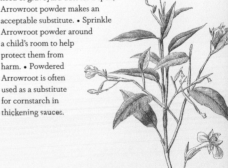

No. 332

Marrubium vulgare

Horehound

Bull's Blood | Common Horehound | Even of the Star | Haran | Hoarhound | Huran | Llwyd y Cwn | Marrubio | Marrubium | *Marrubium album* | *Marrubium apulum* | *Marrubium ballotoides* | *Marrubium germanicum* | *Marrubium hamatum* | *Marrubium hyperleucum* | *Marrubium uncinatum* | *Marrubium vaillantii* | Maruil | *Prasium marrubium* | Seed of Horns | Soldier's Tea | White Horehound

❋ **SYMBOLIC MEANINGS**
Imitation.

❀ **POSSIBLE POWERS**
Air element; Balance; Exorcism; Fire element; Healing; Health; Masculine energy; Mental clarity or power; Mercury; Protection; Purification.

✦ **FOLKLORE AND FACTS**
Carry Horehound to protect yourself against magical fascination and sorcery. • The Horehound plant was named after the Egyptian god Horus. • Horehound was thought to be struck by Donar, the Germanic god of thunder and lightning, which made Horehound incredibly powerful. • Elves, pixies, and fairies are sometimes believed to be obsessed with Horehound flowers.

No. 333

Matricaria chamomilla

German Chamomile

Anthemis vulgaris | Blue Chamomile | Camomile | *Camomilla deflexa* | *Camomilla patens* | *Chamaemelum chamomilla* | *Chamaemelum suaveolens* | *Chamaemelum vulgare* | *Chamomilla chamomilla* | *Chamomilla courrantiana* | *Chamomilla meridionalis* | *Chamomilla officinalis* | *Chamomilla recutita* | *Chamomilla unilateralis* | *Chamomilla vulgaris* | *Chrysanthemum chamomilla* | *Chrysanthemum suaveolens* | *Courrantia chamomilloides* | Hungarian Chamomile | *Leucanthemum chamaemelum* | Manzanilla Amarga | Manzanilla Dulce | Manzanilla Grande | *Manzanilla Matricaria* | *Matricaria bayeri* | *Matricaria capitellata* | *Matricaria chamaemilla* | *Matricaria coronata* | *Matricaria courrantiana* | *Matricaria deflexa* | *Matricaria exigua* | *Matricaria kochiana* | *Matricaria littoralis* | *Matricaria obliqua* | *Matricaria patens* | *Matricaria pusilla* | *Matricaria pyrethroides* | *Matricaria recutita* | *Matricaria salina* | *Matricaria suaveolens* | *Matricaria tenuifolia* | *Pyrethrum hispanicum* | Scented Mayweed | True Chamomile | Wild Chamomile

❋ **SYMBOLIC MEANINGS**
May all your wishes be fulfilled; Patience in adversity.

❀ **POSSIBLE POWERS**
Break a hex or spell; Calm; Heal; Humility; Induces sleepiness; Luck when gambling; Masculine energy; Protection against lightning; Relaxation; Sun; Water element.

✦ **FOLKLORE AND FACTS**
Aromatherapy using German Chamomile essential oil can soothe restlessness and help promote sleep. • German Chamomile's fragrance is similar to that of an apple. • Some believe that the German Chamomile flower is sweeter than the larger Roman Chamomile blossom. • As the legend goes, Woden, who is the god of learning, magic, and poetry, had used German Chamomile as a medicine for people, and thus it became one of the Nine Sacred Herbs of the Anglo-Saxons. • During the Middle Ages, on Midsummer's Eve, there were supposedly great bonfires that included German Chamomile, toward which ill people moved closer to breathe in the smoke they came there for, because they believed it to be healing to them and to their orchards and crops. • German Chamomile wreaths used to be fashioned and then hung on doors on June 24, St. John the Baptist Day, as protection against lightning. • A German legend tells of how the cursed souls of dead soldiers who died for their sins are represented by the number of German Chamomile blossoms blooming. • Wash your hands with an infusion of German Chamomile flowers and rainwater, natural spring water, or distilled water before gambling. • Make, then wear or carry a sachet of German Chamomile, preferably in a wallet or pocket, to draw money to it and increase what money is there. • Sprinkle an infusion of German Chamomile flowers and rainwater, natural spring water, or distilled water all around the house to break all hexes and spells imposed upon it.

M

No. 334

Melaleuca alternifolia ☠🗡

Tea Tree

Honey-Myrtle | Melaleuca | *Melaleuca linariifolia* var. *alternifolia* | Paperbark Tree | Punk Tree | Tea Tree Oil Tree | White Bottlebrush Tree

✹ SYMBOLIC MEANINGS

Communication.

✺ POSSIBLE POWERS

Antibacterial; Antiseptic; Healing; Odor removal.

✵ FOLKLORE AND FACTS

Tea Tree essential oil, which is also simply known as Tea Tree oil, is extracted from the leaves of the *Melaleuca alternifolia* tree. • Tea Tree essential oil is used in home aromatherapy to help remove unpleasant odors. • Tea Tree oil has been determined to have antibacterial and antiseptic properties. It is believed that less than a drop of the essential oil can reduce the size of a painful blind pimple. • Medicinally, Tea Tree oil is attributed to being legitimately helpful in commonly treating the maladies of lice, acne, and dandruff. Tea Tree oil should never be ingested in any quantity, at any dilution, for any reason whatsoever, and it should not be used on children. Tea Tree oil has been used commercially since the 1920s as a remedy for an overly wide variety of ailments that have yet to be validated, and can be extremely dangerous if abided by. • Tea Tree oil has been added into a wide array of products and personal toiletries all around the world. • An endocrinological study presented in 2018 overtly suggested that a previously rare occurrence was becoming increasingly less so. There had been a disconcerting and growing number of cases involving young boys who exhibited prepubertal male gynecomastia, which is a swelling of the breast tissue in a prepubescent male child. The study indicated that the common denominator that linked these young boys was the repeated topical use of the combination of Tea Tree oil with Lavender essential oil. A further study by researchers at the National Institute of Environmental Health Sciences found laboratory evidence that these two essential oils appear to be endocrine-disrupting, having estrogen-like and testosterone inhibiting properties, and they should not be used in combination. • Tea Tree pollen has been attributed to the exacerbation of severe hay fever symptoms in sensitivity-prone individuals.

No. 335

Melaleuca leucadendra ☠🗡

Cajeput

Cajuputi leucadendron | Kajuputi leucadendron | *Leptospermum leucodendron* | Long-Leaved Paperbark | Meladendron leucocladum | Melaleuca amboinensis | Melaleuca mimosoides | Melaleuca rigida | Metrosideros coriacea | Myrtus alba | Myrtus leucadendra | Myrtus saligna | Weeping Paperbark | White Paperbark | White Tea Tree

✹ SYMBOLIC MEANINGS

Sense of flow; Strong inner-self.

✺ POSSIBLE POWERS

Ability to move through a contrary experience; Breaks compulsive habits; Cleans ritual objects; Expels intruding energy; Focuses mind or willpower; Heals; Healing; Health; Insect repellent; Protection; Soothes; Soothes sunburn; Stimulant.

✵ FOLKLORE AND FACTS

Cajeput is one of the ingredients in the iconic ointment known as Tiger Balm. • In Malaysia the Cajeput is considered to be an entire apothecary in one tree. • Cajeput is used in traditional Indonesian medicine. • Cajeput is used to treat fish suffering from bacterial and fungal infections such as fin rot and velveting. Aboriginal people used the peeled bark from the Cajeput tree to cut into long strips to use for tying. It was also used to fashion waterproof canoes and huts. They also used it for wrapping food before placing it in a hole that was dug to be an oven. The bark was used to wrap the bodies of the deceased, too.

No. 336

Melissa officinalis 🗡🍴

Lemon Balm

Balm | Balm Mint | Blue Balm | Citronelle | Cure-All | Dropsy Plant | Elixir of Life | *Faucibarba officinalis* | Garden Balm | Gentle Balm | Harden Balm | Heart's Delight | Honey Leaf | Lemon Balm | Lemon Balsam | Melissa | *Mutelia officinalis* | Oghoul | Sweet Balm | Sweet Mary | Sweet Mary Balm | Sweet Melissa | *Thymus melissa* | Tourengane | Zitronmelisse

✹ SYMBOLIC MEANINGS

Brings love; Cure; Joke; Pleasantry; Regeneration; Social intercourse; Sympathy; Wishes will be fulfilled.

✺ POSSIBLE POWERS

Feminine energy; Healing; Love; Moon; Success; Water.

M

Elizabethan Londoners would often carry posies of Lemon
Balm to sniff throughout the day to mask the stench of
unsanitary filth in the streets. • Carry Lemon Balm to find
love. • Rubbed on a new hive, Lemon Balm will keep the
old bees and attract new bees to it. • Carry Lemon Balm to
promote healing.

No. 337

Mentha × *piperita* 🜨🍴

Peppermint

American Mint | Brandy Mint | Mentha ×
balsamea | Mentha × banatica |
Mentha × concina | Mentha × crispula |
Mentha × durandoana | Mentha × exaltata |
Mentha × fraseri | Mentha × glabrata | Mentha ×
heuffelii | Mentha × hircina | Mentha × hircina | Mentha ×
hortensis | Mentha × hudsoniana | Mentha × kahirina | Mentha × langii |
Mentha × napolitana | Mentha × nigricans | Mentha × odora | Mentha × officinalis |
Mentha × pimentum | Mentha × piperita var. hispidula | Mentha × piperita var. officinalis |
Mentha × piperita var. ouweneelii | Mentha × piperita var. pennsylvanica | Mentha × schultzii |
Mentha × tenuis | Mentha hortensis var. citrata | Vilayati Pudina

☀ SYMBOLIC MEANINGS
Affability; Cordiality; Love; Warmth of feeling.

🌼 POSSIBLE POWERS
Air element; Aphrodisiac; Attracts love; Fire element;
Healing; Love; Masculine energy; Mercury; Pluto; Prophetic
dreaming; Psychic power; Purification; Sleep.

C: FOLKLORE AND FACTS
Sniff fresh Peppermint leaves to help sleep. • Put Peppermint
leaves under the pillow to promote prophetic dreaming.
• Rub Peppermint leaves on walls, furniture, and elsewhere
around the home to rid it of negative energies.
• Peppermint in any area will positively increase the
vibration of the room. • Keep a Peppermint leaf in the
handbag or wallet to encourage money to come to it.
• Peppermint essential oil can be used for aromatherapy
for stimulation to invigorate the senses. • Tuck Peppermint
leaves all over the house to help rid it of negative energy.

No. 338

Mentha spicata 🜨🍴

Spearmint

Brandy Mint | Brown Mint |
Common Mint | Garden Mint |
Green Mint | Green Spine | Lamb
Mint | Lammit | Mackerel Mint |
Mentha atrata | Mentha balsamea |
Mentha brevispicata | Mentha chalepensis |
Mentha crispa | Mentha crispata | Mentha glabra |
Mentha hortensis | Mentha inarimensis | Mentha integerrima |
Mentha laciniosa | Mentha laevigata | Mentha lejeuneana | Mentha
lejeunei | Mentha michelii | Mentha microphylla | Mentha ocymiodora | Mentha pectinata |
Mentha piperella | Mentha pudina | Mentha sieberi | Mentha sofiana | Mentha stenostachya |
Mentha subsessilis | Mentha tomentosa | Mismin | Our Lady's Mint | Spear Mint | Spire Mint |
Yerba Buena

☀ SYMBOLIC MEANINGS
Burning love; Warm feelings; Warm sentiment; Warmth of
sentiment.

🌼 POSSIBLE POWERS
Air element; Aphrodisiac; Attracts love; Enhances sexuality;
Feminine energy; Healing; Hecate; Humble virtue; Love;
Masculine energy; Mental clarity or power; Mercury;
Passion; Pluto; Venus; Virtue; Water element.

C: FOLKLORE AND FACTS
In ancient Rome and Greece, Spearmint was thought to
increase the desire for lovemaking. • In ancient Rome and
Greece, Spearmint was rubbed on banquet tables as a symbol
of hospitality. • In ancient Rome, scholars were encouraged
to wear crowns of Spearmint to stimulate their thinking.
• Smelling Spearmint is supposed to sharpen mental power.
• Spearmint essential oil can be helpful as aromatherapy for
emotional agitation, sluggish concentration, and tension.

M

No. 339
Menyanthes trifoliata ☠☙

Bogbean
Bitterklee | Bog-Bean | Buckbean | Fieberklee | Marsh Clover | Marsh Trefoil | Menyanthes americana | Menyanthes latifolia | Menyanthes palustris | Menyanthes paradoxa | Menyanthes tridentata | Menyanthes trifolium | Menyanthes verna | Water Trefoil

☀ SYMBOLIC MEANINGS
Calm repose; Calmness; Quiet; Repose.

✿ POSSIBLE POWERS
Calmness; Clearing.

☾ FOLKLORE AND FACTS
Thick-rooted Bogbean can be found abundantly growing in bogs, contributing to the development of large quagmires. • Utilizing magical homeopathic rationale, where sometimes a purposeful opposing energy can do much to accomplish a positive result, a Bogbean amulet would be very helpful in clearing the mind of all the tidbits of residual psychic goo that a lot of seriously deep magical thinking can leave lingering behind. The end result of the clearing is much-needed inner calm. • Bogbean was once occasionally used as a substitute for Hops in beer brewing.

No. 340
Monarda didyma ☙❶

Bee Balm
Bergamot | Crimson Beebalm | Monarda coccinea | Monarda kalmiana | Monarda oswegoensis | Monarda purpurascens | Monarda purpurea | Oswego Tea | Scarlet Bee Balm | Scarlet Beebalm | Scarlet Monarda | Wild Bergamot

☀ SYMBOLIC MEANINGS
You change your mind too much; Your whims are unbearable.

✿ POSSIBLE POWERS
Air element; Feminine energy; Healing; Love; Psychic development; Spiritual development; Success.

☾ FOLKLORE AND FACTS
After the rebellious Boston Tea Party, colonists resorted to and popularized *Monarda didyma* Bee Balm tea as a popular, patriotic, temporary substitute for imported teas. • Bee Balm is believed to be able to bring clarity to unclear situations and working order to those situations which are disorderly. • Bee Balm in a love charm will attract romance. • Bee Balm works well in spells focused on healing disorders of the mind. • Don't confuse Bee Balm's other common name of Bergamot with the Bergamot Orange. The only similarity between the two is their fragrance.

M

No. 341
Morus alba ☠✿

White Mulberry

China Mulberry | *Morus alba
pendula* | *Morus alpina* |
Morus atropurpurea | *Morus
bullata* | *Morus byzantina* |
Morus colombassa | *Morus
constantinopolitana* | *Morus
cucullata* | *Morus dulcis* | *Morus
fastigiata* | *Morus furcata* |
Morus guzziola | *Morus heterophylla* | *Morus hispanica* | *Morus intermedia* | *Morus kaki* |
Morus levasseurei | *Morus lhou* | *Morus lucida* | *Morus mariettii* | *Morus membranacea* | *Morus
morettii* | *Morus multicaulis* | *Morus nana* | *Morus nigriformis* | *Morus patavia* | *Morus
patavina* | *Morus pumila* | *Morus romana* | *Morus serotina* | *Morus subalba* | *Morus tatarica* |
Morus tokwa | *Morus tortuosa* | *Morus venassainii* | *Morus venosa* | Russian Mulberry | Sang
Shen Tzu | Silkworm Mulberry | Tuta | Tuti

☀ SYMBOLIC MEANINGS
Kindness; Prudence; Strength; Wisdom.

⟡ POSSIBLE POWERS
Air element; Diana; Masculine energy; Mercury; Minerva;
Protection; San Ku Fu Jen.

☘ FOLKLORE AND FACTS
In ancient times, a forest area that was thick with White
Mulberry trees was considered the most sacred of all
places. • Careful cultivation of the White Mulberry tree
began in China more than 4,000 years ago, for the specific
intention of using the leaves as the preferred food needed
for raising healthy, productive silkworms. • White Mulberry
fruit is edible if it is ripe, with it more often made into
wine. • White Mulberry is an herb used in traditional
Chinese medicine. • The White Mulberry is a multiple
fruit, as is the Pineapple and Jackfruit, with each cluster of
fruits resembling a single Raspberry or Blackberry. Each
minuscule segment in the cluster is actually an individual
seed-bearing fruit that has grown from its own individual
flower, with all the fruits aggregating together to form the
appearance of one whole berry.

No. 342
Murraya koenigii ✿🍴

Curry Leaf Tree

Bergera koenigii | *Camunium koenigii* | *Chalcas koenigii* | *Chalcas siamensis* | Curry Bush |
Curry Leaves | Curry Tree | *Murraya foetidissima* | *Murraya siamensis* | *Nimbo melioides* |
Sweet Neem

☀ SYMBOLIC MEANINGS
Pungent.

⟡ POSSIBLE POWERS
Fire element; Flavor; Health; Healthy; Mars; Masculine
energy; Protection.

☘ FOLKLORE AND FACTS
The fresh leaves of the Curry Leaf Tree are
commonly known as curry leaves, which are a
fundamental part of the cuisine of India and
other regions in Asia. • The Curry Leaf
Tree has been utilized medicinally in
traditional Ayurvedic and Siddha
medicine.

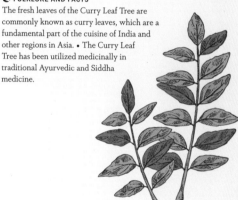

M

No. 343

Myristica fragrans ✴☠☉♊

Nutmeg

Aruana silvestris | Bicuiba Acu | Mace | Myristica amboinensis | Myristica aromatica | Myristica laurella | Myristica moschata | Myristica officinalis | Myristica philippinensis | Palala fragrans | Qoust | Sadhika | Wohpala

✴ **SYMBOLIC MEANINGS**
Clarity of thought.

🌸 **POSSIBLE POWERS**
Aphrodisiac; Attracts love;
Breaks a hex; Fidelity; Fire
element; Health; Increase
clarity of thought; Jupiter;
Luck; Masculine energy;
Mental power; Money;
Protection; Psychic power.

🜨 **FOLKLORE AND FACTS**
Carry or wear a whole
Nutmeg as a good-luck
charm. • Make an amulet
of a whole Nutmeg to wear
or carry to increase clarity of thought. • Nutmeg can be
carried to fend off such ailments as cold sores, neuralgia,
boils, styes, and rheumatism. • If you want a lover to be
faithful, cut a whole Nutmeg into four pieces. Bury one
piece. Burn one piece. Toss one piece off a cliff. Then boil
the last piece in water. Drink one very small sip of the
water, then carry that boiled quarter piece of Nutmeg with
you wherever you go, putting it under your pillow when
you sleep. • Sprinkle Nutmeg on a lottery ticket for good
luck. • Nutmeg has been banned in most prisons because
of it being routinely stolen from the prison kitchens to be
used in bartering for money and cigarettes. • Due to the
medicinal properties and popular use of Nutmeg in the
Middle East, Saudi Arabia classified it as an intoxicant and
a hallucinogen drug and has actually banned it. Apparently,
very small amounts of Nutmeg are permitted to flavor food,
if any could be found somewhere to buy. • The red seed
covering of the Nutmeg seed is processed to make the more
delicate culinary spice known as Mace. • Mace can be
burned like incense to increase one's psychic powers.
• Mace can be burned like incense to purify and consecrate
a ritual area. • Make, then wear or carry a Mace sachet to
improve one's intelligence prior to taking exams.

No. 344

Myroxylon balsamum var. *pereirae* ☠☉

Balsam of Peru

Balsam Tree | Balsamo | Myrospermum balsamiferum | Myrospermum pereirae | Myrospermum punctatum | Myrospermum toluiferum | Myroxylon hanburyanum | Myroxylon pereirai | Myroxylon punctatum | Peru Balsam | Quina | Santos Mahogany

✴ **SYMBOLIC MEANINGS**
Calm.

🌸 **POSSIBLE POWERS**
Aromatic; Healing;
Relaxation; Shade.

🜨 **FOLKLORE & FACTS**
The Balsam of Peru is a very
tall, spreading tree that can
reach heights of 150 feet,
and is most often used to
provide shading on Coffee
plantations. • Balsam of
Peru's sweet fragrance smells
like Vanilla with a hint of
Cinnamon, and it is useful
in aromatherapy to calm

nervous tension and help promote a tranquil environment
in which to relax. • The Balsam of Peru resin from the
Myroxylon balsamum var. *pereirae* tree is obtained by
stripping the bark off the tree and wrapping rags around the
wounded trunk to soak up the resin. The resin is extracted
when the rags are boiled and the fragrant, oily, brown balsam
resin sinks to the bottom of the vessel, where it is collected
and used in perfumes, cosmetics, toiletries, medicinal
products, and for an optical glue for mounting specimens
for use under a microscope. • The Balsam of Peru is also
used as flavoring in a very wide-ranging variety of beverages
and foods. Needless to say, Balsam of Peru is an extremely
versatile and immensely useful herb indeed. • Balsam of
Peru has been identified as one of the top five allergens most
commonly revealed during a skin patch test.

M

No. 345

Myrrhis odorata

Sweet Cicely

Anise Fern | *Chaerophyllum odoratum* | Cicely | Garden Myrrh | Great Chervil | Lindera odorata | Myrrh Plant | *Myrrhis brevipedunculata* | *Myrrhis iberica* | *Myrrhis sulcata* | Saksankirveli | *Scandix odorata* | *Selinum myrrhis* | Sweet Chervil

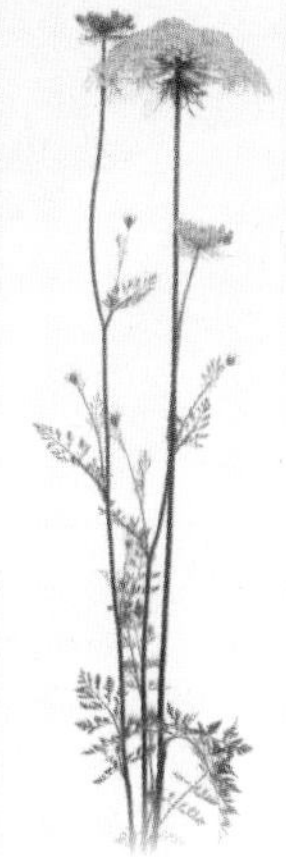

SYMBOLIC MEANINGS

Gladness.

POSSIBLE POWERS

Abundance; Advancement; Protection; Psychic vision; Second sight.

FOLKLORE AND FACTS

In Finland, Sweet Cicely was believed to offer protection against suddenly painful invisible arrows aimed at a human or animal, having been let loose by a malicious elf or a witch attacking with foul intent. • Sweet Cicely was once believed to offer a glimpse of Álfheimr, which is the home of the elves. Álfheimr is better known as Fairyland. • Make, then wear a Sweet Cicely sachet to improve the quality and clarity of psychic visions. • Sweet Cicely is used to flavor akvavit liqueur.

No. 346

Myrtus communis

True Myrtle

Common Myrtle | Corsican Pepper | Myrtle | Myrtus | Sweet Myrtle

SYMBOLIC MEANINGS

Beauty; Chastity; Friendship; Generosity; Good deeds; Happiness; Heartfelt love; Honor; Hope; Immortality; Joy; Justice; Love; Marriage; Memory of the Garden of Eden; Mirth; Modest worth; Money; Peace; Prosperity; Sacred love; Scent of the Garden of Eden; Souvenir of the Garden of Eden; Symbol of the Garden of Eden; Weddings; Youth.

POSSIBLE POWERS

Aphrodite; Artemis; Ashtoreth; Assistance; Astarte; Demeter; Feminine energy; Fertility; Fond memories; Friendship; Harmony; Hathor; Independence; Love; Marian; Material gain; Money; Peace of mind; Peace; Persistence; Purification; Recovery; Restoration; Stability; Strength; Tenacity; Venus; Water element; Youth.

FOLKLORE AND FACTS

True Myrtle is considered to be a sacred plant that is both the symbol and the fragrance of the Garden of Eden. • A sprig of True Myrtle that was in Queen Victoria's bridal bouquet was planted, and, since then, sprigs of that same plant have been included in many different royal bridal bouquets. • Carry True Myrtle wood to preserve youthfulness. • Carry or wear a True Myrtle flower to preserve love. • Grow True Myrtle on each side of a house to promote peace and love within the home. • If a woman plants True Myrtle in a window box, it will become lucky. • According to Arabian traditions, when Adam was forced to leave the Garden of Eden, he took with him three plants, one of them being the True Myrtle so that he could replant it, as it is considered the foremost of all sweetly scented flowers. • According to the Talmudic Jewish tradition, the bough with leaves of a True Myrtle is one of the four species of plants lovingly tied together to be waved in the festival of Sukkot, with the other three being the fruit of a Citron tree, a ripe green closed frond of a Date Palm, and leafy branches from a Willow tree. • True Myrtle flowers are often made into a pleasantly fragrant cologne called *eau d'ange*. • Sweet True Myrtle is occasionally used in a bride's floral head wreath and bouquet to symbolize her chastity. • Sleep on a True Myrtle-filled pillow to attain peace of mind. • Make, then carry or wear a sachet of True Myrtle to attract what hopes to be a potentially true friend. • The fruit of the True Myrtle is aromatic and has been used to flavor some Middle Eastern dishes. The berries can be a milder-flavored replacement for Juniper berries. The leaves can be used to flavor soups.

No. 347

Nandina domestica ☠☕

Heavenly Bamboo

Nandina | Nandina denudata | Nandina tomentosa | Nandina tsermonanten | Sacred Bamboo

✿ SYMBOLIC MEANINGS

Hardship reversal; Sacred celebration; South Heaven.

⦾ POSSIBLE POWERS

Ancestral tributes; Healing.

⦿ FOLKLORE AND FACTS

Nandina domestica is the only species in its genus.
• Heavenly Bamboo is a tall shrub that can grow up to seven feet, but it is not a bamboo, although the leaves are bamboo-like. • The leaves of Heavenly Bamboo will change colors with the seasons. Once they change color, they will not change back but will be eventually replaced by new green leaves. The combination of the colored leaves and the green leaves is quite attractive. • In China, during Chinese New Year, stems of Heavenly Bamboo leaves and berries are sold to be used as altar and temple decorations. • Due to the deep and extensive root runners, once Heavenly Bamboo is established, it is very difficult to remove. It's no surprise that the plant is highly invasive in the southeastern parts of North America, where new plantings are strongly discouraged. • All parts of Heavenly Bamboo are toxic, with the berries being extremely toxic to birds. • Heavenly Bamboo is also associated with Chinese Kitchen Day on December 23. Stems of Heavenly Bamboo are offered to the Kitchen God, who spends most of the year in a little shrine in the kitchen where the offerings are made.

No. 348

Narcissus poeticus ☠☕

Poet's Daffodil

Findern Flower | Leirion | Narcissus poeticus subsp. poeticus | Narcissus poeticus subsp. radiiflorus | Narcissus poeticus subsp. verbanensis | Nargis | Pheasant's Eye | Pinkster Lily | Poet's Narcissus

✿ SYMBOLIC MEANINGS

Annunciation; Appreciation of honesty; Beauty; Chivalry; Clarity of thought; Contentment; Deceitful hopes; Egotism; Energy that comes from being in love; Excessive self-love; Faith; Forgiveness; Formality; Forthrightness; High regards; Honesty; Hope; Inner beauty; Love; New beginnings; Promise of eternal life; Rebirth; Regard; Renewal; Respect; Resurrection and Rebirth; Self-concept; Self-esteem; Self-love; Simple pleasures; Singular love; Stay as sweet as you are; The Sun shines when I'm with you; Sunlight; Sunshine; Truth; Uncertainty; Unrequited love; Vanity; Vanity and death; Vanity and egoism; You're the only one.

⦾ POSSIBLE POWERS

Aphrodisiac; Attracts love; Conception; Eloquence; Emotional expression of thought in words; Faith; Feminine energy; Fertility; Forgiveness; Honesty; Love; Luck; Poetry; Selflessness; Venus; Water element.

⦿ FOLKLORE AND FACTS

The Poet's Daffodil is an herb that is known to have been the first *Narcissus* to be cultivated. • The first mention of the Poet's Daffodil was around 287 CE. • The Poet's Daffodil is believed to be the daffodil often referred to in ancient writings. • The Poet's Daffodil is the flower of the Underworld. • Animals do not eat the Poet's Daffodil flower because the sap contains sharp crystals. • Wear a Poet's Daffodil blossom over your heart for good luck. • During medieval times in Europe, it was thought that if a Poet's Daffodil drooped while it was being looked at, it was an indisputable omen of death. • A Poet's Daffodil is thought to have the power to attract an angel of forgiveness when one is needed the most. • Chicken farmers were superstitious and would not allow Poet's Daffodil into their homes, as they believed they were unlucky and would stop their hens from laying eggs or keep the eggs they did lay from hatching. • In Maine, USA, there is a superstition that if you point at a Poet's Daffodil with your index finger, it will not bloom. • The Chinese believe that the Poet's Daffodil is lucky and will bring good luck for an entire year if it can be forced to bloom during Chinese New Year. • Make a pink sachet with a Poet's Daffodil blossom in it, then tuck it under the mattress to give a loving boost to fertility and conception. • According to myth, the Poet's Daffodil did not start out in the physical world as a flower. It began as the handsome young man, Narcissus, who believed himself to be more handsome than any other. He was constantly unsympathetic and rude to everyone around him. The Greek gods took offense at Narcissus's obnoxious behavior, so they cursed him. They tricked Narcissus to go look into a pool of still water. He went. He looked. What he saw enticed him to quite madly fall head over heels in love with his own reflection. Narcissus refused to leave the pool. His obsession with his reflection led him to die of starvation. At that very spot, the nymphs transformed him into the first *Narcissus* flower, which is believed to be the Poet's Daffodil. • The essential oil of Poet's Daffodil is used in fine perfumery. • The fragrance of Poet's Daffodil is lovely, but it is highly scented and has been known to be much too powerful a fragrance to encounter in a small, closed room. Those who have, have suffered headaches and extreme nausea to the degree of vomiting in response to it.

No. 349
Nardostachys grandiflora ☠️⚗️
Spikenard
Fedia grandiflora | Fedia jatamansi | Muskroot | Nard | Nardin | Nardostachys chinensis | Nardostachys gracilis | Nardostachys grandiflora | Nardostachys jatamansi | Patrinia jatamansi | Pikenard | Valeriana jatamansi

☀ SYMBOLIC MEANINGS
Anoint.

⚜ POSSIBLE POWERS
Calls upon St. Joseph for protection; Feminine energy; Fidelity; Health; Venus; Water element.

☣ FOLKLORE AND FACTS
Spikenard is believed to be the plant that produced the perfume ointment that Mary, the sister of Lazarus, used to anoint Jesus's feet six days before the Passover that preceded his crucifixion. Also, two days before that fateful death, an unnamed woman anointed Jesus's head with the same type of perfume taken from an alabaster jar. The use of this exceptionally expensive perfume on Jesus, rather than being sold for 300 denarii, which would have been about a year's wages, is what incited Judas Iscariot to his betrayal of Jesus, which led to Jesus's arrest and subsequent crucifixion. • Spikenard is often used as an incense.

No. 350
Nasturtium officinale ⚗️🍴
Watercress
Arabis nasturtium | Baeumerta nasturtium | Baeumerta nasturtium-aquaticum | Cardamine aquatica | Cardamine fontana | Cardamine nasturtium | Cardamine nasturtium-aquaticum | Cardaminum nasturtium | Crucifera fontana | Nasturtium fontanum | Nasturtium siifoliu | Radicula nasturtium | Radicula nasturtium-aquaticum | Rorippa nasturtium | Rorippa nasturtium-aquaticum | Rorippa officinalis | Sisymbrium amarum | Sisymbrium cardaminefolium | Sisymbrium fluviatile | Sisymbrium nasturtium | Sisymbrium nasturtium-aquaticum | Stime | Yellowcress

☀ SYMBOLIC MEANINGS
Cure of cures.

⚜ POSSIBLE POWERS
Aphrodisiac; Attracts love; Fertility; Fire element; Healing; Mars; Mind activity; Moon; Moon magic; Sex magic; Strengthens the conscious mind; Water element.

☣ FOLKLORE AND FACTS
Watercress, which was then known as Stime, is one of the Nine Sacred Herbs that was often referred to as the "Cure of Cures." It was originally written of in the dialect of the day used in Wessex, England, around the tenth century. • Peppery Watercress is one of the oldest known, leafy, herbal vegetables in the world. • The Watercress plant has hollow stems that buoyantly float the plant in water. • The first commercial cultivation of Watercress intended to be used for consumption was undertaken in 1808 along the River Ebbsfleet in Kent, England. • The ancient Romans believed that Watercress had the power to cure mental illnesses. • Wild Watercress that is grown anywhere near manure can possibly be infested with bacteria such as *Escherichia coli,* which is more commonly known as *E. coli.* In addition, it can be infected with parasites, such as *Fasciola hepatica,* which is more commonly known as the liver fluke. • Hippocrates is believed to have built the first hospital in Kos, Greece, to deliberately be near water so Watercress could be grown for use as a remedy for his patients.

No. 351
Nepeta cataria ⚗️
Catnip
Calamintha albiflora | Cat | Cat's Wort | Cataria tomentosa | Cataria vulgaris | Catmint | Catnep | Catrup | Catswort | Field Balm | Glechoma cataria | Glechoma macrura | Nepeta | Nepeta americana | Nepeta bodinieri | Nepeta ceretana | Nepeta citriodora | Nepeta laurentii | Nepeta macrura | Nepeta minor | Nepeta mollis | Nepeta ruderalis | Nepeta tomentosa | Nepeta vulgaris | Nip

☀ SYMBOLIC MEANINGS
Courage; Happiness.

⚜ POSSIBLE POWERS
The Arts; Attraction; Bast; Beauty; Cat magic; Feminine energy; Friendship; Gifts; Harmony; Joy; Love; Pleasure; Power; Sensuality; Venus; Water element.

☣ FOLKLORE AND FACTS
Make a little pouch and fill it with Catnip, then give it to your cat in an effort to create a psychic bond. • Catnip

supposedly attracts good spirits and good luck. • It is believed that if you are to hold Catnip in your hand until it becomes warm, then hold another person's hand, that person will be your friend, but only for as long as you keep the Catnip that you used in the friendship spell in a safe place. • Minty Catnip leaves are supposedly a favorite bookmark for magical books. • The fragrance of Catnip essential oil can do much for relieving stress or anxiety.

No. 352
Newbouldia laevis ☠☕

Boundary Tree
Bignonia glandulosa | Ewe | Ewe Akoko | Newbouldia pentandra | Nii Abaa | Nii Nyaba | Spathodea adenantha | Spathodea jenischii | Spathodea laevis | Spathodea pentandra | Spathodea speciosa

☀ SYMBOLIC MEANINGS
Chief seed.

✺ POSSIBLE POWERS
Drive away a bad spirit; Health; Luck; Protection; Repels witches and wizards.

☙ FOLKLORE AND FACTS
The flowering Boundary Tree is planted near shrines and in household gardens because it is considered to be a highly sacred tree. • It is believed by some that witches or wizards flying over a Boundary Tree will fall from the sky to crash to the ground and be gone.

No. 353
Nicandra physalodes ☠☕

Shoo-Fly
Apple of Peru

☀ SYMBOLIC MEANINGS
Go away.

✺ POSSIBLE POWERS
Induces abundance; Induces wealth; Repels flying insects; Repels malicious magic; Repels an unwanted lover.

☙ FOLKLORE AND FACTS
It was believed that the Shoo-Fly plant is an insecticide that will effectively shoo pesky flies away. • Make a sachet of Shoo-Fly flowers or leaves to tuck under the welcome mat at your front door to shoo away an unwanted lover. When the unwanted lover officially becomes the ex-lover by not coming around anymore, the sachet can be discarded by burning or burying it.

No. 354
Nicotiana rustica ☠☕

Wild Tobacco
Aztec Tobacco | Makhorka | Mapacho | Nicotia rustica | Nicotiana andicola | Nicotiana asiatica | Nicotiana brasilia | Nicotiana humilis | Nicotiana humilis | Nicotiana minor | Nicotiana pavonii | Nicotiana pavonii var. rotundifolia | Nicotiana pumila | Nicotiana rugosa | Nicotiana rustica var. asiatica | Nicotiana rustica var. brasilia | Nicotiana rustica var. humilis | Nicotiana rustica var. pavonii | Nicotiana rustica var. pumila | Nicotiana rustica var. texana | Nicotiana scabra | Nicotiana sibirica | Nicotiana tatarica | Nicotiana texana | Nicotiana turcica | Strong Tobacco | Taaba | Tabacca | Taback | Thuoc Lao | Traditional Tobacco

☀ SYMBOLIC MEANINGS
Power.

✺ POSSIBLE POWERS
Healing; Illness; Insecticide; Offerings; Peacefulness following hostilities; Purification; Sealing of bargains and agreements; Strength; Unification.

☙ FOLKLORE AND FACTS
Wild Tobacco has been commonly used for spiritual, religious, ritual, and ceremonial reasons in pipe ceremonies of various intentions, such as sealing an agreement or as a prayerful offering to the creator. • Wild Tobacco has long been regarded as a sacred plant by many Native American and South American tribes. • Indigenous South American tribes use Wild Tobacco for shamanic purposes. One of those purposes being that they believe that smoking Wild Tobacco makes it possible to speak directly with spirits. • The *Nicotiana rustica* Wild Tobacco plant contains up to nine times more nicotine than *Nicotiana tabacum,* or Common Tobacco, making it suitable for use as an insecticide. • The Native American peace pipe ceremony used a very special ceremonial pipe from which Wild Tobacco would be smoked by passing it among those involved. • Except for small crops grown by some Native American tribes to use for both secular and religious ceremonies, rites of passage, alliances, and significant social events, *Nicotiana rustica* is no longer a cultivated crop in North America. • Wild Tobacco is thrown into the water at the beginning of a water journey to appease the Water Spirit.

No. 355

Ñicotiana tabacum ☠☘

Tobacco

Brown Gold | Common Tobacco | Nicotiana alba | Nicotiana alipes | Nicotiana angustifolia | Nicotiana attenuata | Nicotiana capensis | Nicotiana caudata | Nicotiana crispula | Nicotiana doniana | Nicotiana florida | Nicotiana frutescens | Nicotiana fruticosa | Nicotiana gigantea | Nicotiana gracilipes | Nicotiana havanensis | Nicotiana lancifolia | Nicotiana latissima | Nicotiana lehmannii | Nicotiana lingua | Nicotiana loxensis | Nicotiana macrophylla | Nicotiana mexicana | Nicotiana mexicana var. rubriflora | Nicotiana nepalensis | Nicotiana pallescens | Nicotiana petiolaris | Nicotiana petiolata | Nicotiana pilosa | Nicotiana repanda | Nicotiana serotina | Nicotiana tabaca | Nicotiana tabacum var. alipes | Nicotiana tabacum var. angustifolia | Nicotiana tabacum var. attenuata | Nicotiana tabacum var. brasiliensis | Nicotiana tabacum var. goyanum | Nicotiana tabacum var. gracilipes | Nicotiana tabacum var. lancifolia | Nicotiana tabacum var. lingua | Nicotiana tabacum var. loxensis | Nicotiana tabacum var. macrophylla | Nicotiana tabacum var. pallescens | Nicotiana tabacum var. serotina | Nicotiana tabacum var. undulata | Nicotiana tabacum var. verdon | Nicotiana tabacum var. virginica | Nicotiana verdon | Nicotiana virginica | Nicotiana ybarrensis | Tabacum latissimum | Tabacum nicotianum | Tabacum ovatofolium

❇ **SYMBOLIC MEANINGS**
Power.

✸ **POSSIBLE POWERS**
Healing; Illness;
Insecticide; Offerings;
Peacefulness
following
hostilities;
Purification;
Sealing of bargains
and agreements;
Strength; Unification.

✪ **FOLKLORE AND FACTS**
First discovered in pre-Columbian America, where it was ceremonially used by indigenous people, Spaniards carried Tobacco back to Europe, where it quickly became habitual to smoke or use as snuff. • An English colonist living in Jamestown, Virginia, in 1609 by the name of John Rolfe, who eventually was to become the husband of Pocahontas, was the first person to successfully cultivate Tobacco and export the cured leaves to England. The endeavor was the source of his fortune. • As Tobacco was introduced around the world and the addiction to it grew, trade increased, as did the profitability of the herb. Eventually the demand for Tobacco was so great it was used as an excuse to utilize slave labor to meet the need, which helped fuel the slave trade. • By the 1930s in the United States and in England, there was a mysterious rise in lung cancer cases without any certainty of why. Eventually the negative effect that Tobacco has had on the health of those in bondage to it became evident. • A great global movement to curtail Tobacco use occurred, surprisingly beginning in Nazi Germany in 1941, when Tobacco use was being condemned as being detrimental to public health, and it was banned in public places. • A British physiologist by the name of Richard Doll wrote a scientific paper in 1948 as the first of several papers that directly pointed to Tobacco smoking as a cause of lung cancer. • By 1959, Tobacco advertisements began to disappear from billboards, magazines, and television. • It wasn't until the 1980s, after tens of thousands of studies by physicians around the world, that Tobacco was directly linked not only to lung cancer, but to a long list of other diseases and illnesses. From then onward, the persistent push for people to quit smoking Tobacco became a daily plea. • Tobacco use in magical workings is still in practice.

No. 356

Ñigella sativa ☠☘🍯

Black Cumin

Black Caraway | Black Onion Seed | Kalangi | Kalonji | Kolojeera | Nigella | Nigella cretica | Nigella indica | Nigella truncata | Roman Coriander

❇ **SYMBOLIC MEANINGS**
Listen.

✸ **POSSIBLE POWERS**
Aphrodisiac.

✪ **FOLKLORE AND FACTS**
In what is now Turkey, archaeologists discovered Black Cumin seeds, dating to the Bronze Age, inside an ancient Hittite wine flask. Archaeologists also found the seeds in the tomb of Pharaoh Tutankhamun.

No. 357

Nymphaea nelumbo ☠ ⚱

Sacred Lotus

Ambuja | Aravind | Arvind | Baino | Bean of India | Egyptian Lotus | Flower of Hindus and Buddhists | Indian Lotus | Kamal | Kamala | Kunala | Lotus Flower | Lotus Lily | Nalin | Nalini | Neeraj | *Nelumbium album* | *Nelumbium asiaticum* | *Nelumbium caspicum* | *Nelumbium caspium* | *Nelumbium discolor* | *Nelumbium indicum* | *Nelumbium javanicum* | *Nelumbium marginatum* | *Nelumbium nelumbo* | *Nelumbium rheedii* | *Nelumbium speciosum* | *Nelumbium tamara* | *Nelumbium transversum* | *Nelumbium turbinatum* | *Nelumbium venosum* | *Nelumbo caspica* | *Nelumbo indica* | *Nelumbo komarovii* | *Nelumbo nelumbo* | *Nelumbo speciosa* | *Nelumbo speciosa var. alba* | *Nymphaea nelumbo* | Padma | Pankaj | Pankaja | Saroja | *Tamara alba* | *Tamara hemisphaerica* | *Tamara rubra*

SYMBOLIC MEANINGS

Beauty; Chastity; Divine female fertility; Eloquence; Enlightened one in a world of ignorant beings; Estranged love; Estrangement; Evolution; Far from the one who is loved; Forgetful of the past; Mere display; Potential; Purity; Resurrection; Spiritual promises; Truth; Virtuous.

POSSIBLE POWERS

Feminine energy; Fertility; Lock-opening; Longevity; Moon; Protection; Purity; Spirituality; Water element.

FOLKLORE AND FACTS

The Sacred Lotus is highly regarded as a meaningful, sacred plant in Egypt, India, Greece, and Japan as being the mystical symbol of life, spirituality, and the center of the universe. • The pod of the Sacred Lotus holds the seed nutlets which are each individual fruits as a part of the multiple fruit the pod represents. • The viability of Sacred Lotus is quite incredible. If conditions are ideal, the seeds that are viable can last a very long time. How long was never quite established until 1995, when research biologist Jane Shen-Miller successfully germinated Sacred Lotus seeds that had been found in a dry Northeast China lakebed. Using modern technological radiocarbon-dating, those seeds were dated to be 1,288 years old, give or take 250 years. • Most deities of Asian religions are shown sitting upon a Sacred Lotus flower. • It is believed that anyone who breathes in the fragrance of a Sacred Lotus flower will benefit from the flower's inherent blessings and protection. • Carry or wear any part of the Sacred Lotus plant to receive good luck and blessings. • For thousands of years, Hindu worshippers have often offered Sacred Lotus blossoms at the feet of statues of their gods and goddesses. • Hindu worshippers believe that Lord Brahma, who is believed to be the creator of all the universe, was born of a Sacred Lotus flower. • Ancient Egyptians believed that their goddess Isis was also born of a Sacred Lotus flower. • The Sacred Lotus is believed to have the power to cultivate people's thoughts, words, and deeds by way of meditation. • The deeply spiritual enlightenment inspired by the Sacred Lotus is significant in a simple lesson. This most sacred and deeply meaningful flower manages to rise up from the slimy mud at the bottom of a pond to reach the surface, drawn up by the light reflecting upon the water. Once there, it will bud with great promise, filled with the wondrousness to come. Then the blossom unfurls, opening wide to reveal the potential and the completeness of itself and ourselves in the same way. Thus, the Sacred Lotus is a lesson in blossoming into one's full and compete self, regardless of how and where one started out. • The Sacred Lotus is the national flower of India. • String 108 Sacred Lotus seeds together to be used for Hindu, Jain, Sikh, or Buddhist prayer and meditation beads, which is known as a *japamala*. • Sacred Lotus seeds are used in Chinese medicine as Lian Zi Xi.

No. 358

Ocimum basilicum ♂🍵

Basil

Albahaca | American Dittany | Arjaka | Balanoi | Bazil | Brenhinllys | Busuioc | Common Basil | Feslien | Garden Basil | Genovese Basil | Great Basil | Herb of Kings | Herbe Royale | Holy Basil | Kiss Me Nicholas | Luole | Njilika | Ocimum album | Ocimum anisatum | Ocimum barrelieri | Ocimum bullatum | Ocimum caryophyllatum | Ocimum chevalieri | Ocimum ciliare | Ocimum ciliatum | Ocimum citrodorum | Ocimum cochleatum | Ocimum dentatum | Ocimum hispidum | Ocimum integerrimum | Ocimum lanceolatum | Ocimum laxum | Ocimum majus | Ocimum medium | Ocimum minus | Ocimum nigrum | Ocimum odorum | Ocimum scabrum | Ocimum simile | Ocimum thyrsiflorum | Ocimum urticifolium | Our Herb | Plectranthus barrelieri | St. Joseph's Wort | Sweet Basil | Sweet Bazil | The Devil's Plant | Witches Herb

☀ SYMBOLIC MEANINGS

Best wishes; Give me your good wishes; Good luck; Good wishes; Hatred; Hatred of the other; Kingly; Poverty; Romance; Royal; Sacred; Wealth.

🌀 POSSIBLE POWERS

Accidents; Aggression; Anger; Aphrodisiac; Carnal desire; Clear the mind; Conflict; Erzulie; Exorcism; Fire element; Flying; Love; Lust; Machinery; Mars; Masculine energy; Prosperity; Protection; Relaxation; Rock music; Strength; Struggle; Vishnu; War; Wealth; Witch flight.

🜋 FOLKLORE AND FACTS

The ancient Greeks considered Basil to be a strong symbol of hate, misfortune, and poverty. • Carry a Basil leaf in your pocket to bring you money. • In the West Indies, Basil is placed around shops to attract customers. In other parts of the world, a Basil leaf is placed in cash registers and on the entry doors into shops, not only to attract customers but to ensure continued financial success. • In Italy, Basil is a symbol for love and is widely used as a token of love. • Giving a sprig of Basil to a man means, "Be wary, for someone is plotting against you." • According to Jewish legend, if you hold a sprig of Basil while fasting it will help you maintain your strength and resolve to proceed. • In Spain, a pot of Basil on a windowsill indicated that it was a house of ill repute. • The fragrance of Basil is said to promote thoughtful consideration between two unsympathetic people. • Basil given as a gift will bring good luck into a new home. • Add Basil to a bath to promote spiritual purification. • A married couple can share one Basil leaf

between them to rub over their hearts as a request that fidelity will bless their relationship. • In India, the Basil plant is considered to be sacred. • It was believed by many that evil cannot be in the same place as Basil. • The fragrance of Basil can soothe mutual hot tempers. • If you are seeking a job, sprinkle Basil at the front of the building where you are entering for a job interview. • Carry Basil to feel safe moving positively forward despite the threat of peril. • Basil essential oil is useful in aromatherapy to clear groggy dull feelings and sluggish reasoning. • Basil essential oil is useful in aromatherapy for relaxing the mind at the end of a long stressful chaotic day.

No. 359

Ocimum basilicum var. thyrsiflora ♂🍵

Thai Basil

Chi Neang Voang | Cinnamon Basil | Horapha | Horaphā | Hùng Quế | Kmer

☀ SYMBOLIC MEANINGS

Best wishes; Give me your good wishes; Good luck; Good wishes; Hatred; Hatred of the other; Kingly; Poverty; Romance; Royal; Sacred; Wealth.

🌀 POSSIBLE POWERS

Accidents; Aggression; Anger; Aphrodisiac; Carnal desire; Clears the mind; Conflict; Exorcism; Flying; Love; Lust; Machinery; Money; Prosperity; Protection; Relaxation; Rock music; Strength; Struggle; War; Wealth; Witch Flight.

🜋 FOLKLORE AND FACTS

The cinnamon-licorice flavor of fresh Thai Basil leaf is a staple used in much of Asian cuisine. • It is believed by some that if a sprig of Thai Basil is placed in a prospective lover's hand and it immediately withers, it is a sign of promiscuity. • A Thai Basil leaf in a cash register, pocket, wallet, tucked under a computer, or affixed under a desk where the business of making money is transacted, it can pull money to it.

O

No. 360
Onopordum acanthium 🏺

Scottish Thistle

Cotton Thistle | Onopordum acanthifolium |
Onopordum stenostegium | Scotch Thistle |
Scots Thistle | Wooly Thistle

❋ **SYMBOLIC MEANINGS**
Aggressiveness; Alerting;
Austerity; Bravery; Christ's
deliverance; Fierceness;
Hard work; Harshness;
Independence; Nobility; Pain;
Pride; Retaliation; Sternness;
Suffering.

❧ **COMPONENT MEANING**
Seed head: Depart.

✹ **POSSIBLE POWERS**
Assistance; Breaks a hex; Dispels melancholy; Exorcism;
Fertility; Harmony; Healing; Independence; Material gain;
Persistence; Protection; Revelation; Stability; Strength;
Tenacity.

✦ **FOLKLORE AND FACTS**
According to legend, the Scottish Thistle is the national
flower of Scotland, due to a sneaky invasion that was
attempted in 1263 when King Haakon of Norway's fleet of
longships met with a strong gale that forced a few of his ships
to a beach at Largs, in Ayrshire. During the night, barefoot
Norsemen, intent upon sneaking up on the Scots who were
sleeping unaware of trouble coming their way, unwittingly
entered a field where Scottish Thistles poked and prickled
one particular invader enough to shriek in pain when he
stepped on one. This woke up and alerted the Scots, allowing
them enough time to successfully defend themselves and
win the battle, saving many of their lives. From then on, the
Scottish Thistle became honored and sacred to Scotland.
• The Scottish Order of the Thistle's motto is *"Nemo me
impune lacesset,"* which means "No one attacks me with
impunity." • A stylized Scottish Thistle is on Scotland's rugby
team uniforms. • Wear or carry a Scottish Thistle blossom to
rid yourself of feeling melancholy. • A vase of fresh Scottish
Thistle in a room will renew the vitality of all who are within
it. • Grow Scottish Thistle in the garden to fend off thieves.
• Carry a Scottish Thistle blossom for protection against
evil. • A man can carry a Scottish Thistle blossom as an
amulet for a boost to and protection of his lovemaking skills.
• The dried flowers of the Scottish Thistle can be used as
a substitute for rennet. • Carry or wear a Scottish Thistle
amulet for protection against witches and witchery.

No. 361
Ophioglossum vulgatum ☠🏺

Adder's Tongue Fern

Adder's Tongue | Serpent's Tongue |
Snake Tongue | Southern Adder's
Tongue

❋ **SYMBOLIC MEANINGS**
Caution.

✹ **POSSIBLE POWERS**
Cease slanderous gossip;
Divination; Dream
magic; Feminine energy;
Healing; Healing magic;
Moon; Moon magic; Virility; Water element.

✦ **FOLKLORE AND FACTS**
Adder's Tongue Fern is an herb that is so ancient, dating back
so far in prehistory that it can be considered to be a living
fossil. • The short stalk of the Adder's Tongue Fern is thought
to look somewhat like the tongue of a snake, but it only
grows a few inches tall and it only appears in the summer,
between June and August. • To help put an end to slanderous
gossip, put an Adder's Tongue Fern leaf and piece of stalk in
two separate yellow cotton sachets. Carry or wear one and
bury the other in the ground deeply.

No. 362
Origanum majorana 🏺🍴

Marjoram

Amaracus majorana | Knotted Marjoram | Majorana
dubia | Majorana fragrans | Majorana hortensis |
Majorana majorana | Majorana mexicana | Majorana
ovalifolia | Majorana ovatifolia | Majorana suffruticosa |
Majorana tenuifolia | Majorana uncinata | Majorana
vulgaris | Mejorana | Origanum confertum | Origanum
dubium | Origanum majoranoides | Origanum odorum |
Origanum salvifolium | Sweet Marjoram | Thymus
majorana

❋ **SYMBOLIC MEANINGS**
Blushes; Comfort; Consolation;
Happiness; Joy; Love.

✹ **POSSIBLE POWERS**
Air element; Aphrodite; Happiness;
Health; Longevity; Love; Masculine
energy; Mercury; Money;
Protection; Soothes anxiety;
Soothes grief; Venus.

O

It is thought that if someone rubs Marjoram on themselves before falling asleep, he or she will dream of their future spouse. • Ancient Greeks believed Marjoram grew over the grave of a dead person who was happy. • Ancient Greeks and Romans would make Marjoram crowns for marrying couples to wear as symbols of love, happiness, and honor. • When feeling under the weather, Marjoram essential oil may provide comforting aromatherapy and relaxation to facilitate sleep.

• Ancient Greeks would sometimes wear an Oregano crown while they slept for psychic purposes and with the hope of having prophetic dreams. • Put Oregano under the pillow to encourage pleasant dreams. • Place a nosegay of Oregano at a grave as a wish for the peaceful journey of the deceased spirit while transitioning to the afterlife. • Avoid Oregano for two weeks prior to having surgery to avoid complication with bleeding. • Ingesting Oregano oil can be toxic. • Oregano essential oil can be used for cleaning.

No. 363
Origanum vulgare 💀⛏🍴

Oregano

Herb of Magic | *Origanum floridum* | *Thymus origanum* | Wild Marjoram

☀ SYMBOLIC MEANINGS

Brilliant joy of the mountain; Good luck; Happiness; Joy; Soothing; Will banish sadness.

✸ POSSIBLE POWERS

Air element; Good health; Good luck; Happiness; Joy; Mercury; Prophetic dreaming; Protection; Protection against poison; Purification; Repels evil; Reveals the mystical secrets for using black magic.

☙ FOLKLORE AND FACTS

Oregano was virtually unknown in the United States until the end of World War II, when American soldiers who had been stationed in the Mediterranean made a point to bring seeds home with them. • Oregano is considered to be the herb of all herbs. • The ancient Greeks believed that the goddess Aphrodite created and grew Oregano in her garden atop Mount Olympus. • In Greece, Oregano crowns were worn by marrying couples. • Plant Oregano around the house to fend off evil spirits and all types of negative energy.

No. 364
Oxalis acetosella 💀⛏

Wood Sorrel

Acetosella alba | Alleluia | Common Wood Sorrel | Cuckoo Bread | Cuckowe's Meat | Fairy Bells | *Oxalis alba* | *Oxalis fragrans* | *Oxalis nemoralis* | *Oxalis parviflora* | *Oxalis taquetii* | *Oxalis versicolor* | *Oxalis vulgaris* | *Oxys acetosella* | *Oxys alba* | *Oxys pliniana* | *Oxys vulgaris* | Sour Trefoil | Sourgrass | Sours | Wood Sour

☀ SYMBOLIC MEANINGS

Joy; Maternal tenderness.

✸ POSSIBLE POWERS

Earth element; Feminine energy; Good luck; Healing; Health; Prophecy; Venus.

☙ FOLKLORE AND FACTS

The common name of Alleluia was given to Wood Sorrel because the plant will bloom between Easter and Pentecost, which is during the time when nearly all of the songs that are sung in the Christian churches on Sundays seemed to end with the word "Hallelujah." • Wood Sorrel is closely associated with fairies and other spirits of the woods.

Panax ginseng 🕱🍵

Oriental Ginseng

Aralia ginseng | Asian Ginseng | Chinese Ginseng | Ginnsuu | Human Root | Insam | Jên Shên | Jin Chen | Jin-Sim | Korean Ginseng | Long Brain Root | Man Root | Mountain Root | Ninjin | Nin-sin | *Panax verus* | Red Root | Rénshen | Taegeuk Root | Water Root | White Root | Wonder of the World Root

✴ **SYMBOLIC MEANINGS**
Immortality; Strength.

🌼 **POSSIBLE POWERS**
Aphrodisiac; Attracts love; Beauty; Healing; Longevity; Love; Lust; Protection; Sexual healing; Sexual potency; Wishing; Yang stimulation.

🜂 **FOLKLORE AND FACTS**
As a sacred herb, Oriental Ginseng will bring beauty, love, money, sexuality, and health to all who carry it. • An interesting way to make a wish is to carve your wish into an Oriental Ginseng root and then throw it into naturally running water such as a stream or river. • Oriental Ginseng is one of the basic herbs routinely used in traditional Chinese medicine. • Oriental Ginseng is famously known in China to stimulate the Yang.

Panax quinquefolius 🕱🍵

American Ginseng

American Ginseng | Aralia quinquefolia | Ginseng | Ginseng quinquefolium | Panax americanus

✴ **SYMBOLIC MEANINGS**
Immortality; Strength.

🌼 **POSSIBLE POWERS**
Beauty; Fire element; Healing; Longevity; Love; Lust; Protection; Sexual potency; Sun; Wishing; Yin.

🜂 **FOLKLORE AND FACTS**
American Ginseng will bring beauty, love, money, sexuality, and health to all who carry it. • An interesting way to make a wish is to carve it into an American Ginseng root and then throw it into running water, which will carry the wish to where it needs to go. • The Native American Cherokee tribes' medicine bags always included American Ginseng. • Most of the American Ginseng harvested in North America is exported to Asia, where it is considered to be

of the quality they seek. The herb is appreciated for its use in their own traditional Chinese and other folk medicine treatments, which have included *Panax quinquefolius* for thousands of years.

Papaver rhoeas 🕱🍵

Flanders Poppy

Common Poppy | Corn Poppy | Corn Rose | Field Poppy | *Papaver aegadicum* | *Papaver agrivagum* | *Papaver ameristophyllum* | *Papaver anisotrichum* | *Papaver arvatecum* | *Papaver arvense* | *Papaver atropurpureum* | *Papaver balanocarpum* | *Papaver caespitosum* | *Papaver caudatifolium* | *Papaver cereale* | *Papaver chanceliae* | *Papaver chelidonioides* | *Papaver cinerascens* | *Papaver commixtum* | *Papaver cruciatum* | *Papaver dodonei* | *Papaver erraticum* | *Papaver erucifolium* | *Papaver feddeanum* | *Papaver fuchsii* | *Papaver gabrielianae* | *Papaver graecum* | *Papaver guerlekense* | *Papaver hookeri* | *Papaver humifusum* | *Papaver insignitum* | *Papaver integrifolium* | *Papaver interjectum* | *Papaver intermedium* | *Papaver montenegrinum* | *Papaver omphalodeum* | *Papaver osswaldii* | *Papaver paucisetum* | *Papaver propinquum* | *Papaver pseudohaussknechtii Fedde* | *Papaver rapiferum* | *Papaver rhopalothece* | *Papaver robertianella* | *Papaver rumelicum* | *Papaver rusticum* | *Papaver segetale* | *Papaver spurium* | *Papaver stipitatum* | *Papaver subumbilicatum* | *Papaver tenuissimum* | *Papaver thaumasiosepalum* | *Papaver tumidulum* | *Papaver uniflorum* | Red Poppy | Red Weed

✴ **SYMBOLIC MEANINGS**
Avoidance of problems; Consolation; Ephemeral charms; Eternal rest; Eternal sleep; Fun-loving; Good and evil; Life and death; Light and darkness; Love; Pleasure; Remembrance.

🌼 **POSSIBLE POWERS**
Ambition; Attitude; Clear thinking; Demeter; Feminine energy; Fertility; Fruitfulness; Harmony; Higher understanding; Honor and remember; Hypnos; Invisibility; Logic; Love; Luck; Magic; Manifestation in material form; Money; Moon; Remembrance; Sleep; Spiritual concepts; Thought processes; Water element.

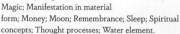

🜂 **FOLKLORE AND FACTS**
The ancient Romans believed that the Flanders Poppy could heal wounds inflicted by love. • Evidence of Flanders Poppy flowers was found in 3,000-year-old Egyptian tombs. • The ancient Greeks believed that corn would not grow without the presence of a Flanders Poppy plant growing nearby. • After World War I, the once battle-pocked fields in Flanders, Belgium, filled up with the Flanders Poppy, which is how the *Papaver rhoeas* received this distinctive common name. • A legend began that the flowers had resulted from the spilt blood of war, making the red Flanders Poppy

P

flower the official World War I remembrance symbol, most especially when worn on Armistice Day and Victory-in-Europe Day at the end of World War II. After the end of World War II, the Flanders Poppy had been imbued with so much symbolic meaning that later the same Flanders Poppy was adopted to wear or display on any of the various days dedicated to the Armed Forces, veterans, and their families. This is entirely because, in both the United States and the United Kingdom, the Flanders Poppy became the official symbolic representation of those who have died while in service to their respective countries while on active duty in any military conflict.

No. 368
Papaver somniferum ☠☠🍴
Opium Poppy
Adormidera | Ahiphenalm | Amapola | Birdseed Poppy | Blind Buff | Blindeyes | Breadseed Poppy | Dormidera | Head Waak | Headaches | Opio | *Papaver album* | *Papaver album-nigrum* | *Papaver amoenum* | *Papaver amplexicaule* | *Papaver glabrum* | *Papaver hortense* | *Papaver indehiscens* | *Papaver nigrum* | *Papaver officinale* | *Papaver opiiferum* | *Papaver paeoniiflorum* | *Papaver sylvestre*

☀ SYMBOLIC MEANINGS
Avoidance of problems; Consolation; Ephemeral charms; Eternal rest; Eternal sleep; Fun-loving; Good and evil; Imagination; Life and death; Light and darkness; Love; Oblivion; Pleasure; Remembrance.

✹ POSSIBLE POWERS
Ambition; Attitude; Clear thinking; Fertility; Fruitfulness; Harmony; Higher understanding; Invisibility; Logic; Love; Luck; Magic; Manifestation in material form; Money; Moon; Sleep; Spiritual concepts; Thought processes; Water element.

☘ FOLKLORE AND FACTS
The ancient Romans believed that Opium Poppy seeds could heal wounds inflicted by hurtful love. • Write a question on a piece of paper. Fold it and tuck it into a sachet with Opium Poppy seeds, then sleep with it under your pillow to dream an answer to your question. • The same poppy seeds that are used on bread and other baked goods and readily sold in a jar on nearly every grocery store shelf come from the Opium Poppy *Papaver somniferum*. Up to ninety percent of the morphine content is removed from the seeds when they are processed in the United States. However, there can possibly be a heavy concentration of residue left on seeds processed in other countries. Not surprisingly, the slice of poppyseed cake or poppyseed-covered bagel consumed even as long as sixty hours before testing can still present trace opioids in urine to result in a false-positive drug test.

No. 369
Pelargonium graveolens ✿
Rose-Scented Geranium
Geraniospermum terebinthinaceum | Geranium asperum | Geranium radula | Geranium terebinthinaceum | Hoarea intermixta | Old Fashion Rose Geranium | Pelargonium asperum | Pelargonium intermdium | Pelargonium terebinthinaceum | Rose-scent Geranium | Scented Geranium | Storksbill

☀ SYMBOLIC MEANINGS
Calm; Folly; Gentility; Happiness; I prefer you; Preference; Spiritual happiness.

✹ POSSIBLE POWERS
Alleviate the negativity that stress instigates; Balances the mind; Calms; Feminine energy; Fertility; Happiness; Health; Love; Prosperity; Protection; Purification; Venus; Water element.

☘ FOLKLORE AND FACTS
Some Rose-Scented Geranium species are said to be able to effectively repel mosquitoes. • Rose-Scented Geranium of all types are protective when grown or brought into the house as cut flowers and put into fresh water. • Pots of red Rose-Scented Geranium offer much protection for the home and health. • *Pelargonium graveolens* Rose-Scented Geranium flowers can be used to flavor vodka to make a home-made liqueur. • Rose-Scented Geranium essential oil for aromatherapy is spiritually uplifting and helps to balance the mind in times of stress, agitation, aggravation, and sadness.

No. 370
Pelargonium odoratissimum ☠✿
Apple Geranium
Apple Pelargonium | *Cortusina odoratissima* | Geraniospermum odoratissimum | Geranium africanum | Geranium odoratissimum | Geranium odoriferum | Malva moschata | Pelargonium odoratum | Pelargonium odorum

☀ SYMBOLIC MEANINGS
Facility; Gentility; Present preference.

P

POSSIBLE POWERS

Feminine energy; Fertility; Health; Love; Protection; Purification; Venus; Water element.

FOLKLORE AND FACTS

Apple Geranium is protective when grown or brought into the house as cut flowers and put into fresh water. • Pots of red Apple Geranium offer a great deal of protection for the home and health. • The fragrance of the Apple Geranium is that of a fresh-cut apple. • The Apple Geranium's essential oil has a delightful apple-scented fragrance that is helpful in alleviating some effects of anxiety and depression.

No. 371

Pelargonium quercifolium ☠🏺

Oakleaf Geranium

Geraniospermum quercifolium | Geranium oxoniense | Geranium quercifolium | Geranium terebinthinaceum | Oak Geranium | Oak-leaf Geranium | Pelargonium karrooense | Pelargonium spinii

SYMBOLIC MEANINGS

Deign to smile; Folly; Friendship; Gentility; Lady; Melancholy mind; True friendship.

POSSIBLE POWERS

Feminine energy; Fertility; Health; Love; Protection; Purification; Venus; Water element.

FOLKLORE AND FACTS

Oakleaf Geranium is protective to the household when grown or when brought into the house as cut flowers and put into fresh water. • The leaves of Oakleaf Geranium are very fragrant and will work well in a potpourri.

No. 372

Perilla frutescens var. *crispa* ☠🏺🍸

Shiso

Acinos sido | Beefsteak Plant | Chinese Basil | Dentidia nankinensis | Dentidia purpurascens | Dentidia purpurea | Ggaetnip | Huihuisū | Japanese Basil | Muslim Perilla | Ocimum acutum | Ocimum crispum | Perilla acuta | Perilla arguta | Perilla crispa | Perilla frutescens var. nankinensis | Perilla Mint | Perilla nankinensis | Perilla ocymoides var. crispa | Perilla Sesame | Purple Mint | Purple Perilla | Rattlesnake Weed | Red Shiso | Red-Leaf Shiso | Soyeop | Su | Summer Coleus | Tía Tô | Wild Basil | Wild Coleus | Wild Sesame | Zǐsū

SYMBOLIC MEANINGS

Meaning of meaning.

POSSIBLE POWERS

Healing; Perfumery; Reawakens courage; Reconnects to life.

FOLKLORE AND FACTS

In the wild, when the dried stalks of the Shiso plant are disturbed when walking past them, they make a strange, somewhat unnerving rattling that sounds like a rattlesnake ready to strike. • The first mention of Shiso in writing was around 500 CE. • Shiso is used in Asian folk medicine. • Shiso flowers were sometimes used in perfumery.

No. 373

Petasites hybridus ☠🏺

Butterbur

Blatterdock | Bog Rhubarb | Boghorns | Butterdock | Capdockin | Cineraria hybrida | Devil's Hat | Flapperdock | Langwort | Pestilence Wort | Petasites georgicus | Petasites officinalis | Petasites ovatus | Petasites pratensis | Petasites vulgaris | Tussilago hybrida | Tussilago petasites | Umbrella Plant

SYMBOLIC MEANINGS

Looking for love.

POSSIBLE POWERS

Love divination; Protection; Psychic power.

FOLKLORE AND FACTS

Butterbur is sometimes used in a very old divination ritual carried out by one who is too desperately seeking to raise their sense of faith and hope in finding out who will be their future mate. The divination is somewhat similar to the Hemp seed divination ritual, the primary difference being that this divination is much more powerful and requires Butterbur seeds. The seeker must be young and never married. Most likely a maid, which also means a virgin. To perform the divination, it must be done very early on a Friday morning in a lonely place thirty minutes before sunrise. The seeds are strew-sown onto the grass while sincerely reciting "I sow, I sow!" Then, "My own dear, come here, come here, and mow and mow." The vision of the future mate may be seen mowing with a scythe within view. But, if the girl is fearful, the vision will immediately disappear. • Butterbur is one plant that has completely separate male or female plants. • Butterbur leaves are heart-shaped and huge, being up to a large as three feet in diameter.

No. 374

Petroselinum crispum 🜍🍴

Parsley

Ammi petroselinoides | Anisactis segetalis | Apium crispum | Apium laetum | Apium latifolium | Apium occidentale | Apium peregrinum | Apium petroselinum | Apium romanum | Apium tuberosum | Apium vulgare | Bupleurum petroselinoides | Carum peregrinum | Carum petroselinum | Carum vulgare | Chinese Lovage | Cnidium petroselinum | Curly Leaf Parsley | Deveseel | Devil's Oatmeal | Flat-leaf Parsley | French Parsley | Garden Parsley | Hamburger Parsley | Helosciadium oppositifolium | Italian Lovage | Italian Parsley | Lavose | Leaf Parsley | Lestyán | Leustean | Levistico | Libbsticka | Libecek | Liebstöckel | Ligusticum peregrinum | Livèche | Lovage | Love Herb | Love Parsley | Love Rod | Love Root | Love Sticklet | Loving Herbs | Lubczyk | Lubestico | Lyubistok | Maggikraut | Maggiplant | Percely | Persil | Petersilie | Petroselinum anatolicum | Petroselinum fractophyllum | Petroselinum hortense | Petroselinum macedonicum | Petroselinum peregrinum | Petroselinum romanum | Petroselinum sativum | Petroselinum selinoides | Petroselinum thermoeri | Petroselinum vulgare | Peucedanum intermedium | Peucedanum petroselinum | Rock Parsley | Root Parsley | Sea Parsley | Selinon | Selinum petroselinum | Siler japonicum | Sison peregrinum | Sium oppositifolium | Sium petroselinum | Turnip-Rooted Parsley | Wydleria portoricensis

✹ SYMBOLIC MEANINGS

Bring love; Death; Evil; Festivity; Fickleness; Love.

⚙ POSSIBLE POWERS

Air element; Aphrodisiac; Attracts love; Attraction; Business transactions; Caution; Cleverness; Communication; Creativity; Faith; Illumination; Initiation; Intelligence; Learning; Love; Lust; Masculine energy; Memory; Mercury; Persephone; Protection; Purification; Science; Self-preservation; Sound judgment; Thievery; Wisdom.

☘ FOLKLORE AND FACTS

Parsley has been cultivated since 300 BCE. • Parsley was valuable to witches because it was believed that Parsley went to the Underworld nine times and back again before sprouting. • If one dreams about cutting Parsley, it is a bad omen for love, indicating that the dreamer will be double-crossed by a lover. • It is believed that to transplant Parsley will bring bad luck for a year. • In medieval times, it was believed that to pluck a sprig of Parsley while speaking an enemy's name had the power to kill. • Ancient Romans and Greeks placed Parsley on dinner plates to protect the food and keep away misfortune during mealtime. • It is believed that adding Parsley to the bath water before going out to meet new people will increase your attractiveness. • Wear a crown of Parsley to prevent or delay drunkenness. • Ancient Romans were wary of Parsley because they considered it to be evil. Even so, they hid a piece of Parsley on or under their togas daily for protection against evil. • The ancient Greeks made Parsley a part of their funeral rituals by using it to strew the tombs of the dead. It was common enough that an impending death was spoken of as there was going to be a need for Parsley.

No. 375

Phlox paniculata 🜍

Phlox

Armeria paniculata | Fall Phlox | Garden Phlox | Panicled Phlox | Perennial Phlox | Phlox acuminata | Phlox acutifolia | Phlox americana | Phlox atrocaulis | Phlox brevifolia | Phlox bridgesii | Phlox broughtonii | Phlox brownii | Phlox canescens | Phlox clarkioides | Phlox cordata | Phlox corymbosa | Phlox cruenta | Phlox decussata | Phlox disticha | Phlox divergens | Phlox elata | Phlox ingramiana | Phlox intermedia | Phlox × laeta | Phlox macrophylla | Phlox missourica | Phlox omniflora | Phlox paniculata var. acuminata | Phlox paniculata var. laxiflora | Phlox philadelphica | Phlox pulchella | Phlox scabra | Phlox sickmannii | Phlox thomsonii | Phlox tigrina | Phlox undulata | Phlox vernoniana | Phlox virginica | Phlox wheeleriana | Summer Phlox

✹ SYMBOLIC MEANINGS

Our souls are united; Sweet dreams; Thinking alike; Unanimity; United hearts; United souls.

⚙ POSSIBLE POWERS

Friendship spells; Healing; Mends a broken friendship; Relationship spells.

☘ FOLKLORE AND FACTS

The highly fragrant Phlox has become so well established that it also grows wild in vacant fields as well as being a favorite plant to grow in gardens, because of its ability to attract butterflies. • Phlox makes a lovely fragrant cut flower to bring into the home. • Gift Phlox flowers to someone with whom you wish to mend a broken friendship. • Phlox was frequently used by Native American tribes for medicinal purposes.

P

No. 376
Phoenix dactylifera ♂

Date

Date Palm | *Encephalartos pungens* | *Palma dactylifera* | *Palma major* | *Phoenix chevalieri* | *Phoenix excelsior* | *Phoenix iberica* | *Zamia pallida*

✹ **SYMBOLIC MEANINGS**
Prosperity; Triumph; Victory.

✺ **POSSIBLE POWERS**
Air element; Apollo; Artemis; Fertility; Hecate; Isis; Masculine energy; Potency; Ra; Spirituality; Strength; Sun.

✤ **FOLKLORE AND FACTS**
In some parts of the world, the Date palm has been grown for over 48,000 years. • The ancient Babylonians ate dried Dates like we now consume candy and other sweets. • In ancient Mesopotamia, Date wine and syrup were both considered to be sacred foods. • Dates presented upon Olive oil-soaked bread was given as offering to the ancient Babylonian deities Anu, Ea, Shamash, and Marduk. • It is believed by some that if a piece of the Date palm frond is carried as an amulet, it will increase fertility. • A Date palm frond placed near the door of the home will keep evil from all sources from entering into it. • Carry a Date pit to regain waning or lost virility. • Dates are referenced in the Bible more than fifty times. They are referenced in the Quran twenty times. • According to Arabian traditions, when Adam was forced to leave the Garden of Eden, he took with him three plants, one of them being the seeds to regrow the Date palm, which is the producer of the foremost of all fruits. • The *Phoenix dactylifera* Date palm has separately sexed trees, with the females being the fruit-bearers of the two. The male plants are only pollinators, which are assisted in accomplishing their task with the help of the wind, and on plantations where there are a limited number of males, with a bit of help utilizing human manual intervention atop tall ladders.

No. 377
Phytolacca americana ☠

Pokeweed

American Pokeweed | Coakum | Cocan | Crowberry | Dragonberries | Garget | Inkberry | Ombú | *Phytolacca decandra* | *Phytolacca vulgaris* | Pigeon Berry | Pocan | Poke | Poke Root | Poke Sallet | Pokeberry | Pokeberry Root | Pokebush | Pokeroot | Polk Root | Polk Salad | Polk Salat | Polk Sallet | Scoke | Virginian Poke

✹ **SYMBOLIC MEANINGS**
Courageousness.

✺ **POSSIBLE POWERS**
Breaks a hex; Courage; Fire element; Hex breaking; Mars; Masculine energy.

✤ **FOLKLORE AND FACTS**
Pokeweed is highly poisonous unless you happen to be a bird. • Make a sachet of Pokeweed leaf to carry or wear for courage when it is most needed. • Make a sachet of Pokeweed leaf and dried berries to break an evil hex. Once you feel the curse has been lifted, destroy the sachet by digging a hole, tossing in the sachet, and burning it there, taking great care not to breathe in any of the smoke. Then cover the ashes over with dirt to bury it. Stomp the soil down hard with one foot then the other. Turn around and walk away from it.

P

No. 378

Pimenta dioica 🍴

Allspice

Caryophyllus pimenta | Clove Pepper | Eugenia micrantha | Eugenia pimenta | Evanesca crassifolia | Jamaica Pepper | Jamaican Pepper | Kurundu | Myrtle Pepper | Myrtus aromatica | Myrtus dioica | Myrtus pimenta | Myrtus piperita | Newspice | Pepper | Pimenta | Pimenta aromatica | Pimenta communis | Pimenta officinalis | Pimenta pimenta | Pimenta vulgaris | Pimentus aromatica | Pimentus geminata | Pimentus vera

☀ SYMBOLIC MEANINGS

Compassion; Languishing; Love; Luck.

🌀 POSSIBLE POWERS

Accidents; Aggression; Anger; Carnal desire; Conflict; Finding treasure; Fire element; Healing; Looking for hidden treasure; Love; Luck; Lust; Machinery; Mars; Masculine energy; Money; Rock music; Strength; Struggle; Treasure hunting; War.

⚄ FOLKLORE AND FACTS

The unripe dried fruit of *Pimenta dioica* is Allspice.
• Allspice is often added to herbal mixtures to attract money or luck. • The name of Allspice started being used around 1621 because the berry tastes like a combination of Clove, Cinnamon, and Nutmeg, considered to be all the important spices of those days. • Allspice is often added to herbal mixtures to attract money or luck. • Birds are responsible for spreading the Allspice trees into the wild. • Christopher Columbus encountered *Pimenta dioica* trees on his second New World voyage, back in the days when it grew wild and could only be found in Jamaica. • When searching for treasure, wear an amulet of Allspice to assist in the hunt.
• As a culinary herb, Allspice is used in both sweet and savory dishes. • Allspice essential oil is often added to a light carrier oil to give it an exotic warm fragrance when used for massage.

No. 379

Pimpinella anisum 🐾🍴

Anise

Aniseed | Anisum odoratum | Anisum officinale | Anisum officinarum | Anisum vulgare | Anix | Anneys | Apium anisum | Carum anisum | Pimpinele anisa | Pimpinella | Ptychotis vargasiana | Selinum anisum | Seseligilliesii | Sison anisum | Sweet Cumin | Tragium anisum | Yanisin

☀ SYMBOLIC MEANINGS

Restoration of youth; Spiritual restoration of youthful exuberance and confidence.

🌀 POSSIBLE POWERS

Air element; Aphrodisiac; Attracts love; Business; Business transactions; Calls on good spirits; Caution; Cleverness; Communication; Creativity; Expansion; Faith; Honor; Illumination; Initiation; Intelligence; Jupiter; Leadership; Learning; Masculine energy; Memory; Politics; Power; Protection; Prudence; Psychic ability; Public acclaim; Purification; Repels evil; Responsibility; Royalty; Science; Self-preservation; Sleep; Sound judgment; Success; Thievery; Wards off the evil eye; Wealth; Wisdom.

⚄ FOLKLORE AND FACTS

Tuck a pouch or sachet filled with Anise seeds under a pillow to help prevent unpleasant dreams. • Fresh Anise leaves will push away evil and are often used around a magic circle to force evil spirits away from the magic practitioner within the circle. • Hang a sprig of fresh or dried Anise or a sachet of Anise seeds over the bed to restore lost youth. • Anise is often used to fend off the evil eye.
• Anise as a culinary herb has transformed many recipes for plain biscotti or tea biscuits into delectable Anise-flavored baked treats.

No. 380

Piper betle ⚱

Betel Leaf

Artanthe hexagyna | Betel | Betel Leaf Vine | Betela mastica | Binglang | Chavica auriculata | Chavica betle | Chavica blumei | Chavica canaliculata | Chavica chuvya | Chavica densa | Chavica siriboa | Cubeba melamiri | Cubeba siriboa | Macropiper potamogetonifolium | Piper anisodorum | Piper bathicarpum | Piper betel | Piper bidentatum | Piper blancoi | Piper blumei | Piper canaliculatum | Piper carnistilum | Piper densum | Piper fenixii | Piper macgregorii | Piper malamiri | Piper malamiris | Piper malarayatense | Piper marianum | Piper philippinense | Piper pinguispicum | Piper potamogetonifolium | Piper puberulinodum | Piper rubroglandulosum | Piper saururus | Piper silletianum | Piper siriboa | Piperi betlum

☀ SYMBOLIC MEANINGS
Love; Loyalty; Strong bond.

⚙ POSSIBLE POWERS
Banishing negativity; Dependability; Fertility; Healing; Intensify; Love; Magnify; Uplift the spirit.

☘ FOLKLORE AND FACTS
The religious, festive, social and personal use of the heart-shaped Betel Leaf is to wrap it around a Betel Nut, then chew them together as has been done for well over 4,000 years. • Two Betel Leaves topped with a Betel Nut, or a preparation of chopped Betel Nut with Tobacco wrapped in a leaf and topped with a coin, is a standard good gift of thanks. It is also for blessings paid to priests, elders, doctors, astrologers, and anyone else to whom respect and a token of such esteemed appreciation is justified. • The Betel Leaf's essential oil is useful for magical purposes. • The Betel Leaf is used to purify the water for nearly all Hindu rituals because, according to Hindi legend, when Sita Devi could not find anything but Betel Leaf to offer Lord Ram, she wove the leaves into a wreath as a token of her appreciation of and delight in him. That was considered to be purely spiritual love tangibly expressed. • The Betel Leaf plays a significant part in many of the religiously oriented legends of India. • Because the combination of chewing Betel Leaf with the Betel Nut is such a religiously connected practice, with deep symbolism connected to love and bonding, it is a custom in some parts of India for an engaged couple to partake of Betel Leaf and Betel Nut while discussing marital plans with the parents. It also celebrates marriage, fertility, and a long life of love together as a couple.

No. 381

Piper cubeba ⚱🍴

Cubeb

Cubeba cubeba | Cubeba officinalis | Cubeba segetum | Java Pepper | Tailed Pepper | Vidanga | Vilenga

☀ SYMBOLIC MEANINGS
Fidelity; Hex breaker; Love.

⚙ POSSIBLE POWERS
Aphrodisiac; Attracts love; Elemental fire; Exorcism; Fire element; Love; Lust; Mars; Masculine energy; Repels evil; Repulses demons; Sex; Wards off incubi.

☘ FOLKLORE AND FACTS
Make two red sachets with Cubeb berries then place under the mattress on both sides of the bed to encourage sexual love. • Cubeb is mentioned in *The Travels of Marco Polo*, with Java being a producer along with other precious spices. • Cubeb berry can be used when needing to add fire to a spell. • Cubeb is used to flavor liqueur, cigarettes, and food in Indonesia. • The people of both China and Europe considered Cubeb to be repulsive to demons. A Catholic priest in the seventeenth century mentions it as being an important element for use in an exorcism to ward off an incubus. • The Cubeb essential oil is used in aromatherapy for calming and uplifting without being overstimulating. • Cubeb is an ingredient used in traditional Chinese medicine.

No. 382

Piper nigrum ⚱🍴

Black Pepper

Marica | Muldera multinervis | Muldera wightiana | Pepe | Peper | Pepper | Peppercorn | Pfeffer | Piper aromaticum | Piper baccatum | Piper colonum | Piper denudatum | Piper glabrispica | Piper glyphicum | Piper laxum | Piper malabarense | Piper nigricans | Piper rotundum | Piper trioicum | Pipor | Pippali | Poivre | Rhyncholepis haeankeana

☀ SYMBOLIC MEANINGS
Fidelity, Hex breaker; Love.

⚙ POSSIBLE POWERS
Banishes the evil eye; Energy; Exorcism; Fire element; Mars; Masculine energy; Protection.

Pistacia vera 🜿

Pistachio

Lentiscus vera | Pista | Pistacchio | Pistacia | *Pistacia badghysi* | Pistacia macrophylla | Pistacia narbonnensis | Pistacia nemausensis | Pistacia nigricans | Pistacia officinarum | Pistacia reticulata | Pistacia trifolia | Pistacia variifolia | Pistáke | Pistákion | Terebinthus pistacia

☀ SYMBOLIC MEANINGS

Good fortune; Happiness; Health.

⊛ POSSIBLE POWERS

Air element; Breaking love spells; Masculine energy; Mercury.

☾ FOLKLORE AND FACTS

Dyeing Pistachio nut shells red was for the purpose of hiding blemishes on the shell. • To bring a zombie out of its trance and allow it to pass into death, give it Pistachio nuts that have been dyed red. • Around 700 BCE, Pistachio trees were supposedly included among the other plants showcased in ancient Babylon's Hanging Gardens. • The Pistachio was brought to Europe by the Romans in the first century CE. • Pistachio trees will grow for approximately ten years before producing a crop. Then they can live and produce fruit for several hundred years. • The shell of a Pistachio is so hard that to bite on it in an attempt to open it can hurt your teeth. • When high-quality Pistachio fruits ripen on the tree, the shell will change from green to a natural yellowish-red and will suddenly split partly open with an audible popping sound. • It takes around seven years for a Pistachio to start producing a good yield of fruit. Once it is established, it will produce for a hundred years or more. • One year the Pistachio tree will produce a bountiful crop, and the following year it won't produce as much. Then the year after that it will be bountiful again. On and on it grows and goes. • Pistachio fruits grow in clusters just like Grapes do. • The ripened fruit surrounding the Pistachio nut needs to be removed and the shells dried within twenty-four hours of their harvest to prevent them from becoming moldy. • There is a myth that the Queen of Sheba forbade peasants from eating a Pistachio because she claimed they were for royalty only.

☾ FOLKLORE AND FACTS

Carry or wear a sachet filled with easy-to-obtain Black Pepper to banish the evil eye. • Black Pepper was prized for trade and highly valued to the extreme that it was once considered a valid form of currency. • Burn a pinch of Black Pepper to clear away negative energy. • Carry or wear a sachet with a bit of Black Pepper within it to protect yourself from having persistent envious thoughts. • Combine equal amounts of Black Pepper along with natural sea salt, then scatter the blend around the perimeter of the entire property to rid it of evil and to help protect it from returning. • In the Middle Ages, Black Pepper was very expensive and usually found only in the homes of royals and aristocrats. • One-fifth of the world's spice trade is concentrated on Black Pepper. • For a purpose unknown, Black Peppercorns were found stuffed into the mummified nose of Ramesses II. • Black Pepper essential oil is very useful in aromatherapy for reducing stress and anxiety to help restore balance to emotions and lifting a dark and heavy mood.

Pistacia lentiscus 🜿

Mastic

Gum Mastic | Lentiscus massiliensis | Lentiscus vulgaris | Mastic Tree | Masticke | Pistachia Galls | *Pistacia brevifolia* | *Pistacia gummifera* | Pistacia multiflora | Pistacia subfalcata | Terebinthus lentiscus

☀ SYMBOLIC MEANINGS

Chew; Gnashing of teeth.

⊛ POSSIBLE POWERS

Abundance; Advancement; Air element; Conscious will; Energy; Friendship; Growth; Healing; Joy; Leadership; Life; Light; Lust; Masculine energy; Natural or psychic power; Success; Sun.

☾ FOLKLORE AND FACTS

Mastic is obtained from the resin of the *Pistacia lentiscus* tree. • Mastic is a vital ingredient in myron, the sacred holy oil used in some orthodox religions' sacred church rituals.

No. 385
Pisum sativum ❦

Garden Pea
English Pea | Green Pea | *Lathyrus oleraceus* | Pissa |
Pisum arvense | *Pisum biflorum* | *Pisum elatius* |
Pisum humile | *Pisum vulgare*

☀ SYMBOLIC MEANINGS
Appointed meeting; Respect.

🌀 POSSIBLE POWERS
Abundance; Beauty; Earth element;
Feminine energy; Friendship; Health; Love; Money; Peace;
Prosperity; Protection; Venus; Water element; Wealth.

☙ FOLKLORE AND FACTS
Bring fortune and profit to a business by shelling Garden
Peas. • One interesting love divination is for an unmarried
woman to find a Garden Pea pod with exactly nine seeds
within it. When this is done, if she hangs the pod over a door,
the first single man who walks beneath it will be her future
husband.

No. 386
Plantago major ❦

White Man's Foot
Broadleaf Plantain | Broad-leaved Plantain | Greater Plantago | Greater Plantain | Llantén |
Plantago adriatica | *Plantago altissima* | *Plantago angustata* | *Plantago borysthenica* |
Plantago bracteata | *Plantago compresscapa* | *Plantago crenata* | *Plantago dentata* |
Plantago dilatata | *Plantago dostalii* | *Plantago dregeana* | *Plantago exaltata* | *Plantago*
fonticola | *Plantago gigas* | *Plantago gouanii* | *Plantago gracilis* | *Plantago humifusa* | *Plantago*
japonica | *Plantago laciniosa* | *Plantago latifolia* | *Plantago limosa* | *Plantago littoralis* |
Plantago longiscapa | *Plantago loureiroi* | *Plantago macronipponica* | *Plantago maxima* |
Plantago minima | *Plantago minor* | *Plantago namikawae* | *Plantago nana* | *Plantago*
officinarum | *Plantago pauciflora* | *Plantago polystachia* | *Plantago polystachya* | *Plantago*
quinquenervis | *Plantago rocae* | *Plantago rosea* | *Plantago sawadae* | *Plantago scopulorum* |
Plantago sinuata | *Plantago sorokini* | *Plantago stylosa* | *Plantago subsinuata* | *Plantago*
tabernaemontani | *Plantago togashii* | *Plantago villifera* | *Plantago vulgaris* | Plantain | Plantén |
Rat's Tail | Waybread | Wegbrade

☀ SYMBOLIC MEANINGS
Never despair.

🌀 POSSIBLE POWERS
Blessings; Earth element; Feminine energy; Heals headache;
Lifts weariness; Protection from an evil spirit, snakes, or
snakebites; Venus.

☙ FOLKLORE AND FACTS
After North America was first
colonized, the Native Americans began
referring to *Plantago major* as white
man's footprint and Englishman's foot
because, to them, it seemed as if the
plant would grow wherever white
men went. This phenomenon occurred
because colonists would bring cereal
crop seeds with them to the New
World, and *Plantago major* seeds were
commonly mixed into the seed bags.
Where settlers would plant cereal crops, which would be
near where they lived, White Man's Foot would grow and
ultimately naturalize. • Hang a pouch with some White
Man's Foot in the car to keep evil from entering into it.
• White Man's Foot, that was then known as Weybrode, is
in the Nine Sacred Herbs healing charm that was originally
written in the dialect used in Wessex, England, around the
time of the tenth century. • Prior to the steady emigration
from England, White Man's Foot was virtually unknown
in North America, until it was introduced into the newly
planted English vegetable gardens in the New World.

No. 387
Plumbago zeylanica ☠❦

Ceylon Leadwort
Bella Emilia | Cape Leadwort | Chitrak | Doctor Bush | Elanitul | *Findlaya alba* | *Molubda*
scandens | Pegosa | *Plumbagidium scandens* | *Plumbago americana* | *Plumbago flaccida* |
Plumbago floridana | *Plumbago juncea* | *Plumbago lactea* | *Plumbago littoralis* | *Plumbago*
maximowiczii | *Plumbago mexicana* | *Plumbago occidentalis* | *Plumbago sarmentosa* |
Plumbago scandens | *Plumbago toxicaria* | *Plumbago viscosa* | *Thela alba* | White Plumbago |
Wild Leadwort | Wild Plumbago

☀ SYMBOLIC MEANINGS
Heavy as lead; Spiritual desire.

🌀 POSSIBLE POWERS
Heavy weight; Immovability; Stubbornness.

☙ FOLKLORE AND FACTS
Ceylon Leadwort's name of leadwort may have been inspired
by the lead-colored stain the sap can create. • Ceylon
Leadwort has been used in folk and Ayurvedic medicine for
thousands of years.

No. 388
Pogostemon cablin ☠⚰

Patchouli

Ellai | Kablin | *Mentha auricularia* | *Mentha cablin* | Patchai | Patchouly | *Pogostemon battakianus* | *Pogostemon comosus* | *Pogostemon hortensis* | *Pogostemon javanicus* | *Pogostemon mollis* | *Pogostemon nepetoides* | *Pogostemon patchouli* | *Pogostemon suavis* | *Pogostemon tomentosus* | Pucha-Pot | Xukloti

☀ SYMBOLIC MEANINGS
Scent.

✸ POSSIBLE POWERS
Abundance; Accidents; Advancement; Aggression; Anger; Binding; Breaks a hex; Building; Carnal desire; Conflict; Conscious will; Death; Earth element; Energy; Feminine energy; Fertility; Friendship; Growth; Healing; History; Joy; Knowledge; Leadership; Life; Light; Limitations; Lust; Machinery; Money; Natural power; Obstacles; Rock music; Saturn; Strength; Struggle; Success; Time; War.

✿ FOLKLORE AND FACTS
A touch of Patchouli oil on money, handbags, and wallets is believed to increase prosperity. • Patchouli essential oil can be used as aromatherapy to help ease nervous tension and worry.

No. 389
Polygala senega ☠⚰

Seneca Snake Root

Milkwort | Mountain Flax | *Polygala albida* | *Polygala rosea* | *Polygala seneka* | Rattlesnake Root | *Senega officinalis* | Senega Snake Root | Seneka | Seneka | Snakeroot | Snakeroot

☀ SYMBOLIC MEANINGS
Hermitage.

✸ POSSIBLE POWERS
Money; Protection.

✿ FOLKLORE AND FACTS
Seneca Snake Root originally received its name from the Seneca Native American tribe when the plant was used as a treatment for snakebite. • Put some of the powdered root in each shoe when venturing into a place where you are worried about walking into trouble. The Seneca Snake

Root will offer protection against evil, tricks, and messes you did not make and are no part of, but that could implicate you anyway. • Make a sachet with a bit of Seneca Snake Root inside of it, then put it inside a wallet, pocket, purse, or household bank to draw money to it.

No. 390
Polygonatum multiflorum ☠⚰

Solomon's Seal

Common Solomon's Seal | *Convallaria ambigua* | *Convallaria govaniana* | *Convallaria multiflora* | David's Harp | Dropberry | King Solomon's Seal | Ladder to Heaven | Lady's Seal | *Polygonatum bracteatum* | *Polygonatum intermedium* | St. Mary's Seal | Sealroot | Sealwort

☀ SYMBOLIC MEANINGS
Be my support.

✸ POSSIBLE POWERS
Air element; Aphrodisiac; Attracts love; Binding magical works; Binding sacred oaths and promises forever; Breaking bad habits; Consecration; Earth element; Exorcism; Feminine energy; Fire element; Gracefully transitioning through changes beyond control; Love; Making difficult decisions; Protection; Saturn; Seeking change; Summoning Air element sylphs; Summoning Earth element gnomes; Summoning Fire element salamanders; Summoning helpful spirits; Summoning Water element nymphs and undines; Water element.

✿ FOLKLORE AND FACTS
There is a legend that Solomon's Seal received its name after King Solomon, who it was said was given extreme wisdom by God, along with a mystical magical seal that gave Solomon the power to command demons without causing harm to himself. Accordingly, legend also tells that King Solomon placed that seal upon a plant to convert it into one that heals and is also magical. • There is a legend that the scars on the roots of Solomon's Seal were placed there by King Solomon to testify to its powerful virtues. • The age of the Solomon's Seal plant can be determined by the number of scars along the root, as each year produces a new stem that dies at the end of each summer to leave a new scar. • One can tell true Solomon's Seal, *Polygonatum multiflorum*, from false Solomon's Seal, *Maianthemum racemosum*, by the fact that *Polygonatum multiflorum* has bell-shaped flowers dangling down along the stem. *Maianthemum racemosum* has flowering plumes at the end of the plant's stems. • Place a

Solomon's Seal root sachet in each of the four corners of your home to protect it. • A Solomon's Seal root can be carried as an amulet to push away malicious spirits. • Solomon's Seal is an appropriate herb for use in autumn equinox rituals. • Solomon's Seal is an herb that can seal a commitment, promise, or sacred oath. It can also seal a spell. In that respect, use it judiciously. • Make an infusion of Solomon's Seal mixed with rainwater, natural spring water, or distilled water to sprinkle or spray around the outside of the home to fend off malicious spirits and negative energies. • A Solomon's Seal root can be carried as an amulet to provide wisdom when wisdom is most important to exercise in difficult decision-making. • Solomon's Seal is an extremely powerful magical herb, having the advantage of all four of the magical elements.

No. 391

Portulaca grandiflora 🕱☙

Portulaca

Aizoon | Garden Jewels | Garden Purslane | Golden Purslane | Hoa Muoi Gio | Moss Rose | Moss-rose Purslane | Portulaca | *Portulaca hilaireana* | *Portulaca immersostellulata* | *Portulaca megalantha* | *Portulaca mendocinensis* | *Portulaca multistaminata* | *Portulaca rupicola* | *Portulaca splendens* | Purslane | Rose Moss | Sun Jewels | Sun Rose | Sunny Jewels | Ten o'Clock Flower | Time Flower | Time Full

✹ SYMBOLIC MEANINGS
Superior merit; Voluptuous love; Voluptuousness.

❧ COMPONENT MEANING
Bud: Confessions of love.

⊛ POSSIBLE POWERS
Aphrodisiac; Attracts love; Feminine energy; Happiness; Love; Luck; Moon; Protection; Sleep; Water element.

☾ FOLKLORE AND FACTS
Prepare a sachet with Portulaca within it and give it to a soldier to carry into a battle for magical protection. • Grow Portulaca to protect the home and bring happiness to it.

No. 392

Potentilla erecta ☙

Tormentil

Biscuits | Common Tormentil | Earthbank | Ewe Daisy | Five Fingers | Flesh and Blood | *Fragaria tormentilla* | *Potentilla dacica* | *Potentilla divergens* | *Potentilla favratii* | *Potentilla laeta* | *Potentilla monacensis* | *Potentilla officinalis* | *Potentilla sciaphila* | *Potentilla strictissima* | *Potentilla sylvestris* | *Potentilla tetrapetala* | *Potentilla tormentilla* | Septfoil | Shepherd's Knot | Thormantle | Tormenti | *Tormentilla adstringens* | *Tormentilla alpina* | *Tormentilla dissecta* | *Tormentilla divergens* | *Tormentilla erecta* | *Tormentilla ericetorum* | *Tormentilla montana* | *Tormentilla nodosa* | *Tormentilla officinalis* | *Tormentilla officinarum* | *Tormentilla orophila* | *Tormentilla parviflora* | *Tormentilla sessilifolia* | *Tormentilla tuberosa*

✹ SYMBOLIC MEANINGS
Power.

⊛ POSSIBLE POWERS
Fire element; Love; Masculine energy; Protection; Sun; Thor.

☾ FOLKLORE AND FACTS
To drive away evil, hang Tormentil somewhere near the center of the home. • To attract love, carry a sprig of Tormentil. • Tormentil can be used to make a red dye. • To prevent evil from entering into the house, hang a Tormentil amulet on the front door.

P

Primula veris ☠☕

Cowslip

Common Cowslip | Cowslip Primrose | English
Cowslip | Key Flower | *Primula brandisii* | *Primula
cordifolia* | *Primula coronaria* | *Primula discolor* |
Primula inflata | *Primula lasiopetala* | *Primula
officinalis* | *Primula pannonica* | *Primula pistillaris* |
Primula praticola | *Primula pyrenaica* | *Primula
velenovskyi* | St. Peter's Herb

✳ SYMBOLIC MEANINGS
Adventure; Birth; Contentment; Death; Doom; Eternal love;
Frivolity; Happiness; Mischief; Modest worth; Pleasure;
Satisfaction; Thoughtlessness; Wantonness.

✾ POSSIBLE POWERS
Feminine energy; Finding treasure; Healing; Love;
Protection; Venus; Water element.

✿ FOLKLORE AND FACTS
Carry a Cowslip flower to attract love. • The Cowslip is
the nightingale's favorite flower. • Carry a Cowslip flower
to cure madness. • Carry or wear a Cowslip flower for good
luck. • Touch a rock with a nosegay of Cowslip flowers with
the intention of splitting it open to find hidden fairy gold.
If you touch it the wrong number of times, it could initiate
doom, although if done correctly it could open the door to
Fairyland, fairy gifts, and fairy gold. • There is a legend that
the Cowslip first grew because St. Peter dropped his keys
from where he was standing guard at Heaven's gate when
he angrily responded to the news that some people were
sneaking into Heaven at a back entrance. The Cowslip is
what grew when St. Peter's keys fell to land on the Earth. The
legend continues that those who can find the flowers might
find the keys that open Heaven's gates. • When fairies are
frightened, they will hide in a Cowslip. • In parts of Southern
England near Somerset, where this children's tradition
began, when Cowslips were in bloom on the seventh Sunday
following Easter, which is Whitsunday, the children would
tie the flower heads together with the stems pointing toward
the middles to make them ball-like. Calling them "tisty-
tosties," the children would tie them on a thin twig and use
them to divine whom they would marry by tossing about the
Cowslip balls and calling out the name of every boy and girl
they would happen to know as a chant to, "Tisty-tosty, tell
me true, who shall I be married to?" When the ball fell, that
was whom they would supposedly marry. A similar Cowslip
flower ball divination by children was also done to determine
how many years of life one would live by counting out the
years.

Primula vulgaris ☠☕

Primrose

Artetyke | Arthritica | Buckles | Common Primrose | Crewel | Cuslyppe | Cuy | Cuy Lippe |
Drelip | Fairy Cup | Frauenschlussel | Himmelschusslechen | Key Flower | Key of Heaven |
Keyflower | Lady's Key | Lippe | Our Lady's Keys | Paigle | Palsywort | Paralysio | Peggle |
Petty Mulleins | Plumrocks | *Primula acaulis* | *Primula atropurpurea* | *Primula bicolor* | *Primula
breviscapa* | *Primula calycantha* | *Primula grandiflora* | *Primula hybrida* | *Primula inodora* |
Primula minima | *Primula odorata* | *Primula pseudoacaulis* | *Primula sylvestris* | *Primula
uniflora* | *Primula variabilis* | *Primula vernalis*

✳ SYMBOLIC MEANINGS
Birth; Consummation; Death;
Most excellent; Wantonness;
Women.

✾ POSSIBLE POWERS
Earth element; Emotional
rebirth; Feminine energy;
Find treasure; Healing;
Love spells; Transformation;
Venus; Youth.

✿ FOLKLORE AND FACTS
The Primrose is considered to be extremely sacred and
connected to emotional rebirth. • Fairies love and protect
the Primrose. • Primrose flowers are considered fairy flowers
in Ireland and Wales. • It is thought that touching a fairy
rock with a Primrose nosegay will open an invisible door
into Fairyland. However, if there are not the proper number
of flowers in the nosegay, there will be certain doom. The
problem is that no one knows for sure what the required
proper number of flowers actually is. • It is also believed
that Primrose helps children find hidden treasures, most
particularly fairy gold. • In Germany, the Primrose is known
as *Himmelschusslechen*, which means the little keys to
Heaven. • If you do not want visitors, put a sprig of Primrose
on the front porch. • Wear or carry Primrose to preserve or
restore your youth. • The phrase "to walk along the Primrose
path" means a life that is pleasurable and self-indulgent.
• Since the Primrose is among the early spring-blooming
flowers, it was given the botanical prefix *prima-*, which
means "first." • When it rains, fairies hurry to be under the
protection of Primrose leaves.

P

No. 395
Prostanthera melissifolia ☙

Balm Mint Bush

Green Mint | *Prostanthera melissifolia var. melissifolia* |
Prostanthera melissifolia var. parviflora

✳ SYMBOLIC MEANINGS
Exciting.

❀ POSSIBLE POWERS
Aphrodisiac; Attract love; Excitement; Good luck; Health;
Insect repellent; Overcome evil or fear of death; Pledge of
love; Purification; Recover from hydrophobia; Scatter snakes.

☙ FOLKLORE AND FACTS
Burn Balm Mint Bush leaves to help promote healing. • To
help promote the healing of a debilitating sickness, make
then carry or wear a Balm Mint Bush sachet that includes a
small amount each of leaf, stem and root • Balm Mint Bush
produces an essential oil that can be used in house cleaning
products. • The Balm Mint Bush essential oil is useful for
purifying the fragrance of the air, as well as warding off pesky
flying insects. It can also brighten the mood to make one ready
for the complications and challenges of the upcoming day.

No. 396
Prunella vulgaris ☠☙

All-Heal

Carpenter-weed | Heal-All | Heart-of-the-Earth | Self-Heal | Sicklewort | Woundwort |
Xia Ku Cao

✳ SYMBOLIC MEANINGS
Hope; Immortality; Strength.

❀ POSSIBLE POWERS
Healing; Hope; Observation; Protection; Protection from the
Devil; Repels the Devil.

☙ FOLKLORE AND FACTS
People once openly declared that God Himself sent the
people of Earth All-Heal to cure them of anything and
everything that ailed them. • All-Heal is still considered by
many people to be a sacred holy herb. • Wearing or carrying
All-Heal will hopefully bring beauty, love, money, sexuality,
and health. • It was believed that All-Heal can drive away
the actual Devil. • At one time, witches made a point of
planting All-Heal hidden in their gardens in a concerted
effort to fend off the Devil. • There was a time when the
Native American Ojibwa tribes' hunters used All-Heal root
with the intent of sharpening their skills of observation
before they went off to hunt.

No. 397
Pteridium aquilinum ☠☙

Bracken Fern

Allosorus acutifolius | *Allosorus aquilinus* | *Allosorus capensis* | *Allosorus tauricus* | *Allosorus
villosus* | *Asplenium aquillinum* | *Bracken* | *Cincinalis aquilina* | *Cincinalis gleditschii* | *Cincinalis
lanuginosa* | Common Bracken | *Eupteris aquilina* | Fern | Fern of God | Fernbrake | *Filix
aquilina* | *Filix-foemina aquilina* | *Filix-foemina vulgaris* | Huckleberry's Blanket | *Onychium
capense* | *Ornithopteris aquilina* | *Paesia aquilina* | *Polypodium austriacum* | *Pteridium
cehegninense* | *Pteridium heredia* | *Pteridium tauricum* | *Pteris aquilina* | *Pteris auriculata* |
Pteris borealis | *Pteris brevipes* | *Pteris firma* | *Pteris foemina* | *Pteris gardneri* | *Pteris heredia* |
Pteris nudicaulis | *Pteris recurvata*

✳ SYMBOLIC MEANINGS
Confidence; Confusion;
Protection; Rain; Wealth.

❀ POSSIBLE POWERS
Air element; Colorize;
Fertility; Healing; Health;
Invisibility; Luck; Magical
powers or qualities;
Masculine energy; Mercury;
Prophetic dreams; Protection; Rain
magic; Riches; Stress relief.

☙ FOLKLORE AND FACTS
It was once believed that after stepping upon Bracken Fern,
a traveler would become disoriented to the point of losing
direction. • Place a frond of Bracken Fern under the pillow
to dream of the solution to a perplexing problem. • Placing a
frond of Bracken Fern under the pillow may help release and
eliminate negativity. • Add Bracken Fern fronds to flower
arrangements to increase protection to the room in which it
was placed. • In England it was once believed that hanging
dried Bracken Fern in the house would protect everyone
who dwelled there from thunder and lightning. • In England
it was also once believed that cutting or burning Bracken
would bring on rain. • It was believed that Bracken seed
would provide magic powers, such as invisibility, but only
if it is carried around in a pocket. • A vegetable dye using
Bracken will produce colors ranging from green to brown.
• The Bracken Fern is believed to hold the monogram of
Jesus Christ within its stem. • Bracken Fern magic power
is strong enough to prevent witchcraft because it is potent
enough for a witch to fear its presence nearby. • To discover
who one's true love may be, slice open the stem of a Bracken
Fern, then try to discern what letter or letters can be seen
within it. • A divination that was once used to prove the
existence of God was to slice a Bracken Fern into three
sections and look to see if one section each might actually
reveal the letters G, O, and D.

No. 398

Pulmonaria officinalis ☠⚱

Lungwort

Bethlehem Sage | Jerusalem Cowslip | Joseph and Mary | Lungenkraut | Medunitza | Miodunka | Pulmonaria alpina | Pulmonaria cordatofolia | Pulmonaria gallorum | Pulmonaria maculata | Pulmonaria mollis | Pulmonaria pauciflora | Pulmonaria tridentina | Pulmonaria vulgaris | Soldiers and Sailors | Spotted Dog

✸ SYMBOLIC MEANINGS
You are my life.

❁ POSSIBLE POWERS
Protection when traveling by air.

❦ FOLKLORE AND FACTS
Lungwort leaves are sometimes used to represent diseased lungs during healing magic. • Lungwort seems to be one of the rare few plants able to resist the toxic effects of the Black Walnut tree, which will chemically render the ground under and around it inhospitable to other plants. • Make a Lungwort sachet to carry or wear for protection when journeying by air.

No. 399

Pulsatilla vulgaris ☠⚱

Pasqueflower

Anemone acutipetala | Anemone bogenhardiana | Anemone collina | Anemone intermedia | Anemone pratensis | Anemone pulsatilla | Anemone sylvestris | Anemone tenuifolia | Backsippa | Common Pasque Flower | Easter Flower | European Pasqueflower | Lännekylänkukka | Meadow Anemone | Opret Kobjælde | Pasque Flower | Passe Flower | Prairie Crocus | Pulsatilla amoena | Pulsatilla aperta | Pulsatilla bogenhardiana | Pulsatilla intermedia | Pulsatilla media | Pulsatilla oenipontana | Pulsatilla propera | Pulsatilla recta | Pulsatilla transsilvanica | Purple Cowbell | Shamefaced Maiden | Stor Kubjelle | Thunderbolt | Windflower

✸ SYMBOLIC MEANINGS
Every gardener's pride; Fading youth; I have no claims; Immortal love; Staunch love; Undying love; Unfading love; You have no claims.

❁ POSSIBLE POWERS
Adonis; Anemos; Decision-making; Easter; Feminine energy; the Four Winds; Healing; Health; Mercury; Protection; Protection against negative magic or sickness; Spring equinox; Venus; Water element.

❦ FOLKLORE AND FACTS
In England's Cotswolds region, there is a public protected area that is abundant with Pasqueflower plants that is known as the Gloucestershire Wildlife Trust's Pasqueflower Reserve. • The Pasqueflower is the state flower of South Dakota. • Make a sachet of dried Pasqueflower petals to carry or wear when feeling indecisive and needing to make a firm decision.

No. 400

Punica granatum 🐾🍴

Pomegranate

Anaar | Anar | Apple of Granada | Carthage Apple | Daalim | Garnet Apple | Granada | Granado |
Granatapfel | *Granatum punicum* | Grenadier | Johm | Malicorio | Malum Granatum | Malum
Punicum | Melagrana | Melograno | Nhm | Pomme-grenade | Pound Garnet | *Punica florida* |
Punica grandiflora | *Punica nana* | *Punica spinosa* | *Rhoea punica*

☀ SYMBOLIC MEANINGS
Abundance; Ambition; Compassion; Conceit; Conceited;
Elegance; Fertility; Foolishness; Foppery; Fruitfulness;
Fullness; Good luck; Good things; Housewarming gift;
Kabbalah; Marriage; Mysteriousness; Mystical experience;
Offspring; Paradise; Prosperity; Resurrection; Righteousness;
Suffering; Suffering and resurrection; Summer; Sweetness of
the heavenly kingdom.

⚜ POSSIBLE POWERS
Abundance; Aphrodisiac; Attracts love; Binding; Ceres;
Creative power; Divination; Elegance; Fertility; Fire element;
Immortality; Incarceration; Intellectual ability; Love; Luck;
Masculine energy; Mature elegance; Passion; Persephone;
Sensuous love; Unreciprocated love magic; Venus; Wealth;
Wishing.

✺ FOLKLORE AND FACTS
Make a sachet filled with bits of Pomegranate husk to
carry or wear to increase fertility. • Use a forked branch of
Pomegranate as a divining rod to search for and find hidden
wealth. • Pomegranates symbolize the Kabbalah as being
the mystical entryway into the Garden of Pomegranates.
• It is traditional to eat Pomegranate seeds on Rosh
Hashanah because the many seeds represent fruitfulness.
• A fun divination for a girl to try to find how many children
she might have is to throw a Pomegranate fruit onto the
ground hard enough to break
it open. However many
seeds fall out of the
fruit are the number
of children she will
someday have.
• In Greece, it is
customary to give
a Pomegranate as
a housewarming gift,
which is placed on or
under the home's
altar as a blessing of
abundance, good
luck, and fertility.
• In the Book of

Exodus, the robe worn by the Hebrew high priest had
decorative Pomegranates embroidered all around the bottom
near the hem. • According to Jewish law, the Pomegranate is
one of the Seven Species that require a blessing before being
eaten. • Hang a Pomegranate tree branch over a doorway
to fend off evil. • Pomegranates have been cultivated in the
Mediterranean region for thousands of years. • As a spice,
ground dried Pomegranate seeds are known as anar dana.

No. 401

Pyrus communis ☠🐦

Pear

Crataegus excelsa | European Pear | *Malus communis* | *Pyrenia pyrus* | *Pyrus achras* | *Pyrus
ambrosiaca* | *Pyrus amphigenea* | *Pyrus balansae* | *Pyrus dasyphylla* | *Pyrus domestica* | *Pyrus
pyraster* | *Pyrus rossica* | *Pyrus salviati* | *Sorbus pyrus* | Wild Pear

☀ SYMBOLIC MEANINGS
Affection; Health; Hope.

⚜ POSSIBLE POWERS
Colorize; Comfort; Feminine energy; Long life; Love; Lust;
Venus; Water element.

✺ FOLKLORE AND FACTS
Pear wood is desirable for constructing a magic wand. • Pear
wood is one of the woods favored for use in the construction
of higher-quality woodwind instruments. • Dye using Pear
leaves and twigs can produce an attractive, yellowish-tan
color. • As is the same with Apple seeds, Pear seeds are
toxic. • There is archeological evidence in several European
Neolithic and Bronze Age sites that Pears were gathered in
the wild. • Make, then carry or wear a sachet of Pear blossom
and leaf to encourage a long, loving, comfortable life.

No. 402

Quassia amara ☠☢

Quassia

Amargo | Bitter Ash | Bitter Bark | Bitter Quassia | Bitterholz | Bitter-Wood | Bois Amer | Bois de Quassia | Crucete | Cuassia | Fliegenholz | Guabo | Hombre Grande | Jamaica Bark | Jamaica Quassia | Kashshing | Marauba | Marupa | Palo Muneco | Pau Amarelo | *Quassia amara* var. *paniculata* | Quassia Bark | Quassia de Cayenne | Quassia Wood | Quassiaholz | Quassiawood | Quassie | Quina | Ruda | Simaba | Simaruba | Simarubabaum | Suriname Wood

☀ SYMBOLIC MEANINGS
Bitter; Bitterness.

✹ POSSIBLE POWERS
Healing; Health.

☾ FOLKLORE AND FACTS
The bitterness extracted from Quassia bark is used in the making of Angostura Bitters. • In beer making, it is possible to substitute Quassia bark extract for Hops.

No. 403

Quercus alba ☠☢

White Oak

Celestial Tree | Duir | Pren-Awr | *Quercus candida* | *Quercus nigrescens* | *Quercus ramosa* | *Quercus repanda* | *Quercus retusa*

☀ SYMBOLIC MEANINGS
Endurance; Hospitality; Liberty; Noble presence; Personal finances; Regal power; Wealth.

⚘ COMPONENT MEANINGS
Acorn: Fruition of long, hard labor; Good luck; Immortality; Life; Patience.
Leaves: Bravery; Strength; Welcome.
Sprig: Hospitality.

✹ POSSIBLE POWERS
Abundance; Advancement; Air element; Aphrodisiac; Attracts love; Autumn; Business; Conscious will; Earth element; Energy; Expansion; Female energy; Fertility; Fire element; Friendship; the Four Winds; Growth; Healing; Health; Honor; Insight; Joy; Leadership; Life; Light; Love; Luck; Masculine energy; Money; Natural power; Politics; Potency; Power; Protection; Public acclaim; Responsibility; Royalty; Spring; Success; Summer; Water element; Wealth; Winter.

☾ FOLKLORE AND FACTS
Although there were other oak trees, the Druids would perform rituals only under a White Oak tree, most particularly if there was Mistletoe growing on its branches. • The White Oak tree has been revered, even worshipped, since prehistoric times. • The White Oak has been known to live for hundreds of years. Although many have been cut for lumber, as it is a very hard wood suitable for furniture, one specimen has been dated to be 600 years old. • Although it is called White Oak, bark lighter than the usual light gray is a rare find. Even so, the finished wood is very light.

• A very powerful protector against evil is a cross whittled from White Oak wood made from equal lengths that are tied together in the center with red thread and hung in the house. The resulting cross predates Christianity and is known as the equal-armed cross, the balanced cross, the Greek cross, and the peaceful cross. The symbol of that cross represents the Earth, male and female, the Four Winds, the four seasons, and the four elements. Sometimes it is found in a circle; when it is, the cross represents the Earth, such as would be found on an astrological natal birth chart. • Carry a small piece of White Oak wood as protection from harm and as a good luck charm. • If you happen to catch a falling autumn White Oak leaf, it is believed that you will not have a cold for all of winter. • Wear a White Oak acorn amulet for protection against aches, pains, and illnesses. • Wear a White Oak acorn as an amulet to promote youthfulness. • Wear a White Oak acorn as an amulet to encourage longevity and even immortality. • Wear a White Oak acorn as an amulet to increase fertility. • Wear a White Oak acorn as an amulet to improve sexual powers. • A White Oak tree is able to grow up to one hundred feet tall with a massive canopy of branches that spread widely. White Oak trees growing in a forest will be much taller and wider than those growing in open areas. • The Mingo White Oak was measured to be 145 feet tall. It was cut down in 1945. • White Oaks that grow in extremely high altitudes will not grow to be much taller than a little shrub. • A magic wand that has been lovingly fashioned by its intended user from a length of White Oak wood, then properly charged before putting it into service, will provide powerful magic that offers tremendous protection supported by strength, endurance, and great luck. • A White Oak wood wand will be useful in fending off evil. • There was a time when holding a splinter between the teeth that was obtained from a White Oak tree that had been struck by lightning was supposed to be the best cure for a toothache. • The ancient Greeks once believed that stirring water with a White Oak branch would make it rain. • The only part of the White Oak tree that is edible are the acorns after they have been processed by roasting or by boiling and drying. At that point, they are best used after grinding into a flour.

No. 404

Quercus robur ☠☙

English Oak

Common Oak | European Oak | King of the Forest | Pedunculate Oak | *Quercus longaeva*

✹ SYMBOLIC MEANINGS
Endurance; Hospitality; Liberty; Love; Noble presence; Personal finances; Regal power; Supreme being; Wealth.

🌱 COMPONENT MEANINGS
Acorn: Fruition of long, hard labor; Good luck; Immortality; Life; Patience.
Leaves: Bravery; Strength; Welcome.
Sprig: Hospitality.

⬡ POSSIBLE POWERS
Abundance; Advancement; Aphrodisiac; Attracts love; Autumn; Business; Colorize; Conscious will; Cybele; Dagda; Dianus; Earth element; Energy; Erato; Expansion; Female energy; Fire element; the Four Winds; Friendship; Growth; Healing; Health; Hecate; Heme; Honor; Janus; Joy; Jupiter; Leadership; Life; Light; Luck; Masculine energy; Money; Natural power; Pan; Politics; Potency; Power; Protection; Public acclaim; Responsibility; Rhea; Royalty; Spring; Success; Summer; Sun; Thor; Wealth; Winter; Zeus.

☙ FOLKLORE AND FACTS
The English Oak tree has been revered, even worshipped, as an emblem of the Supreme Being by significant cultures and people since prehistoric times. • A very powerful protector against evil is a cross whittled from English Oak

wood made from equal lengths that are tied together in the center with red thread and hung in the house. The resulting cross predates Christianity and is known as the equal-armed cross, the balanced cross, the Greek cross, and the peaceful cross. The symbol of that cross represents the Earth, male and female, the Four Winds, the four seasons, and the four elements. Sometimes it is found in a circle; when it is, the cross represents the Earth, such as would be found on an astrological natal birth chart. • Carry a small piece of English Oak wood as protection from harm and as a good luck charm. • If in autumn you happen to catch a falling English Oak leaf, the divination is that you will not have a cold for all of winter. • Wear an English Oak acorn amulet for protection against aches, pains, and illnesses. • Wear an English Oak acorn as an amulet to promote youthfulness. • Wear an English Oak acorn as an amulet to encourage longevity and even immortality. • Wear an English Oak acorn as an amulet to increase fertility. • Wear an English Oak acorn as an amulet to improve sexual powers. • With the proper mordant, English Oak can produce a rich, dark gray dye for fabric. • The only part of the English Oak tree that is edible are the acorns after they have been processed by roasting or by boiling and drying. At that point, they are best used after grinding into a flour.

No. 405
Reseda odorata ☙

Mignonette

Little Darling | *Reseda neilgherrensis*

❋ **SYMBOLIC MEANINGS**
Moral and mental beauty; Worth and loveliness.

🌼 **POSSIBLE POWERS**
Beautification; Mental health.

🜨 **FOLKLORE AND FACTS**
Mignonette's sweet, penetrating fragrance helps mask the stench of rotting garbage, sewage, and who-knows-what awful other odors wafting about. Back in the 1700s, when the stink of rivers and trash was strong enough to induce indiscreet retching, the lovely and very fragrant Mignonette became an exceptionally popular plant that was widely grown in pots to place on windowsills and on balconies throughout London and Paris, with the intent of perfuming the area as much as possible. • A yellow vegetable dye can be obtained from the Mignonette plant.

No. 406
Rhamnus cathartica ☠☙

Buckthorn

Buckthorn | *Cervispina cathartica* | Common Buckthorn | European Buckthorn | Hart's Thorn | Hartsthorn | Highwaythorn | Purging Buckthorn | Rams Thorn | Ramsthorn | *Rhamnus cadevalii* | *Rhamnus hydriensis* | *Rhamnus spinosa* | *Rhamnus sylvatica* | *Rhamnus uninervis* | *Rhamnus wichellii* | *Rhamnus wicklia* | *Rhamnus wihhor* | *Rhamnus willdenowiana* | *Rhamnus xanthocarpa*

❋ **SYMBOLIC MEANINGS**
Branch of thorns; Thorn branch; Thorny branch.

🌼 **POSSIBLE POWERS**
Colorize; Elf magic; Exorcism; Feminine energy; Force away an enchantment; Legal matters; Luck in a legal matter in court; Magical working; Protection; Saturn; Water element; Wishing.

🜨 **FOLKLORE AND FACTS**
To drive away all sorceries and all enchantments from the home and its occupants, place branches of Buckthorn near the windows and doors. • Carry or wear a Buckthorn sachet to undertake legal matters, including being in the courtroom. • Carry or wear Buckthorn to create good luck. • Buckthorn will produce a vegetable dye color ranging from pink to a rusty shade of red. • To make a strong wish, first make an

infusion of Buckthorn bark mixed with rainwater, natural spring water, or distilled water. Face east, sprinkle a bit of the infusion, concentrate on the wish. Turn left to face north, repeat. Turn left again to face west, repeat. Turn left again to face south, repeat. Turn left again to face east, once more sprinkle the infusion and wish the wish one last time. Believe the wish will come true in good time.

No. 407
Rhamnus purshiana ☠☙

Cascara Sagrada

Bitter Bark | *Cardiolepis obtusa* | Cascara | Cascara Buckthorn | Cascara Sagrada | Chittam | Chittam Bark | Chitticum | Cittim Bark | Ecorce Sacree | *Rhamnus alnifolia* | *Rhamnus purshiana* | Sacred Bark | Yellow Bark

❋ **SYMBOLIC MEANINGS**
Patience; Providence.

🌼 **POSSIBLE POWERS**
Legal matters; Money; Money spell; Protection; Protection against a hex.

🜨 **FOLKLORE AND FACTS**
To help win a court case, before going to court, sprinkle around the home an infusion of Cascara Sagrada that has been mixed with rainwater, natural spring water, or distilled water. Then make, then carry or wear a sachet of Cascara Sagrada to court to invite a positive outcome of the case. • Make, then carry or wear a sachet of Cascara Sagrada to help concentrate. • A vase or bowl with leafy stems of Cascara Sagrada on the desk near to where thoughtful work is done can help with well-focused concentration. • Carry or wear Cascara Sagrada to fend off hexes and evil.

No. 408
Rheum officinale ☠☙

Medicinal Rhubarb

Chinese Rhubarb | Eastern Rhubarb | Indian Rhubarb | Klernbak | *Rheum baillonii* | Yào Yòng Dà Huáng

❋ **SYMBOLIC MEANINGS**
Need.

🌼 **POSSIBLE POWERS**
Earth element; Incense; Purgative; Venus.

🜨 **FOLKLORE AND FACTS**
Medicinal Rhubarb has been used in traditional Chinese medicine for thousands of years. • Make a Medicinal Rhubarb sachet or amulet to wear on a string around the neck to help rid aches in the stomach.

R

No. 409

Rhodiola rosea ☠⚗

Midsummer Men

Aaron's Rod | Arctic Root | Golden Root | Hóng Jǐng Tiān | Kings Crown | Lignum Rhodium | Orpin Rose | *Rhodia officinarum* | *Rhodiola arctica* | *Rhodiola borealis* | *Rhodiola elongata* | *Rhodiola hideoi* | *Rhodiola iremelica* | *Rhodiola krivochizhinii* | *Rhodiola maxima* | *Rhodiola minor* | *Rhodiola odora* | *Rhodiola odorata* | *Rhodiola roanensis* | *Rhodiola sachalinensis* | *Rhodiola scopolii* | *Rhodiola sibirica* | *Rhodiola tachiroei* | *Rhodiola telephioides* | Rose Root | Roseroot | *Sedum altaicum* | *Sedum arcticum* | *Sedum caerulans* | *Sedum capitatum* | *Sedum dioicum* | *Sedum elongatum* | *Sedum ledebourii* | *Sedum rhodiola* | *Sedum rhodioloides* | *Sedum roanense* | *Sedum rosea* | *Sedum sachalinense* | *Tetradium odoratum* | *Tolmachevia krivochizhinii*

✳ SYMBOLIC MEANINGS
Golden roses.

⚘ POSSIBLE POWERS
Alleviates anxiety and depression; Alleviates fatigue; Healing; Increases sex drive; Mental performance; Physical endurance; Stimulate immune system; Weight loss.

☙ FOLKLORE AND FACTS
Midsummer Men can be cultivated to become an attractive groundcover. • Although Midsummer Men has been effectively used in traditional medicine for various disorders, the United States Food and Drug Administration issued warnings that the claims to the safety and effectiveness of *Rhodiola rosea* in dietary supplements for weight management and conditions were falsely misleading and extremely unsafe unless prescribed by qualified physicians. • Based on the false hype, the Midsummer Men plant in the wild has been disturbingly diminishing on such a grotesquely industrial scale that it is now illegal to harvest the plant in many protected areas. • When cutting into the root of Midsummer Men, it gives off the aroma of rose. • Greek physician Dioscorides wrote of Midsummer Men as *Rhodiola rosea* in 77 CE. • It is believed that Russian cosmonauts may have relied on Midsummer Men's beneficial medicinal effects when going into outer space. • Midsummer Men has been used in traditional Chinese medicine for thousands of years. • Midsummer Men has been used for hundreds of years in Scandinavia and Russia to help cope with the stressfully cold climate.

No. 410

Rhododendron groenlandicum ☠⚗

Ledum

Bog Labrador Tea | Hudson's Bay Tea | Indian Plant Tea | Labrador Tea | *Ledum canadense* | *Ledum groenlandicum* | *Ledum latifolium* | *Ledum pacificum* | Muskeg Tea | Muskekopukwan | Swamp Tea

✳ SYMBOLIC MEANINGS
Harmony.

⚘ POSSIBLE POWERS
Balance; Calms nervousness; Cleansing; Energy flow; Harmony; Healing; Sleep.

☙ FOLKLORE AND FACTS
Native American tribes often used Ledum leaves to brew teas as beverages and for medicinal purposes. • When Ledum essential oil is used for aromatherapy, it may help the flow of energy that allows an ease of relaxation that promotes sleep and alleviates nervousness.

No. 411

Rhus coriaria ☠⚗🍴

Sumac

Elm-leaved Sumach | Og Ha-bursaka'im | *Rhus amoena* | *Rhus coriaria* var. *zebaria* | *Rhus heterophylla* | *Rhus sumac* | *Rhus variifolia* | Samak | Samaka | Sicilian Sumac | Sumak | Sumaq | Sumok | Tamtam | Tanner's Sumach | Tatrak | Tatri | Timtima | *Toxicodendron coriaria*

✳ SYMBOLIC MEANINGS
Intellectual excellence; Splendid; Splendor.

⚘ POSSIBLE POWERS
Addresses difficulty; Elemental fire energy; Energy of wild nature; Facilitates harmony among people; Intellect; Life; Movement.

☙ FOLKLORE AND FACTS
Tangy ripe Sumac fruit, which is dried, crushed, then used as a spice, was introduced to Europeans long before the Lemon was. • Nine Sumac berries in the pocket will help get a lighter sentence if found guilty in a court trial. • A three-foot-long branch of Sumac wood that is approximately one-half-inch thick, with a puff of downy eagle feathers attached on one end, will suffice as a suitable Navajo shamanistic healing wand called a nahikàï. • The toxic Sumac leaves have been used since ancient times to tan leather.

No. 412

Rosa acicularis 🌿

Prickly Rose

Arctic Rose | Bristly Rose | Prickly Wild Rose |
Rosa alpina | *Rosa amurensis* | *Rosa baicalensis* |
Rosa carelica | *Rosa fauriei* | *Rosa gmelinii* | *Rosa granulosa* | *Rosa korsakoviensis* | *Rosa polyphylla* |
Rosa sichotealinensis | *Rosa stevenii* | *Rosa taquetii* | Wild Rose

✹ SYMBOLIC MEANINGS
A poetic person.

🌐 COLOR MEANINGS
Pink: Confidence; Desire; Elegance; Energy; Everlasting joy; Gentility; Grace; Gratitude; Happiness; Indecision; Joy; Joy of life; Love; Passion; Perfect happiness; Perfection; Please believe me; Pure; Pure and lovely; Romance; Romantic love; Secret love; Sweetness; Thank you; Thankfulness; Trust; You are young and beautiful; You're so loved; Youth.
Dark pink: Thank you.

🌀 POSSIBLE POWERS
Meaningful words from the heart; Potential invisibility; Venus; Water element.

🜂 FOLKLORE AND FACTS
It is believed that a fairy is supposedly able to render itself invisible by eating a Prickly Rose hip, then turning counterclockwise three times. To become visible again, the fairy would need to eat another Prickly Rose hip then turn clockwise three times.

No. 413

Rosa × alba 🌿

White Rose

Backyard Rose | Mother of Roses | Nesri | *Rosa × christii* | *Rosa × collina* | *Rosa × incarnata* |
Rosa × lloydii | Sufaid Gulab | White Oil-Bearing Rose | White Rose of York

✹ SYMBOLIC MEANINGS
Delicate; Honor; Innocence; Innocence between two souls; Joy; Loyalty; Peace; Purity; Reverence; Secrecy; Timeless journey of love; Worthiness.

🌐 COLOR MEANINGS
Bridal White: Bliss; Happiness; Happy love.
White: Charm; Eternal love; Exorcism; Girlhood; a Heart ignorant of love; the Heart that knows not love; Heavenly; Humility; I am worthy of you; I would be single; Innocence; Purity; Reverence; Secrecy; Silence; Too young to love; Too young to marry; Virtue; Wistfulness; Worthiness; You're heavenly; Youthfulness.

🍃 COMPONENT MEANINGS
Bouquet in full bloom: Gratitude.
Bud: Beauty; Confessed love; Confession of love; a Heart innocent of love; Innocence; Virginity; Young girl; Youth.
Crown: Beware of virtue; Reward of merit; Reward of virtue; Superior merit; Virtue.
Full-blown: You are beautiful.
Full-blown flower placed over two buds: Secrecy.
Garland: Beware of virtue; Reward of merit; Reward of virtue; Symbol of superior merit.

🌀 POSSIBLE POWERS
Adonis; Aurora; Beauty; Cupid; Demeter; Divination; Eros; Feminine energy; Hippocrates; Hathor; Healing; Isis; Love; Peace; Protection; Psychic power; Purification; Venus; Virgin Mary; Virtue; Water element; Wholesomeness.

🜂 FOLKLORE AND FACTS
The ancient Greeks and ancient Romans were the first to cultivate *Rosa × alba*, the magnificent sweetly scented, ancient White Rose of unknown parentage. • Aromatic water that is called nesri water is made in Tunisia from the *Rosa × alba*. • White Rose essential oil is used in perfume and cosmetics. • White Rose has been the favorite of bridal bouquets and wedding flower arrangements. • According to legends, the White Rose was the first rose created to evolve into all the other colors over time as they were needed to exist. • According to Greek myth, every rose was a White Rose until Aphrodite, the goddess of love, pricked her finger on a rose thorn. Her blood upon the White Rose that she held turned it red. • The White Rose is said to be a reflection of the Mystical Rose of Heaven, who is the holy Virgin Mary. • A long, bloody royal British power-struggling conflict between the House of Lancaster and the House of York in the fifteenth century CE was known as the Wars of the Roses. It ended after the victory of King Henry VII at the Battle of Bosworth Field, when he finally married Elizabeth of York on January 18, 1486. That marriage between the two ruling houses united the Red Rose with the White Rose to become the symbolic Tudor Rose, a combination herald of both badges. Since then, the White Rose itself has become an enduring symbol of honor, loyalty, and peace.

No. 414

Rosa canina ❧

Dog Rose

Dog Berry | Itburunu | Kusburnu | *Rosa aciphylla* | *Rosa adenocalyx* | *Rosa adscita* | *Rosa afzeliana* | *Rosa agraria* | *Rosa albolutescens* | *Rosa amansii* | *Rosa analoga* | *Rosa armata* | *Rosa armoricana* | *Rosa aspratilis* | *Rosa belgradensis* | *Rosa calvatostyla* | *Rosa cariotii* | *Rosa catalaunica* | *Rosa caucasea* | *Rosa caucasica* | *Rosa cinerascens* | *Rosa cinerosa* | *Rosa cladoleia* | *Rosa communis* | *Rosa controversa* | *Rosa cuneata* | *Rosa curticola* | *Rosa diddensis* | *Rosa dilucida* | *Rosa disparilis* | *Rosa dollineriana* | *Rosa dumosa* | *Rosa edita* | *Rosa eriostyla* | *Rosa erythrantha* | *Rosa exilis* | *Rosa fallens* | *Rosa firmula* | *Rosa fissispina* | *Rosa flavidifolia* | *Rosa flexibilis* | *Rosa flexuosa* | *Rosa fraxinoides* | *Rosa frivaldskyi* | *Rosa frondosa* | *Rosa generalis* | *Rosa glaberrima* | *Rosa globularis* | *Rosa heterostyla* | *Rosa hirtella* | *Rosa horridula* | *Rosa inconspicua* | *Rosa intercedens* | *Rosa kalmiussica* | *Rosa laxifolia* | *Rosa leucantha* | *Rosa lioclada* | *Rosa litigiosa* | *Rosa lonaczevskii* | *Rosa ludibunda* | *Rosa lutetiana* | *Rosa macroacantha* | *Rosa macrostylis* | *Rosa maialis* | *Rosa marisensis* | *Rosa mediata* | *Rosa mexicana* | *Rosa mollardiana* | *Rosa montezumae* | *Rosa montivaga* | *Rosa mygindii* | *Rosa myrtilloides* | *Rosa nemophila* | *Rosa nervulosa* | *Rosa novella* | *Rosa oblongata* | *Rosa occulta* | *Rosa oenensis* | *Rosa oreades* | *Rosa oxyphylla* | *Rosa penchinatii* | *Rosa polyodon* | *Rosa porrectidens* | *Rosa praeterita* | *Rosa pratincola* | *Rosa prutensis* | *Rosa pseudoblondeana* | *Rosa psilophylla* | *Rosa pubens* | *Rosa raui* | *Rosa retusa* | *Rosa rorida* | *Rosa rougeonensis* | *Rosa rubelliflora* | *Rosa rubescens* | *Rosa sarmentacea* | *Rosa sazilliacensis* | *Rosa scabrata* | *Rosa semibiserrata* | *Rosa senticosa* | *Rosa separabilis* | *Rosa sepium* | *Rosa seposita* | *Rosa sosnovskyi* | *Rosa sphaerica* | *Rosa spuria* | *Rosa stenocarpa* | *Rosa stipularis* | *Rosa subertii* | *Rosa sylvularum* | *Rosa systylomorpha* | *Rosa touranginiana* | *Rosa trichoneura* | *Rosa tyraica* | *Rosa venosa* | *Rosa verlotii* | *Rosa vinealis* | *Rosa vinetorum* | *Rosa viridicata* | *Rosa wettsteinii* | *Rosa willibaldii* | Steinnype | Stenros | Witches Briar

❀ SYMBOLIC MEANINGS

Ferocity; Honesty; Pain and pleasure; Simplicity.

❀ COLOR MEANINGS

Light pink: Admiration.

Pink: Confidence; Desire; Elegance; Energy; Everlasting joy; Gentility; Grace; Gratitude; Happiness; Indecision; Joy; Joy of life; Love; Passion; Perfect happiness; Perfection; Please believe me; Pure; Pure and lovely; Romance; Romantic love; Secret love; Sweetness; Thank you; Thankfulness; Trust; You are young and beautiful; You're so loved; Youth.

White: Charm; Eternal love; Exorcism; Girlhood; a Heart ignorant of love; the Heart that knows not love; Heavenly; Humility; I am worthy of you; I would be single; Innocence; Purity; Reverence; Secrecy; Silence; Too young to love; Too young to marry; Virtue; Wistfulness; Worthiness; You're heavenly; Youthfulness

❧ POSSIBLE POWERS

Adonis; Aurora; Beauty; Cupid; Demeter; Divination; Eros; Feminine energy; Hippocrates; Hathor; Healing; Isis; Longevity; Love; Peace; Protection; Psychic power; Purification; Venus; Water element.

❧ FOLKLORE AND FACTS

The Dog Rose is a climbing wild rose. • The Dog Rose root was once believed to remedy the bite from a mad, rabid dog. • The rose that was stylized and used on various heralds in Europe was designed using the Dog Rose as the model. • The Dog Rose is the county flower of Hampshire, England. • The Dog Rose has a long-lived legend surrounding a climbing display up the wall of the Cathedral of the Assumption of Mary, located in Hildesheim, Germany. The legend is that it is the Thousand-year Rose that was planted back when the diocese was first established in the year 815 CE.

No. 415

Rosa × centifolia ❧

Hundred-Petaled Rose

Cabbage Rose | Hundred-Leaved Rose | Provence Rose | *Rosa × burgundica* | *Rosa × centifolia* var. *semiduplex* | *Rosa × dijoniensis* | *Rosa × muscosa* | *Rosa × parvifolia* | *Rosa × pulchella* | Rose de Mai

❀ SYMBOLIC MEANINGS

Ambassador of love; Dignity of mind; Gentleness; Graces; Love's ambassador; Passion; Pride.

❀ COLOR MEANINGS

Blush: If you love me, you will discover it; If you love me, you will find me out.

Coral: Desire; Enthusiasm; Happiness; Passion.

Light pink: Admiration.

Pink: Confidence; Desire; Elegance; Energy; Everlasting joy; Gentility; Grace; Gratitude; Happiness; Indecision; Joy; Joy of life; Love; Passion; Perfect happiness; Perfection; Please believe me; Pure; Pure and lovely; Romance; Romantic love; Secret love; Sweetness; Thank you; Thankfulness; Trust; You are young and beautiful; You're so loved; Youth.

Dark pink: Thank you.

Lavender: Enchantment; Love at first sight; Magic.

Orange: Desire; Enthusiasm; Fascination; Passion; Pride; Wonder; Passion; Protection; Respect; Romance; Well done.

Peach: Appreciation; Closing of the deal; Gratitude; Immortality; Let's get together; Modesty; Sincerity.

Red: Beauty; Congratulations; Courage; Desire; Healing; I love you; Job well done; Love;

White: Charm; Eternal love; Exorcism; Girlhood; a Heart
ignorant of love; the Heart that knows not love; Heavenly;
Humility; I am worthy of you; I would be single; Innocence;
Purity; Reverence; Secrecy; Silence; Too young to love; Too
young to marry; Virtue; Wistfulness; Worthiness; You're
heavenly; Youthfulness.

Pale yellow: Friendship.

Yellow: Apology; Caring; Dying Love; Friendship; Gladness;
Infidelity; Jealousy; Joy; Love; Platonic love; Remember me;
Welcome; Welcome back.

❧ COMPONENT MEANINGS

Bouquet in full bloom: Gratitude.

Bud: Beauty; Confessed love; Confession of love; a Heart
innocent of love; Innocence; Virginity; Young girl; Youth.

Crown: Beware of virtue; Reward of merit; Reward of virtue;
Superior merit; Virtue.

Full-blown: You are beautiful.

Full-blown flower placed over two buds: Secrecy.

Garland: Beware of virtue; Reward of merit; Reward of virtue;
Symbol of superior merit.

❀ POSSIBLE POWERS

Adonis; Aurora; Beauty; Cupid; Demeter; Diminish anger;
Divination; Eros; Feminine energy; Hippocrates; Hathor;
Healing; Isis; Love; Nourishing love; Passion; Peace;
Penetrating love; Protection; Psychic power; Purification;
Romance; Venus; Water element.

⬥ FOLKLORE AND FACTS

The Hundred-Petaled Rose is believed be a sacred herb. The
entire plant and especially the flower have a spiritual and
psychic vibration higher than that of any other flower. • The
fragrant Hundred-Petaled Rose is cultivated in France for
use in perfumes. • The ancient Romans believed that Flora,
their goddess of Springtime, created the Hundred-Petaled
Rose. • Hundred-Petaled Rose essential oil is useful in
aromatherapy to reduce stress and anxiety and help relieve
depression.

No. 416

$\mathcal{R}osa \times damascena$ ❦

Damascus Rose

Damask | Damask Rose | Gole Mohammadi | Rose of Castile | Rose Otto

✳ SYMBOLIC MEANINGS

Bashful love; Brilliant complexion; Close friendship; Divine
love; Freshness; Inspiration for love; Refreshing love.

🌀 COLOR MEANINGS

Blush: If you love me, you will discover it; If you love me, you
will find me out.

Light pink: Admiration.

Pink: Confidence; Desire; Elegance; Energy; Everlasting joy;
Gentility; Grace; Gratitude; Happiness; Indecision; Joy; Joy
of life; Love; Passion; Perfect happiness; Perfection; Please
believe me; Pure; Pure and lovely; Romance; Romantic love;
Secret love; Sweetness; Thank you; Thankfulness; Trust; You
are young and beautiful; You're so loved; Youth.

Dark pink: Thank you.

Red: Beauty; Congratulations; Courage; Desire; Healing; I
love you; Job well done; Love; Passion; Protection; Respect;
Romance; Well done.

❧ COMPONENT MEANINGS

Bouquet in full bloom: Gratitude.

Bud: Beauty; Confessed love; Confession of love; a Heart
innocent of love; Innocence; Virginity; Young girl; Youth.

Crown: Beware of virtue; Reward of merit; Reward of virtue;
Superior merit; Virtue.

Full-blown: You are beautiful.

Full-blown flower placed over two buds: Secrecy.

Garland: Beware of virtue; Reward of merit; Reward of virtue;
Symbol of superior merit.

❀ POSSIBLE POWERS

Adonis; Aurora; Beauty; Cupid; Demeter; Divination;
Domestic happiness or peace; Eros; Feminine energy;
Fertility; Hippocrates; Hathor; Healing; Isis; Long-lasting

relationship; Love; Peace; Protection; Protection of loved ones; Psychic power; Purification; True and lasting love; Venus; Water element.

🜨 FOLKLORE AND FACTS
The Damascus Rose is an ancient sacred plant with a large, beautiful, fragrant flower that originated in Iran and is revered in the Middle East. • The Damascus Rose is the source of a pure essential oil that is used in some religious ceremonies. • Damascus Rose essential oil is pleasant in aromatherapy for relaxation and peace of mind. • The fragrance of the Damascus Rose can attract angels. • It is believed that Lord Vishnu used a Damascus Rose to create the goddess Lax. • The Damascus Rose has been associated with the nightingale in Persian art and poetry. • A long-stem length of the gentle Damascus Rose wood that has had the thorns trimmed off will make a magic wand that can be applied to love magic in a manner that will magically bless true and lasting love, encourage fertility, offer protection to loved ones, and tap into psychic powers. • The Damascus Rose is a fragrant, wonderfully exotic, flavorful ingredient used in many Middle Eastern dishes. It is a favorite as a flavoring or as a seasoning in desserts, ice cream, jam, the sweet confection known as Turkish delight, rice pudding, yogurt, teas, and other beverages, as well as being a necessary ingredient in a Moroccan seasoning mixture known as ras el hanout. Powdered dried Damascus Rose petals or fragrant rose water is frequently sprinkled over dishes. • Damascus Rose petals can be brush painted with reconstituted meringue powder then sugared to transform them into a sparkly garnish decoration for cakes and candies. • It is believed that it was Allah himself who named the white Damascus Rose the Queen of Flowers.

No. 417
Rosa foetida 🜨
Persian Yellow Rose
Austrian Briar Rose | Austrian Copper Rose | Capucine Briar Rose | Copper | Corn Poppy Rose | *Rosa bicolor* | *Rosa chlorophylla* | *Rosa lutea* | *Rosa punicea* | Rose Comtesse | Rosier Eglantier | Vermilion Rose of Austria

✱ SYMBOLIC MEANINGS
Decrease of love; Friendship; Infidelity; Jealousy; Joy; Loveliness; Platonic love; Try to care; Unfaithfulness; Very lovely; You are all that is lovely.

🌼 COLOR MEANINGS
Pale yellow: Friendship.
Yellow: Apology; Caring; Dying Love; Friendship; Gladness; Infidelity; Jealousy; Joy; Love; Platonic love; Remember me; Welcome; Welcome back.

🌸 POSSIBLE POWERS
Adonis; Aurora; Beauty; Cupid; Demeter; Diminishment of trust; Divination; Eros; Feminine energy; Friendship; Hathor; Healing; Hippocrates; Isis; Love; Peace; Protection; Psychic power; Purification; Venus; Water element.

🜨 FOLKLORE AND FACTS
The Persian Yellow Rose is a prolifically blooming, rambling briar with very pretty, vivid yellow flowers that has a somewhat peculiar boiled-linseed-oil fragrance. • The Persian Yellow Rose was the first yellow rose in Europe.

No. 418
Rosa gallica 🜨
Gallic Rose
Apothecary's Rose | Fair Rosamond's Rose | French Rose | Garnet Stripe Rose | Gemengte Rose | Hungarian Rose | Monday Rose | Mundi Rose | Mundy Rose | Officinal Rose | Provence Rose | Queen of Flowers | *Rosa arvina* | *Rosa assimilis* | *Rosa atropurpurea* | *Rosa austriaca* | *Rosa austriaca var. officinalis* | *Rosa belgica* | *Rosa cordata* | *Rosa cordifolia* | *Rosa crenatula* | *Rosa crenulata* | *Rosa czackiana* | *Rosa elata* | *Rosa gallica var. mahesca* | *Rosa gallica var. officinalis* | *Rosa gallica var. pontii* | *Rosa gallica var. pumila* | *Rosa gallica var. ranunculus* | *Rosa gallica var. versicolor* | *Rosa grandiflora* | *Rosa heteracantha* | *Rosa hispida* | *Rosa holosericea* | *Rosa humilis* | *Rosa minimalis* | *Rosa mirogojana* | *Rosa oligacantha* | *Rosa olympica* | *Rosa pinnatifida* | *Rosa portlandica* | *Rosa provincialis* | *Rosa pumila* | *Rosa pumila var. holosericea* | *Rosa pumila var. officinalis* | *Rosa pumila var. rosamundi* | *Rosa pumila var. subnigra* | *Rosa pumila var. tricolor* | *Rosa pygmaea* | *Rosa racemosa* | *Rosa repens* | *Rosa rubra* | *Rosa ruralis* | *Rosa sylvatica* | *Rosa tenuis* | *Rosa velutiniflora* | *Rosa versicolor* | *Rosa virescens* | Rose Mundi | Rose of Provins | Rosemonde | Rosemondi | Rosemunde | Striped Rose of France

✱ SYMBOLIC MEANINGS
Innermost temple; Variety; You are merry.

🌼 COLOR MEANING
Striped or variegated: Immediate affection; Love at first sight; Warmth of heart.

🌸 POSSIBLE POWERS
Adonis; Aurora; Beauty; Cupid; Cures depression; Demeter; Divination; Eros; Feminine energy; Hathor; Healing; Heart as the temple; Hippocrates; Introspection; Isis; Love; Options; Peace; Protection; Psychic power; Purification; Venus; Water element.

Believed to have been indigenous to Iran, where it was cultivated for an untold number of centuries, the Gallic Rose was one of the first *Rosa* species cultivated in Europe. • The Greek poet Sappho described the Gallic Rose as the Queen of Flowers. • The sixth-century BCE Romans included the Gallic Rose in all of their celebrations. • It was the Persian physician Avicenna who, sometime just before 1037 CE, invented rosewater using the Gallic Rose essential oil and pure rainwater to do so. • The Gallic Rose has flower petals that are striped in such a way that they appear hand-colored. • There is a legend that the Gallic Rose was given the name Rose Mundi after one of King Henry II's mistresses. • The Gallic Rose was a popular rose in medieval monastery herb gardens. • Gallic Rose essential oil has been used for aromatherapy to help induce a sense of calm to help alleviate depression.

No. 419

Rosa moschata ☙

Musk Rose

Rosa arborea | Rosa broteroi | Rosa brownii | Rosa glandulifera | Rosa manuelii | Rosa opsostemma | Rosa pissardii | Rosa ruscinonensis

☀ SYMBOLIC MEANINGS

Capricious beauty; Fickle.

🌺 COLOR MEANINGS

White: Charm; Eternal love; Exorcism; Girlhood; a Heart ignorant of love; the Heart that knows not love; Heavenly; Humility; I am worthy of you; I would be single; Innocence; Purity; Reverence; Secrecy; Silence; Too young to love; Too young to marry; Virtue; Wistfulness; Worthiness; You're heavenly; Youthfulness.

🌿 COMPONENT MEANINGS

Cluster: Capricious beauty; Charming.

🌺 POSSIBLE POWERS

Adonis; Aurora; Beauty; Charm; Cupid; Demeter; Divination; Eros; Feminine energy; Flirtatiousness; Hathor; Healing; Hippocrates; Isis; Love; Peace; Protection; Psychic power; Purification; Venus; Water element.

☙ FOLKLORE AND FACTS

The Musk Rose is believed to have originated in the Himalayas. • The rose that William Shakespeare mentioned in *A Midsummer Night's Dream* is thought to be the Musk Rose, since it was a favorite garden rose of his time. • The Musk Rose is prickly, five-petaled, and very fragrant.

No. 420

Rosa rubiginosa ☙

Eglantine Rose

Rosa almeriensis Rouy | Rosa camberiensis | Rosa chailletii | Rosa comosa | Rosa densa | Rosa dolorosa | Rosa echinocarpa | Rosa eglanteria | Rosa floribunda | Rosa grandiflora | Rosa gremlii | Rosa kurganica | Rosa minuscula | Rosa moutinii | Rosa resinosa | Rosa rotundifolia | Rosa suavifolia | Rosa tanaitica | Rosa uliginosa | Rosa umbellata | Rosa walpoleana | Rosa zamensis | Shakespeare's Eglantine *|* Sweet Briar *|* Sweet Brier *|* Sweetbriar

☀ SYMBOLIC MEANINGS

Healing a wound; Poetry; Simplicity; Spring; Sympathy.

🌺 COLOR MEANINGS

Light pink: Admiration.

White: Charm; Eternal love; Exorcism; Girlhood; a Heart ignorant of love; the Heart that knows not love; Heavenly; Humility; I am worthy of you; I would be single; Innocence; Purity; Reverence; Secrecy; Silence; Too young to love; Too young to marry; Virtue; Wistfulness; Worthiness; You're heavenly; Youthfulness.

🌺 POSSIBLE POWERS

Adonis; Aurora; Beauty; Cupid; Demeter; Divination; Eros; Feminine energy; Hathor; Healing; Hippocrates; Isis; Love; Marriage; Peace; Protection; Psychic power; Purification; Romance; Venus; Water element.

☙ FOLKLORE AND FACTS

At one time, the Eglantine Rose was strictly a well-tended garden rose until it escaped all boundaries to naturalize wildly along roadsides throughout Europe. • The thickly dense growth of the Eglantine Rose makes it a good candidate for an effective hedge that is also pretty and fragrant. • The Eglantine Rose is considered to be critically endangered in Portugal. • The crushed foliage of the Eglantine Rose has the fragrance of an Apple. • A romantic love-oriented pink and red sachet to try can be made by drying the petals of an Eglantine Rose for at least a week, until dry enough to blend the crumbled petals into a few blanched Sweet Almonds that have been crushed into it. Add a few Orange blossoms or a drop of Orange blossom essential oil if desiring that the romance results in a marriage. Carry or wear this sachet until achieving the desired result.

No. 421
Rosa rugosa
Rugged Rose
Haedanghwa | Hamanashi | Hamanasu | Japan Rose | Japanese Rose | Ramanas Rose | *Rosa andreae* | *Rosa coruscans* | *Rosa fastuosa* | *Rosa ferox* | *Rosa kamtchatica* | *Rosa maikwai* | *Rosa pubescens* | *Rosa regeliana* | Rose Hip Rose | Rugosa Rose

☀ SYMBOLIC MEANINGS
Beauty is not your only attraction.

❀ COLOR MEANINGS
Dark pink: Thank you.

❁ POSSIBLE POWERS
Adonis; Aurora; Beauty; Cupid; Demeter; Divination; Endurance; Eros; Feminine energy; Fortitude; Hathor; Healing; Hippocrates; Isis; Love; Peace; Protection; Psychic power; Purification; Strength; Tenacity; Venus; Water element.

☾ FOLKLORE AND FACTS
Growing best in sandy seaside areas to stabilize the dunes and help protect against erosion, the thorny Rugged Rose has gorgeous large fragrant flowers, and they are the source of the best-quality, edible, vitamin C–rich rose hips.

No. 422
Rubia tinctorum ☠☕
Madder
Common Madder | Dyer's Madder | *Galium rubia* | *Rubia acaliculata* | *Rubia iberica* | *Rubia sativa* | *Rubia sylvestris* | *Rubia tinctoria*

☀ SYMBOLIC MEANINGS
Calumny; Talkative.

❁ POSSIBLE POWERS
Colorize; Flirt; Sensuality.

☾ FOLKLORE AND FACTS
Since ancient times, the root of the Madder plant has been used to create exquisite red dyes for natural fibers and leather. • A bit of the Madder plant in a red sachet to be worn or carried while wearing an attractive red garment or accessory will activate one's inner sensuality to make it clearly visible and recognizable beyond one's own inner realm of presence.

No. 423
Rumex acetosa ☠☕🍴
Common Sorrel
Acetosa agrestis | *Acetosa amplexicaulis* | *Acetosa angustata* | *Acetosa bidentula* | *Acetosa fontanopaludosa* | *Acetosa hastifolia* | *Acetosa hastulata* | *Acetosa magna* | *Acetosa officinalis* | *Acetosa olitoria* | *Acetosa pratensis* | *Acetosa subalpina* | Garden Sorrel | Juopmu | Kuzu Kulağı | *Lapathum acetosa* | *Lapathum pratense* | Little Vinegar Plant | Macris | Narrow-leaved Dock | Rugstyne | *Rumex acetosus* | *Rumex acidus* | *Rumex acuminatus* | *Rumex agrestis* | *Rumex amplexicaulis* | *Rumex angustatus* | *Rumex bidentula* | *Rumex biformis* | *Rumex bulbosus* | *Rumex commersonianus* | *Rumex commersonii* | *Rumex fontanopaludosus* | *Rumex hastatulus* | *Rumex hispanicus* | *Rumex hortensis* | *Rumex micranthus* | *Rumex mutabilis* | *Rumex oblongus* | *Rumex olitoria* | *Rumex oxyotus* | *Rumex planellae* | *Rumex pratensis* | *Rumex pseudoacetosa* | *Rumex sagittifolius* | *Rumex stenophyllus* | *Rumex triangularis* | Shchavel | Sorrel | Sóska | Spinach Dock | Stevie | Szczaw | Wild Sorrel

☀ SYMBOLIC MEANINGS
Affection; Ill-timed wit; Parental affection; Refreshes the spirit; Wit.

❁ POSSIBLE POWERS
Healing; Health.

☾ FOLKLORE AND FACTS
The sour-tasting Common Sorrel has been cultivated for centuries to be used in soups, stews, and even batter-dipped and deep-fried. • Common Sorrel can be used to make a red dye for fabric. • Make, then carry or wear a Common Sorrel sachet to refresh the inner spirit.

No. 424
Rumex acetosella ☠☕
Sheep Sorrel
Acetosa acetosella | *Acetosa hastata* | *Acetosa parva* | *Acetosa repens* | *Acetosa sterilis* | *Acetosella acetosella* | *Acetosella vulgaris* | Field Sorrel | *Lapathum acetosella* | *Lapathum arvense* | *Pauladolfia acetosella* | Red Sorrel | *Rumex arvensis* | *Rumex falcarius* | *Rumex fascilobus* | *Rumex infestus* | *Rumex tenuifolius* | Sangre de Toro | Sheep's Sorrel | Sour Weed

☀ SYMBOLIC MEANINGS
Affection; Ill-timed wit; Parental affection; Refreshes the spirit; Wit.

❁ POSSIBLE POWERS
Affection; Healing; Health; Joy; Luck; Maternal tenderness; Spiritual healing.

☾ FOLKLORE AND FACTS
The male and female Sheep Sorrel flowers are on different plants that are pollinated by the wind rather than by insects. • Make, then wear or carry a dried Sheep Sorrel leaf sachet for good luck.

R

No. 425
Rumex crispus ☠☙

Yellow Dock

Curled Dock | Curly Dock | *Lapathum crispum* | Narrow Dock | *Rheum crispum* | *Rumex coreanus* | *Rumex elongatus* | *Rumex fauriei* | *Rumex kunthianus* | *Rumex kunthii* | *Rumex lingualus* | *Rumex longifolius* | *Rumex luederi* | *Rumex turcicus* | Sour Dock

✵ SYMBOLIC MEANINGS
Curled; Curls; Curly.

⊛ POSSIBLE POWERS
Air element; Fertility; Healing; Jupiter; Masculine energy; Money.

⟐ FOLKLORE AND FACTS
Yellow Dock can grow quite large, having leaves that are long, narrow, hairless, and edible. The seeds are also edible, being best dried before grinding into a flour. • To help a woman conceive a child, place a small amount of Yellow Dock seeds in a small cotton pouch and tie it to her left arm.

No. 426
Rumex scutatus ☠☙🍴

French Sorrel

Acetosa alpestris | *Acetosa hortensis* | *Acetosa scutata* | Buckler Sorrel | Buckler-Leaf Sorrel | Green-Sauce Sorrel | *Lapathum alpestre* | *Lapathum scutatum* | *Rumex acmophorus* | *Rumex aetnensis* | *Rumex alpestris* | *Rumex bellojocensis* | *Rumex glaucus* | *Rumex hastatus* | *Rumex hastifolius* | *Rumex pubescens* | *Rumex subvirescens* | Shield-Leaf Sorrel

✵ SYMBOLIC MEANINGS
Affection; Ill-timed wit; Parental affection; Refreshes the spirit; Wit.

⊛ POSSIBLE POWERS
Affection; Heal heartbreak; Healing; Health; Joy; Luck; Maternal tenderness; Protection; See a fairy; Spiritual healing.

⟐ FOLKLORE AND FACTS
The lemony French Sorrel leaves are edible for use in salads as well as for soups, stews, and sauces. Make, then carry or wear a sachet of French sorrel leaves to heal the wearer from heartbreak. • Carrying or wearing French sorrel is believed to make it possible to see a fairy.

No. 427
Ruta graveolens ☠☙

Rue

Bashoush | Common Rue | Garden Rue | German Rue | Herb of Grace | Herb of Repentance | Herbygrass | Hreow | Mother of the Herbs | Peganon Rewe | Ruda | Ruda de Huerta | Ruta | *Ruta altera* | *Ruta ciliata* | *Ruta crithmifolia* | *Ruta divaricata* | *Ruta diversifolia* | *Ruta holopetala* | *Ruta hortensis* | *Ruta intermedia* | *Ruta macrophylla* | *Ruta officinalis* | *Ruta subtripinnata* | Witches Bane

✵ SYMBOLIC MEANINGS
Fecundity of fields; Grace; Regret.

⊛ POSSIBLE POWERS
Aradia; Break a hex; Diana; Endurance; Exorcism; Fire element; Healing; Health; Love; Mars; Masculine energy; Mental clarity or patience; Powers; Protection; Purification; Repel a witch or cats; Virginity.

⟐ FOLKLORE AND FACTS
The Rue plant is a sacred herb. • Catholic priests used to sprinkle holy water off a Rue branch. • A Rue plant can live for hundreds of years. • There was once a time when Lithuanian brides would wear Rue wreaths at their weddings. • In medieval times, Rue was hung in the windows to keep any evil entity from coming into the house. • In medieval times, Rue was worn in a small bunch at the waist to repel witches. • There was a time when a Rue leaf was placed on the forehead to relieve a headache. • There was a time when people would rub fresh Rue leaves on the floor to revert any negative spells back to whoever cast them. • Make and then carry or wear a sachet of Rue to repel a negative spell back to who cast it. • It was believed that you can fend off werewolves by carrying a sprig of Rue. • William Shakespeare wrote Rue into his works many times, naming it the Herb of Grace. • Christian church attendees in the sixteenth century were most likely sprinkled with holy water from a Rue swab-like branch. • In the Middle Ages, Rue was believed to have the power to cure the afflicted from suffering the plague. It was also used as a strewing herb during that time for the same purpose. • Rue essential oil for aromatherapy can send one off to imagine being at the mountains to unwind after a long day elsewhere. • There is an unproven belief that, by holding a nosegay of self-gathered sprigs of Rue, Broom, Maidenhair Fern, Agrimony, and Ground Ivy, one can gain profound intuition of who is and who is not a practicing witch.

R

No. 428
Saccharum officinarum 🍶

Sugar Cane
Arundo saccharifer | Caña Costeña | Caña de Azúcar | Kō | Saccharifera officinalis | Saccharum atrorubens | Saccharum fragile | Saccharum hybridum | Saccharum infirmum | Saccharum occidentale | Saccharum officinale | Saccharum rubicundum | Saccharum violaceum | Sugar | Sugarcane

☀ SYMBOLIC MEANING
Sweet love; Sweeten; Sweetest love; Sweets for celebration.

✹ POSSIBLE POWERS
Aphrodisiac; Attracts love; Celebration; Feminine energy; Love; Lust; Stimulant; Venus; Water element.

✿ FOLKLORE AND FACTS
Sugar Cane was once considered to be a spice. • Sugar Cane has been used in medicines for hundreds of years. • Sugar Cane and other sweet herbs are frequently falling out of favor, with blame being centered upon it as being the cause of many ills, and research deepening into cause and effect, ongoing and controversial. • Sometime around 800 BCE, Sugar Cane was first cultivated in New Guinea. • Approximately seventy percent of the world's sugar is produced by the Sugar Cane plant *Saccharum officinarum*. • Sugar Cane was carried to North America on Christopher Columbus's second journey in 1493. • A paste of granulated brown pure cane sugar mixed with water and some freshly squeezed lemon juice goes back to the ancient Egyptians, who used it to remove hair. The same method of using this sugar paste is still being employed by many people as a depilatory that is better known as sugaring. • To instill lust where it may seem to be waning, mix granulated or brown sugar and some coconut oil together to make a coarse paste then use it in the shower as a body scrub that will smooth and sweetly fragrance the skin. • *Saccharum officinarum* and its hybrids are not only being grown for sugar, but also to be further processed into ethanol.

No. 429
Salicornia europaea ☠🍶

Glasswort
Chicken Toe | Common Glasswort | Marsh Samphire | Pickle Weed | Salicornia annua | Salicornia biennis | Salicornia brachystachya | Salicornia herbacea | Salicornia simonkaiana | Salicornia stricta | Saltwort | Sea Asparagus | Sea Pickle

☀ SYMBOLIC MEANING
Salt horn.

✹ POSSIBLE POWERS
Grounding; Healing; Regeneration; Renewing; Seasoning.

✿ FOLKLORE AND FACTS
Glasswort is a salt-tolerant, edible, flowering annual succulent that can be found in some salt marshes, among the mangroves, and on beach dunes. • The salty Glasswort was utilized for a very long time as a source of soda ash that was instrumental in the making of glass up until the beginning of the nineteenth century.

No. 430
Salix babylonica 🍶

Weeping Willow
Babylon Willow | Chuí Liŭ | Ficus salix | Napoleon Will | Peking Willow | Salix cantoniensis | Salix capitata | Salix chinensis | Salix dependens | Salix jeholensis | Salix jishiensis | Salix lasiogyne | Salix lenta | Salix matsudana | Salix napoleona | Salix napoleonis | Salix neolasiogyne | Salix ohsidare | Salix pendula | Salix perpendens | Salix pingliensis | Salix propendens | Salix pseudogilgiana | Salix pseudolasiogyne | Salix pseudomatsudana | Salix subfragilis | Salix yuhkii

☀ SYMBOLIC MEANINGS
Bendable but not breakable; Divination; Forsaken; Healing; Love; Melancholy; Metaphysicality; Moon magic; Mourning; Sadness; Tenacity.

✹ POSSIBLE POWERS
Colorize; Divination; Healing.

✿ FOLKLORE AND FACTS
Weeping Willow wood is sacred to all goddesses of the Moon and will make a powerful magic wand. It should be cut and properly fashioned by the intended user. After it has been charged and worked under the light of the Moon, the Weeping Willow wand's strength will greatly increase. • Weeping Willow can be used to produce a yellow dye. • The flexibility of Weeping Willow branches make it useful for basketry, sculpture, and woven furniture. • There was a time when a feverish person would be directed to send their

S

affliction into a Weeping Willow tree by going to the tree with a handful of thick mud, without crossing over water or speaking a word. Then they would make a gash in the bark, breathe deeply into the gash three times, and close it over quickly with the mud poultice and a prayer of gratitude for taking on the fever before hurrying away from the tree without looking back to it. • The forerunner of modern day aspirin was found in the leaves of the Weeping Willow that had been used medicinally for pain relief for over 2,400 years.

No. 431

Salvia apiana 🕱☸

Sacred Sage

Audibertia polystachya | Audibertiella polystachya | Bee Sage | Ramona polystachya | Sage | Salvia californica | White Sage

☀ SYMBOLIC MEANINGS

Air element; Esteem; Jupiter; Virtuous industry.

⚜ POSSIBLE POWERS

Artistic ability; Banishes evil or negativity; Business; Cleanses the aura; Consecration; Expansion; Female fidelity; Great respect; Healing; Holiness; Honor; Immortality; Leadership; Longevity; Memory; Politics; Power; Prosperity; Protection; Public acclaim; Purification; Responsibility; Royalty; Settles a lawsuit; Snake; Snakebites; Success; Wards off evil; Wealth; Wisdom; Wishing.

☘ FOLKLORE AND FACTS

Salvia apiana is the sage of choice for smudging. • For healing or prosperity, Sacred Sage is burned as incense, worn as an amulet, or used as an ingredient in a sachet. • Burning Sacred Sage will purify an area by removing negativity, spiritual impurities, and banishing evil, thus consecrating the area and providing protection. • Before entering a courtroom with the hopes of settling a lawsuit, write the names of the Christian Twelve Apostles on Sacred Sage leaves. Put them all into the shoes and enter the courtroom with confidence of gaining a positive outcome. • Due to the massive over-harvesting of wild Salvia apiana, the herb is quickly becoming endangered. It is highly recommended that easy-to-grow Salvia apiana is planted in home gardens instead.

No. 432

Salvia officinalis 🕱☸🍴

Sage

Alba | Aurea | Berggarten | Broadleaf Sage | Common Sage | Culinary Sage | Dalmatian Sage | Extrakta | Garden Sage | Golden Sage | Icterina | Kitchen Sage | Purple Sage | Red Sage | Savior | Sawge | Tricolor | True Sage

☀ SYMBOLIC MEANINGS

Agelessness; Air element; Alleviate grief; Domestic virtue; Esteem; Good health; Holiness; Holy; Immortality; Jupiter; Long life; Sacred; Wisdom.

⚜ POSSIBLE POWERS

Air element; Artistic ability; Banishes evil or negativity; Business; Cleanses the aura; Consecration; Expansion; Female fidelity; Great respect; Healing; Holiness; Honor; Immortality; Jupiter; Leadership; Longevity; Masculine energy; Memory; Politics; Power; Prosperity; Protection; Public acclaim; Purification; Responsibility; Royalty; Snakebite; Snakes; Success; Wards off evil; Wealth; Wisdom; Wishing.

☘ FOLKLORE AND FACTS

The ancient Romans believed that Sage was holy and quite powerful enough to create immortal life. • It was once believed that Sage would thrive only in gardens of homes controlled by a woman. • Sage was often planted in cemeteries because it was believed that it would easily thrive on neglect and therefore live and grow forever. • Since ancient times, Sage has been used to ward off evil and more. • Sage was a major ingredient in a medieval magical medicinal concoction called Four-Thieves Vinegar, which was supposedly used to ward off the plague. • For a chance at immortality, eat Sage daily throughout the month of May. • If you write a wish on a Sage leaf, put it under your pillow, then sleep upon it for three consecutive nights and you dream of the wish coming true, it will come true. If you do not dream of that wish coming true, you must take that leaf and bury it immediately so that it brings you no harm. • Native Americans and most new-agers prefer Salvia apiana for smudging. However, the energy from burning any other Sage species, such as Salvia officinalis, is still the same. Although the fragrance when burning Salvia officinalis for smudge smoke isn't quite as pleasant, even so, in a pinch—most especially in a negative energy emergency—any Sage can certainly be used for blessing and cleansing the negative energy from any space as a smudge, wash, or sachet. • Salvia officinalis essential oil is readily available and can also be mixed into rainwater, natural spring water, or distilled for a shake and spray infusion for cleansing an area of negative energy as a substitute for Sacred Sage.

S

No. 433

Salvia rosmarinus 🕱⚕️🍴

Rosemary

Compass Weed | Dew of the Sea | Elf Leaf | Guardrobe | Herb of Remembrance | Incensier |
Libanotis | Miss Jessopp's Upright | Old Man | Polar Plant | Romarin | Romero | Ros Maris |
Rose of Mary | Rosemarie | Rosmarin | *Rosmarinus angustifolius* | *Rosmarinus communis* |
Rosmarinus flexuosus | *Rosmarinus latifolius* | *Rosmarinus laxiflorus* | *Rosmarinus ligusticus* |
Rosmarinus officinalis | *Rosmarinus palaui* | *Rosmarinus rigidus* | *Rosmarinus serotinus* |
Rosmarinus tenuifolius | *Salvia fasciculata* | Sea Dew | Severn Sea Rosemary | Sissinghurst Blue

✺ SYMBOLIC MEANINGS

Affectionate remembrance; Attraction of love; Constancy;
Death; Fidelity; Fire element; Friendship; Love; Loyalty;
Memory; Power of rekindling extinct energy; Remembrance;
Restore balance of domestic power; Vitality; Wedding herb.

❀ POSSIBLE POWERS

Abundance; Advancement; Conscious will;
Divination; Emotions; Energy; Exorcism;
Fertility; Fire element; Friendship;
Generation; Growth; Healing;
Inspiration; Intuition; Joy; Leadership;
Life; Light; Love; Love charm; Lust;
Masculine energy; Mental clarity or
power; Moon; Natural power; Protection;
Protection from illness; Psychic ability;
Purification; Repels a witch or nightmares;
Sea; Sleep; Subconscious mind; Success; Sun; Tides; Travel
by water; Water element; Youth.

☙ FOLKLORE AND FACTS

Rosemary is native to the Mediterranean. It can grow into a
large bush, large enough to prune into topiary forms. It has
needle-like leaves and blue, pink, purple, or white flowers
and is extremely fragrant when simply brushing past it.
• Rosemary was first mentioned on a stone tablet in
cuneiform glyphs that date back to 5000 BCE. • To fragrance
the house during the holidays, Rosemary was commonly
strewn upon the floor during the Middle Ages. Stepping
upon it would release the pleasant aroma while also
perfuming the hems of long gowns and robes. • It is believed
that anyone who smells the aroma of Rosemary on Christmas
Eve will have happiness throughout the coming year. • Since
ancient times, when the practice was started in Greece,
Rosemary has been used in both funeral and marriage rituals.
• Students in ancient Greece would tuck sprigs of Rosemary
behind an ear or in their hair to enhance their memories
during academic exams. • Rosemary has been liberally
used in wedding flowers because the plant was thought to
encourage the bridal couple to remember and stay true to
their marriage vows. • It was believed that one would fall in
love if touched on the finger by a sprig of Rosemary.

• A sprig of Rosemary under the pillow is supposed to be a
remedy for nightmares. • Back in the time of ancient Egypt,
Rosemary was part of funeral rituals and also used in the
embalming process. • In medieval times, it was thought
that one must be righteous to grow Rosemary in their own
garden. • In Australia, a sprig of Rosemary is worn on Anzac
Day to remember the war dead of World War I. • Rosemary
is supposedly grossly offensive to evil spirits. • Be sure to
plant Rosemary in a garden that is intended to please the
fairies. • In the Middle Ages, a newlywed couple would plant
a branch of Rosemary. If the branch did not thrive, it was
a bad omen for the marriage and the family. • A Rosemary
plant on each side of an entry door to a home is said to repel
witches. • A popular Rosemary-scented perfume known as
hungry water was distilled back in the fourteenth century.
• Rosemary essential oil for aromatherapy can be helpful for
remembering and for remaining alert. • Rosemary essential
oil is used to add fragrance to soap and other toiletry
products. • To preserve youth, make a box from Rosemary
wood to open and smell from time to time. • Fresh Rosemary
sprigs are regularly used to flavor foods, most especially
roasted meat. The leaves can be dried and added to infuse
Olive oil to use for dipping bread. The dried leaves can be
also ground into a powder to be used to season foods without
having the needle-like leaves in the dish. • Rosemary can
easily be raised in pots that are grown in a sunny spot outside
or inside the home.

No. 434

Salvia sclarea 🕱⚕️

Clary Sage

Aethiopis sclarea | Clary | *Salvia altilabrosa* | *Salvia calostachya* |
Salvia coarctata | *Salvia haematodes* | *Salvia lucana* | *Salvia
pamirica* | *Salvia simsiana* | *Salvia turkestanica* | *Sclarea vulgaris*

✺ SYMBOLIC MEANINGS

Clarify; Clear the mind; Cool; Lift the
spirit; Uplifting.

❀ POSSIBLE POWERS

Emotions; Fertility; Generation;
Inspiration; Intuition; Psychic ability;
Sea; Subconscious mind; Tides; Travel by
water.

☙ FOLKLORE AND FACTS

Clary Sage is primarily grown for its essential oil, which
is used in perfumery as well as to flavor muscatel wine,
vermouth, and liqueurs. • Clary sage essential oil is
sometimes considered to be a woman's herb because of the

S

calming and centering effect the fragrance can have on potentially fluctuating emotions just prior to and during menstruation. • Clary Sage's medicinal use is documented back to ancient Greece during the fourth century BCE.

No. 435
Sambucus canadensis ☠☕

Common Elder

Absolute | Alhuren | American Black Elderberry | Battree | Black Elder | Bore Tree | Bour Tree | Boure Tree | Canada Elderberry | Elder Bush | Elder Flower | Elderberry | Eldrum | Ellhorn | European Black Elderberry | European Elder | European Elderberry | Frau Holle | Hildemoer | Hollunder | Hylan Tree | Hylder | Lady Ellhorn | Old Gal | Old Lady | Pipe Tree | Rob Elder | *Sambucus bipinnata* | *Sambucus canadensis* subsp. *laciniata* | *Sambucus canadensis* var. *laciniata* | *Sambucus canadensis* var. *rubella* | *Sambucus canadensis* var. *submollis* | *Sambucus canadensis* var. *tarda* | *Sambucus cerulea* var. *arizonica* | *Sambucus eberhardtii* | *Sambucus humilis* | *Sambucus intermedia* var. *insularis* | *Sambucus nigra* subsp. *canadensis* | *Sambucus nigra* var. *canadensis* | *Sambucus orbiculata* | *Sambucus orbiculata* var. *glabr* | *Sambucus orbiculata* var. *puberula* | *Sambucus planteriensis* | *Sambucus planteirensis* | *Sambucus rehderiana* | *Sambucus repens* | *Sambucus simpsonii* | Sureau | Sweet Elder | Tree of Doom | Yakori Bengeskro

✷ SYMBOLIC MEANINGS
Compassion; Creativity; Cycles; Death; Endings; Humility; Kindness; Protection against evil dangers; Rebirth; Regeneration; Renewal; Transformation; Zeal; Zealousness.

⚙ POSSIBLE POWERS
Aphrodisiac; Attracts love; Colorize; Death; Exorcism; Feminine energy; Good luck; Healing; Holda; Kills a serpent; Magic; Prosperity; Protection; Protection against a witch or evil spirit; Sends away a thief; Sleep; Venus; Water element.

☙ FOLKLORE AND FACTS
A sweet kitchen-brewed mix of Common Elderberries, cane sugar, and water simmered down to a basic syrup can be made to save and use throughout the autumn and winter as a folk medicine remedy for colds and coughs. If the sugar is not added, it is simply reduced to a syrup using the natural sugars present in the berries; the healing syrup is traditionally known as "elderberry rob." • The cooked Common Elderberries are edible and can be used to make jam, jelly, pie filling, marmalade, and wine. • Common Elder is associated with witches. • When the dead were once buried, Common Elder branches were planted with the body to protect it from evil spirits. • Stone Age arrowheads were shaped to look like

Common Elder leaves. • A cross made of Common Elder wood then attached to stables is supposed to keep evil away from the animals. • Cradles were not to be ever made of Common Elder wood because the baby would either fall out of it, not be able to sleep, or be pinched by fairies. • The English believe that burning Common Elder wood logs will bring the Devil into the house. • Before pruning a Common Elder tree, one must ask the tree's permission, then spit three times before making the first cut. • Common Elder leaves gathered on April 30 can be attached to doors and windows to keep witches from entering the home. • Common Elder trees or Elderberry hedges grown near a home's entrance will supposedly keep evil from entering. • An amulet of a piece of Common Elder wood on which the Sun has never directly shone is tied inside a small pouch that is held between two knots to be worn around the neck as a pendant protection against evil. • Common Elderberries will produce a blue dye that can be used on fabric. • Common Elder essential oil aromatherapy might help to alleviate anxiety and calm irritability. It may even help lift one up from the kind of depression that one may be suffering for a valid reason.

No. 436
Sanguinaria canadensis ☠☕

Bloodroot

Belharnosia canadensis | Belharnosia mesochora | Bloodroot | Bloodwort | Coon Root | Indian Paint | Indian Plant | Indian Red Paint | Paucon | Pauson | Red Paint Root | Red Puccoon Root | Red Pucoon | Redroot | *Sanguinaria acaulis* | *Sanguinaria australis* | *Sanguinaria dilleniana* | *Sanguinaria grandiflora* | *Sanguinaria mesochora* | *Sanguinaria rotundifolia* | *Sanguinaria stenopetala* | *Sanguinaria vernalis* | *Sanguinaria virginiana* | Snakebite | Sweet Slumber | Tetterwort

✷ SYMBOLIC MEANING
Protective love.

⚙ POSSIBLE POWERS
Fire element; Love; Mars; Masculine energy; Protection; Purification.

☙ FOLKLORE AND FACTS
When Bloodroot is worn in an amulet it will attract love and repel evil spells as well as all types of negativity. • Make Bloodroot sachets to put near the windows and doors to protect the home.

S

No. 437

Sanguisorba minor 🌿🍴

Burnet

Garden Burnet | Italian Pimpernel | *Pimpinella minor* | *Pimpinella sanguisorba* | *Poterium sanguisorbens* | *Poterium anceps* | *Poterium collinum* | *Poterium dictyocarpum* | *Poterium duriaei* | *Poterium glaucescens* | *Poterium guestphalicum* | *Poterium maroccanum* | *Poterium minus* | *Poterium sanguisorba* | Salad Burnet | Salada Burnet | *Sanguisorba dictyocarpa* | *Sanguisorba guestphalica* | *Sanguisorba maroccana* | *Sanguisorba pimpinella* | *Sanguisorba sanguisorba* | Small Burnet

☀ SYMBOLIC MEANING
A merry heart.

🌐 POSSIBLE POWERS
Consecration of ritual accoutrements; Countering magic; Lifts depressive feelings; Penetrates despondency; Protection.

🜋 FOLKLORE AND FACTS
Because at the beginning of summer Burnet plants will flower early, the blossoms are cut and used in spiritually and psychologically uplifting floral arrangements for the home, while the leaves are encouraged to grow on for culinary and other magical uses. When flowering, Burnet is at its best vibration and yet its briefest window of opportunity, so be sure to put what cut Burnet flowers might be available in the rooms of those who may be in great need to have the weight of depression lifted up off of them. It may be of help.
• Burnet can be used to counter an unwanted magical effect.
• Burnet can be used to consecrate magical tools with an infusion of rainwater or natural spring water.

No. 438

Sanicula europaea ☠🌿

Sanicle

Astrantia diapensia | *Caucalis capitata* | *Caucalis sanicula* | European Sanicle | Herbe aux Charpentiers | Herbe aux Chênes | Herbe aux Vaches | Herbe de St. Laurent | Poolroot | Sanicle d'Europe | Sanicle | *Sanicula officinalis* | *Sanicula officinarum* | *Sanicula sylvatica* | *Sanicula trilobata* | *Sanicula vulgaris* | Saniculae Herba | Sanicule | Self-Heal | Wood Sanicle

☀ SYMBOLIC MEANING
Own healer.

🌐 POSSIBLE POWERS
Exorcism; Fire element; Healing; Health; Healthy; Horus; Mars; Masculine energy; Water element.

🜋 FOLKLORE AND FACTS
In 1836, John Jacob wrote a passage in his book *West Devon and Cornwall Flora,* taking a few lines to mention that Sanicle was esteemed in Germany as a plant remedy that cured mouth ulcers. To also quote a German proverb that praised the herb: "He who has Sanicle and Self-heal needs neither physician nor surgeon."

No. 439

Santalum album 🌿

Sandalwood

Indian Sandalwood Tree | Sandal | Santal | *Santalum ellipticum* | *Santalum myrtifolium* | *Santalum ovatum* | *Sirium myrtifolium* | White Sandalwood | White Saunders | Yellow Sandalwood

☀ SYMBOLIC MEANING
Deep meditation.

🌐 POSSIBLE POWERS
Business; Caution; Cleverness; Communication; Creativity; Emotions; Exorcism; Faith; Feminine energy; Fertility; Generation; Healing; Illumination; Initiation; Inspiration; Intelligence; Intuition; Learning; Love; Memory; Moon; Protection; Protection against a dog bite; Protection against a ghost; Protection against a snake bite; Protection against drunkenness; Protection against sorcery; Prudence; Psychic ability; Purification; Science; Sea; Self-preservation; Sound judgment; Spirituality; Subconscious mind; Thievery; Tides; Transactions; Travel by water; Water element; Wisdom; Wishing.

S

Wooden beads made of Sandalwood are believed to be protective and facilitate spiritual awareness whenever they are worn. • Sandalwood is a threatened species in the wild. • Sandalwood is one of the most expensive woods in the world. • When you enter a temple, it will most likely smell like Sandalwood. • Sandalwood essential oil used in aromatherapy does much to calm agitations and relieve tension.

No. 440

Santolina chamaecyparissus ☠⚗

Lavender Cotton

Abrotanum foemina | Achillea chamaecyparissus | Cotton Lavender | Santolina | Santolina brevidentata | Santolina cupressiformis | Santolina dentata | Santolina linearifolia | Santolina lobata | Santolina marchii | Santolina pallida | Santolina pecten | Santolina provincialis | Santolina ruscinonensis | Santolina sericea | Santolina tomentosa

❋ SYMBOLIC MEANING
Virtue.

❀ POSSIBLE POWERS
Air element; Fends off insects; Masculine energy; Mercury.

FOLKLORE AND FACTS
The Pennsylvania Amish use dried Lavender Cotton herb where they store their food to fend off infestations of weevils. At the end of summer they will also pull up whole plants and hang them upside-down in their root cellars, which will not only fend off insects, but control odors with its pleasantly strong fragrance. • Lavender Cotton is often dried and used in dried floral arrangements and potpourri. • Make a large sachet filled with dried Lavender Cotton to use as an insect repellent in various areas of the home, to fend off bugs.

No. 441

Saponaria officinalis ☠⚗

Soapwort

Booti vulgaris | Bootia saponaria | Bouncing-Bet | Common Soapwort | Crow Soap | Fuller's Herb | Lychnis officinalis | Lychnis saponaria | Saponaria hybrida | Saponaria nervosa | Saponaria officinarum | Saponaria vulgaris | Săpunele | Silene saponaria | Soapweed | Wild Sweet William

❋ SYMBOLIC MEANINGS
Delicate; Gentleness; Soap.

❀ POSSIBLE POWERS
Cleanliness; Gentleness; Washing.

FOLKLORE AND FACTS
The lather that can be obtained from the Soapwort plant is known to be what was once used to clean extremely delicate textiles.

No. 442

Sassafras albidum ☠⚗

White Sassafras

Gumbo Filé | Laurus albida | Laurus diversifolia | Laurus salsafraz | Laurus sassafras | Laurus variifolia | Persea sassafras | Red Sassafras | Sassafras | Sassafras officinale | Sassafras officinarum | Sassafras rubrum | Sassafras triloba | Silky Sassafras | Tetranthera albida

❋ SYMBOLIC MEANING
Lucky wood.

❀ POSSIBLE POWERS
Fire element; Healing; Health; Jupiter; Masculine energy; Money.

FOLKLORE AND FACTS
Make a White Sassafras sachet of a leaf or a few pinches of filé powder, then carry it in the purse or wallet to attract money. • Cajun cuisine's filé powder is made from the tiny, newly growing leaves of the White Sassafras tree, which are dried and ground into a fine powder. In the 1960s, the US Federal Department of Agriculture determined that White Sassafras leaves contain safrole, which has been determined to be carcinogenic. Thus, White Sassafras was banned from being in foods, which theoretically made filé powder illegal, and yet filé powder is still readily available. Filé powder is also known as gumbo filé, which is a prime ingredient in Louisiana Cajun cuisine's iconic gumbo and filé gumbo dishes. • Filé powder was first devised by the Native

S

American Choctaws, who used it to thicken stews. • White Sassafras essential oil has been banned from use in food or medicines due to its toxicity and carcinogenic outcome.

No. 443
Satureja hortensis 🫕🍴

Summer Savory

Clinopodium hortense | Clinopodium pachyphyllum | Garden Savory | Herbe de St. Julien | Satureja altaica | Satureja brachiata | Satureja filicaulis | Satureja officinarum | Satureja pachyphylla | Satureja viminea | Satureja zuvandica | Thymus cunila

✸ SYMBOLIC MEANING
Interest.

❀ POSSIBLE POWERS
Aphrodisiac; the Arts; Attracts love; Attraction; Beauty; Friendship; Gifts; Harmony; Joy; Love; Love charm; Mental clarity; Mental power; Pleasure; Sensuality; Sex magic; Sexuality; Strength.

✥ FOLKLORE AND FACTS
Carry or wear a sprig of Summer Savory to strengthen your mind's clarity and power. • The peppery nature of Summer Savory has given it an abiding reputation as the herb of love. • The ancient Romans used Summer Savory to make their favorite love potions. • The sensual reputation of Summer Savory was such that monasteries were absolutely forbidden to grow the herb because the monks could fall under its alluring spell and become sexually corrupted by it.

No. 444
Satureja montana 🫕🍴

Winter Savory

Clinopodium montanum | Micromeria montana | Mountain Savory | Saturiastrum montanum | Thymus montanus

✸ SYMBOLIC MEANING
Interest.

❀ POSSIBLE POWERS
Air element; Anti-flatulent; Antiseptic; Diminishes sexual desire; Mercury; Seasoning herb.

✥ FOLKLORE AND FACTS
Winter Savory was used by the ancient Greeks and Romans at least 2,000 years ago. • Winter Savory is occasionally planted with bean plants to fend off bean weevil seed beetles to keep them from damaging the plants. • While Summer Savory is thought to be an aphrodisiac, Winter Savory is thought to have the exact opposite effect on the libido.

No. 445
Scrophularia nodosa ☠🫕

Knotted Figwort

Carpenter's Square | Escrophularia | Figwort | Kernalwort | Rosenoble | Scrophula Plant | Scrophularia capitata | Scrophularia cechica | Scrophularia foetida | Scrophularia halleri | Scrophularia hemschinica | Scrophularia italica | Scrophularia major | Scrophularia sckellii | Scrophularia serrulata | Scrophularia ternata | Scrophularia wirtgenii | Throatwort

✸ SYMBOLIC MEANINGS
Health; Protection.

❀ POSSIBLE POWERS
Feminine energy; Health; Protection; Protection against the evil eye; Venus; Wards off a witch; Water element.

✥ FOLKLORE AND FACTS
Make an amulet using pieces of Knotted Figwort flower, leaf, stem, and root to wear around the neck for strong protection against the evil eye. • Make an amulet using pieces of Knotted Figwort flower, leaf, stem, and root to hang around the neck of a cow to protect it from the evil eye and from malicious witches.

S

No. 446

Scutellaria baicalensis 🐾☠

Baikal Skullcap

Chinese Skullcap | Golden Herb Root | Huang Qin Root | Huángqín |
Skullcap | Scutellaria adamsii | Scutellaria davurica | Scutellaria
lanceolaria | Scutellaria macrantha | Scutellaria speciosa

✴ SYMBOLIC MEANING
Yellow herb.

🌼 POSSIBLE POWERS
Feminine energy; Fidelity; Healing;
Health; Love; Peace; Saturn; Water
element.

✿ FOLKLORE AND FACTS
Another of the fifty fundamental Chinese medicine herbs
used for more than 2,000 years is Baikal Skullcap, *Scutellaria
baicalensis*. • Official study is ongoing into the potential
antibacterial and antiviral applications of *Scutellaria
baicalensis* in medicine for treating colds and bacterial
pneumonia in particular.

No. 447

Scutellaria galericulata 🐾☠

Common Skullcap

American Skullcap | Cassida galericulata | Cassida major |
European Skullcap | Greater Skullcap | Helmet Flower |
Hooded Skullcap | Hooded Willow Herb | Hoodwort | Marsh
Skullcap | Quaker Bonnet | Scutellaria adamsii | Scullcap |
Skullcap | Scutellaria epilobiifolia | Scutellaria pauciflora

✴ SYMBOLIC MEANINGS
Faithfulness; Restoration.

🌼 POSSIBLE POWERS
Assistance; Eases anxiety; Fertility;
Fidelity; Harmony; Independence;
Love; Material gain; Peace; Persistence;
Restorative after assault via magic;
Restorative after spiritual working;
Stability; Strength; Tenacity.

✿ FOLKLORE AND FACTS
When a woman wears or carries a sprig of Common
Skullcap, she believes she is protecting her husband against
the enticing charms of another woman. • Common Skullcap
is useful as a restorative power in recovering from a magical
attack. It is also restorative following any demanding
spiritual working. • A pinch of dried Common Skullcap in a
lover's shoes is believed to stop a search for a different lover.

No. 448

Sedum acre ☠

Stonecrop

Biting Stonecrop | Common Stonecrop | Gold Moss | Golden Stonecrop | Goldmoss |
Goldmoss Sedum | Mossy Stonecrop | Sedum drucei | Sedum erectum | Sedum glaciale |
Sedum krajinae | Sedum neglectum | Sedum procumbens | Sedum wettsteinii |
Stone Crop | Wallpepper

✴ SYMBOLIC MEANING
Sharp.

🌼 POSSIBLE POWERS
Healing; Repels
lightning.

✿ FOLKLORE AND FACTS
Stonecrop is creeping
groundcover that is matted and
tufted with tiny yellow, white,
pink, or red flowers with reddish-
brown stems. It can grow on the
thinnest covering of dry soil, like that
found on dry stone, masonry cracks,
rooftops, and other dry sandy places.
• In some places, Stonecrop was planted on
rooftops because it was believed it had the
power to repel lightning strikes.

S

No. 449
Senegalia senegal ☠️⚗️
Gum Arabic
Acacia cufodontii | Acacia Gum | Acacia oliveri | Acacia oxyosprion | Acacia platyosprion | Acacia pseudoglauca | Acacia pseudoglaucophylla | Acacia rostrata | Acacia rupestris | Acacia senegal | Acacia senegal var. kerensis | Acacia senegal var. rostrata | Acacia senegalensis | Acacia spinosa | Acacia trispinosa | Acacia unispinosa | Acacia verek | Acacia virchowiana | Acacia volkii | Arabic Gum | Cape Gum | Egyptian Thorn | Gum Arabic Tree | Gum Arcacia | Gum Senegal Tree | Hashab Gum | Kikwata | Meska | Mgunga | Mimosa senegal | Mimosa senegalensis | Mkwatia | Mokala | Rfaudraksh | Senegalia oliveri | Senegalia retusa | Senegalia senegal var. kerensis | Senegalia senegal var. rostrata

✳ SYMBOLIC MEANING
Platonic love.

✤ POSSIBLE POWERS
Air element; Astarte; Diana; Ishtar; Masculine energy; Money; Osiris; Platonic love; Protection; Psychic powers; Purification; Purify evil or negativity; Ra; Spiritual enhancement; Spirituality; Sun; Wards off evil.

✣ FOLKLORE AND FACTS
The highest quality of the Gum Arabic resin is from Sudan. • Gum Arabic is used to anoint and consecrate all the accoutrements used in carrying out magical rituals of all types. • The thick, gummy sap is harvested by cutting slashes into a branch, stripping out the bark in the wound, then waiting several weeks for the resinous gum to collect in the gash and harden.
• The term "Gum Arabic" dates back to when it was used in the Middle East, from around the ninth century CE. • Among its many uses, Gum Arabic acts as a binder, thickening agent, stabilizer, or emulsifier in the manufacturing of certain food products, confections, and beverage syrups. • Because it is water soluble, Gum Arabic is a valuable binder used for watercolor paints.

No. 450
Senna alexandrina ☠️⚗️
Alexandrian Senna
American Senna | Cassia acutifolia | Cassia alexandrina | Cassia angustifolia | Cassia lanceolata | Cassia lenitiva | Cassia senna | East Indian Senna | Egyptian Séné de la Palthe | Fan Xia Ye | Fan Xie Ye | Locust Plant | Rajavriksha | Senna | Senna acutifolia | Senna angustifolia | Senna Pot | Senna sophera | Tinnevelly Senna | Wild Senna

✳ SYMBOLIC MEANING
Purging.

✤ POSSIBLE POWERS
Love; Lust; Powerful purge; Purgative.

✣ FOLKLORE AND FACTS
There is a written entry made by two Arabian doctors that dates back to the ninth century in the Middle East noting Alexandrian Senna as being *Cassia senna.* • Make two red sachets filled with Alexandrian Senna. To promote lust in a romantic relationship, carry or wear one of them. Tuck the second under the mattress.
• When Alexandrian Senna was harvested in far-off places such as Nubia and the Sudan, it was first sun-dried then packed to be transported by camel to the nearest port. From there, the herb was further transported by boat, to eventually float along the Nile River to finally reach Alexandria, Egypt. From there, it was sent by various modes of transport to places far beyond.

No. 451
Senna auriculata ☠️⚗️
Tanner's Cassia
Avārai | Avaram | Avaram Senna | Avarike | Awala | Cassia auriculata | Cassia densistipulata | Matura Tea Tree | Ranawara | Tagedu | Tamgēdu | Tangedi | Tarwad | Tarwar

✳ SYMBOLIC MEANING
Transform.

✤ POSSIBLE POWERS
Air element; Healing; Hide tanning; Love; Masculine energy; Mercury.

✣ FOLKLORE AND FACTS
Tanner's Cassia is the state flower of Telangana, India. • Tanner's Cassia is especially attractive when it is in full bloom with yellow flowers, or later when it is full of pea-like green seed pods. • The bark of the Tanner's Cassia is often used for tanning fine-quality sheep and goat hides. • Tanner's cassia has been used in traditional Ayurveda and Sidha medicine in India for thousands of years.

S

No. 452

Serenoa repens 💀🜍

Saw Palmetto

Brahea serrulata | Cani | Chamaerops serrulata | Corypha obliqua | Corypha repens | Guana | Palmetto | Sabal serrulata | Serenoa serrulata | Taalachob | Tala | Talimushi

☀ SYMBOLIC MEANING
Cover over.

❋ POSSIBLE POWERS
Aphrodisiac; Attracts love; Health; Lust; Romance; Sexuality.

☙ FOLKLORE AND FACTS
Saw Palmetto is a creeping palm that will spread to completely cover a field as time goes by. • Evidence of Saw Palmetto fibers have been uncovered in archeological investigations of ancient indigenous camps to determine that there may have been trading between the southern and northern areas of North America long before Europeans were involved. • Traditional Seminole dolls made out of Saw Palmetto fiber are a child's toy and beloved iconic South Florida souvenir. • The Miccosukee and Seminole craftspeople make traditional dance fans and ceremonial rattles from the Saw Palmetto. • Saw Palmetto fronds have been used for thatching the roofs of Seminole chickee huts. • Hand-woven palm-leaf hats that are made from Saw Palmetto fronds make the best sun-shielding hats for protection from the hot sun of South Florida. Consequently, the hats become an iconic souvenir of a tourist's visit.

No. 453

Sesamum indicum 🜍🍴

Sesame

Ajonjoli | Anthadenia sesamoides | Benne | Bonin | Ellu | Gergelim | Gingli | Hoholi | Ilu | Jaljala | Kunjid | Kunzhut | Logowe | Sesamum africanum | Sesamum auriculatum | Sesamum brasiliense | Sesamum edule | Sesamum foetidum | Sesamum hopkinsii | Sesamum luteum | Sesamum malabaricum | Sesamum mulayanum | Sesamum occidentalis | Sesamum oleiferum | Sesamum orientale | Sesamum somalense | Sesamum tavakarii | Sesamum trifoliatum | Sesemt | Shaman shammi | Shamash-Shammu | Shawash-Shammu | Shumshema | Simsim | Strobilanthes gentiliana | Sumsum | Til | Ufuta | Volkameria orientalis | Volkameria sesamoides | Ziele

☀ SYMBOLIC MEANINGS
Purge; Reveal.

❋ POSSIBLE POWERS
Aphrodisiac; Attracts love; Conception; Finds hidden treasure; Fire element; Ganesha; Lust; Masculine energy; Money; Opens a locked door; Protection; Reveals a secret path; Success in business; Sun.

☙ FOLKLORE AND FACTS
Every month, put fresh Sesame seeds in a small jar in the house and leave the lid off of it to draw money to it. • One of the oldest crops in the world that was raised for use as an oil is Sesame. • Sesame can grow in harsh conditions and in very poor soils that cannot support other types of crops. • Sesame seeds are used as a topping for many types of baked goods, including as a primary ingredient in others. • Ground Sesame seeds make the tahini that is a necessary ingredient in the iconic mashed Chickpea spread that is known as hummus.

No. 454

Silene dioica 💀

Catchfly

Agrostemma sylvestre | Campion | Lychnis arvensis | Lychnis dioecia | Lychnis dioica | Lychnis diurna | Lychnis preslii | Lychnis rosea | Lychnis rubra | Lychnis silvestris | Lychnis sylvestris | Lychnis vespertina | Melandrium dioicum | Melandrium diurnum | Melandrium preslii | Melandrium purpureum | Melandrium rubrum | Melandrium stenophyllum | Saponaria dioica | Silene diurna | Silene hornemannii | Silene latifolia | Silene rubra

☀ SYMBOLIC MEANINGS
Betrayed; Caught at last; Gentleness; I fall victim; Night; Only deserve my love; Snare; Youthful love.

❋ POSSIBLE POWERS
Divination; Laundry.

☙ FOLKLORE AND FACTS
A diviner of the Xhosa tribe of South Africa will gather wild Catchfly for use during a full Moon divining ritual. • The pretty little dark-pink to red Catchfly flowers can be found throughout most of the British Isles. • A serviceable laundry soap substitute can be extracted from the roots of the *Silene dioica* plant by simmering the roots in hot water. • On the Isle of Man, picking Catchfly is in violation of a local taboo, believing that it is very bad luck to do so, will vex the fairies and bring down fairy wrath to fall upon them all.

No. 455
Silphium laciniatum

Compass Plant

Carpenter's Weed | Compass Flower | Compassplant | Cup Plant | Cup Rosinweed | Cut-Leaf Silphium | Gum Weed | Indian-Cup | Pilot Weed | Polarplant | Prairie Compass Plant | Rosinweed | *Silphium gummiferum* | *Silphium spicatum* | Squareweed | Turpentine Plant

✹ SYMBOLIC MEANINGS
Align; Contain; Direction; Faith.

✸ POSSIBLE POWERS
Finding north.

☾ FOLKLORE AND FACTS
Amazingly, like a magnet, the tips of the leaves of the living Compass Plant align north to south. New leaf growth will emerge randomly. However, within a few weeks they, too, will be aligned in the same direction as all the other leaves on the plant. • It is said that traveling settlers moving across the Great Plains could determine the direction they were headed by following the leaves. • To avert a strike by lightning during an electrical storm, burn Compass Plant. • Legend tells that God created the Compass Plant to aid travelers. • The presumed earliest possible mention of there being such a thing as a "compass" plant is in a description of a hunting trip in May 1843, when the *Silphium laciniatum* common name appears to be coined by William Clark Kennerly and those in his party.

No. 456
Silybum marianum

Milk Thistle

Blessed Milk Thistle | *Carduus lactifolius* | *Carduus mariae* | *Carduus marianus* | *Carduus versicolor* | *Carthamus maculatus* | *Centaurea dalmatica* | *Cirsium maculatum* | Holy Thistle | *Mariacantha maculosa* | Marian Thistle | *Mariana lactea* | *Mariana mariana* | Mary Thistle | Mediterranean Milk Thistle | Our Lady's Thistle | St. Mary's Milk Thistle | St. Mary's Thistle | *Silybum intermedium* | *Silybum leucanthum* | *Silybum maculatum* | *Silybum mariae* | *Silybum pygmaeum* | Sow Thistle | Variegated Thistle | Wild Artichoke

✹ SYMBOLIC MEANING
Physical love.

✸ POSSIBLE POWERS
Assistance; Fertility; Fire element; Harmony; Independence; Mars; Masculine energy; Material gain; Persistence; Snake enraging; Stability; Strength; Tenacity.

☾ FOLKLORE AND FACTS
The legend for this prickly Milk Thistle plant is that the white veins on the leaves manifested when a drop of the Virgin Mary's milk fell upon the leaves. • There is an old Anglo-Saxon belief that if a man were to wear Milk Thistle around his neck any snakes anywhere within his presence will become enraged and begin to fight. • Milk Thistle was virtually unknown in North America before it was introduced into the gardens of immigrants from England. • Milk Thistle seeds can viably linger in the ground for nine years. It is a constant toxic threat to pasturing sheep and cattle. In Washington, USA, Milk Thistle is a Class A Noxious Weed that is on the list to be persistently eradicated throughout the state. • Milk Thistle has a considerable amount of existing scientific investigation regarding the potential of the mainstream medicinal healing power of its active ingredient, silymarin, which is extracted from the leaves of the *Silybum marianum* plant.

No. 457
Simmondsia chinensis

Jojoba

Brocchia dichotoma | *Buxus californica* | *Buxus chinensis* | *Celastrus obtusatus* | Coffeeberry | Dear Nut | Goat Nut | Gray Fox Bush | Hohowi | Jojoba Bean | Pignut | Quinine Nut | *Simmondsia californica* | *Simmondsia pabulosa* | Wild Hazel

✹ SYMBOLIC MEANING
Soothe.

✸ POSSIBLE POWERS
Cleansing; Conditioning; Healing; Moisturizing; Smoothing; Softening; Soothing.

☾ FOLKLORE AND FACTS
Of all the seed oils, it is believed that the oil extracted from the Jojoba seed is the closest to human sebum that nature can provide. • Jojoba oil is very often used to condition dry hair and dry skin. • Scientific study has determined that Jojoba oil is rare in that it is more similar to whale oil than it is to vegetable oil.

S

No. 458
Sinapis alba

White Mustard
Bonannia officinalis | Brassica alba | Brassica hirta | Crucifera lampsana | Eruca alba | Field Mustard | Leucosinapis alba | Mustard Plant | Napus leucosinapsis | Raphanus alba | Rhamphospermum album | Rorippa coloradensis | Sinapis foliosa | Wild Mustard

✳ **SYMBOLIC MEANINGS**
Charity; Indifference.

🌱 **COMPONENT MEANINGS**
Seed: Good luck charm; Indifference; Visible faith.

🌀 **POSSIBLE POWERS**
Banishes negativity; Ending relationships; Endings; Fertility; Fire element; Mars; Mental clarity or power; Protection.

🜂 **FOLKLORE AND FACTS**
White Mustard is cultivated for its seeds, which provide the mustard element to the yellow mustard recipe that is commonly used as the zingy iconic hotdog and hot soft pretzel condiment in the United States. • White Mustard leaves can be harvested before the plant blooms, to be prepared and cooked as a leafy green vegetable or added to soups.
• Carry White Mustard seed in a red cloth pouch to increase your mental powers. • In northern California, during the White Mustard plant's blooming season, there may be an occasional mustard festival or two to celebrate it.
• Bury White Mustard seeds under or near your doorstep to keep supernatural beings from coming into your home.

No. 459
Sisymbrium officinale ☙

Singer's Plant
Chamaeplium officinale | Crucifera sisymbrium | Erysimum officinale | Erysimum runcinatum | Erysimum vulgare | Hedge Mustard | Hesperis niagarensis | Hesperis officinalis | Hesperis ruderalis | Kibera officinalis | Nasturtium nasturtium | Phryne vulgaris | Sisymbrium niagarense | Sisymbrium officinarum | Valarum officinale | Velarum leiocarpum | Velarum officinale | Velarum tzvelevii

✳ **SYMBOLIC MEANINGS**
Cool; Smooth.

🌀 **POSSIBLE POWERS**
Healing.

🜂 **FOLKLORE AND FACTS**
The ancient Greeks once believed that Singer's Plant was not only a medicine for sore throats but also an antidote for every poison. Alas, it was not quite as healing as that. • In Great Britain and Northern Europe, Singer's Plant is cultivated for its leaves, which are prepared as a leafy green vegetable or added to soups. The mustard seeds are ground into a paste condiment familiar in European markets.

No. 460
Smilax ornata ☠☙

Sarsaparilla
Ba Qiajupicanga | Honduran Sarsaparilla | Jamaican Sarsaparilla | Khao Yen | Liseron Epineux | Salsaparrilha | Salsepareille | Saparna | Sarsa | Smilace | Smilax | Smilax regelii | Smilax utilis | Sweet Sarsaparilla | Zarzaparrilla

✳ **SYMBOLIC MEANINGS**
Loveliness; Lovely; Mythology.

🌀 **POSSIBLE POWERS**
Fire element; Jupiter; Love; Masculine energy; Money.

🜂 **FOLKLORE AND FACTS**
Sarsaparilla is a vintage-style beverage that requires Sarsaparilla as a necessary ingredient. It is also an ingredient in the brewing of the old-fashioned traditional beverage known as root beer.

S

No. 461

Smyrnium olusatrum 🌿🍽

Alexanders

Alisanders | Black Lovage | Black Potherb | Horse Parsley | Pot Herb of Alexandria | *Smyrnium maritimum* | *Smyrnium vulgare*

✴ SYMBOLIC MEANINGS
Manly; Repel; Warrior.

❀ POSSIBLE POWERS
Earth element; Mars; Masculine energy; Protection against the enemy.

❦ FOLKLORE & FACTS
In Alexander the Great's time, Alexanders was a very popular herb that was consumed as a vegetable and used in many different dishes. • Roman soldiers fancied all parts of Alexanders so much that they would carry the plant along with them wherever they traveled.

No. 462

Solidago odora 🌿

Sweet Goldenrod

Anise-scented Goldenrod | Blue Mountain Tea | European Goldenrod | Fragrant Goldenrod | Gizisomukiki | Golden Rod | Goldenrod | Missouri Goldenrod | Sweet-scented Goldenrod

✴ SYMBOLIC MEANINGS
Be cautious; Encouragement; Good fortune; Good luck; Precaution; Strength; Success; Treasure.

❀ POSSIBLE POWERS
Air element; Divination; Feminine energy; Luck; Money; Prosperity; Venus.

❦ FOLKLORE AND FACTS
The flowers and the leaves of Sweet Goldenrod can be brewed into teas. • Witches frequently used Sweet Goldenrod in their potions. • It was believed that if you wear a sprig of Sweet Goldenrod one day, your future love will appear to you on the next day. • It was believed by some that Sweet Goldenrod can be utilized as a simple divining device, citing that if you hold a floral stem in your hand the flowers will nod in the direction of the lost or hidden object, perhaps even toward treasure. • If Sweet Goldenrod suddenly grows near a door at your house in a place where it did not grow before, expect an abundance of good fortune for the entire household. • Sweet Goldenrod is the state herb of Delaware, USA. • Sweet Goldenrod is the state flower of both Kentucky and Nebraska, USA.

No. 463

Sorbus aucuparia ☠🌿

European Rowan

American Mountain Ash | Cascade Mountain Ash | Delight of the Eye | Dwarf Rowan | Esserteau's Rowan | European Mountain Ash | European Rowan | Greene Mountain Ash | Greenland Mountain Ash | Harrow Rowan | Hubei Rowan | Japanese Rowan | Kashmir Rowan | Kite-Leaf Rowan | Ladder Rowan | Madeira Rowan | Moon Tree | Mountain Ash | Quickbane | Quickbeam | Ran Tree | Roden-Quicken | Rowan Tree | Roynetree | Sargent's Rowan | Service Tree | Showy Mountain Ash | Sitka Mountain Ash | Small-Leaf Rowan | Sorb | Sorb Apple | Sorb Tree | Thor's Helper | Tsema Rowan | Vilmorin's Rowan | White-Fruited Rowan | Whitty | Whitty Pear | Wicken-Tree | Wiggin | Wiggy | Wiky | Wild Ash | Witch Bane | Witchbane | Witchen | Witchwood

✴ SYMBOLIC MEANINGS
Balance; Connection; Courage; Harmony; Mystery; Prudence; Transformation; With me you are safe.

❀ POSSIBLE POWERS
Abundance; Communication with the spirit world; Defiance; Determination; Divination; Fends off malicious witchcraft; Fends off malicious fairy magic; Fertility; Fire element; Healing; Inner strength; Intuition; Love; Lucky; Masculine energy; Power; Prosperity; Protection; Psychic power; Resilience; Strength when facing an adversity; Success; Sun; Thor; Visions; Wards off evil or sorcery; Wisdom.

❦ FOLKLORE AND FACTS
The European Rowan is the Celtic tree of life. • To the ancient Celts, the European Rowan tree is believed to be the most powerful of all trees. • European Rowan trees are not true Ash trees. • A European Rowan tree that is growing near a stone circle is the most potent of all. • Carry European Rowan wood to increase your psychic powers. • European Rowan wood is often a preferred choice in the making of a magical wand. • It is believed that European Rowan is sacred to Thor, god of thunder and lightning, and that lightning will only rarely ever strike it. • An effective divining rod can be made using a forked European Rowan branch. • Carry European Rowan berries or bark to help recuperate from an illness. • There is a huge European Rowan tree in Moravia, Czechia, that is estimated to be approximately 418 years old. • In Europe, for hundreds of years, protective crosses have been made from European Rowan twigs that

S

have been tied together with red thread and then carried.
• European Rowan walking sticks help those who do a lot
of walking at night. • Plant European Rowan on a grave to
keep the deceased's ghost from haunting. • European Rowan
branches near a house can often be found pinned to grow
over doorways in order to ward off evil and sorcery from
entering into the dwelling. • The European Rowan is the tree
of the Queen of the Fairies. • The European Rowan is closely
associated with the spirit world, offering its protection when
journeying there. • European Rowan wood is the traditional
wood of choice to use for carving a set of divination runes.
• A magic wand made of European Rowan wood is a
powerful wand for any witch. It is best used for protection
by placing it above a doorway to guard the home from all
evil spirits attempting to enter it. • A European Rowan
wood magic wand can bring about success when used for
divination, healing, and aiding psychic power. • On the
day of the winter solstice and again on the summer solstice,
branches of European Rowan were often placed across the
door and window lintels to bring good fortune to the home.
• A piece of European Rowan wood that is carried around
in a pocket is rumored to be a cure for rheumatism. • Evil
spirits are believed to dread, fear, and shun the fearsome
power of the European Rowan tree. • A European
Rowan tree is reported growing in most of the oldest
Welsh churchyards as a defense against evil spirits. • The
Druids planted circles of European Rowan around their
encampments to offer protection against the dark powers
that threatened all within them. • During the winter solstice,
the sparkly frost on the clustered branches of the European
Rowan tree can sometimes give the illusion of twinkling
stars.

No. 464

Spartium junceum ☠☙

Spanish Broom

Cytisus junceus | Genista acutifolia | Genista
americana | Genista hispanica | Genista
juncea | Genista odorata | Genista
odoratissima | Ginesta |
Retamo | Retamo de Olor |
Rush Broom | Spartianthus
americanus | Spartianthus
junceus | Spartium acutifolium |
Spartium americanum | Spartium
japonicum | Spartium odoratissimum | Spartium odoratum | Weaver's Broom

❀ SYMBOLIC MEANING
Cleanliness.

✿ POSSIBLE POWERS
Air element; Healing; Mars; Masculine energy.

❦ FOLKLORE AND FACTS
Since ancient times, a stiff tool has been needed to brush
ash out from a fireplace, as well as being able to move debris
and dust across a bare floor then out into an entranceway.
Dried Spanish Broom plants have been used for the creation
of such a useful tool as is the broom. • Spanish Broom fibers
have been used to make cloth. • Spanish Broom can produce
a yellow dye for fabric.

No. 465

Spinacia oleracea ☙

Spinach

Acelga | Bayam | Bo Cai | Buai Leng | Chenopodium oleraceum | Chhurika | Chieftain of Leafy
Greens | Common Spinach | Epinard | Espinaca | Espinada | Espinafre | Goli Spinat | Horenso |
Houreson | Isfanahk | Ispanahk | Ispanak | Ispany | Paalak | Palak | Palang | Palong Sak |
Paraj | Pasala | Pinaatti | Pinni | Raïs Al-Buqūl | Rau Chan Vit | Sabanekh |
Shi Geum Chi | Shi Gum Chi | Sigmchi | Spanaki | Spenat | Spinacia
domestica | Spinacia glabra | Spinacia inermis | Spinacia oleracea |
Spinacia sessiliflora | Spinacia spinosa | Spinat | Spinazie |
Tered | Tered Hagina

❀ SYMBOLIC MEANINGS
Power; Strength.

S

POSSIBLE POWERS
Earth element; Jupiter; Powerfulness.

FOLKLORE AND FACTS
Spinach is high up on the list of plants that are edible and consumed either fresh, frozen, or canned as a leafy green vegetable. • The nautical cartoon character introduced in 1932 known as Popeye the Sailor Man, claimed Spinach as responsible for his strength. • Spinach was referenced in three different writings dating from the tenth century CE. • Dreaming about Spinach could mean a subconscious feeling of repression due to a sense of dread at being forced to do something that would be good to do, against your will.

No. 466

Spiraea ulmaria 🌿

Meadowsweet

Bridewort | Dollof | *Filipendula denudata* | *Filipendula megalocarpa* | *Filipendula subdenudata* | Lady of the Meadow | Meadow Queen | Meadow Sweet | Meadow-Wort | Meadowt | Pride of the Meadow | Queen of the Meadow | *Spiraea contorta* | *Spiraea denudata* | *Spiraea glauca* | *Spiraea obtusiloba* | *Spiraea odorata* | *Spiraea palustris* | *Spiraea ulmarioides* | *Spiraea unguiculata* | Ulmaria | *Ulmaria denudata* | *Ulmaria glauca* | *Ulmaria obtusiloba* | *Ulmaria palustris* | *Ulmaria pentapetala* | *Ulmaria spiraea-ulmaria* | *Ulmaria variegat* | *Ulmaria vulgaris*

SYMBOLIC MEANINGS
Usefulness; Uselessness.

POSSIBLE POWERS
Air element; Divination; Happiness; Jupiter; Love; Masculine energy; Peace.

FOLKLORE AND FACTS
Meadowsweet is edible and used to flavor wines, beers, and vinegars. It is also added to jams to season them with a hint of an Almond-like flavor. • Meadowsweet was the preferred floor-strewing herb of Queen Elizabeth I of England. • Dried Meadowsweet flowers can be added to potpourri blends. • A black vegetable dye can be created from Meadowsweet roots. • In Wales, there was found archeological evidence of Meadowsweet along with cremated remains that date back to the Bronze Age.

No. 467

Stachys sylvatica ☠🌿

Hedge Woundwort

Hedge Nettle | *Stachys canariensis* | *Stachys cordata* | *Stachys cordatifolia* | *Stachys foetida* | *Stachys glaucescens* | *Stachys trapezuntea* | Whitespot | Woundwort

SYMBOLIC MEANINGS
Love; Surprise.

POSSIBLE POWERS
Colorize; Guard against harm; Healing of body and soul; Love; Protection; Protection against witchcraft and sorcery; Purification; Wards off an evil spirit or evil magic.

FOLKLORE AND FACTS
When the leaves of the Hedge Woundwort are crushed, the fragrance is extremely unpleasant. • Since the seventeenth century CE, Hedge Woundwort has been used to heal wounds. • Hedge Woundwort is a favorite food of foraging honeybees. • Hedge Woundwort can be used to produce a yellow vegetable dye for fabric.

S

No. 468

Stellaria media 🐝☠

Chickweed

Alsine apetala | Alsine avicularum | Alsine barbata | Alsine bipartita | Alsine brachypetala | Alsine elongata | Alsine gussonii | Alsine media | Alsine repens | Alsine vulgaris | American Starwort | Arenaria vulgaris | Holosteum alsine | Starwort | Stellaria alpicola | Stellaria alsinoides | Stellaria bertolae | Stellaria caroliniana | Stellaria cerastium | Stellaria chlorotica | Stellaria cucubaloides | Stellaria decandra | Stellaria dichotoma | Stellaria duthiei | Stellaria elisabethiae | Stellaria glabella | Stellaria glabra | Stellaria grandiflora | Stellaria hiemalis | Stellaria latifolia | Stellaria latisepala | Stellaria modesta | Stellaria monogyna | Stellaria murmuria | Stellaria oligandra | Stellaria pilosa | Stellaria umbrosa | Stellaria vernalis | Stellaria vulgaris | Stellaria xanthanthera | Stellularia media | Stitchwort

✴ SYMBOLIC MEANINGS
Cheerfulness in old age; Welcome to a stranger.

✸ POSSIBLE POWERS
Encourage good to enter; Feminine energy; Moon; Protection; Protection against ghosts or witches; Repels a hex; Repels evil; Water element.

✥ FOLKLORE AND FACTS
The small Chickweed flowers are white and star-shaped. • It appears to be that all the Pennsylvania Dutch hex symbols that look like flowers are, in fact, stylized Chickweed blossoms. • Prior to the steady emigration from England, Chickweed was virtually unknown in North America until it was introduced into the newly planted English gardens in the New World.

No. 469

Stevia rebaudiana ☠

Stevia

Candyleaf | Eupatorium rebaudianum | Ka'a He'ê | Sugarleaf | Sweetleaf

✴ SYMBOLIC MEANINGS
Sweet herb; Sweet leaf; Sweet treat.

✸ POSSIBLE POWERS
Sweeten.

✥ FOLKLORE AND FACTS
The Guaraní people of South America used Stevia 1,500 years ago. The extremely sweet leaves of the Stevia plant have been used for the purpose of sweetening tea in Brazil and Paraguay for hundreds of years. • Starting in Japan in the early seventies, awareness of Stevia as a natural alternative sweetener to Cane Sugar steadily increased until it was readily available around the world.

No. 470

Stillingia sylvatica 🐝☠

Queen's Delight

Excoecaria sylvatica | Queen's Root | Sapium sylvaticum | Stillingia angustifolia | Stillingia lanceolata | Stillingia salicifolia | Stillingia smallii | Stillingia spathulata | Stillingia sylvatica var. angustifolia | Stillingia sylvatica var. genuina | Stillingia sylvatica var. salicifolia | Stillingia sylvatica var. spathulata | Stillingia sylvatica subsp. tenuis | Stillingia tenuis | Stillingia treculeana | Yaw Root

✴ SYMBOLIC MEANINGS
Find; Locate.

✸ POSSIBLE POWERS
Locate lost things; Psychic power.

✥ FOLKLORE AND FACTS
Follow the smoke from burning Queen's Delight to find something that was lost. • Make a sachet of Queen's Delight to wear when needing to tap into one's own psychic ability. • Contrary to some belief, according to the Sloan Kettering Institute, which is a top cancer treatment facility in the USA, there is no supporting evidence that Stillingia sylvatica is a viable treatment for cancer. Nor is the herb a viable treatment for infections or other medical conditions. Even so, as in the past, alternative healers have used and are using this herb for medicinal purposes.

No. 471

Styphnolobium japonicum 🐝☠

Pagoda Tree

Anagyris chinensis | Anagyris foetida | Anagyris sinensis | Chinese Scholar Tree | Japanese Pagoda Tree | Macrotropis foetida | Ormosia esquirolii | Pongamia chinensis | Radiusia chinensis | Robinia mitis | Sophora angustifoliola | Sophora japonica | Sophora korolkowii | Sophora mairei | Sophora pendula | Sophora pubescens | Sophora sinica | Sophora vaniotii | Sophora vestita | Zuihuai

✴ SYMBOLIC MEANING
Scholarly.

✸ POSSIBLE POWERS
Education; Health; Studiousness.

✥ FOLKLORE AND FACTS
The flowers and leaves of the Pagoda Tree are one of the fifty essential herbs used in traditional Chinese medicine. • Since Emperor Chongzhen, who was the last emperor of the Chinese Ming dynasty, hanged himself from a Beijing Pagoda Tree in 1644, the tree became known as the Guilty Chinese Scholar Tree. The tree itself is now a Chinese national landmark and tourist attraction in Jingshan Park. It has been replaced many times since its day of infamy. And

S

yet, the current Pagoda Tree is already 150 years old. • Well known as one of the original Old Lions, a Pagoda Tree that is still standing was planted in Kew Gardens in 1762 and was the first of its species in England. • The name "pagoda" tree might have been originally inspired because they were often planted around Buddhist temples. • A yellow and a gray vegetable dye can be made from the bark and leaves of the Pagoda Tree.

No. 472

Styrax benzoin ☠☕

Gum Benjamin Tree

Ben | Benzoin officinale | Benzoina vera | Cyrta dealbata | Gum Benjamin | Gum Benzoin | Kemenyan | Loban | Onycha | Plagiospermum benzoin | Siam Benzoin | Siamese Benzoin | Styrax benjuifer | Styrax dealbatus

✻ SYMBOLIC MEANINGS
Good luck; Protection.

❀ POSSIBLE POWERS
Abundance; Advancement; Aphrodisiac; Astral travel; Attracts love; Binding; Building; Business transactions; Calming anger; Caution; Cleverness; Communication; Conscious will; Creativity; Death; Energy; Enhances concentration; Faith; Friendship; Growth; Healing; History; Illumination; Initiation; Intelligence; Joy; Knowledge; Leadership; Learning; Life; Light; Limitations; Manifestation of spirits; Memory; Natural power; Obstacles; Promotes generosity; Prosperity; Protects the flying spirit during astral travel; Provides focus; Prudence; Purification; Relaxing irritability and stress; Relief from depression; Relief from resentment; Relieves sexual fears; Science; Self-preservation; Shape-shifting; Sound judgment; Success; Thievery; Time; Travel; Wisdom.

☙ FOLKLORE AND FACTS
The combined scents of Benzoin, Cinnamon, and Basil could attract customers to a place of business. • Styrax benzoin is cultivated in parts of Asia for its resin, which is also known as sambrami, loban, or benzoin resin. It is collected after piercing the bark to allow the sap to accumulate. • The Gum Benjamin benzoin resin is used in some cosmetics as well as being a stabilizing fixative in perfumery. It is also a vital ingredient in incense that is commonly burned in Asia. • Benzoin resin was used in the ancient Egyptian mummification process. • Benzoin essential oil is helpful in aromatherapy in lifting depression and helping with relaxation.

No. 473

Succisa pratensis ☠☕

Devil's Bit

Asterocephalus succisa | Asterocephalus tomentosus | Devil's Bit Scabious | Djævelsbid | Lepicephalus succisa | Ofbit | Scabiosa borealis | Scabiosa glabrata | Scabiosa hirsuta | Scabiosa praemorsa | Scabiosa prolifera | Scabiosa succisa | Scabiosa succisa var. arenaria | Scabiosa succisa var. grandifolia | Scabiosa succisa var. ovalis | Stúfa | Succisa altissima | Succisa angustula | Succisa aurigerana | Succisa beugesiaca | Succisa brevisv | Succisa cagiriensis | Succisa cuspidata | Succisa dentata | Succisa elliptica | Succisa fuchsii | Succisa fuscescens | Succisa gigantea | Succisa glabrata | Succisa gracilescens | Succisa incisa | Succisa laetevirens | Succisa microcephala | Succisa palustris | Succisa parvula | Succisa platyphylla | Succisa praemorsa | Succisa pratensis subsp. hirsuta | Succisa pratensis subsp. scotiaca | Succisa pratensis var. arenaria | Succisa pratensis var. grandifolia | Succisa pratensis var. ovalis | Succisa pratensis var. subacaulis | Succisa prativaga | Succisa procera | Succisa propera | Succisa pyrenaica | Succisa rhodanensis | Succisa sabauda | Succisa stricta | Succisa subacaulis | Succisa sylvatica | Succisa tardans | Succisa viretorum | Succisa vogesiaca | Succisa vulgaris | Succise des Prés | Teuflassabbiss

✻ SYMBOLIC MEANING
Scratch my itch.

❀ POSSIBLE POWERS
Exorcism; Love; Luck; Mars; Masculine energy; Moon; Protection; Venus; Water element.

☙ FOLKLORE AND FACTS
Butterflies and bees feed on Devil's Bit flowers in hedgerows all over Europe. • The plant can produce a green vegetable dye that was used to color the wool used for some tartans. In folk tales, the short black roots of the Devil's Bit plant are the result of the Devil biting off the roots in anger after hearing a rumor that the plant may have had curative powers against the bubonic plague. • Devil's Bit was once used as a folk remedy to treat a body infestation of the Sarcoptes scabiei itch mite. • Roll up an intact stem of Devil's Bit that includes the flower and two leaves, then gently tuck into a white cotton pouch to make an amulet that intends to help your spirit recover from a violent trauma. In ink, in your best handwriting on no more than one sheet of good paper, write a brief explanation of what you endured and how you intend to expel that lingering energy from your psyche with the help of the amulet's protective energy. Fold the paper small, kiss it goodbye, then tuck it into the pouch before closing it. Hang that pouch amulet over the head of your bed. Leave it there until the anxiety of the experience dissipates to a tolerable degree, which can occur if you allow it to.

S

No. 474
Symphytum officinale ☠⚱
Comfrey

Assear | Black Wort | Bruisewort | Comphrey | Consohada | *Consolida major* | Consound | Cultivated Comfrey | Gavez | Gum Plant | Healing Herb | Karakaffes | Knit Back | Knit Bone | Knitbone | Miracle Herb | Quaker Comfrey | Slippery Root | Slipperyroot | Smeerwartel | *Symphytum album* | *Symphytum ambiguum* | *Symphytum besseri* | *Symphytum bohemicum* | *Symphytum coccineum* | *Symphytum commune* | *Symphytum consolida* | *Symphytum elatum* | *Symphytum majus* | *Symphytum microcalyx* | *Symphytum molle* | *Symphytum patens* | *Symphytum peregrinum* | *Symphytum rakosiense* | *Symphytum stenophyllum* | True Comfrey | Wallwort | Yalluc | Ztworkost

✽ SYMBOLIC MEANINGS
Protection; Restoration; Safety.

🌸 POSSIBLE POWERS
Ensures safety during travel; Feminine energy; Healing; Heals broken bones; Money; Restoration of virginity; Saturn; Water element.

🜂 FOLKLORE AND FACTS
Comfrey worn or tucked into a pocket will provide safe travel. • A piece of Comfrey root in each suitcase will protect luggage while traveling. • Due to its toxicity, several countries have declared Comfrey enough of an unsafe herb to either restrict its use or ban it entirely. • Prior to the steady emigration from England, Comfrey was virtually unknown in North America until it was introduced into the newly planted English gardens in the New World.

No. 475
Symplocarpus foetidus ☠⚱
Skunk Cabbage

Clumpfoot Cabbage | *Dracontium foetidum* | Eastern Skunk Cabbage | Foetid Pothos | *Ictodes foetidus* | Meadow Cabbage | Pole Cat Weed | Polecat Weed | *Pothos foetidus* | *Pothos putorii* | Skunk Cabbage | Skunk Weed | *Spathyema angusta* | *Spathyema foetida* | *Spathyema lanceolata* | *Spathyema latifolia* | Suntull | Swamp Cabbage

✽ SYMBOLIC MEANINGS
Good luck; Move forward; Proceed forward.

🌸 POSSIBLE POWERS
Feminine energy; Fertility; Good fortune; Legal matters; Saturn; Water element.

🜂 FOLKLORE AND FACTS
The Iroquois Native Americans would pass a bouquet of Skunk Cabbage over a woman's pelvis to wish fertility with conception upon her.

No. 476
Syringa vulgaris ⚱
Lilac

Common Lilac | Field Lilac | French Lilac | *Lilac caerulea* | *Lilac cordatifolia* | *Lilac suaveolens* | *Lilac vulgaris* | Lilak | *Liliacum album* | *Liliacum vulgare* | Nila | Nilak | Paschalia | *Syringa alba* | *Syringa albiflora* | *Syringa amoena* | *Syringa bicolor* | *Syringa carlsruhensis* | *Syringa cordifolia* | *Syringa latifolia* | *Syringa nigricans* | *Syringa philemon* | *Syringa rhodopea* | *Syringa versaliensis* | *Syringa virginalis*

✽ SYMBOLIC MEANINGS
Disappointment; Do you still love me? First emotion of love; Fraternal love or sympathy; Humility; Love; Love's first emotions; Memory; Remember me; Reminder of young love; Youthful innocence.

S

COLOR MEANINGS

Pink: Acceptance; Youth.
Purple: First emotions of love; First love; Infatuation; Obsession.
White: Candor; Children; First dream of love; Youth; Youthful innocence; Youthful looks.

POSSIBLE POWERS

Exorcism; Feminine energy; Protection; Purification; Venus; Water element.

FOLKLORE AND FACTS

Plant or strew Lilac flowers where you wish to drive away evil. • In New England, Lilac bushes were originally planted to fend evil from properties. • Fresh Lilac flowers can help clear out a haunted house of ghosts and haunting energies. • The Lilac is the state bush of New York, USA. Lilac wood is feminine and ruled by Venus, so it is associated with love, beauty, balance, and harmony in all things. • A well-charged Lilac wood magic wand will do a fine job of driving away evil and unwanted lurking ghosts from a home.

No. 477

Syzygium aromaticum 🌿🍴

Clove

Bol del Dlavo | Carenfil | *Caryophyllus aromaticus* | *Caryophyllus hortensis* | *Caryophyllus silvestris* | Cengkeh | Cengkih | Clavo de Olor | Clou de Girofle | Cravo da India | Cravo das Molucas | Cravo de Doce | Dlavero Giroflé | *Eugenia aromatica* | *Eugenia caryophyllata* | *Eugenia caryophyllus* | Gewürznelkenbaum | Giroflier | Grampoo | *Jambosa caryophyllus* | *Karabu Nati* | Kirambu | Kruidnagel | Laong | Laung | Lavang | Lavanga | Lavangam | Lawang | Mykhet | *Myrtus caryophyllus*

SYMBOLIC MEANINGS

Dignity; Lasting friendship; Love; Money; Restraint.

POSSIBLE POWERS

Aphrodisiac; Abundance; Advancement; Conscious will; Energy; Exorcism; Fire element; Friendship; Growth; Healing; Joy; Jupiter; Leadership; Life; Light; Love; Masculine energy; Mental clarity; Money; Natural power; Protection; Purification; Success.

FOLKLORE AND FACTS

A Clove is the dried flower bud of the *Syzygium aromaticum* tree. It is used as a fragrant spice that is a favorite in cooking with meats and fruits as well as in baking. • Worn or carried tucked in a pocket, the magical properties and fragrance of a whole Clove will attract the opposite sex. • Worn as an amulet or carried in a pocket, the whole Clove will comfort someone who suffered an emotional loss and is bereaved. • If Clove is burned as an incense, it will stop people gossiping, attract riches, drive away hostility, turn away negative energies, and produce positive spiritual energy, all while it is also purifying wherever the fragrance goes. • The seventeenth century CE trade wars between European nations and the Maluku Islands of Indonesia precipitated the planting of Clove trees wherever in the world they would grow. • Clove essential oil mixed in a spray bottle of distilled water can make a good cleaner for the home when there is illness. • A time-honored home remedy found in the spice cabinet is a whole Clove to chew on to offer some relief from the pain of a toothache. • An easily successful herbal craft project is to make an old-fashioned pomander ball for a bowl by decoratively embellishing an unblemished, firm Orange by poking it all over with dried Clove buds. • During the winter holiday celebrations, the aromatherapy of the warm spicy fragrance of essential Clove oil can bring the nature of the holidays into the home.

No. 478

Tagetes patula ☠☗

French Marigold

Dao Ruang Lek | French Marygold | Garden Marigold | Marigold | Marygold | Rainy Marigold | Tagetes corymbosa | Tagetes lunulata | Tagetes remotiflora | Tagetes signata | Tagetes tenuifolia

✹ SYMBOLIC MEANINGS
Creativity; Grief; Jealousy; Passion; Spreading; Storm; Uneasiness.

✹ POSSIBLE POWERS
Amorousness; Colorize; Dream magic; Evil thoughts; Fire element; Helps with seeing fairies; Legal matters; Love charms; Masculine energy; Prediction; Prophetic dreams; Protection; Psychic power; Rebirth; Sleep; Sun; Tages.

✹ FOLKLORE AND FACTS
Early Christians would offer French Marigold blossoms around statues of the Virgin Mary instead of coins. • The Welsh believed that French Marigold could be used to predict stormy weather if the flowers did not open in the morning. • French

Marigold essential oil is often used as an insect repellent, most especially against bedbugs. • French Marigold is occasionally added to the feed of home-farmed chickens to intensify the color of the yolks and to cast a yellow tint to the chicken skin. • Make, then wear or carry a sachet of French Marigold petals with a Bay Laurel leaf to quiet gossip being passed around about you. • In the Republic of Georgia's cuisine, dried powdered French Marigold petals are used as a favorite seasoning, as well as being included in a seasoning blend known as khmeli suneli. • French Marigold flower heads follow the sun like Sunflowers do. • French Marigold is considered to be one of the most sacred herbs of India, with the flower heads being commonly strung into garlands and used in temples and at weddings.

No. 479

Tanacetum annuum ☠☗

Blue Tansy

Balsamita annua | Balsamita multifida | Psanacetum annuum | Vogtia annua

✹ SYMBOLIC MEANINGS
To soothe.

✹ POSSIBLE POWERS
Expansiveness; Protective; Speaking one's own truth; Unconditional love; Uplifting.

✹ FOLKLORE AND FACTS
To enliven one's life, make, then carry or wear a sachet of Blue Tansy to lift the mood and the personality to help "get back into the swing of things." • *Tanacetum vulgare* is not the same as thujone-free Blue Tansy, which is *Tanacetum annuum*. • Blue Tansy essential oil is useful in aromatherapy for clearing and calming.

No. 480

Tanacetum balsamita ☗🌿

Costmary

Alecost | Balsam Herb | Balsamita balsamita | Balsamita major | Balsamita suaveolens | Balsamita vulgaris | Bible Leaf | Chamaemelum balsamita | Chrysanthemum apetalum | Chrysanthemum balsamita | Chrysanthemum majus | Leucanthemum balsamita | Matricaria apetala | Matricaria balsamita | Mint Geranium | Patagonian Mint | Pyrethrum balsamita | Pyrethrum majus | Pyrethrum tanacetum | Tanacetum balsamitum | Tanacetum ovatifolium | Tanacetum simplicifolium

✹ SYMBOLIC MEANINGS
Gentility; Virtue.

✹ POSSIBLE POWERS
Holy reference; Peace in the home; Protection at sea.

✹ FOLKLORE AND FACTS
A sprig of Costmary was used in medieval times as a place marker in Bibles. • Carry or wear a Costmary amulet if traveling by sea.

No. 481

Tanacetum cinerariifolium

Pyrethrum Daisy

Chrysanthemum cinerariifolium | *Chrysanthemum rigidum* | *Chrysanthemum turreanum* | Dalmatian Daisy | Dalmatian Pellitory | *Pyrethrum cinerariifolium* | *Pyrethrum elongatum* | *Pyrethrum turreyanum* | *Pyrethrum willemotii*

SYMBOLIC MEANINGS

Fire element.

POSSIBLE POWERS

Insecticide.

FOLKLORE AND FACTS

For centuries, the crushed flowers of the Pyrethrum Daisy were used as a powerful, effective insecticide that is still an active ingredient in many flea, tick, and lice remedies.

No. 482

Tanacetum parthenium

Feverfew

Altamisa | Altamiza | Amargosa | Bachelor's Button | Bride's Button | *Chamaemelum parthenium* | *Chrysanthemum parthenium* | *Chrysanthemum praealtum* | Featherfew | Featherfoil | Febrifuge Plant | Flirtwort | *Leucanthemum parthenium* | Manzanilla | *Matricaria eximia* | *Matricaria latifolia* | *Matricaria partheniifolia* | *Matricaria praealta* | *Matricaria vulgaris* | Mum | Mutterkraut | *Pontia matricaria* | *Pyrethrum buschianum* | *Pyrethrum divaricatum* | *Pyrethrum fruticosum* | *Pyrethrum grossheimii* | *Pyrethrum latilobum* | *Pyrethrum parthenium* | *Pyrethrum praealtum* | *Pyrethrum sevanense* | *Tanacetum glanduliferum* | *Tanacetum kubense* | *Tanacetum persicum* | *Tanacetum sevanense* | Wild Chamomile

SYMBOLIC MEANINGS

Good health.

POSSIBLE POWERS

Masculine energy; Protection; Venus; Water element.

FOLKLORE AND FACTS

It is believed by some that bees do not like the scent of Feverfew, so one might choose to carry a sachet of Feverfew flowers to fend off bees. • Feverfew is good at keeping insects away from plants, so it is often planted around gardens for pest control. • A woman can attract a man by wearing a Feverfew flower. • Carry a sprig of Feverfew for protection against fevers and accidents.

No. 483

Taraxacum officinale

Dandelion

Blowball | Cankerwort | Canker-Wort | Chicoria | *Chondrilla taraxacum* | Common Dandelion | Dandelion | Dent de Lion | Diente de León | Faceclock | Irish Daisy | Lechuguilla | *Leontodon taraxacum* | *Leontodon vulgaris* | Lion's Tooth | Milk-Witch | Monk's Head | Pee-a-Bed | Piss-a-Bed | Priest's Crown | Puffball | Puff-Ball | Swine Snout | Swine's Snout | *Taraxacum dens-leonis* | *Taraxacum taraxacum* | *Taraxacum vulgare* | Tharakhchakon | Wet-a-Bed | White Endive | Wild Endive | Yellow Gowan

SYMBOLIC MEANINGS

Coquetry; Faithfulness; Happiness; Oracle; Prosperity; Wishing; Wishing for love.

POSSIBLE POWERS

Air element; Calling spirits; Depart; Divination; Hecate; Jupiter; Love's oracle; Masculine energy; Moon; Oracle; Purification; Rustic oracle; Spirit magic; Water element; Wish magic; Wishes come true; Wishing.

FOLKLORE AND FACTS

Bury a Dandelion seed ball in the northwest corner of your house to bring desirable winds. • A curious divination is that, if you blow the seeds off a Dandelion seed ball, you will supposedly live for as many years as there are seeds that remain on the stem head. Also, for every Dandelion ball that you blow the seeds off, you will be granted a wish. • To send a message to your loved one, visualize the message then blow on the Dandelion seed ball in his or her direction. • Fossilized Dandelion from the Pliocene Epoch has been found in Southern Russia. • Dandelion seed was brought on the Mayflower to North America. Prior to the steady emigration from England, Dandelion was virtually unknown in North America until it was introduced into the newly planted English gardens in the New World. • Dandelion has been used in Chinese medicine for more than 1,000 years. • Dandelion pollen provides the first food for bees in the spring. • The entire Dandelion *Taraxacum officinale* plant is edible, as it has been since prehistoric gatherers included it in their foraging. It is still enjoyed by many people who recognize its sustainability and relative availability for use as a versatile leafy green. • The natural latex that a Dandelion excretes has many of the same properties as that which is obtained from a Rubber Tree. In that respect, there has been a great deal of interest in the different ways the Dandelion sap can be developed. • A natural vegetable dye can be produced using the blossoms to produce a yellow color. • The New York State University of Rochester's official flower is the

Dandelion, with one of their official school colors and the title of their school song being The Dandelion Yellow. • There is an annual Dandelion Festival in White Sulphur Springs, West Virginia, USA, where the city emblem is five Dandelions.

No. 484
Teucrium scorodonia 🌿

Woodland Germander

Ambroise | Ambrose | Garlic Sage | Hind Heal | Large-Leaved Germander | *Monochilon cordifolius* | Sage-leaved Germander | *Scorodonia heteromalla* | *Scorodonia solitaria* | *Scorodonia sylvestris* | *Scorodonia trivialis* | *Teucrium salviifolium* | *Teucrium sylvestre* | Wood Sage

✹ SYMBOLIC MEANINGS
Faithfulness.

✹ POSSIBLE POWERS
Protection against offensive magic; Snake repellent.

✹ FOLKLORE AND FACTS
Bitter-flavored Woodland Germander was once, and occasionally still is, used in the making of beer as a substitute for Hops. • During the Middle Ages, Woodland Germander was used as a strewing herb, believed to be able to keep snakes from entering the house.

No. 485
Thalictrum flavum ☠🏺

Common Meadow-Rue

Thalictrum altissimum | *Thalictrum anonymum* | *Thalictrum belgicum* | *Thalictrum capitatum* | *Thalictrum commutatum* | *Thalictrum controversum* | *Thalictrum exaltatum* | *Thalictrum flaccidum* | *Thalictrum flavum var. euskarum* | *Thalictrum friesii* | *Thalictrum glaucovirens* | *Thalictrum glomerulosum* | *Thalictrum gracile* | *Thalictrum heterophyllum* | *Thalictrum hybridum* | *Thalictrum latifolium* | *Thalictrum linnaeanum* | *Thalictrum nigricans* | *Thalictrum nutans* | *Thalictrum obtusatum* | *Thalictrum pauperculatum* | *Thalictrum porrectum* | *Thalictrum princeps* | *Thalictrum prorepens* | *Thalictrum pseudoflavum* | *Thalictrum purpurascens var. rugosum* | *Thalictrum riparium* | *Thalictrum rufinerve* | *Thalictrum rugosum* | *Thalictrum sphaerocarpum* | *Thalictrum udum* | *Thalictrum vaginatum* | *Thalictrum wallrothianum* | Yellow Meadow-Rue

✹ SYMBOLIC MEANINGS
Flourish.

✹ POSSIBLE POWERS
Colorize; Divination; Love.

✹ FOLKLORE AND FACTS
Common Meadow-Rue can make a yellow dye for fabric. • At one time, Common Meadow-Rue was used for medicinal and ceremonial purposes by the Native American Navajo tribe.

No. 486
Theobroma cacao ☠🏺

Cacao

Cacahuatl | Cacao | *Cacao minus* | *Cacao sativa* | *Cacao theobroma* | Cocoa | Cocoa Tree | Kakaw | Food of the Gods | *Theobroma caribaeum* | *Theobroma integerrimum* | *Theobroma kalaguum* | *Theobroma leiocarpum* | *Theobroma pentagonum* | *Theobroma salzmannianum* | *Theobroma sapidum* | *Theobroma sativum* | *Theobroma sphaerocarpum*

✹ SYMBOLIC MEANINGS
Food of the gods; Love; Sensual.

✹ POSSIBLE POWERS
Aphrodisiac; the Arts; Attracts love; Attraction; Awakens creativity; Awakens the inner self; Beauty; Clarifies thoughts; Develops creativity; Enhances energy; Friendship; Gifts; Harmony; Healing; Healthy; Joy; Love; Meditation; Opening the heart; Peace; Peacefulness; Pleasures; Sensuality; Vibrancy; Wisdom.

✹ FOLKLORE AND FACTS
In some areas of Mexico, such as the Yucatan, Cacao beans were used as currency until as recently as the late 1800s. • The discovery that there was something inside of the Cacao pod that was edible on the Cacao tree was made over 2,000 years ago by indigenous people, who lived deep in the tropical rainforests in Central America. God bless them for their curiosity. • Processing a Cacao bean is a lot more involved than most people realize, requiring multiple consecutive steps, among which include fermentation, roasting, and grinding. • The fatty cocoa butter is extracted and favored for use in cosmetics. Long before there was an effort to transform the Cacao in what is known and loved as "chocolate", Cacao beans were used in religious, cultural, and magical ancient Maya and Aztec ceremonial rituals. • According to mythology, it was the Maya deity the Plumed Serpent who gave Cacao to the Maya.

T

No. 487

Thymus serpyllum 🍶

Creeping Thyme

Breckland Thyme | Breckland Wild Thyme | Elfin Thyme | Mother of Thyme | Mother of Time | *Origanum serpyllum* | *Serpyllum vulgare* | *Thymus campestris* | Wild Creeping Thyme | Wild Thyme

✹ SYMBOLIC MEANINGS

Action; Activity; Affection; Bravery; Courage; Daring; Death; Elegance; Energy; Ensures restful sleep; Happiness; Swift movement; Thriftiness.

❀ POSSIBLE POWERS

Ability to see fairies; Aphrodisiac; the Arts; Attracts love; Attraction; Beauty; Courage; Friendship; Gifts; Harmony; Healing; Health; Irresistibility; Joy; Love; Pleasure; Psychic power; Purification; Sensuality; Sleep; Venus; Water element.

☘ FOLKLORE AND FACTS

Dense, low-mounding Creeping Thyme plants are not much higher than three inches. Their random sprawl can be quite impressive when thickly covered over with lavender flowers when the herb is in full bloom. • Make, then carry or wear a sachet of Creeping Thyme with the intention of seeing a fairy. • Make, then carry or wear a sachet of Creeping Thyme to enhance psychic power. • Make, then carry or wear a red sachet of creeping thyme to attract sensual love.

No. 488

Thymus vulgaris 🍶🍴

Thyme

Common Thyme | English Wild Thyme | Garden Thyme | *Origanum thymus* | *Thymus collinus*

✹ SYMBOLIC MEANINGS

Action; Activity; Affection; Bravery; Courage; Daring; Death; Elegance; Energy; Ensures restful sleep; Happiness; Healing; Health; Love; Psychic power; Purification; Restful sleep; Sleep; Spontaneous emotion; Strength; Swift movement; Thriftiness.

❀ POSSIBLE POWERS

Ability to see fairies; Aphrodisiac; the Arts; Attracts love; Attraction; Beauty; Courage; Feminine energy; Friendship; Gifts; Harmony; Healing; Health; Irresistibility; Joy; Love; Pleasure; Protection; Psychic power; Purification; Sensuality; Sleep; Venus; Water element.

☘ FOLKLORE AND FACTS

Because Thyme was a symbol of bravery and courage in medieval times, it was common for knights on their way to the Crusades to carry a scarf or wear a tunic that had the image of a sprig of Thyme embroidered upon it by their fair lady. • In ancient Greece, Thyme was burned as an incense to purify the temples. • It was once thought that, if a woman were to tuck a sprig of Thyme in her hair, it would render her irresistible. • Thyme was once used in nosegays to ward off disease and to also help mask any encountered bad odors. • Thyme placed under the pillow might help repel nightmares. • Thyme was once commonly worn by both men and women to ward off negativity and evil as they went about their daily business. • Thyme is thought to provide a home for fairies and a pleasant place for them to be able to dance near to it. • Wear a sprig of Thyme to attract good health. • Wear a sprig of Thyme to be able to see fairies. • Be sure to plant Thyme in a garden that is intended to please the fairies. • When a member of the Order of Oddfellows is buried, Thyme is tossed into his grave. • It is believed that it is possible to cleanse yourself of all the ills and sorrows of the past every spring by taking a purifying bath that has had crushed Thyme and Sweet Marjoram leaves added to the water until it is utterly fragrant.

No. 489

Tilia × *europaea* ☠🍶

Linden

Basswood | Common Lime | Common Linden | Lime | Lime Tree | Linnflowers | *Tilia* × *acuminata* | *Tilia* × *banatica* | *Tilia* × *bohemica* | *Tilia* × *carnuntiae* | *Tilia* × *communis* | *Tilia* × *croatica* | *Tilia* × *eriostylis* | *Tilia* × *floribunda* | *Tilia* × *hybrida* | *Tilia* × *intermedia* | *Tilia* × *officinarum* | *Tilia* × *oxycarpa* | *Tilia* × *pseudobliqua* | *Tilia* × *subparvifolia* | *Tilia* × *vulgaris*

✹ SYMBOLIC MEANINGS

Conjugal affection or love; Love; Luck; Marriage; Matrimony.

❧ COMPONENT MEANINGS

Sprig: Conjugal love.

❀ POSSIBLE POWERS

Air element; Fire element; Immortality; Jupiter; Lada; Love; Luck; Masculine energy; Prevents intoxication; Protection; Sleep; Sun; Venus.

T

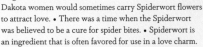

FOLKLORE AND FACTS

It is believed that one can prevent intoxication by having a few Linden leaves in the pocket. • Effective good luck charms can be carved from Linden wood. • A magic wand fashioned from Linden wood is very strongly connected to medicine, healing, and justice. Properly charged for a useful service, a Linden-wood wand is a positive magical wand full of light that is perfectly suited for white magic.

No. 490

Trachyspermum ammi ☠️🍶🍴

Ajwain

Ajowan | Ajowan Caraway | Ajwain | Ammi cicutarium | Ammi copticum | Ammi glaucifolium | Ammios muricata | Apium ammi | Athamanta ajowan | Bishop's Weed | Bunium aromaticum | Bunium copticum | Carom Seed | Carum ajawain | Carum ammi | Carum aromaticum | Carum copticum | Carum korolkowii | Cyclospermum ammi | Daucus anisodorus | Daucus copticus | Deverra korolkowii | Helosciadium ammi | Ligusticum ajawain | Ligusticum ajowan | Petroselinum sativum | Pituranthos korolkowii | Ptychotis ajawain | Ptychotis coptica | Selinum copticum | Seseli ammoides | Seseli foeniculifolium | Seseli gilliesii | Sison ammi | Thymol Seeds | Trachyspermum copticum

SYMBOLIC MEANINGS

Truthful communication.

POSSIBLE POWERS

Harmony; Healing; Protection.

FOLKLORE AND FACTS

The Ajwain fruit is often mistaken to be a seed. • Make, then wear or carry a sachet of Ajwain leaf and fruit to eject negative energy. • Ajwain can be added to a healing spell to increase the healing energy. • Wear or carry a sachet of Ajwain to encourage the truth in a conversation of any kind. • Wear or carry a sachet of Ajwain to remove bad luck and the lingering negative energy of a past illness.

No. 491

Tradescantia virginiana ☠️🍶

Spiderwort

Common Spiderwort | Ephemerum congestum | Knowlesia spicata | Leiandra divaricata | Spider Lily | Spider Wort | Tradescantia albida | Tradescantia axillaris | Tradescantia barbata | Tradescantia brevicaulis | Tradescantia caricifolia | Tradescantia crinigera | Tradescantia cristata | Tradescantia divaricata | Tradescantia elata | Tradescantia flexuosa | Tradescantia glabra | Tradescantia levigata | Tradescantia pilosissima | Tradescantia pumila | Tradescantia rupestris | Tradescantia speciosa | Tradescantia spicata | Tradescantia splendens | Tradescantia trachyloma | Tradescantia villosissima | Tradescantia virginica

SYMBOLIC MEANINGS

Esteem not love; Love; Momentary happiness; Transient felicity.

POSSIBLE POWERS

Abundance; Love.

FOLKLORE AND FACTS

Single Native American Dakota women would sometimes carry Spiderwort flowers to attract love. • There was a time when the Spiderwort was believed to be a cure for spider bites. • Spiderwort is an ingredient that is often favored for use in a love charm. • Make a red sachet of Spiderwort flowers to wear or carry to attract love. • Sprinkle an infusion of rainwater, natural spring water, or distilled water and Spiderwort flowers and leaves around the outside of the home and at the threshold of the front door to remove negative spirits. • Plant Spiderwort in your garden to attract an abundance of love to the home.

No. 492

Trichosanthes kirilowii ☠️🍶

Chinese Snake Gourd

Anguina japonica | Anguina kirilowii | Chinese Cucumber | Eopepon aurantiacus | Eopepon vitifolius | Guālóu | Gymnopetalum japonicum | Trichosanthes japonica | Trichosanthes obtusiloba | Trichosanthes palmata | Trichosanthes quadricirrha | Trichosanthes vitifolia

SYMBOLIC MEANINGS

Shaggy.

POSSIBLE POWERS

Feminine energy; Healing; Illumination; Moon; Water element.

FOLKLORE AND FACTS

The Chinese Snake Gourd plant has an unusual, pretty white flower with long strands of white wafting from the petals. • Chinese Snake Gourd oil is sometimes used as a lamp fuel. The Chinese Snake Gourd is one of the fifty essential plants used in traditional Chinese medicine. • Researchers are studying *Trichosanthes kirilowii* as a potential treatment for HIV, the AIDS virus.

T

No. 493
Trifolium dubium ☠🏺

Shamrock
Chrysaspis dubia | Clover | Honey | Honeystalks | Lesser Hop Trefoil | Lesser Trefoil | Little Hop Clover | Shamrock Clover | Suckling Clover | Three-Leaved Grass | Trefoil | Trifoil | *Trifolium dubium var. microphyllum* | *Trifolium flavum* | *Trifolium luteolum* | *Trifolium minus var. microphllum* | *Trifolium praticola*

✹ SYMBOLIC MEANINGS
I promise; Lightheartedness; Promise; Think of me.

❀ POSSIBLE POWERS
Air element; Good luck; Happy marriage with good luck; Joyfulness; Marital longevity with happiness and good fortune; Masculine energy; Mercury; Prosperity; Protection; Virility.

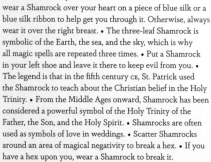

❦ FOLKLORE AND FACTS
If love has broken your heart, wear a Shamrock over your heart on a piece of blue silk or a blue silk ribbon to help get you through it. Otherwise, always wear it over the right breast. • The three-leaf Shamrock is symbolic of the Earth, the sea, and the sky, which is why all magic spells are repeated three times. • Put a Shamrock in your left shoe and leave it there to keep evil from you. • The legend is that in the fifth century CE, St. Patrick used the Shamrock to teach about the Christian belief in the Holy Trinity. • From the Middle Ages onward, Shamrock has been considered a powerful symbol of the Holy Trinity of the Father, the Son, and the Holy Spirit. • Shamrocks are often used as symbols of love in weddings. • Scatter Shamrocks around an area of magical negativity to break a hex. • If you have a hex upon you, wear a Shamrock to break it.

No. 494
Trifolium pratense 🏺

Red Clover
Beebread | Broadleaved Clover | Carretón | Cleaver Grass | Clover | Cow Grass | Honeysuckle Clover | *Lagopus pratensis* | Marl Grass | Meadow Clover | Peavine Clover | Purple Clover

✹ SYMBOLIC MEANINGS
I promise; Industry; Provident; Revenge.

❀ POSSIBLE POWERS
Air element; Consecration; Exorcism; Fidelity; Love; Masculine energy; Mercury; Money; Protection; Rowen; Success.

❦ FOLKLORE AND FACTS
The Red Clover's leaves and flowers are edible and used in soups or prepared like a leafy green vegetable. • If love has broken your heart, wear Red Clover over your heart on a piece of blue silk or blue silk ribbon to help get you through it. Otherwise, always wear it over the right breast. • Brides and grooms should enter into marriage with any three-leaf Red Clover (better yet, a four-leaf Red Clover!) tucked into each shoe. • The Druids considered all Red Clover to be sacred and magical plants. To them, the three-leaf Red Clover is symbolic of the Earth, the sea, and the sky, which is why all spells are repeated three times. • Red Clover is the state flower of Vermont, USA. • Wear Red Clover before signing a financial contract of any kind.

No. 495
Trigonella foenum-graecum ☠🏺🍴

Fenugreek
Abesh | Alholva | Bird's Food | Bockhornsklöver | Bockshornklee | *Buceras foenum-graecum* | *Buceras odoratissima* | Chandrika | Fenogreco | *Foenugraeci Semen* | *Foenum-graecum officinale* | *Foenum-graecum sativum* | *Folliculigera graveolens* | Greek Clover | Greek Hay | Greek Hay Seed | Halba | Hilbeh | Holba | Hu Lu Ba | Medhika | *Medicago foenugraeca* | Menthya | Menti | Methi | Methya | Ram's Horn Clover | Sénégrain | Shanballeh | *Telis foenum-graecum* | *Trigonella ensifera* | *Trigonella graeca* | *Trigonella haussknechtii* | *Trigonella jemenensis* | *Trigonella rhodantha* | *Trigonella tibetana* | Uluhaal | Uluva | Vendayam | Woo Lu Bar | *Xiphostylis erectus*

✹ SYMBOLIC MEANINGS
Growth; Transformation; Youth.

❀ POSSIBLE POWERS
Air element; Apollo; Masculine energy; Mercury; Money; Prosperity; Wealth.

❦ FOLKLORE AND FACTS
One easy way to bring money into the house fund is to add Fenugreek seeds to the water you mop the floors with. • Fenugreek was once believed to have the magical power of being able to transform an old man back into a young man.

T

No. 496

Tuber melanosporum 🌿🍴

Black Truffle

Black Diamond | French Black Truffle | French Truffle | Périgord Truffle | Summer Truffle | *Tuber aestivum*

✳ **SYMBOLIC MEANINGS**
Luxury; Refinement.

🌐 **POSSIBLE POWERS**
Aphrodisiac; Decadence; Love;
Love magic; Lust; Luxury;
Sensuality; Sex; True love magic;
Venus; Water element.

🜊 **FOLKLORE AND FACTS**
Best found in France, where they are most likely to grow, is the exquisite beloved Black Truffle. • The Black Truffle is one of the many counterfeited spices. The high price that the Black Truffle commands makes it a target for someone to try to slip in the much less valuable Chinese *Tuber indicum*. To avoid the disruption in the truffle market due to mis-marking the two species or, of course, blatant outright attempts at fraud, a DNA genetic test was devised to definitively identify one from the other. • In parts of France, Spain, and Italy, the Black Truffle naturally develops in the ground. • The fragrance of the Black Truffle intensifies when it is heated, unlike the white truffle, which becomes less so. • Grown to be close to the size of a Potato, with a pungent earthiness to its aroma, the Black Truffle is extremely difficult to find because of its strict growing requirements, which could be artificially or even naturally perfect in every possible way and still fail to support the growth of a Black Truffle. And, even if one is successfully harvested, the Black Truffle will spoil after only five days, which is the primary reason they are so extremely expensive and considered to be the most expensive food in the world. • The Black Truffle is most likely to be found between November and April. • Nowadays, farmers in search of uncovering Black Truffles to harvest will tend to use highly trained dogs to sniff out the tasty *Fungi* treasures, rather than employing the traditional male truffle hog. Even so, it can be argued that a truffle hog will be devoted to its owner as well as exhibit superior skill in finding Black Truffles by using its superb sense of smell, its natural rooting behavior, and its powerful sex hormone of androstenol, which can also be found in a Black Truffle. On the other hand, truffle hunters who employ a trained truffle dog's skills are quick to remind that the dog is less likely to try to eat the Black Truffle before the hunter takes hold of it, while holding a pig back away from its found treasure takes some doing. However, seeking a Black Truffle driven by desire that is doubly fueled by a naturally occurring sex hormone seems like it would be *much* more powerful, as magic goes, than taking home a Black Truffle found by a smart dog's trained behavior, which is naturally rewarded by much praise and a beloved treat pulled out from a truffle hunter's pocket. The treat was well earned. However, the Black Truffle located by the lusting pig will be a much, *much* more powerful herb ideally suited for mutually enjoyed love magic. Indeed. Even so, any Black Truffle will be magical, as will it being powdered or in an oil.

No. 497

Tussilago farfara ☠🌿

Coltsfoot

Ass's Foot | Bechichie | Bechie | Bechion | British Tobacco | Bull's Foot | Chamæleuce | *Cineraria farfara* | Coughwort | Farfara | *Farfara radiata* | Foal's Foot | Foalswort | Horse Foot | Pas d'Ane | Pes Pulli | *Petasites farfara* | Sponnc | Tash Plant | *Tussilago alpestris* | *Tussilago generalis* | *Tussilago radiata* | *Tussilago ruderalis* | *Tussilago rupestris* | *Tussilago umbertina* | *Tussilago vulgari* | Ungula Caballina | Winter Heliotrope

✳ **SYMBOLIC MEANINGS**
Justice; Justice shall be done; Justice shall be done you; Love; Maternal Love; Political power.

🌐 **POSSIBLE POWERS**
Feminine energy; Healing; Love; Prosperity; Psychic vision; Venus; Visions; Water element; Wealth.

🜊 **FOLKLORE AND FACTS**
A Coltsfoot sachet can be worn or carried to induce tranquility and peacefulness. • A Coltsfoot sachet can be made or worn to encourage the manifestation of a psychic vision.

No. 498
Ulex europaeus ☠🏺

Gorse

Broom | Common Gorse | Frey | Furse | Furze | Fyrs | *Genista europaea* | Gorst | Goss | Prickly Broom | Ruffet | Whin

☀ SYMBOLIC MEANINGS
Anger; Despair; Endearing affection; Hopelessness; Independence; Industry; Intelligence; Light; Love for all occasions or seasons; Love in all seasons; Vibrancy.

🌀 POSSIBLE POWERS
Colorize; Fire element; Masculine energy; Money; Protection.

🌙 FOLKLORE AND FACTS
Gorse hedges in Wales were originally planted as a preventative against fairy invasions because a fairy cannot get through the prickly row of bushes. • Gorse can produce a nice yellow dye for fabrics.

No. 499
Ulmus procera ☠🏺

English Elm

Atinian Elm | Common Elm | Elm | Elven | European Elm | Field Elm | Horse May | *Ulmus ambigua* | *Ulmus anglica* | *Ulmus araxina* | *Ulmus asperrima* | *Ulmus asymmetrica* | *Ulmus aurea* | *Ulmus carpinifolia* | *Ulmus coritana* | *Ulmus corylifolia* | *Ulmus cucullata* | *Ulmus densa* | *Ulmus diversifolia* | *Ulmus elliptica* | *Ulmus fastigiata* | *Ulmus foliacea* | *Ulmus fungosa* | *Ulmus georgica* | *Ulmus glabra* | *Ulmus grossheimii* | *Ulmus major* | *Ulmus modiolina* | *Ulmus monumentalis* | *Ulmus nana* | *Ulmus nemoralis* | *Ulmus nemorosa* | *Ulmus nitens* | *Ulmus nuda* | *Ulmus planereoides* | *Ulmus plotii* | *Ulmus pseudocoritana* | *Ulmus purpurea* | *Ulmus reticulata* | *Ulmus rosseelsii* | *Ulmus rotundifolia* | *Ulmus sativa* | *Ulmus sowerbyi* | *Ulmus sparsa* | *Ulmus suberosa* | *Ulmus surculosa* | *Ulmus tetrandra* | *Ulmus tiliifolia* | *Ulmus tortuosa* | *Ulmus uzbekistanica* | *Ulmus virens* | *Ulmus vulgaris* | *Ulmus wheatleyi* | *Ulmus wyssotzky* | Vanishing Elm | Water Elm | White Elm | Zelkova

☀ SYMBOLIC MEANINGS
Achievement of a goal; Death; Dignity; Dignity and grace; Life; Patriotism; Rebirth; Victory.

🌀 POSSIBLE POWERS
Attracts love; Balances the emotions; Energizes the mind; Feminine energy; Love; Odin; Protection; Rebirth; Saturn; Tunes psychic powers; Water element.

🌙 FOLKLORE AND FACTS
English Elm is known to be a favorite tree of elves who diligently guard burial mounds. • Carry bits of English Elm bark or leaves in a pink and red sachet to attract love. • The English Elm tree has been associated with the Underworld.

U

No. 500

Ulmus rubra ☠️🍯

Slippery Elm

Gray Elm | Indian Elm | Moose Elm | Red Elm | Soft Elm | *Ulmus dimidiata* | *Ulmus fulva* | *Ulmus pendula* | *Ulmus pinguis* | *Ulmus pubescens* | *Ulmus tridens* | *Ulmus triserrata*

✹ SYMBOLIC MEANINGS
Independence; Smooth and silky.

✹ POSSIBLE POWERS
Air element; Feminine energy; Halts gossip; Invisibility; Saturn.

✹ FOLKLORE AND FACTS
A rainwater powder to sprinkle upon oneself and anything else needing to disappear can supposedly be made by grinding together a mix of magically prescribed equal amounts of dried powdered Slippery Elm, Myrrh, Marjoram, Poppyseed, and Maidenhair Fern. • To stop idle gossip, tie knots along a length of yellow thread then tie the thread around a few rolled Slippery Elm leaves before tossing it into a fire. • Packaged medicinal herbal teas for the treatment of sore throats often contain Slippery Elm. • Women who are pregnant or think they might be pregnant should not use Slippery Elm in any form.

No. 501

Umbellularia californica ☠️🍯

California Bay Laurel

Balm of Heaven | California Bay | California Laurel | Cinnamon Bush | *Drimophyllum pauciflorum* | Headache Tree | *Litsea californica* | Mountain Laurel | Myrtlewood Tree | Oregon Myrtle | *Oreodaphne californica* | *Oreodaphne regalis* | Peppernut Tree | Pepperwood | *Persea causticans* | Pōl'-Cum Ōl | Sō-ē'-bā | Spicebush | *Tetranthera californica* | *Tetranthera causticans*

✹ SYMBOLIC MEANINGS
Agitation; Ambition; Ambitious; Beware; Danger.

✹ POSSIBLE POWERS
Banishing; Learning who is against you; Power; Power to overcome enemies; Stirring up agitation.

✹ FOLKLORE AND FACTS
The fine-grained, hard California Bay Laurel wood is a known tonewood that is also known as myrtlewood and is thereby used to make the backs and the sides of acoustic guitars. • The leaf of the more intensely pungent California Bay Laurel is used to flavor soups, stews, and casseroles in the same way as a *Laurus nobilis* leaf.

No. 502

Uncaria rhynchophylla ☠️🍯

Cat's Claw

Diào Gōu Téng | Life-Giving Vine of Peru | *Nauclea rhynchophylla* | *Ourouparia rhynchophylla* | Uña de Gato

✹ SYMBOLIC MEANINGS
Feline helper.

✹ POSSIBLE POWERS
Finance; Gate opening; Health; Increases energy flow through the self; Journeys; Releases blockages; Rites of passage; Vision quests.

✹ FOLKLORE AND FACTS
Make a white Cat's Claw sachet to carry or wear or put under the pillow to help open a gate between the physical and the spiritual realms.

No. 503

Urtica dioica ☠☢

Stinging Nettle

Bull Nettle | Burning Nettle | Burning Weed | California Nettle | Common Nettle | Fire Weed | Jaggy Nettle | Nettle | Ortiga | Ortiga Ancha | Ortiga Mayor | Slender Nettle | Stiðe Nettle | Tall Nettle | *Urtica dioecia* | *Urtica eckloniana* | *Urtica haussknechtii* | *Urtica major* | *Urtica microphylla* | *Urtica radicans* | *Urtica sicula* | *Urtica submitis* | *Urtica tibetica* | Wergulu

✴ **SYMBOLIC MEANINGS**
Cruelty; Slander.

❀ **POSSIBLE POWERS**
Ambition; the Arts; Attitude; Attraction; Beauty; Clear thinking; Exorcism; Fire element; Friendship gifts; Harmony; Healing; Higher understanding; Joy; Logic; Love; Lust; Manifestation in material form; Mars; Masculine energy; Pleasures; Protection; Sensuality; Spiritual concepts; Thor; Thought processes.

☕ **FOLKLORE AND FACTS**
Carry Stinging Nettle in a pouch to remove a curse and send it back to whoever created it. • Stinging Nettle can make a yellow vegetable dye. • Prior to the steady emigration from England, Stinging Nettle was virtually unknown in North America until it was introduced into the newly planted English gardens in the New World.

U

No. 504

Vachellia farnesiana ♂

Sweet Acacia

Acacia acicularis | Acacia farnesiana | Acacia indica | Acacia lenticellata | Acacia minuta | Aroma | Cascalotte | Casha | Casha Tree | Cashaw | Cashia | Cassia | Cassic | Cassie | Cassie Flower | Cuntich | Cushuh | Dead Finish | Ellington's Curse | Farnese Wattle | *Farnesia odora* | *Farnesiana odora* | Golden Wattle | Honey-Ball | Huisache | Iron Wood | Mealy Wattle | *Mimosa acicularis* | Mimosa Bush | *Mimosa farnesiana* | *Mimosa indica* | *Mimosa suaveolens* | Mimosa Wattle | Needle Bush | Northwest Curara | Opoponax | *Pithecellobium acuminatum* | *Pithecellobium minutum* | Popanax farnesiana | Popinac | *Poponax farnesiana* | Prickly Mimosa Bush | Prickly Moses | Sheep's Briar | Sponge Wattle | Sweet Briar | Texas Huisache | Thorny Acacia | Thorny Feather Wattle | Wild Briar

✴ SYMBOLIC MEANINGS

Chaste love; Concealed love; Decrease of love; Elegance; Endurance of the soul; Friendship; Immortality; Let us forget; Platonic love; Poetry; Pure and platonic love; Purity; Resurrection; Secret love; Sensitiveness.

🌀 POSSIBLE POWERS

Abundance; Advancement; Banishing; Business transactions; Caution; Cleverness; Communication; Conscious will; Creativity; Divination; Energy; Exorcism; Faith; Feminine energy; Friendship; Growth; Healing; Illumination; Initiation; Intelligence; Joy; Leadership; Learning; Life; Light; Love; Memory; Money; Natural power; Prophetic dreams; Protection; Prudence; Purification; Repels demons or ghosts; Saturn; Science; Self-preservation; Sound judgment; Success; Thievery; Water element; Wisdom.

🜂 FOLKLORE AND FACTS

Use Sweet Acacia incense to consecrate boxes and cabinets where magical ritual tools are to be stored. • Sweet Acacia has been used in perfumery dating back thousands of years. • The Sweet Acacia tree has been associated with Egyptian mythology's Tree of Life. Legend tells that the Sweet Acacia tree could have been the burning bush that Moses encountered in Exodus 3:2 of the Bible. • It is also thought that the Ark of the Tabernacle was constructed of Sweet Acacia wood. • Jesus Christ's crown of thorns is thought to have been fashioned from thorny Sweet Acacia stems. • A sprig of Sweet Acacia over a bed or on a hat will supposedly ward off evil. • Sweet Acacia will purify an area of evil and negativity. • Sweet Acacia wood is sacred in India and all areas in the Middle East. • Sacred ritual fires will burn Sweet Acacia wood. • Many temples in India are built using Sweet Acacia wood. • Burn Sweet Acacia wood with Sandalwood

to raise psychic vibrations and increase psychic perception and reception. • Sweet Acacia bark smoke is believed by some to have the power to repel ghosts, demons, and all manners of evil spirits.

No. 505

Valeriana officinalis ☠♂

Valerian

Amantilla | *Astrephia chinensis* | Bloody Butcher | Capon's Trailer | Cat's Valerian | Common Valerian | English Valerian | Fragrant Valerian | Garden Heliotrope | Garden Valerian | Phu | Red Valerian | St. George's Herb | Set Well | *Valeriana altissima* | *Valeriana baltica* | *Valeriana exaltata* | *Valeriana lucida* | *Valeriana major* | *Valeriana multiceps* | *Valeriana palustris* | *Valeriana pinnata* | *Valeriana pseudoumbrosa* | *Valeriana sinensis* | *Valeriana sylvestris* | *Valeriana vulgaris* | Vandal Root

✴ SYMBOLIC MEANINGS

Accommodating disposition; Facility; Good disposition; Readiness.

🌀 POSSIBLE POWERS

Aphrodisiac; Applying knowledge; Astral plane; Attracts love; Controlling lower principles; Feminine energy; Finding lost objects; Love; Overcoming evil; Protection; Purification; Regeneration; Removing depression; Sensuality; Sleep; Uncovering secrets; Venus; Victory; Water element.

🜂 FOLKLORE AND FACTS

Valerian can be occasionally found in relaxation and sleep teas that are blended with Chamomile. • Valerian has been used for protection against lightning by hanging it in the home. Place a sprig of Valerian under the pillow to use as a sleep aid. • If a woman wears a sprig of Valerian, men will follow her. • Valerian placed in the room of a quarreling couple will calm their disagreements. • Valerian placed under a window will repel evil. • A bridegroom in Sweden will sometimes wear a sprig of Valerian to fend off envious elves from disrupting the marriage ceremony and wedding festivities.

Vanilla planifolia 🌿🍴

Vanilla Orchid

Banilje | Bourbon Vanilla | *Epidendrum rubrum* | Flat-Leaved Vanilla | Madagascar Vanilla | *Myrobroma fragrans* | *Notylia planifolia* | *Notylia salvia* | *Notylia sylvestris* | Pompona | Tlilxochitl | Vanilla | *Vanilla aromatica* | *Vanilla bampsiana* | *Vanilla duckei* | *Vanilla fragrans* | *Vanilla rubra* | *Vanilla sativa* | *Vanilla sylvestris* | *Vanilla viridiflora* | West Indian Vanilla

✹ SYMBOLIC MEANINGS
Elegance; Innocence; Purity.

❁ POSSIBLE POWERS
Aphrodisiac; Attracts love; Energy; Feminine energy; Love; Lust; Mental clarity or power; Venus; Water element.

❧ FOLKLORE AND FACTS
Vanilla Orchids bloom after the flowers are fully grown, opening in the morning and closing late that same afternoon, never to reopen. If the Vanilla Orchid flower is not pollinated by a certain type of bee or hummingbird or by hand on the day that the flower opens, it will fall off the next day. • A Vanilla Orchid fruit, erroneously called a bean, will take eight to nine months to ripen. The fragrance of the Vanilla Orchid fruit is believed to be an aphrodisiac and able to induce lust. • Carry a Vanilla Orchid fruit for mental clarity and improved energy. • The sap from a Vanilla Orchid can cause a severe rash when in contact with skin.

Verbascum thapsus ☠🌿

Mullein

Aaron's Rod | Blanket Leaf | Candlewick Plant | Clot | Common Mullein | Doffle | Feltwort | Flannel Plant | Hag's Tapers | Hedge Taper | Jupiter's Staff | Lady's Foxglove | Leiosandra cuspidata | Old Man's Fennel | Peter's Staff | Shepherd's Club | Shepherd's Herb | *Thapsus linnaei* | *Thapsus schraderi* | Torches | Velvet Plant | Velvetback | *Verbascum alatum* | *Verbascum angustius* | *Verbascum bracteatum* | *Verbascum canescens* | *Verbascum decurrens* | *Verbascum elongatum* | *Verbascum indicum* | *Verbascum intermedium* | *Verbascum kickxianum* | *Verbascum lanatum* | *Verbascum linnaei* | *Verbascum majus* | *Verbascum mas* | *Verbascum neglectum* | *Verbascum officinarum* | *Verbascum pallidum* | *Verbascum plantagineum* | *Verbascum schraderi* | *Verbascum seminigrum* | *Verbascum spectabile* | *Verbascum subalpinum* | *Verbascum tapsus* | *Verbascum thapsum* | White Mullein

✹ SYMBOLIC MEANINGS
Good nature; Good-natured; Immortality.

❁ POSSIBLE POWERS
Calling a spirit; Courage; Curses; Divination; Exorcism; Feminine energy; Fire element; Health; Invoking a spirit; Jupiter; Love; Protection from nightmares; Protection from sorcery; Protection from wild animals; Saturn.

❧ FOLKLORE AND FACTS
Make a sachet of Mullein to wear as an amulet for courage. • Sleep on a pillow stuffed with Mullein to fend off nightmares. • In India, Mullein is considered to be the most powerful protection against magic and evil spirits. It is believed to be effective in banishing negativity and demons, so it is often worn, carried, and hung over doors and in windows. • A love divination used at one time by the young men of the Ozark Mountains area was to find a live Mullein plant and then bend it toward the object of his love. If the girl loved him in return, then the Mullein would grow back upright again. If she loved someone else, the plant would die. • Carry or wear a sachet or amulet of Mullein to attract love. • Native Americans would sometimes use the smoke from Mullein to revive an unconscious person. • In an emergency away from home, Mullein's soft, wooly leaves were used as wound bandages by Native Americans. • Prior to the steady emigration from England, Mullein was virtually unknown in North America until it was introduced into the newly planted English gardens in the New World. • Mullein seeds can remain viable for up to one hundred years. • Ancient Roman soldiers would light grease-dipped Mullein for use as torches. • The early American colonists would sometimes use the large, fuzzy Mullein leaves in their shoes to help keep their feet warm.

No. 508
Verbena officinalis ☠️🏺

Vervain

Bijozakura | Blue Vervain | Brittanica | Common Verbena | Common Vervain | Devil's Bane | Echtes Eisenkraut | Enchanter's Plant | Herb of Grace | Herb of the Cross | Holy Herb | Ijzerhard | Juno's Tears | Laege-Jernurt | Mosquito Plant | Pigeon's Grass | Pigeonwood | Rohtorautayrtti | Simpler's Joy | Tears of Isis | Van-Van | *Verbena domingensis* | *Verbena macrostachya* | Vervan | Wild Hyssop | Zeleznik Lekársky

☀️ SYMBOLIC MEANINGS
Hope in darkness; Pray for me; Pure affection; You enchant me.

🌐 COLOR MEANINGS
Pink: Family union.
Scarlet: Church unity;
  Unite against evil.
Purple: I am so sorry;
  I weep for you; Regret.
White: Pray for me.

🌸 POSSIBLE POWERS
Abilities; Aradia; Beauty; Chastity; Cooperativeness; Divine forces; Divine offering; Earth element; Enchantment; Feminine energy; Feminine power; Healing; Inspires artistry or creativity; Instills a love of and for learning; Isis; Juno; Jupiter; Kerridwen; Love; Mars; Money; Peace; Problems; Protection; Protection against depression; Protection from negative emotions; Protection from vampires; Protection from witchcraft; Purification; Remedy for over-enthusiasm; Repels evil intentions; Repels negativity; Repels a vampire; Repels witches; Rest; Safety; Security; Sensibility; Sensitiveness; Sleep; Sorcery; Supernatural forces; Thor; Venus; Water element; Women's power; Youth.

🜍 FOLKLORE AND FACTS
There is a legend that Vervain was used to stop the bleeding of Jesus's crucifixion wounds after he was taken down from the cross. • In ancient Rome, Vervain would be bundled together as whisk brooms then used to sweep altars clean of dust, debris, and negative energy. • Carry a piece of Vervain as an amulet. • Use Vervain in the home as protection against destructive storms and lightning. • Scatter Vervain around the home to bring peace inside. • Grow Vervain to encourage the other plants to produce abundantly. • Carry a sprig of Vervain to encourage everlasting youth. • Vervain placed under the bed or pillow offers protection from harmful dreams. • To determine if someone has stolen something from you, wear a sprig of Vervain then ask if the suspect did the crime. The suspect will not be able to lie about it without revealing a tell as a perceptible hint that will reveal the truth of the statement.

No. 509
Viburnum opulus ☠️🏺

Guelder Rose

Common Snowball | Crampbark | European Cranberrybush | Guelder-Rose | Kalina | Kalyna | *Opulus edulis* | *Opulus glandulosa* | *Opulus lobatofolia* | *Opulus oxycoccos* | *Opulus palustris* | *Opulus vulgaris* | Snowball Bush | Snowball Tree | *Viburnum glandulosum* | *Viburnum lobatum* | *Viburnum nanum* | *Viburnum opuloides* | *Viburnum oxycoccos* | *Viburnum palustre* | *Viburnum pinnina* | *Viburnum primina* | *Viburnum rosaceum* | *Viburnum roseum* | Water Elder

☀️ SYMBOLIC MEANINGS
Blood; Coolness; Eroticism; Family roots; Home; Love; Love separation; Native land; Passionate love of a maiden.

🌸 POSSIBLE POWERS
Eroticism.

🜍 FOLKLORE AND FACTS
The original medicinal intention of Guelder Rose bark was to use it to relieve women's menstrual cramps. • Guelder Rose is very much an integral part of Ukrainian folk traditions, in which it is called Kaylna and which began to be depicted in art, music, poetry, and even embroidery as far back as the start of Slavic paganism 1,000 years ago. • According to legends, Guelder Rose is associated with the beginning of the universe. • The Ukrainian army's insignia is a stylized cluster of Guelder Rose *Viburnum opulus* berries. • The Guelder Rose fruit is also called Kalina, which is a national symbol in Russia. • Stylized depictions of Guelder Rose berries, leaves, and flowers on a Russian national woodcraft known as *khokhloma* are common and culturally important.

No. 510
Viburnum prunifolium ☠⚱

Black Haw

American Sloe | Blackhaw |
Blackhaw Viburnum | Devil's
Shoestring | Stag Bush |
Stagberry | Stagbush | Sweet
Haw | *Viburnum bushii* | *Viburnum pyrifolium*

🌟 **SYMBOLIC MEANINGS**
Coolness; Retain.

🌼 **POSSIBLE POWERS**
Calm hysterics; Employment; Exorcism; Fire element;
Gambling; Good luck; Luck; Mars; Masculine energy; Power;
Protection.

🜂 **FOLKLORE AND FACTS**
Carry or wear a sachet or pouch of Black Haw to increase
luck when job seeking. • Carry or wear a sachet or pouch
of Black Haw when speaking to an employer regarding any
work-related issue or requesting a raise. • Carry or wear a
sachet or pouch of Black Haw to increase positive results
when collecting money owed.

No. 511
Vicia sativa ☠⚱

Vetch

Common Vetch | Faba | Garden Vetch | Tare | Winter Tares

🌟 **SYMBOLIC MEANINGS**
Fidelity; I cling to thee;
Shyness; Vice.

🌼 **POSSIBLE POWERS**
Fidelity.

🜂 **FOLKLORE AND FACTS**
A sachet of Vetch tucked
under both sides of
the mattress will help
maintain faithfulness
and commitment in a
monogamous relationship.

No. 512
Vigna unguiculata ☠⚱

Black-Eyed Pea

Alasandalu | Alsande Kalu | Asparagus Bean | Augenbohne | Black Eye | Black-Eyed Bean |
Catjang | Chawli | Cow Pea | Cowpea | Crowder Pea | *Dolichos capitatus* | *Dolichos catjang* |
Dolichos cylindricus | *Dolichos echinatulus* | *Dolichos hastatus* | *Dolichos hastifolius* | *Dolichos
leucomelas* | *Dolichos lubia* | *Dolichos melanophthalmus* | *Dolichos monachalis* | *Dolichos
obliquifolius* | *Dolichos sesquipedalis* | *Dolichos sinensis* | *Dolichos sphaerospermus* | *Dolichos
subracemosus* | *Dolichos tranquebaricus* | Dolico Esparrago | Dolique | Fasolita | Feijao Frade |
Haricot Dolique | Inek Nokhudu | Kacang Tolo | Kacang Tunggak | Karamani | Korovi Gorokh |
Korovyachi Gorokh | Kuherbse | Lathanay Dha Beeja | *Liebrechtsia scabra* | Lobia | Lobiya |
Lobya | Long Bean | Lovia | Lubiyo | *Phaseolus cylindricus* | *Phaseolus ellipticus* | *Phaseolus
sphaerospermus* | Purple Hull Pea | Rongi | *Scytalis catjang* | Thattapayaru | *Vigna catjang* |
Vigna cylindrica | *Vigna hastata* | *Vigna monachalis* | *Vigna scabra* | *Vigna scabrida* | *Vigna
sinensis* | *Vigna tranquebarica* | *Vigna unguiculata*

🌟 **SYMBOLIC MEANINGS**
Good luck and prosperity for all the new year.

🌼 **POSSIBLE POWERS**
Good luck; Plenty; Prosperity.

🜂 **FOLKLORE AND FACTS**
In most of the Southern United States of America, wishing
goodness for the upcoming new year while eating three
Black-Eyed Peas on New Year's Day is an annual tradition.
One for luck. One for fortune. One for romance. • Black-
Eyed Peas must be cooked until tender before eating them.

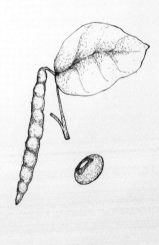

No. 513

Viscum album ☠♀

Mistletoe

Affolter | American Mistletoe | Bocksfutter | Common Mistletoe | Drudenfua | Elfklatte | European Mistletoe | Geiakrut | Golden Bough | Guatrice | Gui | Gui Commun | Gui de Druides | Guomol | Hexenbesen | Holy Wood | Immergrune | Kluster | Leimmistel | Marenklatte | Marentaken | Mischgelt | Mischgle | Misple | Mistel | Muerdago | Nistle | Pania | Scoaggine | *Stelin album* | Thunderbesom | Uomol | Vescovaggine | Vischio | *Viscum dichotomum* | *Viscum polycoccon* | *Viscum stellatum* | Vogelchrut | Vogelklab | Vogellim | Vogelmistel | Wasp | Wespe | Wintergrun | Wispen

✱ SYMBOLIC MEANINGS

Affection; Difficulties; Give me a kiss; Hunting; I surmount difficulties; I surmount everything; Kiss me; Looking; Love; Obstacles to be overcome; To surmount difficulties.

✿ POSSIBLE POWERS

Air element; Apollo; Exorcism; Fertility; Freya; Frigga; Healing; Health; Hunting; Love; Masculine energy; Odin; Protection; Sun; Venus.

✾ FOLKLORE AND FACTS

The ancient Greeks believed that Mistletoe had mystical powers. • Mistletoe is one of the most magical plants, encompassing all European folk beliefs since it was thought to be able to cure diseases, make poisons harmless, reproduce animals to enormous herds and flocks, protect one against witchcraft, protect houses from ghosts, even to force a ghost to speak when so desired, and more. • Mistletoe was believed to bring good luck to anyone who possessed it. • The ancient Celts hung Mistletoe to ward off evil and to welcome a new year at the winter solstice. • The ancient Celts would hang Mistletoe over a baby's cradle to protect the child from being stolen away by fairies. • During Christmastime, if a girl is standing under Mistletoe and is not kissed, she cannot expect to be married the coming year. • It was believed that the golden bough of Aeneas, who is considered to be the ancestor of the Romans, was Mistletoe. • The Druids considered the winter solstice to be the beginning of a new year because that is when their sacred Mistletoe would bear fruit. Thus, Mistletoe was part of their immortality rites. • Legend tells that Baldr, a Norse god, was murdered with Mistletoe. • As long as the bough of the White Oak tree from which the sacred Mistletoe was gathered did not touch the ground, the Mistletoe power would be potently strong enough to wear a very small sprig of it as a talisman around the neck for protection against malicious magical intentions.

• Mistletoe is the state flower of Oklahoma, USA. • If Mistletoe is gathered and hung up in the windows on the eve of St. John's Day, the protection is effective against storms, thunder, evil spirits, witchcraft, and a wide variety of other unpleasant phantoms.

No. 514

Vitis vinifera ♀

Grape

Chicco d'Uva | *Cissus vinifera* | Common Grape Vine | *Maerklinia viridis* | Mata de Uva | *Noachia macrophylla* | *Palatina dichotoma* | *Palatina dissecta* | *Palatina macrocarpa* | *Palatina oblonga* | *Palatina septemloba* | *Palatina sinuata* | *Palatina sylvestris* | *Palatina tilicefolia* | *Palatina wisilocensis* | Parra | *Schamsia ligustrica* | *Sickleria brevicirrhata* | *Thalesia rubrivenia* | *Tyrtamia revoluta* | Vid | *Vitis apiana* | *Vitis apiifolia* | *Vitis apyrena* | *Vitis bosturgaiensis* | *Vitis cebennensis* | *Vitis corinthiaca* | *Vitis cylindrica* | *Vitis densiflora* | *Vitis farinosa* | *Vitis gmelinii* | *Vitis guilelmii* | *Vitis hyrcanica* | *Vitis laciniosa* | *Vitis laxiflora* | *Vitis mensarum* | *Vitis moschata* | *Vitis praecox* | *Vitis saccharina* | *Vitis silvestris* | *Vitis sinuosa* | *Vitis succinea* | *Vitis sylvestris* | *Vitis tinctoria* | *Vitis turbinata* | *Vitis usunachmatica* | *Zaehringia nobilis*

✱ SYMBOLIC MEANINGS

Celebration; Charity; Faith needed for growth or to prosper; Fertility; Initiation; Intemperance; Joy; Meekness; Pleasure; Rural felicity; Transformation.

✿ POSSIBLE POWERS

Abundance; Bacchus; Colorize; Dionysus; Feminine energy; Fertility; Garden magic; Hathor; Kindness; Life; Mental clarity or power; Money; Moon; Mystical transformation; Water element.

✾ FOLKLORE AND FACTS

There are nearly 10,000 varieties of Grape. • Paint pictures of grapevines with fruiting Grapes on garden walls to promote fertility. • Wild Grapes have been harvested since Neolithic times. • Grape pip seeds have been found that date back to 6000 BCE. • Up until the seventh century CE, Grapes were primarily grown and sold in the Middle East. • Grapes are grown everywhere in the world except in the Arctic regions. • Since ancient times, nearly every culture that knew of the Grape regarded it as being sacred. • In the Bible, Jesus turns jugs of water into fine Grape wine while attending a wedding in Cana with his mother. As the event is written, it was the first tangible miraculous act that Jesus manifested.

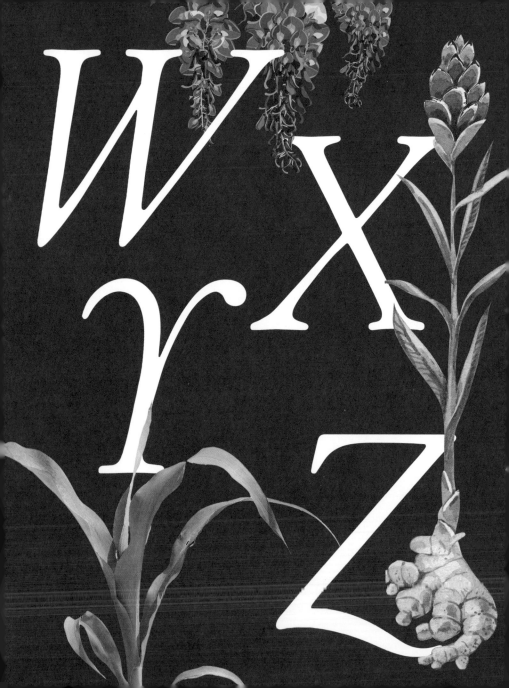

No. 515
Warszewiczia coccinea ☠️🏺

Wild Poinsettia

Aegiphila macrophylla | Calycophyllum coccineum | Chaconia | Cuetlaxochitl | Macrocnemum coccineum | Mussaenda coccinea | Pride of Trinidad and Tobago | Warszewiczia macrophylla | Warszewiczia maynensis | Warszewiczia poeppigiana | Warszewiczia pulcherrima | Warszewiczia schomburgkiana | Warszewiczia splendens

✺ **SYMBOLIC MEANINGS**
Celebration; Good cheer;
Imperishability of life; Mirth;
Purity.

🌀 **POSSIBLE POWERS**
Aphrodisiac; Attracts love;
Celebration; Wishing.

🜨 **FOLKLORE AND FACTS**
The Wild Poinsettia was considered to be a symbol of purity to the ancient Aztecs. • Botanist Joel Roberts Poinsett was the first United States Ambassador to Mexico who recognized something special about the plants. Poinsett brought the first Wild Poinsettia plants to South Carolina in the 1820s. • During the fourteenth through the sixteenth centuries, the Wild Poinsettia bracts were used to make a reddish dye. • The Wild Poinsettia is the national flower of both Trinidad and Tobago. • Because Wild Poinsettia could not be grown in the high altitude of Mexico City, the last ancient Aztec king, Moctezuma II, would have the flowers brought to him by caravan.

No. 516
Wasabia japonica ☠️🏺🍴

Wasabi

Alliaria wasabi | Cochlearia wasabi | Eutrema japonicum | Eutrema koreanum | Eutrema okinosimense | Eutrema wasabi | Japanese Horseradish | Lunaria japonica | Wasabia pungens | Wasabia wasabi

✺ **SYMBOLIC MEANINGS**
Pungent awakening.

🌀 **POSSIBLE POWERS**
Flavoring; Healing; Health.

🜨 **FOLKLORE AND FACTS**
As pungent as Horseradish, Wasabi root is ground into a light-green paste for use as a condiment for Asian dishes, most particularly for sushi. • Due to the mass appeal

of sushi and the condiment Wasabi that lends itself to it so well, it has been difficult to keep up the cultivation of Wasabi plants to meet the demand for this culinary herb. As a consequence, an extremely common condiment substitute blend of Horseradish, Mustard, and a starch such as Rice flour is mixed with some green food coloring. This is packaged in a container labeled as "wasabi" to be commercially offered to the insatiable sushi-devouring public of the Western Hemisphere. There is most likely no actual Wasabi plant added to be even part of the mix. The fake Wasabi tastes somewhat similar, but it will burn hotter and longer than true Wasabi. • It is rare to find true Wasabi plants anywhere outside Japan. • Outside Japan, true Wasabi paste is usually only found at very high-end Japanese-style sushi restaurants or high-end specialty stores. • The difference between fake and true Wasabi is that the fake is creamy smooth, while true Wasabi has a grated, gritty mouth feel. True Wasabi is served freshly and finely grated. The fake version is prepared from the aforementioned type of powder.

No. 517
Wisteria floribunda ☠️🏺

Wisteria

Chinese Wisteria | Glycine sinensis | Kraunhia sinensis | Rehsonia sinensis | Wistaria | Wisteria polystachya

✺ **SYMBOLIC MEANINGS**
Let's be friends; Welcome,
fair stranger; Your friendship
is agreeable to me.

🌀 **POSSIBLE POWERS**
Bliss; Conflict; Devotion;
Immortality; Longevity;
Love; Overcome an
obstacle; Promotes psychic
receptiveness; Prosperity;
Raises the vibration;
Sensitivity; Sensuality;
Support; Tenderness.

🜨 **FOLKLORE AND FACTS**
Wisteria can live for a very long time. The average is around one hundred years. There is a Wisteria in Japan that is supposedly 1,200 years old. • There is a Korean legend about the origin of Wisteria that involves two sisters discovering they were both in love with the same warrior. They threw themselves into a pond and turned into Wisteria when they died.

No. 518

Withania somnifera ☠☿

Ashwagandha

Ajagandha | Amukkuram | Ashwagandha |
Ashwagandha Root | Chinese Lantern | Indian Ginseng |
Kanaje Hindi | *Physalis somnifera* | Poison Gooseberry |
Samm Al Ferakh | Winter Cherry | Winter Cherry Herb |
Withania kansuensis | *Withania microphysalis*

❋ **SYMBOLIC MEANINGS**
Deception; Enlightenment;
Illumination.

✿ **POSSIBLE POWERS**
Fertility spell; Love spell; Matters of the heart; Vitality.

✦ **FOLKLORE AND FACTS**
In Sanskrit, the common name of Ashwagandha means
"smell of a horse," which adequately describes the fragrance
of *Withania somnifera*. • Put the lantern-shaped husk of
Ashwagandha in a sachet and place the sachet under the
pillow to bring enlightenment to the status of a relationship
as it is revealed in dreams. • To assist in illuminating a dark
spot in a romance and help return trust and friendship back
into the relationship, place stems of Ashwagandha in a
copper container on a Friday, then place the arrangement in
the center of the table that receives the most natural light.

No. 519

Xanthium strumarium ☠☿

Xanthium

Acanthoxanthium | Cockle Burr | Cockle Burro | Cocklebur | Donkey Burr | Stickers

❋ **SYMBOLIC MEANINGS**
Prickled.

✿ **POSSIBLE POWERS**
Fends off witchcraft; Healing;
Protection.

✦ **FOLKLORE AND FACTS**
It was believed that if Xanthium is placed under the head of
a sleeper, it must be removed for the sleeper to fully awaken.
• Xanthium will offer protection against negativity if it is
scattered around the perimeter of one's home. • Make, then
carry a Xanthium sachet in a pocket or wear it around
the neck or at the waist for protection against witchery.
• Xanthium is believed to determine if a witch is present or
nearby. • Xanthium is believed to be able to offer protection
against evil, poison, and goblins as well as banish negative
energies and negative spirits.

No. 520

Yucca filamentosa ☠☿

Yucca

Adam's Needle | Adam's Needle and Thread | Bear-Grass | Common Yucca | Ghosts in the
Graveyard | Needle Palm | Needle-Palm | Silk-Grass | Spanish Bayonet | Spoonleaf Yucca |
Spoon-Leaf Yucca | Yuca | *Yucca filamentosa var. bracteata* | *Yucca filamentosa var. laevigata* |
Yucca filamentosa var. mexicana | *Yucca filamentosa var. recurvifolia*

❋ **SYMBOLIC MEANINGS**
Best friends; a Friend in need.

✿ **POSSIBLE POWERS**
Fire element; Hex removal; Loyalty;
Mars; Masculine energy; New
opportunities; Protection; Purification;
Purity; Transmutation.

✦ **FOLKLORE AND FACTS**
Yucca is commonly found in rural
Midwestern American graveyards. When they are blooming,
the flowers appear to be floating apparitions or ghosts.
• Yucca fibers twisted into a cross then placed in the center
of the home will protect the house from evil. • Yucca is the
state flower of New Mexico, USA. • It was believed by some
that if a person jumps through a loop of twisted Yucca, he
will magically transmute into an animal.

No. 521

Zanthoxylum piperitum ☠☿❶

Szechuan Pepper

Chinese Pepper | Chinese Prickly Ash | Chopi | Fagara | *Fagara piperita* | Huājiāo | Japanese
Pepper | Japanese Pepper Tree | Japanese Prickly-Ash | Korean Pepper | Mala Pepper | Rattan
Pepper | Sanshō | Sichuan Pepper | *Zanthoxylum ovalifoliolatum*

❋ **SYMBOLIC MEANINGS**
Numbing.

✿ **POSSIBLE POWERS**
Fire element; Flavoring; Healing; Mars; Masculine energy;
Numbing spiciness.

✦ **FOLKLORE AND FACTS**
The lemony-tasting Szechuan Pepper is not a pepper.
• Szechuan Pepper is one of the main ingredients in the
multi-spice blend known as *shichimi togarashi* and can also
be found in Chinese five-spice powder. • The Szechuan
Pepper has been used in traditional Chinese medicine for
many centuries.

No. 522

Zea mays 🌿

Corn

Giver of Life | Maize | *Mays americana* | *Mays zea* | *Mayzea cerealis* | Mealie | Mielie | Milho | Sacred Mother | Seed of Seeds | *Thalysia mays* | *Zea segetalis*

☀ SYMBOLIC MEANINGS
Abundance; Quarrel; Riches.

🌱 COMPONENT MEANINGS
Broken: Quarrel.
Ear: Delicacy.

🜨 POSSIBLE POWERS
Divination; Earth element; Feminine energy; Luck; Protection; Venus.

☾ FOLKLORE AND FACTS
Some believe that to place an ear of Corn in an infant's cradle will protect the baby from negative energies and forces. • A bundle of Corn husks over a mirror will bring good luck into the house. • The Corn Mother is the goddess of fertility and plenty revered by Native American tribes in North America. • Ancient North Americans would toss Corn pollen into the air in an attempt to call down the rain. • Cornstarch, which is also known as cornflour, is obtained from the *Zea mays* Corn kernel for use as a thickener for soups and sauces. Cornstarch is also used to make Corn syrup. In addition, it is used medicinally when mixed with a liquid for a paste poultice, or as a talcum substitute for use as a body powder, particularly for babies. Cornstarch is also used as an anti-stick powder for latex gloves, condoms, and other plastic products.

No. 523

Zingiber officinale 🌿🍴

Ginger

Amomum angustifolium | *Amomum zingiber* | *Amomum zinziba* | Ginger Root | Gingerroot | *Zingiber aromaticum* | *Zingiber cholmondeleyi* | *Zingiber missionis* | *Zingiber sichuanense*

☀ SYMBOLIC MEANINGS
Aromatic; Comforting; Diversity; Pleasant; Safe; Strength; Unlimited wealth; Warming; Wealth.

🜨 POSSIBLE POWERS
Abundance; Accidents; Advancement; Aggression; Anger; Breaks a hex; Carnal desire; Conflict; Conscious will; Energy; Fire element; Friendship; Growth; Healing; Health; Joy; Leadership; Legal matters; Life; Light; Love; Lust; Machinery; Mars; Masculine energy; Money; Natural power; Power; Protection; Psychic power; Rock music; Strength; Struggle; Success; War.

☾ FOLKLORE AND FACTS
Carry or wear a sachet of Ginger to foster your psychic abilities. • Carry or wear a sachet of Ginger to pull in good luck to you. • Put Ginger into a leather pouch with silver coins then carry it in a pocket or purse to bring in more money. • To promote lust, sprinkle Ginger around the home. • When Ginger ale, Ginger candy, and Ginger tea don't soothe a flustered belly as well as one hopes for, the one first-aid remedy that usually works better than "like magic" for almost any kind of irritated digestion issues is just one capsule of powdered Ginger root with a glass of water or milk.

WORKS
CONSULTED

———•◦•———

Acamovic, T, C.S. Stewart, and T.W Pennycott, ed., *Poisonous Plants and Related Toxins* (Cabi, 2004).

Ancient Wisdom Foundation, "Herbs: A–Z List: The Medicinal, Spiritual and Magical Uses," http://www.ancient-wisdom.com/herbsaz.htm

Arrowsmith, Nancy, Calantirniel, et al, *Llewellyn's 2010 Herbal Almanac* (Llewellyn Publications, 2010)

Australian National Botanic Gardens Centre for Australian National Biodiversity Research, https://www.cpbr.gov.au

Bailey, L.H., Ethel Zoe Bailey, Staff of Liberty Hyde Bailey Hortotorium, and David Bates, *Hortus Third: A Concise Dictionary of Plants Cultivated in the United States and Canada* (Macmillan, 1976)

Baynes, Thomas Spencer, Day Otis Kellogg, and William Robertson Smith, *Encyclopedia Britannica* (Encyclopedia Britannica, 1897)

Behind the Name, "The Etymology and History of First Names," https://www.behindthename.com

Beyerl, Paul, *A Compendium of Herbal Magick* (Phoenix Publishing Inc., 1998)

Biodiversity Heritage Library, https://www.biodiversitylibrary.org

Blanchan, Neltje, *Wildflowers Worth Knowing,* (Doubleday, 1917)

Bremness, Lesley, *Herbs*, DK Smithsonian Handbooks, 1994

Brickell, Christopher, *The Royal Horticultural Society A–Z Encyclopedia of Garden Plants,* (Dorling Kindersley Publishers Ltd., 1996)

Buhner, Stephen Harrod and Brooke Medicine Eagle, *Sacred Plant Medicine: The Wisdom in Native American Herbalism* (Bear & Company, 2006)

California Department of Food & Agriculture, http://www.cdfa.ca.gov

Coats, Alice M. and John L. Creech, *Garden Shrubs and Their Histories* (Simon & Schuster, 1992)

Connecticut Botanical Society, https://www.ct-botanical-society.org

Coombes, Allen J., *The Collingridge Dictionary of Plant Names* (Hamlyn, 1985)

Cullina,William, *The New England Wildflower Society Guide to Growing and Propagating Wildflowers of the United States and Canada* (Houghton Mifflin Harcourt, 2000)

Culpeper, Nicholas, *The Complete Herbal* (1662 edition), https://www.bibliomania.com

Culpepper, Nicholas, M.D., *The Complete Herbal;* (London: A. Cross, 1652)

Cunningham, Scott, *Cunningham's Encyclopedia of Magical Herbs* (Llewellyn Publications, 1985)

Cunningham, Scott, *Magical Herbalism: The Secret Craft of the Wise* (Llewellyn's Practical Magick, 1986)

Delaware Valley Unit of the Herb Society of America, https://www.delvalherbs.org

Delforge, Pierre, *Orchids of Europe, North Africa and the Middle East* (Timber Press, 2006)

Dobelis, Inge N., *Magic and Medicine of Plants* (Reader's Digest, 1986)

Duke, James A., Peggy-Ann K. Duke, and Judith L. duCellie, *Duke's Handbook of Medicinal Plants of the Bible* (CRC Press, 2007)

eFloras.org, https://www.efloras.org

Endocrine Society, "Chemicals in lavender and tea tree oil appear to be hormone disruptors," https://www.endocrine.org/news-and-advocacy/news-room/2018/chemicals-in-lavender-and-tea-tree-oil-appear-to-be-hormone-disruptors

Fairchild Tropical Botanic Garden, http://www.fairchildgarden.org

FDA Poison Plant Data Base, https://www.fda.gov/food/science-research-food/fda-poisonous-plant-database

Fielding, Robert O., *Spices: Their Histories*, (The Trade Register, 1910)

Folkard, Richard Jr. *Plant Lore, Legends, and Lyrics: Embracing Myths, Traditions, Superstitions, and Folk-Lore of the Plant Kingdom* (R. Folkard and Son, 1884)

Francis, Rose, *The Wild Flower Key: A Guide to Plant Identification in the Field* (Frederick Warne & Co., 1981)

Gardening Channel, "List of Herbs from A to Z", https://www.gardeningchannel.com/list-of-herbs-from-a-to-z/

Garland, Sarah, *The Complete Book of Herbs and Spices*, (Viking Press, 1979)

Grieve, Maud, Mrs., *A Modern Herbal* online, https://botanical.com

Harner, Michael J., ed., *Hallucinogens and Shamanism* (Oxford University Press, 1973)

Harvard University Herbaria & Libraries, https://kiki.huh.harvard.edu/databases/botanist_index.html

Hazlitt, William Carew, and John Brand, *Faiths and Folklore and Facts: A Dictionary* (Charles Scribner's Sons, 1905)

Hoffman, David, *The Complete Illustrated Holistic Herbal: A Safe and Practical Guide to Making and Using Herbal Remedies*, (Element Books Ltd, 1996)

Hohman, John George, *Pow-Wows or The Long Lost Friend: A Collection of Mysterious and Invaluable Arts and Remedies*, (1820)

Howard, Michael, *Traditional Folk Remedies: A Comprehensive Herbal* (Century, 1987)

Hutchens, Alma R., *Indian Herbalogy of North America: The Definitive Guide to Native Medicinal Plants and Their Uses* (Shambhala, 1991)

Ildrewe, Miss, *The Language of Flowers* (De Vries, Ibarra, 1865)

Ingram, John, *The Language of Flowers, or Flora Symbolica* (Frederick Warne and Company, 1897)

Invasive Species Compendium, https://www.cabi.org/isc/

Johnson, Arthur Tysilio and Henry Augustus Smith, *Plant Names Simplified* (W. H. & L. Collingridge Ltd., 1931)

Keightley, Thomas, *The Fairy Mythology: Illustrative of the Romance and Superstition of Various Countries*; (George Bell & Sons, 1892)

Kepler, Angela Kay, *Hawaiian Heritage Plants* (University of Hawaii Press, 1998)

Kew Royal Botanic Gardens, "World Checklist of Selected Plant Families (WCSP)," http://plantsoftheworldonline.org

Kew Royal Botanic Gardens, Kew Science, "Plants of the World Online (POWO)," http://wcsp.science.kew.org/home.do

Kilmer, John, *The Perennial Encyclopedia* (Crescent Books, 1989)

Lad, Dr. Vasant K., *Ayurveda: The Science of Self-Healing* (Lotus Press, 1985)

Lust, John, *The Herb Book: The Most Complete Catalog of Herbs Ever Published* (Bantam Books, 1979)

Mairet, Ethel M., *A Book On Vegetable Dyes* (Douglas Pepler at the Hampshire House Workshops, Hammersmith W, 1916)

Mairet, Ethel M., *Vegetable Dyes: Being A Book of Recipes and Other Information Useful to the Dyer*, (Ditchling Press, 1938)

McCormick & Company, Importers and Grinders of Spices, *Spices: A Text-Book For Teachers* (McCormick & Co., 1915)

McGuffin, Michael, *American Herbal Products Association's Botanical Safety Handbook* (American Herbal Products Association)

McKenny, Margaret and Roger Tory Peterson, *A Field Guide to Wildflowers of Northeastern and North-central North America* (Houghton Mifflin Company, 1968)

Mehl-Madrona, Lewis, M.D. and William L. Simon, *Coyote Medicine: Lessons from Native American Healing* (Scribner, 1997)

Missouri Botanical Garden, http://www.missouribotanicalgarden.org/gardens-gardening.aspx

National Capital Poison Center Poison Control, "Poisonous and Non-Poisonous Plants," https://www.poison.org/articles/plant#poisonousplants

Nations Online, http://www.nationsonline.org

Natural Medicinal Herbs,
http://www.naturalmedicinalherbs.net/herbs/natural/

Northcote, Lady Rosalind, *The Book of Herbs*,
(Turnbull & Spears, 1903)

Ody, Penelope, *The Complete Medicinal Herbal*
(Dorling Kindersley, 1993)

Phillips, Roger, *The Photographic Guide to More than 500
Trees of North America and Europe* (Random House,
Inc., 1979)

Plants for a Future, https://pfaf.org

Puri, H.S., *Neem: The Divine Tree Azadirachta Indica*
(CRC Press, 1999)

Robinson, Nugent, *Collier's Encyclopedia of Commercial
and Social Information and Treasury of Useful and
Entertaining Knowledge* (P. F. Collier, 1892)

Rohde, Eleanour Sinclair, *The Old English Herbals*,
(Longmans, Green and Co. 1922)

Rushforth, Keith, *Trees of Britain and Europe* (Collins Wild
Guide, 1999)

Simonetti, Gualtiero and Stanley Schuler, ed., *Simon &
Schuster's Guide to Herbs and Spices* (Simon & Schuster,
1990)

Simoons, Frederick J., *Plants of Life, Plants of Death*
(University of Wisconsin Press, 1998)

Smithsonian National Museum of Natural History,
"Index Nominum Genericorum (ING),"
https://naturalhistory2.si.edu/botany/ing

Theoi Project, "Flora 1: Plants of Greek Myth,"
https://www.theoi.com/Flora1.html

Thiselton-Dyer, T.F., *The Folk-Lore of Plants* (New York:
D. Appleton, 1889)

Tisserand, Robert B. *The Art of Aromatherapy: The Healing
and Beautifying Properties of the Essential Oils of Flowers
and Herbs*, (Healing Arts Press, 1978)

University of California, "Safe and Poisonous Garden
Plants," https://ucanr.edu/sites/poisonous_safe_plants/

University of Rochester Medical Center,
"A Guide To Common Medicinal Herbs,"
https://www.urmc.rochester.edu/encyclopedia/content.
aspx?contenttypeid=1&contentid=1169

USDA (United States Department of Agriculture) Natural
Resources Conservation Service,
https://www.nrcs.usda.gov/wps/portal/nrcs/site/
national/home

Valnet, Jean Dr., *The Practice of Aromatherapy*, translated
from French by Robin Campbell and Libby Houston,
(Random House, UK 1982; Vermilion, 2011)

Wichtl, Max, *Herbal Drugs and Phytopharmaceuticals:
A Handbook* (Medpharm, 2004)

ACKNOWLEDGMENTS

A special thanks goes to my beloved daughter, Melanie, who was extremely encouraging while I was working on this book. Without her, all the rest of the goodness that came along with her would not have happened as specially as it has. It is with a mind and heart full of love that I wholeheartedly dedicate this book about *The Complete Language of Herbs* to everyone in my entire growing family. I most especially dedicate this new book to my very young great-granddaughter, Daphne, who fell in love with *The Complete Language of Flowers* on my birthday. And to her darling sisters, little Maggie and baby Ruby, who will surely discover my books someday, too, and hopefully love them just as much.

Special thanks to Wellfleet Press and all things Quarto Publishing Group USA. Everyone I have worked with has been outstanding. Thank you to Quarto's brilliant Publisher, Rage Kindelsperger, and Senior Managing Editor, Cara Donaldson, for their overall vision and ongoing encouragement. Thanks to Wellfleet's Editor, Elizabeth You, for her guidance. To Copyeditors Tara Trubela and Helena Caldon for their careful attention to the text. To Creative Director Laura Drew and the entire Art Team for creating such beautiful books. Thanks to James Jayo for his editorial contribution, and also to John Foster, who invited me to consider herbs with a wide-open mind. You are all amazing people. I wish everyone who is affiliated with Quarto, in any capacity, all the very best in every way imaginable.

To my dear friend Robert, who I dearly adore. God bless you always.

To all of the Plant-loving People of the World: look up, look down, look all around. Peace and love to you all.

ABOUT
THE AUTHOR

———•◦•———

Spring, summer, and autumn container gardening on a small apartment balcony is all the more appreciated during the short growing season in the Enchanted Mountains of Western New York State, where eclectic artist and writer S. Theresa Dietz makes her home. Her fascination with all things magical and mysterious, along with a deep abiding love of trees, plants, and flowers, motivates her to continue learning more about them.

PHOTO
CREDITS

————◆◆◆————

Unless otherwise listed below, all images © Shutterstock.com

© Alamy Stock Photo: 403 (*Quercus alba*)

© Alamy Stock Photo/Image BROKER: 075 (*Avena sativa*), 326 (*Lythrium salicaria*), 463 (*Sorbus aucuparia*)

© Alamy Stock Photo: Florilegius, 402 (*Quassia amara*), 443 (*Satureia hortensis*)

© Alamy Stock Photo/The Natural History Museum: 416 (*Rosa × damascena*)

© GettyImages: 303 (*Kigelia africana*)

© GettyImages/ilbusca: 210 (*Cymbopogon nardus*)

© GettyImages/Sepia Times: K chapter opener (*Galanga*)

© GettyImages/SUPER: 356 (*Nigella sativa*)

© Getty Images/ZU_09: 354 (*Nicotiana rustica*)

List of
CULINARY HERBS

No. 087 Achiote *Bixa orellana*

No. 118 Ají Cito Pepper *Capsicum baccatum*

No. 490 Ajwain *Trachyspermum ammi*

No. 109 Aleppo Pepper *Capsicum annum*

No. 461 Alexanders *Smyrnium olusatrum*

No. 378 Allspice *Pimenta dioica*

No. 049 Angelica *Angelica archangelica*

No. 379 Anise *Pimpinella anisum*

No. 331 Arrowroot *Maranta arundinacea*

No. 235 Asafoetida *Ferula assa-foetida*

No. 110 Banana Pepper *Capsicum annuum*

No. 358 Basil *Ocimum basilicum*

No. 307 Bay Laurel *Laurus nobilis*

No. 340 Bee Balm *Monarda didyma*

No. 111 Bell Pepper *Capsicum annuum*

No. 157 Bergamot Orange *Citrus bergamia*

No. 112 Bird's Eye Chili *Capsicum annuum*

No. 156 Bitter Orange *Citrus × aurantium*

No. 356 Black Cumin *Nigella sativa*

No. 093 Black Mustard *Brassica nigra*

No. 382 Black Pepper *Piper nigrum*

No. 496 Black Truffle *Tuber melanosporum*

No. 298 Black Walnut *Juglans nigra*

No. 089 Borage *Borago officinalis*

No. 092 Brown Mustard *Brassica juncea*

No. 437 Burnet *Sanguisorba minor*

No. 171 Calamint *Clinopodium menthifolium*

No. 108 Caper *Capparis spinosa*

No. 126 Caraway *Carum carvi*

No. 221 Cardamom *Elettaria cardamomum*

No. 208 Carrot *Daucus carota* subsp. *sativus*

No. 158 Cassia *Cinnamomum cassia*

No. 113 Cayenne Pepper *Capsicum annuum*

No. 055 Celeriac *Apium graveolens* var. *rapaceum*

No. 054 Celery *Apium graveolens* var. *graveolens*

No. 052 Chervil *Anthriscus cerefolium*

No. 147 Chicory *Cichorium intybus*

No. 035 Chives *Allium schoenoprasum*

No. 181 Cilantro *Coriandrum sativum*

No. 151 Cinnamon *Cinnamomum verum*

No. 162 Citron *Citrus medica*

No. 477 Clove *Syzygium aromaticum*

No. 423 Common Sorrel *Rumex acetosa*

No. 182 Coriander *Coriandrum sativum*

No. 480 Costmary *Tanacetum balsamita*

No. 381 Cubeb *Piper cubeba*

No. 192 Cumin *Cuminum cyminum*

No. 342 Curry Leaf Tree *Murraya koenigii*

No. 048 Dill *Anethum graveolens*

No. 143 Edible Chrysanthemum *Chrysanthemum coronarium*

No. 032 Egyptian Tree Onion *Allium cepa* var. *proliferum*

No. 029 Elephant Garlic *Allium ampeloprasum*

No. 308 English Lavender *Lavandula angustifolia*

No. 033 Everlasting Onion *Allium fistulosum*

No. 495 Fenugreek *Trigonella foenum-graecum*

No. 426 French Sorrel *Rumex scutatus*

No. 114 Friggitello *Capsicum annuum*

No. 034 Garlic *Allium sativum*

No. 037 Garlic Chives *Allium tuberosum*

No. 523 Ginger *Zingiber officinale*

No. 016 Grains of Paradise *Aframomum melegueta*

No. 163 Grapefruit *Citrus × paradisi*

No. 119 Habanero Chili *Capsicum chinense*

No. 062 Horseradish *Armoracia rusticana*

No. 120 Hot Pepper *Capsicum chinense*

No. 281   Hyssop *Hyssopus officinalis*

No. 115   Jalapeño Pepper *Capsicum annuum*

No. 300   Juniper *Juniperus communis*

No. 166   Kabosu Papeda *Citrus sphaerocarpa*

No. 155   Key Lime *Citrus* × *aurantiifolia*

No. 015   Korarima *Aframomum corrorima*

No. 320   Koseret *Lippia abyssinica*

No. 100   Large-Flowered Calamint
          Calamintha grandiflora

No. 056   Leaf Celery *Apium graveolens* var. *secalinum*

No. 028   Leek *Allium ampeloprasum*

No. 160   Lemon *Citrus* × *limon*

No. 336   Lemon Balm *Melissa officinalis*

No. 040   Lemon Verbena *Aloysia citrodora*

No. 199   Lemongrass *Cymbopogon citratus*

No. 261   Licorice *Glycyrrhiza glabra*

No. 313   Lovage *Levisticum officinale*

No. 158   Makrut Lime *Citrus hystrix*

No. 164   Mandarin Orange *Citrus* × *reticulata*

No. 362   Marjoram *Origanum majorana*

No. 343   Nutmeg *Myristica fragrans*

No. 031   Onion *Allium cepa*

No. 368   Opium Poppy *Papaver somniferum*

No. 363   Oregano *Origanum vulgare*

No. 116   Paprika *Capsicum annuum*

No. 374   Parsley *Petroselinum crispum*

No. 337   Peppermint *Mentha* × *piperita*

No. 159   Persian Lime *Citrus* × *latifolia*

No. 117   Pimiento *Capsicum annuum*

No. 400   Pomegranate *Punica granatum*

No. 161   Pomelo *Citrus maxima*

No. 036   Rocambole *Allium scorodoprasum*

No. 122   Rocoto Pepper *Capsicum pubescens*

No. 433   Rosemary *Salvia rosmarinus*

No. 188   Saffron *Crocus sativus*

No. 432   Sage *Salvia officinalis*

No. 453   Sesame *Sesamum indicum*

No. 030   Shallot *Allium ascalonicum*

No. 372   Shiso *Perilla frutecens* var. *crispa*

No. 338   Spearmint *Mentha spicata*

No. 286   Star Anise *Illicium verum*

No. 167   Sudachi *Citrus sudachi*

No. 411   Sumac *Rhus coriaria*

No. 443   Summer Savory *Satureja hortensis*

No. 345   Sweet Cicely *Myrrhis odorata*

No. 240   Sweet Fennel *Foeniculum vulgare*

No. 165   Sweet Orange *Citrus* × *sinensis*

No. 521   Szechuan Pepper *Zanthoxylum piperitum*

No. 121   Tabasco Pepper *Capsicum frutescens* var. *tabasco*

No. 168   Tangerine *Citrus tangerina*

No. 066   Tarragon *Artemisia dracunculus*

No. 359   Thai Basil *Ocimum basilicum* var. *thyrsiflora*

No. 488   Thyme *Thymus vulgaris*

No. 095   Turnip *Brassica rapa* var. *rapa*

No. 194   Turmeric *Curcuma longa*

No. 506   Vanilla Orchid *Vanilla planifolia*

No. 516   Wasabi *Wasabia japonica*

No. 350   Watercress *Nasturtium officinale*

No. 458   White Mustard *Sinapis alba*

No. 444   Winter Savory *Satureja montana*

Index of
COMMON HERB
NAMES

━━━━◦◉◦━━━━

L

Lady's Bedstraw, *248*

Lady's Mantle, *023*

Lantana, *305*

Large-Flowered
  Calamint, *100*

Lavender Cotton, *440*

Lawn Daisy, *081*

Leaf Celery, *056*

Ledum, *410*

Leek, *028*

Lemon, *160*

Lemon Balm, *336*

Lemon Myrtle, *078*

Lemon Verbena, *040*

Lemongrass, *199*

Licorice, *261*

Lilac, *476*

Lily-of-the-Valley, *180*

Linden, *489*

Liverwort, *270*

Locoweed, *072*

Logwood, *264*

Loosestrife, *326*

Loquat, *226*

Lovage, *313*

Love Lies Bleeding, *044*

Lungwort, *398*

M

Maca, *310*

Mace, *342*

Madagascar Periwinkle,
  128

Madder, *422*

Maiden Pink, *211*

Makrut Lime, *158*

Mandarin Orange, *164*

Mandrake, *330*

Mānuka Myrtle, *312*

Marijuana, *107*

Marjoram, *362*

Mastic, *383*

Mayflower, *124, 185*

Meadow Geranium, *255*

Meadowsweet, *466*

Medicinal Rhubarb, *408*

Midsummer Men, *409*

Mignonette, *405*

Milk Thistle, *456*

Miner's Lettuce, *169*

Mistletoe, *513*

Moonwort, *091*

Morning Glory, *290*

Mountain Balm, *130*

Mountain Knotgrass, *014*

Mugwort, *068*

Mullein, *507*

Musk Mallow, *001*

Musk Rose, *419*

Muskroot, *349*

Myrrh, *179*

Myrtle, *346*

N

Neem, *077*

Nepali Paper Plant, *205*

Northern Maidenhair
  Fern, *011*

Nutmeg, *343*

O

Oakleaf Geranium, *371*

Oat, *075*

Oil Palm, *220*

Onion, *031*

Opium Poppy, *368*

Orange Daylily, *269*

Oregano, *363*

Oregon Grape, *328*

Oriental Ginseng, *365*

Orris Root Iris, *292*

Oxeye Daisy, *144*

P

Pagoda Tree, *471*

Palmarosa, *200*

Palo Santo, *098*

Paprika, *116*

Papyrus, *203*

Parsley, *374*

Pasqueflower, *399*

Patchouli, *388*

Pear, *401*

Peppermint, *337*

Periwinkle, *128*

Persian Lime, *159*

Persian Yellow Rose, *417*

Peyote Cactus, *321*

Phlox, *375*

Pimiento, *117*

Pineapple, *046*

Pink Mempat, *186*

Pistachio, *384*

Poet's Daffodil, *348*

Poinsettia, *515*

Pokeweed, *377*

Pomegranate, *400*

Pomelo, *161*

Portulaca, *391*

Prickly Rose, *412*

Pumpkin, *191*

Index of
COMMON MEANINGS
& POWERS

Chastity, 046, 149, 165,
185, 190, 225, 265, 306,
308, 346

Cheer, 081, 142, 143, 144,
164, 168, 188

Cleansing, 071, 078, 082,
085, 094, 097, 102, 156,
192, 278, 307, 410, 457

Colorize, 020, 026, 031,
038, 082, 086, 102, 134,
135, 180, 184, 186, 244,
248, 264, 274, 288, 294,
298, 299, 301, 397, 401,
406, 422, 430, 435, 467,
478, 485, 498, 514

Communication,
126, 183, 199, 201, 205,
213, 214, 223, 261, 301,
308, 324, 329, 334, 374,
379, 439, 463, 472

Courage, 005, 006, 010,
037, 045, 049, 089,
103, 174, 177, 195, 216,
219, 223, 240, 280, 306,
311, 377

Creativity, 081, 110, 111,
113, 114, 115, 116, 117,
121, 122, 126, 234, 261,
324, 374, 379, 439, 478

Cupid, 193, 413, 414, 415,
416, 417, 418, 419, 420,
421

Death, 001, 022, 132, 152,
178, 179, 193, 206, 213,
214, 276, 279, 284, 300,
307, 330, 388, 393, 394,
395, 435, 472, 487, 488,
499

Demeter, 273, 346, 367,
413, 414, 415, 416, 417,
418, 419, 420, 421

Diana, 065, 068, 183, 341,
427, 449

Dionysus, 237, 240, 514

Divination, 005, 006, 016,
018, 038, 081, 086, 144,
149, 183, 210, 212, 234,
237, 239, 259, 265, 271,
280, 286, 297, 361, 400,
413, 414, 415, 416, 417,
418, 419, 420, 421, 430,
433, 454, 462, 463, 466,
483, 485, 522

Dreams, 019, 068, 071,
101, 282, 283, 297, 321,
361, 363

Earth element, 004, 064,
068, 072, 075, 079, 083,
086, 095, 145, 171, 191,
193, 198, 223, 224, 233,
260, 262, 273, 322, 326,
327, 328, 364, 385, 386,

388, 390, 394, 403, 408,
461, 465, 508, 522

Emotions, 009, 020, 084,
106, 149, 189, 433, 434,
439

Energy, 090, 110, 111, 113,
114, 115, 116, 117, 121,
122, 137, 138, 151, 179,
210, 285, 298, 300, 307,
310, 331, 382, 383, 388,
403, 410, 433, 472, 488,
506

Eros, 188, 307, 413, 414,
415, 416, 417, 418, 419,
420, 421

Evil, 007, 014, 019, 020,
024, 048, 101, 110, 112,
113, 114, 115, 116, 117,
119, 120, 121, 122, 132,
214, 220, 225, 235, 240,
251, 381, 382

Exorcism, 005, 006, 021,
028, 029, 031, 032, 034,
035, 049, 058, 062, 064,
090, 153, 179, 192, 217,
225, 235, 240, 257, 267,
268, 280, 300, 315, 329,
330, 332, 358, 359, 360,
381, 382, 390, 406, 427,
433, 435, 438, 439, 473,
476, 477, 493, 503, 504,
507, 510, 513

Faith, 081, 092, 093, 126,
138, 144, 180, 261, 292,
308, 315, 330, 348, 374,
379, 439, 455, 472, 504

Feminine energy, 002,
005, 009, 011, 018, 023,
026, 039, 041, 043, 057,
060, 064, 068, 069,
073, 075, 081, 083, 085,
086, 091, 095, 102, 103,
107, 108, 124, 128, 134,
145, 149, 160, 169, 178,
179, 190, 193, 196, 206,
213, 214, 216, 221, 223,
224, 225, 227, 230, 233,
234, 243, 245, 246, 248,
249, 250, 253, 254, 255,
256, 261, 262, 268, 271,
273, 276, 292, 293, 295,
296, 306, 315, 322, 324,
326, 327, 328, 336, 338,
340, 346, 348, 349, 351,
357, 361, 364, 367, 369,
370, 371, 385, 386, 388,
390, 391, 393, 394, 399,
401, 406, 413, 414, 415,
416, 417, 418, 419, 420,
421, 428, 439, 445, 446,
462, 468, 474, 475, 476,
492, 497, 499, 500, 504,
505, 506, 508, 514, 522

Fertility, 009, 022, 059,
071, 075, 085, 086, 093,
095, 124, 149, 153, 172,
183, 185, 189, 190, 191,
194, 197, 198, 207, 208,
224, 237, 238, 239, 243,

255, 258, 273, 297, 298,
299, 310, 317, 329, 330,
346, 348, 350, 357, 360,
367, 368, 369, 370, 371,
376, 380, 388, 397, 400,
403, 416, 425, 433, 434,
439, 447, 456, 458, 463,
475, 513, 514, 518

Fidelity, 058, 101, 112, 118,
119, 120, 133, 142, 143,
192, 198, 261, 277, 284,
343, 349, 382, 431, 432,
446, 447, 493, 511

Fire element, 010, 016,
028, 029, 030, 031, 034,
043, 046, 047, 048,
049, 053, 054, 055, 056,
058, 061, 062, 063, 065,
072, 079, 084, 088,
090, 092, 093, 096,
098, 103, 109, 110, 111,
112, 114, 115, 116, 117,
118, 119, 120, 121, 122,
135, 139, 142, 143, 147,
151, 153, 155, 156, 159,
164, 166, 167, 168, 171,
172, 181, 185, 188, 192,
202, 208, 210, 217, 235,
237, 240, 244, 246, 247,
251, 257, 265, 270, 278,
280, 281, 291, 298, 299,
300, 301, 307, 314, 319,
330, 332, 337, 343, 350,
358, 366, 377, 378, 381,
382, 390, 392, 400, 403,
411, 427, 433, 436, 438,
442, 453, 456, 458, 460,
463, 477, 478, 481, 498,
503, 507, 520, 521, 522

Friendship, 002, 003, 006,
040, 068, 090, 125, 133,
137, 138, 145, 151, 160,
176, 179, 255, 259, 275,
300, 306, 307, 326, 346,
351, 385, 388, 403, 417,
433, 472, 477, 486, 487,
504, 522

G

Gratitude, 020, 069, 104,
210, 212

Grounding, 005, 013, 106,
187, 223, 429

Growth, 022, 071, 090,
137, 138, 151, 179, 300,
388, 403

H

Happiness, 019, 021, 139,
142, 143, 169, 180, 185,
188, 197, 198, 234, 238,
254, 276, 280, 290, 291,
362, 384, 391, 393, 466

Harmony, 006, 019, 040,
068, 103, 125, 145, 153,
172, 250, 271, 326, 351,
360, 367, 368, 410, 443,
447, 456, 487, 488,
490, 503

Hathor, 330, 413, 414, 415,
416, 417, 418, 419, 420,
421, 514

Healing, 005, 006, 008,
009, 013, 014, 026, 027,
031, 032, 034, 035, 036,
039, 043, 044, 047,
049, 059, 063, 065, 067,
068, 071, 072, 074, 075,
077, 078, 088, 090,
096, 097, 102, 103, 106,
107, 110, 111, 114, 115,
116, 117, 121, 122, 128,
129, 130, 132, 134, 137,
138, 148, 150, 151, 153,
159, 161, 162, 169, 170,
175, 178, 179, 180, 181,
186, 187, 188, 190, 193,
195, 202, 210, 211, 212,
213, 214, 218, 220, 222,
226, 227, 229, 230, 240,
244, 249, 250, 255, 258,
262, 263, 264, 266, 267,
272, 273, 274, 278, 281,
283, 286, 292, 295, 300,
302, 303, 304, 307, 309,
319, 325, 329, 332, 333,
334, 335, 336, 337, 338,
340, 344, 347, 350, 354,
355, 360, 361, 364, 366,
372, 375, 378, 380, 388,
393, 394, 396, 397, 399,
402, 403, 409, 410, 413,
414, 415, 416, 417, 418,
419, 420, 421, 423, 424,
425, 426, 427, 429, 430,
431, 432, 433, 435, 438,
439, 442, 446, 448, 451,
457, 459, 464, 467, 474,
477, 486, 490, 492,
497, 508, 513, 521, 522

Health, 006, 047, 068,
070, 075, 086, 101, 126,
148, 149, 181, 191, 210,
218, 226, 244, 253, 280,
291, 295, 298, 299, 300,
302, 304, 307, 309, 310,
312, 314, 319, 325, 330,
332, 335, 342, 343, 349,
352, 362, 363, 364, 369,
370, 371, 384, 385, 395,
397, 399, 402, 403, 423,
424, 426, 427, 438, 442,
445, 446, 452, 471, 486,
502, 507, 513, 516, 522

Hecate, 034, 073, 330, 338,
376, 483

Hexes, 020, 021, 024, 050,
053, 079, 112, 118, 119,
120, 145, 153, 172, 206,
250, 251, 252, 277, 291,
300, 302, 333, 343, 360,
377, 381, 382, 388, 407,
427, 468, 520, 522

Hippocrates, 413, 414, 415,
416, 417, 418, 419, 420,
421

I

Immortality, 043, 099,
102, 133, 134, 142, 143,
159, 181, 193, 205, 240,
282, 307, 365, 366, 400,
403, 404, 431, 432, 517

Independence, 153, 163,
172, 360, 447, 456, 498,
500

Insects, 005, 077, 078, 199, 200, 201, 254, 283, 302, 335, 353, 354, 355, 395, 440, 481

Invisibility, 011, 043, 044, 147, 268, 311, 367, 368, 397, 500

Isis, 031, 179, 237, 376, 413, 414, 415, 416, 417, 418, 419, 420, 421, 508

J

Joy, 006, 040, 057, 068, 100, 101, 125, 137, 138, 139, 145, 151, 179, 180, 232, 249, 300, 304, 307, 351, 388, 403, 413, 424, 426, 443, 486, 487, 503, 504

Juno, 237, 292, 315, 508

Jupiter, 004, 020, 021, 061, 084, 089, 146, 193, 210, 237, 238, 257, 269, 270, 281, 286, 343, 379, 425, 432, 442, 460, 465, 466, 477, 483, 507, 508

L

Leadership, 084, 090, 137, 138, 151, 179, 227, 297, 307, 308, 379, 403, 431, 432

Life, 022, 090, 137, 138, 151, 179, 198, 213, 214, 307, 403, 404, 499, 514

Longevity, 002, 003, 004, 068, 079, 099, 101, 160, 193, 238, 240, 258, 308, 310, 320, 357, 362, 365, 366, 414, 431, 432, 517

Love, 001, 004, 005, 006, 009, 010, 011, 012, 015, 016, 021, 023, 028, 029, 034, 040, 047, 048, 050, 054, 056, 057, 059, 064, 065, 066, 068, 069, 071, 073, 081, 083, 084, 088, 091, 096, 107, 108, 110, 111, 112, 114, 115, 116, 117, 118, 119, 120, 121, 122, 124, 125, 126, 133, 134, 137, 138, 144, 145, 146, 150, 151, 155, 156, 159, 160, 165, 169, 170, 178, 180, 181, 182, 185, 188, 191, 192, 195, 196, 197, 198, 199, 208, 210, 212, 216, 217, 221, 228, 231, 237, 239, 243, 244, 248, 249, 251, 252, 253, 255, 256, 257, 258, 261, 270, 273, 276, 277, 280, 284, 289, 290, 291, 295, 296, 297, 302, 307, 308, 309, 310, 313, 314, 315, 324, 329, 330, 336, 337, 338, 340, 343, 346, 348, 351, 358, 359, 362, 365, 366, 367, 368, 369, 370, 371, 373, 374, 378, 379, 380, 381, 382,

384, 385, 390, 391, 392, 393, 394, 395, 400, 401, 403, 404, 413, 414, 415, 416, 417, 418, 419, 420, 421, 427, 428, 430, 433, 435, 436, 439, 446, 447, 450, 451, 452, 453, 456, 460, 463, 466, 467, 473, 477, 478, 479, 485, 486, 487, 488, 489, 491, 493, 496, 497, 498, 499, 503, 504, 505, 506, 507, 508, 513, 515, 517, 518

Luck, 006, 009, 014, 015, 016, 030, 039, 046, 060, 079, 094, 098, 102, 104, 137, 138, 145, 147, 148, 150, 155, 159, 169, 175, 180, 181, 182, 183, 194, 210, 212, 226, 238, 239, 242, 243, 244, 251, 262, 275, 282, 286, 319, 331, 343, 348, 352, 358, 359, 363, 364, 367, 368, 378, 391, 395, 397, 400, 403, 424, 426, 462, 463, 473, 493, 510, 512, 522

Lust, 009, 010, 015, 016, 021, 031, 032, 034, 048, 054, 056, 064, 071, 081, 108, 126, 146, 151, 159, 181, 182, 188, 197, 199, 201, 207, 208, 217, 221, 243, 261, 271, 279, 284, 295, 302, 329, 330, 358, 359, 365, 366, 374, 378, 381, 401, 428, 433, 450, 452, 453, 496, 503, 506

M

Marriage, 005, 155, 210, 346, 489, 493

Mars, 010, 016, 028, 029, 030, 031, 034, 047, 053, 058, 062, 065, 088, 092, 093, 096, 103, 109, 110, 111, 112, 114, 115, 116, 117, 118, 119, 120, 121, 122, 153, 172, 181, 185, 192, 202, 208, 217, 235, 244, 247, 251, 274, 291, 350, 358, 377, 378, 381, 382, 427, 436, 438, 456, 458, 461, 464, 473, 503, 508, 510, 520, 521

Masculine energy, 004, 010, 016, 020, 021, 028, 030, 031, 034, 040, 046, 047, 048, 049, 053, 054, 055, 056, 058, 061, 062, 063, 064, 065, 071, 072, 079, 084, 088, 089, 090, 093, 096, 098, 103, 109, 110, 111, 112, 113, 114, 55115, 116, 117, 118, 119, 120, 121, 122, 126, 132, 135, 138, 139, 142, 143, 146, 147, 151, 153, 157, 162, 172, 180, 181, 183, 185, 188, 192, 199, 202, 208, 210, 217, 232, 235, 237, 238, 240, 244, 247, 251, 257, 265, 270, 274, 278, 280, 281, 284, 286, 289, 290, 291, 298, 300, 301, 307, 308, 314, 318, 319, 330,

332, 333, 337, 338, 341,
342, 343, 358, 362, 374,
376, 377, 378, 379, 381,
382, 383, 384, 392, 397,
400, 403, 427, 432, 433,
436, 438, 440, 442,
449, 451, 453, 456, 460,
461, 463, 464, 466, 473,
477, 478, 482, 483, 493,
495, 498, 503, 510, 513,
520, 521, 522

Mercury, 040, 048, 054,
055, 056, 064, 126, 132,
157, 169, 171, 180, 183,
194, 195, 199, 240, 289,
308, 319, 330, 332, 337,
338, 341, 362, 363, 374,
384, 397, 399, 440,
444, 451, 493, 495

Money, 004, 009, 010, 015,
016, 031, 032, 046, 048,
060, 074, 075, 091,
094, 096, 137, 138, 145,
146, 150, 157, 182, 184,
216, 233, 234, 245, 247,
278, 280, 291, 293, 297,
302, 319, 322, 328, 330,
343, 346, 359, 362, 367,
368, 378, 385, 388, 389,
403, 407, 425, 442, 449,
453, 460, 462, 474,
477, 493, 495, 498, 508,
514, 522

Moon, 009, 018, 039, 060,
091, 095, 103, 132, 149,
160, 161, 171, 151, 190,
191, 230, 245, 248, 250,
260, 262, 269, 296, 297,

309, 315, 322, 324, 326,
329, 336, 350, 357, 361,
367, 368, 391, 430, 433,
439, 468, 473, 483,
492, 514

N

Negativity, 003, 019, 020,
026, 031, 059, 095

Neptune, 244

P

Passion, 071, 126, 150, 151,
195, 212, 295, 338, 400,
415

Peace, 019, 103, 106, 111,
128, 238, 249, 255, 268,
272, 290, 308, 326, 346,
413, 414, 415, 416, 417,
419, 420, 421, 446, 447,
466, 486, 508

Pisces, 146, 183, 237, 343

Politics, 084, 227, 297, 308,
379, 403, 431, 432

Power, 084, 150, 194, 215,
217, 227, 251, 256, 280,
297, 308, 311, 324, 351,
379, 403, 431, 432, 463

Prophetic dreaming, 018,
031, 032, 033, 037, 068,
101, 314, 478

Prosperity, 026, 103, 110,
111, 113, 114, 115, 116,
117, 121, 122, 150, 157,
164, 168, 191, 218, 234,
238, 239, 242, 244, 322,
328, 358, 385, 435, 462,
463, 495, 512

Protection, 001, 002, 005,
006, 009, 010, 014,
020, 024, 026, 028,
029, 031, 032, 033, 034,
035, 036, 037, 038, 039,
040, 041, 042, 043,
044, 047, 048, 049,
050, 053, 058, 060, 061,
063, 064, 065, 068,
079, 084, 086, 090,
092, 093, 095, 096,
099, 101, 102, 110, 111,
113, 114, 115, 116, 117,
118, 121, 122, 123, 126,
131, 132, 134, 136, 139,
142, 143, 147, 148, 150,
151, 153, 157, 159, 160,
169, 170, 172, 177, 178,
179, 181, 182, 183, 191,
192, 193, 195, 197, 198,
206, 210, 212, 213, 214,
215, 217, 225, 227, 230,
233, 235, 236, 238, 239,
240, 244, 245, 246, 247,
250, 254, 256, 262, 265,
267, 268, 270, 272, 273,
276, 280, 281, 282, 287,
289, 292, 300, 302, 307,
308, 309, 315, 319, 320,
321, 324, 325, 326, 329,
330, 331, 332, 333, 341,
342, 343, 345, 352, 357,
358, 359, 360, 362, 363,

365, 366, 370, 371, 373,
379, 382, 385, 386, 389,
390, 391, 392, 393, 396,
397, 398, 399, 403, 406,
407, 413, 414, 415, 416,
417, 419, 420, 421, 426,
427, 431, 433, 435, 436,
437, 439, 445, 449, 453,
458, 463, 467, 468, 473,
474, 476, 477, 478, 482,
484, 490, 493, 498,
499, 503, 505, 507, 508,
510, 519, 520, 522

Psychic ability, 005, 006,
009, 018, 019, 020, 033,
035, 037, 041, 054, 056,
063, 065, 068, 086,
089, 094, 101, 106, 149,
150, 151, 162, 177, 188,
189, 199, 201, 227, 232,
245, 277, 286, 289, 296,
297, 300, 302, 309, 314,
319, 337, 340, 343, 345,
373, 379, 413, 414, 415,
417, 418, 419, 420, 421,
433, 434, 439, 449, 463,
470, 478, 487, 488,
497, 499, 517, 522

Purification, 026, 030,
031, 032, 040, 062, 064,
078, 084, 085, 090,
098, 137, 138, 160, 172,
179, 194, 195, 217, 230,
235, 236, 240, 249, 257,
272, 281, 292, 300, 308,
314, 315, 319, 331, 332,
337, 346, 354, 355, 363,
370, 371, 395, 413, 414,
415, 416, 417, 418, 419,